The Veterans' Tale

This is a unique account of the ways in which British veterans of the Second World War remembered, understood, and recounted their experiences of battle throughout the post-war period. Focusing on themes of landscape, weaponry, the enemy, and comradeship, Frances Houghton examines the imagery and language used by war memoirists to reconstruct and review both their experiences of battle and their sense of wartime self. Houghton also identifies how veterans' memoirs became significant sites of contest as former servicemen sought to challenge what they saw as unsatisfactory official, scholarly, and cultural representations of the Second World War in Britain. Her findings show that these memoirs are equally important both for the new light they shed on the memory and meanings of wartime military experience among British veterans, and for what they tell us about the cultural identity of military life-writing in post-war British society.

Frances Houghton is Lecturer in Modern British History at the University of Manchester. She has contributed chapters to several edited volumes and her work has been published in the *Journal of War and Culture Studies*.

Studies in the Social and Cultural History of Modern Warfare

General Editor
Jay Winter, *Yale University*

Advisory Editors
David Blight, *Yale University*
Richard Bosworth, *University of Western Australia*
Peter Fritzsche, *University of Illinois, Urbana-Champaign*
Carol Gluck, *Columbia University*
Benedict Kiernan, *Yale University*
Antoine Prost, *Université de Paris-Sorbonne*
Robert Wohl, *University of California, Los Angeles*

In recent years the field of modern history has been enriched by the exploration of two parallel histories. These are the social and cultural history of armed conflict, and the impact of military events on social and cultural history.

Studies in the Social and Cultural History of Modern Warfare presents the fruits of this growing area of research, reflecting both the colonization of military history by cultural historians and the reciprocal interest of military historians in social and cultural history, to the benefit of both. The series offers the latest scholarship in European and non-European events from the 1850s to the present day.

A full list of titles in the series can be found at:
www.cambridge.org/modernwarfare

The Veterans' Tale

British Military Memoirs of the Second World War

Frances Houghton

University of Manchester

CAMBRIDGE
UNIVERSITY PRESS

CAMBRIDGE
UNIVERSITY PRESS

University Printing House, Cambridge CB2 8BS, United Kingdom

One Liberty Plaza, 20th Floor, New York, NY 10006, USA

477 Williamstown Road, Port Melbourne, VIC 3207, Australia

314–321, 3rd Floor, Plot 3, Splendor Forum, Jasola District Centre,
New Delhi – 110025, India

79 Anson Road, #06-04/06, Singapore 079906

Cambridge University Press is part of the University of Cambridge.

It furthers the University's mission by disseminating knowledge in the pursuit
of education, learning, and research at the highest international levels of
excellence.

www.cambridge.org
Information on this title: www.cambridge.org/9781108496919
DOI: 10.1017/9781108690164

© Frances Houghton 2019

This publication is in copyright. Subject to statutory exception and to the
provisions of relevant collective licensing agreements, no reproduction of any
part may take place without the written permission of Cambridge University
Press.

First published 2019

Printed and bound in Great Britain by Clays Ltd, Elcograf S.p.A.

A catalogue record for this publication is available from the British Library.

ISBN 978-1-108-49691-9 Hardback

Cambridge University Press has no responsibility for the persistence or
accuracy of URLs for external or third-party internet websites referred to in
this publication and does not guarantee that any content on such websites is, or
will remain, accurate or appropriate.

For my grandpa, Kenneth Austin Houghton, whose courage, kindness, and sense of humour touched so many lives, especially my own.

Per Ardua Ad Astra

Contents

Contents

Acknowledgements

I have been extremely privileged throughout my research to be guided by my two brilliant PhD supervisors, Jeremy Crang and Jonathan Wild. To these scholars an enormous and inexpressible debt of gratitude is owed, as it is entirely due to their unfailing patience, support, and faith in both project and researcher that this book was ever given life. Thanks are also due to Paul Addison and Gary Sheffield for their critiques as viva voce examiners, and for generously sharing their time and experience in helping me to get the book off the starting blocks. I have also benefitted greatly from the University of Edinburgh's Principal's Career Development Scholarship which funded the research on which this book is based. Thanks also go to the anonymous reviewers of the book manuscript at Cambridge University Press' 'Studies in the Social and Cultural History of Modern Warfare' series for their feedback and suggestions.

I am deeply appreciative of the assistance that staff at the National Library of Scotland, Special Collections of the University of Reading, the Imperial War Museum, Churchill Archives Centre, and The National Archives have given me throughout the process of researching veteran memoirs. I am also grateful to the Master and Fellows of Churchill College, Cambridge, who have given me permission to quote from materials held in the Churchill Archives. I would especially like to acknowledge my gratitude to the family of Leo Cooper, who kindly granted me permission to quote from his correspondence in this book. The Leo Cooper Archive, which is held in the University of Reading's Special Collections, provided a treasure trove of documents which illustrate the travails of a military history publisher's life. Rummaging through quantities of letters exchanged with his authors, I was consistently struck by the tolerance and good humour with which Leo Cooper treated his ageing and sometimes rather eccentric veteran-memoirists, and I hope that this book will stand as testament to his long and rich service to the British publishing industry.

Among the numerous individuals who have helped and advised me, I should particularly like to thank Wendy Ugolini, Juliette Pattinson,

Lucy Noakes, and Linsey Robb, whose editorial suggestions on the various draft chapters and articles stemming from this research project about Second World War military memoirs that have appeared elsewhere, provided invaluable assistance in honing and deepening this book's more comprehensive consideration of the veterans' tale. Special thanks are due to Malcolm Craig, Mark McLay, and Louise Settle for their provision of practical support by reading endless drafts, and their constant friendship on our long voyage together since the beginning of the PhD. To other friends including Yvonne and Dave McKean, Emma Austin, Gemma Brown, Bernard Kelly, Adrienne Miller McLaughlin, Teri Deighton, Kim Deighton, and Jaqui Booth, who have felt the presence of this research in their own lives, I would like to say a heartfelt 'thank you' for all the tea, cake, and laughter which helped me to keep my sanity. Thank you to Ann Sturdy, Annabel Leakey, and Emily Wilsdon for providing me with places to stay during research trips, and for shepherding me so gracefully around London. Huge thanks also to my new colleagues Eloise Moss, Laure Humbert, Max Jones, Julie-Marie Strange, Ana Carden-Coyne, Kerry Pimblott, and Peter Gatrell at the University of Manchester, who provided much-appreciated support and encouragement during the final push to finish the book.

Finally, my family, who have lived and breathed this book for such a long time that it has practically become another family member are owed the greatest debt of thanks. I am deeply thankful to my parents, Sue and Steve Houghton, and my sister Becky Houghton, for their limitless love, fortitude, and cheerful optimism throughout the rollercoaster of researching and writing a book, and I simply could not have done it without them. My grandparents, too, have been an important part of this process. This book is about creating literary memorials to loved ones, and it seems fitting that in part it should serve as a salutation to the memories of my nana, Joyce Houghton, and my grandpa, Robert Hird, who would have been so proud to see it published. Thanks too, to my grandma, Marjorie Hird, whose indomitable enthusiasm for this research has remained undiminished. Sadly, my wonderful grandpa, Ken Houghton, died shortly before he could see the book finished. His own mischievous anecdotes of service in the RAF provided an impetus to begin this book, whilst his love and support enabled me to battle on with it and to complete it in his memory. The Veterans' Tale is really his book.

Abbreviations

BNB	British National Bibliography
CO	Commanding Officer
CW	Commission Warrant
DFC	Distinguished Flying Cross
FEPOW	Far East Prisoners of War
GHQ	General Headquarters
HF/DF	High Frequency Direction Finding
LMF	Lack of Moral Fibre
Me.109	Messerschmitt Bf. 109
MEF	Mediterranean Expeditionary Force
MC	Military Cross
MM	Military Medal
MOD	Ministry of Defence
MTB	Motor Torpedo Boat
NCO	Non-Commissioned Officer
ORB	Operational Record Book
OTU	Operational Training Unit
POW	Prisoner of War
RAF	Royal Air Force
RAFVR	Royal Air Force Volunteer Reserve
RASC	Royal Army Service Corps
RFC	Royal Flying Corps
RN	Royal Navy
RNVR	Royal Naval Volunteer Reserve
RSM	Regimental Sergeant Major
SAS	Special Air Service
VC	Victoria Cross

Abbreviations

Introduction

> Dear Graeme
>
> I have read your manuscript with the greatest of interest. You have
> recorded your experiences in a way that is perhaps not possible in
> more formal histories, and, while not departing from the authenticity
> of events, by your personal reactions you have added an outstanding
> account of the human factors which are ultimately so important.[1]

In 1963, Second World War veteran Graeme Ogden's memoir of wartime naval service entered a fast-flowing tide of personal narratives
published by British military personnel who had fought in that conflict. Throughout the seven decades since the end of the Second World
War, increasing numbers of these books appeared in print and became
cemented into what Graham Dawson identifies as an enduring popular 'pleasure-culture of war' in Britain.[2] Yet as Rear-Admiral Rupert
Sherbrooke's foreword to Ogden's *My Sea Lady* articulates, they also
proffer an immense value to the social and cultural historian of warfare.
Positioning published veteran memoirs as repositories of vital information about the ways in which former servicemen remembered, understood, and mediated their war, *The Veterans' Tale* establishes the unique
contribution of post-war published military memoirs to the aggregate
of scholarship of modern war and memory. The veterans' memoirs of
the Second World War belong to a lengthy cultural tradition of telling
and receiving old soldiers' stories in Britain. Indeed, when prophesying
his soldiers' creation of memories of Agincourt, William Shakespeare's
'Henry V' sagely observes, 'Old men forget: yet all shall be forgot,/ But

---

[1] Rear-Admiral Rupert Sherbrooke, foreword to Graeme Ogden, *My Sea Lady: The Story of H. M. S. Lady Madeleine From February 1941 to February 1943* (London: Hutchinson, 1963), p. 9.
[2] Graham Dawson, *Soldier Heroes: British Adventure, Empire and the Imagining of Masculinities* (London: Routledge, 1994), p. 4.

he'll remember with advantages/ What feats he did that day.'[3] The play-wright alluded here to the veterans' recollections of fighting, and the emotional meanings that they later came to ascribe to battle. The same process of remembering with 'advantages', of finding order and signifi-cance in combat during the reflective leisure of peacetime, also drove the creation of the Second World War veterans' stories.

That wily bird, Shakespeare, was well aware of the fighting man's love of telling a good story. The embellishments, the factual discrepancies, the shifting and conflicting memories which naturally occur within the narratives of the soldier-raconteur and are wryly identified by the play-wright as 'advantages' of the veteran's memory, might easily be regarded as maddening *dis*advantages to the historical researcher. *The Veterans' Tale*, however, suggests that these inconsistencies of recall and evident subjectivities of veteran war stories are precisely what make them a fas-cinating and rich source of evidence about the experience of war as it is lived and remembered throughout a former soldier's lifetime. Old sol-diers may forget much about their lives, but as Shakespeare remarks, they also often remember and retell their participation in the great events of war for a long time after that war has ended. Rather like the Battle of Agincourt in *Henry V*, a distinctive and spellbinding national mythology was tightly woven around the Second World War in Britain. Swathed in popular images and discourses of the nation's intense pride in attaining victory over the evils of Nazi fascism, the Second World War represented a conflict in which the British ex-serviceman could legitimately exhibit personal pride in his own participation. Unravelling the individual and collective tales of battle that British veterans narrated and published between 1950 and 2010, this book trains fresh sights upon the experi-ence and meaning of the Second World War to those who won it.

As the Second World War slides out of living memory in Britain, *The Veterans' Tale* examines the lived, remembered, and recorded experience of battle within veteran memoir. Traditionally, scholarly investigation of military memoirs has been enacted within the discipline of literary crit-icism, a field which includes such notable works as Paul Fussell's *The Great War and Modern Memory* (1975) and Samuel Hynes' *The Soldiers' Tale* (1998).[4] Fussell's research marked the beginning of new scholarly attitudes towards war literature, playing a pivotal role in shaping under-standings of the canon of First World War texts as part of a broader

---

[3] William Shakespeare, *Henry V*, in *William Shakespeare: The Complete Works*, (ed.) W. J. Craig (London: Magpie Books, 1993), p. 491.

[4] Paul Fussell, *The Great War and Modern Memory* (London: Oxford University Press, 1975); Samuel Hynes, *The Soldiers' Tale: Bearing Witness to Modern War* (London: Pimlico, 1998). A more recent addition to this list is Alex Vernon (ed.), *Arms and the Self: War, the Military and Autobiographical Writing* (Kent (Ohio): Kent State University Press, 2005).

myth-making process within twentieth-century British society. His analysis of the interplay between war, personal narrative, and memory uncovered the ways in which British experience on the Western Front between 1914 and 1918 was 'remembered, conventionalized and mythologized' in literary form.[5] This approach proved 'revolutionary' to furthering scholarly understandings of war, since it demonstrated that battlefield literature offered a vehicle for the expression of collective experience.[6] *The Veterans' Tale* absorbs these ideas to examine how the veteran-memoirists of the Second World War also engaged in a proprietorial form of myth-making in order to shape scholarly, cultural, and official remembrance of 'their' war. In mapping the literary scholarship of military memoirs, Hynes' work provided a subsequent landmark text within the field, making a staunch effort to survey British and American servicemen's memoirs from the First and Second World Wars, and the Vietnam conflict of the 1960s and 1970s. Expanding upon the limited number of sources interrogated by Fussell, Hynes insisted upon the importance of privileging the narratives of the 'one-book men', authors who told their story and then dropped quietly back into anonymity again.[7] Despite this laudable objective, a serious drawback of Hynes' study is its over-reliance upon the more 'literary' and self-conscious popular texts from the Second World War, which does little to rescue the critical mass of military memoirs still consigned to relative oblivion. Building on Hynes' foundations, *The Veterans' Tale* thus extends its scope of enquiry to include a much wider range of these books. Nevertheless, Hynes' consideration of some of the formal qualities of military memoir underpins the identification of narratives examined in this book, which also acknowledges Hynes' salutary reminder that war memoirists are invariably a self-selecting group. Correspondingly, it is contended here that attention must be paid to the reasons why these authors, whether they were prolific writers or 'one-book men', made a decision to pen and make public a narrative of their combat experiences.

To these path-finding literary scholars, especially Hynes, a considerable debt is acknowledged in my own study. However, whilst some of their techniques of literary criticism structurally underpin my own analysis of war memoirs, *The Veterans' Tale* situates itself firmly in the cultural-military history camp. Addressing themes of war, memory, and emotions in relation to veteran-memoirists, this study is intended to fill a critical and inexplicable gap in the rapidly expanding field of historical enquiry into military life-writing. In recent years, military memoirs have come to exert an evident appeal for a growing number of researchers across

[5] Paul Fussell, *The Great War and Modern Memory*, rev. ed. (Oxford: Oxford University Press, 2000), p. ix.
[6] Susanna Rustin, 'Hello to all that', *The Guardian*, 31 July 2004.
[7] Hynes, *The Soldiers' Tale*, p. xv.

the fields of history and social geography. Under the 'war and society' umbrella, military memoirs have become increasingly promoted as an essential means of recovering the experience of battle and understanding the complex relationship between war, the soldier, and society. In 2008, Brian Bond's *Survivors of a Kind* combined the perspectives of cultural and military historians in his approach to British First World War memoirs spawned by the Western Front.[8] Crucially, Bond established that the long-term effects of the conflict upon combatants could be assessed through their personal narratives. This view exerts a formative influence over *The Veterans' Tale*, which examines the ways in which post-1950 military memoirs of the Second World War recorded the enduring impact of battle upon veterans. As a result of a recent cultural turn towards military life-writing, the chronological margins of studying war memoirs have been considerably expanded outwards. Neil Ramsey and Catriona Kennedy have traced soldiers' narratives of the Revolutionary and Napoleonic Wars, whilst Yuval Noah Harari proffers a comprehensive examination of Renaissance military memoirs. Directing scholarly attention towards the more recent twentieth century, the works of K. Neil Jenkings, and Rachel Woodward address contemporary soldiers' life-writing from wars in the Falklands, the Gulf, Northern Ireland, Afghanistan, and Iraq.[9] In this book, a slightly different emphasis is placed on the identity of the military memoirist as an ex-serviceman, or an old soldier, whose authorship is reflective and constructive rather than one of straightforward reportage. This allows for the long-term physical, psychological, and emotional impact of war upon an ex-combatant to be significantly opened up. The central pillar of this book is a scrutiny of the unique identity of the post-war military memoir which 'records the remembered war that persists in the mind through a lifetime.'[10] This

---

[8] Brian Bond, *Survivors of a Kind: Memoirs of the Western Front* (London: Continuum, 2008).

[9] Neil Ramsey, *The Military Memoir and Romantic Literary Culture, 1780–1835* (Farnham: Ashgate, 2011); Catriona Kennedy, *Narratives of the Revolutionary and Napoleonic Wars: Military and Civilian Experience in Britain and Ireland* (Basingstoke: Palgrave Macmillan, 2013); Yuval Noah Harari, *Renaissance Military Memoirs: War, History, and Identity, 1450–1600* (Woodbridge: Boydell Press, 2004); Harari, 'Armchairs, Coffee, and Authority: Eye-Witnesses and Flesh-Witnesses Speak about War, 1100–2000', *Journal of Military History*, 74:1 (January 2010), 53–78; Vernon, *Arms and the Self*; Rachel Woodward and K. Neil Jenkings, 'Soldiers' bodies and the contemporary British military memoir', in *War and the Body: Militarisation, Practice and Experience* (ed.) Kevin McSorley (London: Routledge, 2013), 152–64; K. Neil Jenkings and Rachel Woodward, 'Communicating War through the Contemporary British Military Memoir: The Censorships of Genre, State, and Self', *Journal of War & Culture Studies* 7:1 (2014), 5–17.

[10] Samuel Hynes, 'Personal Narratives and Commemoration', in *War and Remembrance in the Twentieth Century*, (eds.) Jay Winter and Emmanuel Sivan (Cambridge: Cambridge University Press, 1999), p. 211.

book thus represents the first extended scholarly treatment of *veteran* memoirs, situating these texts as particularly valuable to historians of warfare because of their capacity to shed light upon the ex-combatant's retrospective remembrance and understanding of battle.

Surprisingly, the voices of British Second World War veteran-memoirists have yet to be heard on a collective scale within the field of scholarship of war, memory, and personal narratives. Towards the end of the market that caters for more popular histories of wartime martial experience, historians have relied heavily on mining these accounts of soldiers, sailors, and aircrew for the vivid details and human emotions that lend colour to battle for wider reading audiences.[11] Among the extensive terrain of Second World War historiography, the post-war memoirs of former servicemen have been dotted here and there, but their use has been mostly restricted to the provision of salient anecdotes or fleeting descriptions of battle conditions. Given both the fruitful and expanding nature of scholarly enquiry into military life-writing and the Second World War's continued resonance within British national culture, the gaping hole in academic scholarship of the myriad war memoirs generated by the 1939–45 conflict is remarkable. To date, despite a burgeoning literature examining the memoirs of British military captivity in the Far East during the war, no single purpose-built work exclusively addresses British military memoirs of the Second World War.[12] Where they have been cursorily utilised, these books are often somewhat crudely sandwiched into wider discussions that focus upon the narratives of First World War and Vietnam soldiers as a twentieth century literature of disillusionment. Within recent years, Yuval Noah Harari has deservedly become an authority on the genre of Renaissance military memoirs, but the clarity and insight that he brings to his approach to these documents is not entirely matched by his use of twentieth century military life-writing in order to exhibit the distinctive design in structure

---

[11] See, for example, Patrick Bishop, *Fighter Boys: Saving Britain 1940* (London: HarperCollins, 2003); Brian Lavery, *In Which They Served: The Royal Navy Officer Experience in the Second World War* (London: Conway, 2008); Glyn Prysor, *Citizen Sailors: The Royal Navy in the Second World War* (London: Viking, 2011); Michael G. Walling, *Forgotten Sacrifice: The Arctic Convoys of World War II* (Oxford: Osprey Publishing, 2016); Kevin Wilson, *Men of Air: The Doomed Youth of Bomber Command, 1944* (London: Weidenfeld & Nicolson, 2007).

[12] See, for example, Frances Houghton, '"To the Kwai and Back": Myth, Memory and Memoirs of the "Death Railway" 1942–1943', *Journal of War and Culture Studies*, 7:3 (2014), 223–35; Lizzie Oliver, *Prisoners of the Sumatra Railway: Narratives of History and Memory* (New York: Bloomsbury, 2018); Sibylla Jane Flower, 'Captors and Captives on the Burma-Thailand Railway', in Bob Moore and Kent Fedorowich (eds.), *Prisoners of War and their Captors in World War II* (Oxford: Berg, 1996), pp. 227–52; Roger Bourke, *Prisoners of the Japanese: Literary Imagination and the Prisoner-of-War Experience* (Queensland: University of Queensland Press, 2006).

and content of the earlier accounts. Although this method allows a number of valuable conclusions about Renaissance testimonies to be drawn, it also results in a collection of rather frustrating generalisations about the later personal narratives of combat. Harari's broad claim that scholars studying twentieth-century war memoirs 'have reached the almost unanimous conclusion that ... soldiers have become disillusioned with war, and their own image has partly changed from that of heroes to that of victims' is not particularly helpful to any investigation of Second World War memoirs.[13] The veterans' tale of frontline service between 1939 and 1945 shows no sign at all of the disenchantment or betrayal of ideals which may be typically read into the canon of First World War and Vietnam soldiers' testimonies. In fact, the Second World War veteran-memoirists were inordinately proud of their wartime service and clearly subscribed to a concept of the 1939–45 conflict as a 'Good War'.[14] Any public or private suggestion that these men ought to feel guilty or victimised by their wartime experiences typically received extremely short shrift from them.

The theoretical orientation of this book is rooted in a number of fields, weaving together key tenets from memory studies, auto/biographical studies, and the emergent field of history of the emotions to suggest an innovative approach to discussing military memoirs. Within the extant scholarship, valuable new ways of understanding the wider relationship between war and society were offered by a 'boom' in studies of memory which occurred during the 1980s.[15] Academics from multi-disciplines shifted interpretations of private and 'collective' memory from passive to active, relocating the changeability, flexibility, and permeability of memory as a source of interest and advantage to the scholar. Fundamentally, war memoirists came to be viewed within this context as 'makers' who create narratives of remembrance in which meaning is emergent rather than fixed, and Jay Winter and Samuel Hynes have emphasised a need to open up investigation of the place of soldiers' tales in relation to broader historical remembrance.[16] *The Veterans' Tale* responds to this need by enquiring more deeply into the relationship between military memoirs and wider official, scholarly, and cultural remembrance of the Second World War. To a great extent, this study of veteran memoirs is thus informed by the ideas of leading scholars within the field of memory

---

[13] Yuval Noah Harari, 'Martial Illusions: War and Disillusionment in Twentieth-Century and Renaissance Military Memoirs', *Journal of Military History*, 69:1 (2005), 43.

[14] Studs Terkel, *'The Good War': An Oral History of World War Two* (New York: Pantheon, 1984).

[15] Jay Winter, *Remembering War: The Great War Between Memory and History in the Twentieth Century* (New Haven: Yale University Press, 2006), p. 1.

[16] Ibid., p. 9; Hynes, 'Personal Narratives and Commemoration', pp. 205–6.

studies. In particular, it draws upon the theories of Maurice Halbwachs, who demonstrates that memories do not simply exist within a vacuum, but are instead composed within 'social frameworks' that exert an influence upon the recall, recognition, and localization of memory.[17] Standing at the intersection of private and public memory, the published veteran memoir is thus ideally placed to illumine the shifting and often conflicting affinity between individual and 'collective' remembrance of the Second World War in Britain. In analysing the production and reproduction of veteran memory in published literary form, this study also relies heavily upon the work of Henri Rousso, who identifies any source that proposes a deliberate reconstruction of an event for a social purpose as 'carriers' or 'vectors' of memory.[18] Weaving these ideas into its approach towards published veteran memoirs, *The Veterans' Tale* locates these narratives as precious sites from which the veterans could dictate and contest representations of the Second World War.

Oral histories have also come to occupy an important place in examining narratives of war and memory during the twentieth century. In many ways, an oral history bears a marked similarity to a written memoir in that both reconstruct experience from memory and attempt to access an often long-past voice from the situation of the present. Consequently, *The Veterans' Tale* engages with key ideas produced from within the domain of oral histories of war. Alistair Thomson's ground-breaking *Anzac Memories* (1994) explores the processes through which Australian veterans of the First World War composed their memories of war across a lifetime, and how their own later-life experiences and understandings influenced their recollections.[19] Thomson's examination of the ways in which meanings about the past evolved for the old soldiers whom he interviewed thus highlights the necessity to bear in mind that lived and remembered experiences of battle are shared points on the continuum of a lifetime. *The Veterans' Tale* also considers the work of Penny Summerfield in terms of the composure and articulation of wartime self and experience. Summerfield's study of women's oral histories of the Second World War reminds that personal testimony is always inter-subjective, drawing from generalised discourse to construct the particular personal subject.[20]

---

[17] Maurice Halbwachs, *On Collective Memory*, trans. Lewis Coser (Chicago: University of Chicago Press, 1992), p. 38.

[18] Henri Rousso, *The Vichy Syndrome: History and Memory in France since 1944*, trans. Arthur Goldhammer (Cambridge (MA): Harvard University Press, 1991), p. 219.

[19] Alistair Thomson, *Anzac Memories: Living With the Legend* (Oxford: Oxford University Press, 1994)

[20] Penny Summerfield, *Reconstructing Women's Wartime Lives: Discourse and Subjectivity in Oral Histories of the Second World War* (Manchester: Manchester University Press, 1998), p. 15.

Bearing this in mind, *The Veterans' Tale* maintains a particular focus upon the wider discourse, language, and imagery that was available to the veteran-memoirist to reconstruct both his experiences of battle and his sense of wartime self.

This book also examines the question of what the veteran-memoirist consciously and subconsciously remembered of his wartime experiences, and which memories found their way into his personal narrative. In doing so, it draws upon a number of studies rooted in the neurosciences. In their comprehensive study of war and remembrance in the twentieth century, Jay Winter and Emmanuel Sivan pulled together major lines of scientific understandings of memory, finding that most experiences leave long-term memory traces, although these may differ in density. The weight of a memory determines how well it may be recollected, and density is moulded by the degree of drama or uniqueness of an experience. Perhaps unsurprisingly, these scholars found that memories of combat were particularly dense, and therefore long-lasting, because the experience was intensely personal and dramatic. Harrowing moments conferred further density upon a memory.[21] In his study of over 1,000 Second World War British veterans, psychologist Nigel Hunt also found that many of the strongest memories held by these men pertained to battle. The sheer horror of their experiences on the battlefield remained active and tenacious in their recollections.[22] Among the field of neurosciences, links between emotion and memory are now well-established. Ulrike Rimmele *et al.* find that 'emotion enhances the subjective sense of remembering', granting an increased subjective intensity of memory and higher confidence in the accuracy of remembering.[23] Broadly speaking, therefore, the reconstructive nature of individual memory means that experience is transformed into recollection by uniqueness, importance, imaginative elaboration, and confabulation.[24] Not all of the serviceman's time was spent in close proximity to violence and danger; indeed a common aphorism holds that war is 90 per cent boredom and 10 per cent action. It is that 10 per cent of violent, exciting, terrifying experience which is remembered and recorded in the Second World War veterans' tale – as one memoirist of Bomber Command mused, 'who the hell can

---

[21] Jay Winter and Emmanuel Sivan, 'Setting the Framework', in *War and Remembrance in the Twentieth Century*, p. 12.

[22] Nigel C. Hunt, *Memory, War and Trauma* (Cambridge: Cambridge University Press), pp. 140–3.

[23] Ulrike Rimmele, Lila Davachi, Radoslav Petrov, Sonya Dougal, Elizabeth A. Phelps, 'Emotion enhances the subjective feeling of remembering, despite lower accuracy for contextual details', *Emotion*, 11:3 (2011), 553.

[24] Hunt, *Memory, War and Trauma*, p. 118.

write a book about boredom?'[25] *The Veterans' Tale* thus takes as its focus that 10 per cent of remembered and recorded experience 'at the sharp end' of war.

Beneath the surface of personal recollection lurks the sharp rock of war-related trauma, upon which a veteran's memory may easily founder. Dominick LaCapra identifies trauma as 'a disruptive experience that disarticulates the self and creates holes in existence.'[26] Furthermore, as Hunt and Robbins note, trauma – such as may be sustained on the battlefield – disrupts the processing of memory, existing as an unconscious, dissociated recollection which later may be prompted into consciousness through stimulation of reminders.[27] As such, it is necessary to keep in mind Paul Ricoeur's caution of the necessity of acknowledging that individual memory may prove an inherently unstable source.[28] Sometimes it is difficult to identify whether a veteran-memoirist's memory has been corrupted or simply erased by traumatic experience. Equally, it is possible to over-identify trauma in these narratives and attribute every silence or inaccuracy to psychological damage. Nevertheless, *The Veterans' Tale* argues that it is possible to navigate these challenges, frequently with the help of the veteran-memoirist himself. A number of the authors in this study endured psychological breakdown, or some form of what is now termed 'post-traumatic stress disorder', and their accounts proffer important evidence about the impact of wartime trauma and 'battle fatigue' upon the author's own sense of self. Rather than lamenting the ways in which trauma erases memory, therefore, it is more productive to consider how the act of creating a memoir helped traumatised veterans to articulate recoverable memories as an act of catharsis.

As Thomson pointed out in a recent new edition of *Anzac Memories*, the field of 'memory studies' has become closely enmeshed with an 'autobiographical age' among historiography of war and society.[29]As works of life-writing, war memoirs have a distinctive family connection to the literature of auto/biographical studies. Theories connected to the field of auto/biographical study prove enormously helpful in approaching the veterans' tale, particularly in terms of helping to move past a thorny 'truth' versus 'fiction' problem which lingers around these narratives.

[25] John Wainwright, *Tail-End Charlie* (London: Macmillan, 1978), p. 26.
[26] Dominick LaCapra, *Writing History, Writing Trauma* (Baltimore: Johns Hopkins University Press, 2001), p. 41.
[27] Nigel C. Hunt and Ian Robbins, 'Telling Stories of the War: Ageing Veterans Coping with Their Memories through Narrative', *Oral History*, 26:2 (1998), p. 59.
[28] Paul Ricoeur, *Memory, History, Forgetting* (Chicago: University of Chicago Press, 2004), p. 80.
[29] Alistair Thomson, *Anzac Memories: Living with the Legend*, rev. ed., (Monash: Monash University Publishing, 2013), p. 1.

Fussell suggests that the war memoir is not in fact a personal history but is rather 'a kind of fiction', in which the imposition of literary devices of lexis, syntax, structure, and plot when turning memory into linear prose narrative undermine the 'truth' of lived experience.[30] Auto/biographical theory suggests differently, positing that attempting to recover an individual's past solely by matching up a person's recollection with established 'fact' severely limits the usefulness of these texts. As Mark Freeman notes, 'if we think of "truth" in this context only in terms of its faithful correspondence to what was, then autobiographical texts must indeed be deemed illusory and fictional.' Crucially, therefore, he argues that there is little reason to think of truth in such a 'limited and simplistic' way.[31] Similarly, Laura Marcus muses that very few critics of auto/biographical writing would demand that auto/biographical truth should be viewed solely in terms of literal verifiability. She suggests that the seemingly intractable problem of 'referentiality' – the kind and degree of 'truth' that can be expected from autobiographical writing – may be resolved by discussion of the author's intentions and motivations. If the autobiography is 'sincere' in an attempt to understand self and experience, and to make these clear to others, then the 'auto/biographical intention' must be received seriously.[32] A key line of enquiry in *The Veterans' Tale* is thus to interrogate the intention and function of war memoir, deconstructing the veterans' motives for recovering and communicating experience, and the processes by which they attempted to retain the integrity of their narratives in order to bear witness as 'truthfully', in accordance with their own views, as possible.

Furthermore, within the field of auto/biographical study, it has long been recognised that life-writing is a process of 'collusion' between past and present.[33] The creation of an autobiographical text stems from, as James Olney has argued, 'the vital impulse to order that has always caused man to create.'[34] *The Veterans' Tale* thus posits that penning a war memoir allowed the veteran to shape and order his recollections of the past, imposing pattern and coherency upon experience. The narrativisation and emplotment of memory on paper granted a precious second reading of experience, offering the former serviceman a valuable space for reflection

---

[30] Fussell, *The Great War and Modern Memory*, p. 310.
[31] Mark Freeman, *Rewriting the Self: History, Memory, Narrative* (London: Routledge, 1993), p. 32.
[32] Laura Marcus, *Auto/Biographical Discourses: Theory, Criticism, Practice* (Manchester: Manchester University Press, 1994), p. 3.
[33] Roy Pascal, *Design and Truth in Autobiography* (London: Routledge & Keegan Paul, 1960), p. 11.
[34] James Olney, *Metaphors of Self: The Meaning of Autobiography* (Princeton: Princeton University Press, 1972), p. 3.

upon wartime combat. Indeed, Georges Grusdorf argues that, in its
provision of a second opportunity to read experience, autobiographical
writing may actually produce a 'truer' representation than the first as it
adds consciousness to experience.[35] Freeman also notes that 'the central
feature of rewriting the self [is] the process of conferring new meanings
on the past in the light of the present.' In this sense, engaging in an act of
autobiography enables a man to reassemble himself in his own likeness
at a certain moment of his history.[36] His image is fixed for eternity, which
grants him the opportunity to cogitate at length upon the changes sustained to that self. Whether this process of inner reflection is implicit or
explicit in a war memoir, self-knowledge is invariably bound up in autobiographical writing and so the historian gains a valuable glimpse into the
veteran's self-fashioning of past and present identities. Dialogue between
a memoirist's past and present constructions of self thus reveals something important about the veteran's fashioning of that self at the time of
writing. *The Veterans' Tale* therefore concurs with Jay Winter's suggestion
that the stories related by soldiers tell us of their experiences, whilst the
act of narration informs us of who they are at the time of telling.[37] War,
as Elaine Scarry notes, forces the combatant to set aside his normative
peacetime identity, divesting himself of 'a learned and deeply embodied set of physical impulses regarding his relation to any other person's
body.' According to Scarry, through his consent to kill for the nation,
the soldier's identity becomes fragmented: war 'unmakes' his sense of
self.[38] Once the soldier stepped back from the battlefield into peacetime
civilian life, memoir functioned as a mirror in which to reassemble these
pieces. *The Veterans' Tale* engages with these ideas to demonstrate that,
for veterans of the Second World War, autobiographical writing offered
a valuable opportunity to reassemble shattered notions of masculine self
into a coherent and meaningful image. The interiority and linearity of
these narratives is thus an important focus of this study.

Representations of war constitute a pillar of this research. Focusing
on core themes of landscape, weaponry, the enemy, and comradeship,
this book examines the imagery used by Second World War veteran-
memoirists to depict their experiences of battle. It maintains a firm
focus on change and continuity within the veterans' tale. As such, it
also engages with a body of scholarship which focuses more widely on

---

[35] Georges Grusdorf, 'Conditions and Limits of Autobiography', in *Autobiography: Essays Theoretical and Critical*, (ed.) James Olney (Princeton: Princeton University Press, 1980), p. 38.
[36] Ibid., p. 43.
[37] Winter, *Remembering War*, p. 116.
[38] Elaine Scarry, *The Body in Pain* (Oxford: Oxford University Press, 1985), p. 122.

cultural representations and images of the Second World War. As Mark Connelly observes, the Second World War is 'a visual war above all else.'[39] Connelly's analysis of the 'peculiar and particular history and memory' that the British nation continues to hold of this war highlights the vast range of books, newspapers, films, documentaries, and artwork which perennially inform Britain's 'popular, national culture.'[40] It was within this context that the veterans' tale of the Second World War was produced over the course of nearly seventy years, and the memoirists' immersion in this collection of visual images and symbols invariably shaped their own descriptions of 'what it was like' to serve in wartime. In his excellent cultural history of the wartime RAF, Martin Francis demonstrates that 'key myths about the flyer were already in place long before 1945.' His outline of how RAF aircrew in particular negotiated cultural images and stereotypes that many found 'simultaneously compelling and repellent' opens the door to similar interrogation of the mediation of self-image and cultural tropes in the memoirs of soldiers and sailors.[41] *The Veterans' Tale* thus provides an audit of how veteran-memoirists subscribed to, and challenged, a wider cultural iconography of battle during the Second World War in their depictions of wartime experience.

The veterans' narratives are inspected here through a prism of war as a series of separate but interrelated psychological relationships with landscape, weaponry, the enemy, and comrades. *The Veterans' Tale* particularly focuses upon the war memoirists' portrayal of their emotional responses to these four dimensions of frontline experience. As such, this book also contributes to the blossoming field of studies in the history of emotions. As emotionally- saturated documents, war memoirs have much to offer this branch of historical enquiry. For British servicemen prior to 1939, a basic 'language of instincts' was used to describe emotions in war. By the 1960s, a new 'fashionably self-conscious, psychoanalytical style' of war memoirs encouraged a more introspective and confessional narrative of battlefield stories and sensations.[42] There is thus much to be gleaned from these documents about how the veteran-memoirist self-identified and interpreted his emotional and physiological responses to combat. In a recent endeavour to open up further research in the area of the history of emotions, Jan Plamper's introduction to this field

[39] Mark Connelly, *We Can Take It! Britain and the Memory of the Second World War* (Harlow: Pearson Education, 2004), p. 6.
[40] Ibid., p. 14.
[41] Martin Francis, *The Flyer: British Culture and the Royal Air Force, 1939–1945* (Oxford: Oxford University Press, 2008), p. 7.
[42] Joanna Bourke, 'Fear and Anxiety: Writing about Emotion in Modern History', *History Workshop Journal*, 55 (2003), 120.

suggested that the history of emotion might be aligned with the study of oral history.[43] When oral history first gained momentum as a discipline during the 1980s, it gave birth to numerous important theories about how to approach memory as an historical source, a number of which have informed the fashioning of *The Veterans' Tale*.[44] Moving oral history under the umbrella of the history of emotion similarly raises questions pertaining to the relationship between emotion and memory.[45] Whilst Plamper rightfully cautions a need to be mindful of the temporal difference between the experience and memory of emotion, this is the same potentially tricky issue that the historian seeking to distinguish between a veteran-memoirist's lived and remembered experience of war must navigate. In both instances, the answer arguably remains the same. War memoirs are by nature retrospective and have much to say about what a veteran thought he felt, and what he wanted to put on record at the time of writing and publishing his account. If we can accept this as a baseline from which to unravel these documents, we also stand a good chance of further illuminating the emotional significance that the veteran-memoirist attached to his wartime experiences.

The veterans' tale contains a wealth of emotional recollection encoded in emotive language. As historian Barbara Rosenwein observes, such language proffers considerable 'grist for the historian's mill.'[46] A key objective of this book is therefore to analyse the imagery and language that veteran-memoirists used to recover and record their experiences in battle. It is also imperative to critically explore the language and imagery which military memoirists select to frame experiences of combat in their narratives as these choices reveal not only the ways in which the veteran comprehended his experiences but also the ways in which he wanted his audience to understand them. On those occasions where language is viewed as inadequate to convey feelings of anguish or shame, silence itself might also be viewed as symbolic. As Jay Winter reminds, silence is frequently a deliberate construction; an active choice may be made to remain silent for a multitude of reasons.[47] Since superficially unemotional content in these documents is just as revealing as the overtly emotional,

---

[43] Jan Plamper, *The History of Emotions: An Introduction*, trans. Keith Tribe (Oxford: Oxford University Press, 2015), p. 289.

[44] Ibid., p. 289.

[45] Ibid.

[46] Barbara H. Rosenwein, 'Problems and Methods in the History of Emotions', *Passions in Context: International Journal for the History and Theory of Emotions*, www.passionsincontext.de/?id=557.

[47] Jay Winter, 'Thinking about Silence', in Efrat Ben-Ze'ev, Ruth Gino and Jay Winter (eds.), *Shadows of War: A Social History of Silence in the Twentieth Century* (Cambridge: Cambridge University Press, 2010), pp. 4–11.

it is salutary to follow Rosenwein's advice to 'read the silences' in veteran memoirs.[48] The war memoirist's choices and balance of language and silence in his depiction of battle are thus scrutinised in this book as signifiers of the physical, psychological, and emotional impact of combat upon the veteran. Rosenwein's concept of 'emotional communities' – shared systems of feeling in networks of human beings – also exerts a formative influence upon this investigation of veteran memoirs. Published post-war memoirs operated as textual links between an emotional community of military veterans, and it is also possible to identify separate emotional communities within the wider community of post-war veteran memoirists. Published memoirs communicated affective bonds between author and other veterans based on shared experiences of battle during the Second World War. These narratives also functioned as vehicles of communication with a number of other audiences including family, friends, and a wider audience of unknown public readers. Not least, they sought to extend reassurance and guidance to future generations of combatants. Furthermore, Rosenwein's suggestion that emotional communities may avoid expression of some emotions altogether, or only discuss certain emotions within a specific and limited context, also holds import for unpacking veteran memoirs.[49] The unusual punctuation in the title of *The Veterans' Tale* signifies its core argument that these narratives ought to be read on a collective, as well as an individual, level. Borrowing and moving on from Hynes' evocative title of *The Soldiers' Tale*, the placing of the apostrophe opens up discussion of a 'notional tale', or 'one huge story', of the combatant and war.[50] It also establishes the war memoirist's claims to possession of his individual tale, and to his right as spokesman for the masses of former combatants who were never given the chance to tell their stories; a theme which is strongly emergent in this particular category of military life-writing.

Emotive and sensory depictions of battle have been closely woven into the identity of the modern military memoir ever since its birth in the mid-eighteenth century. Although soldiers' stories are as old as war itself, and the British twentieth-century military memoir has its roots in a long tradition of military life-writing which extends back to the Greco-Roman world, the soldier's tale in its modern form began to emerge from the middle of the eighteenth century.[51] At this time an unprecedented outpouring of military life-writing witnessed a number of key changes in

---

[48] Rosenwein, 'Problems and Methods in the History of Emotions'
[49] Ibid.
[50] Hynes, *Soldiers' Tale*, p. xiii.
[51] Yuval Noah Harari, 'Military Memoirs: A Historical Overview of the Genre from the Middle Ages to the Late Modern Era', *War in History*, 14:3 (2007), p. 295.

the nature of soldiers' memoirs. Whereas Renaissance military memoirs comprised mostly of facts rather than experiences, and were generally not written by the lower ranks, during the French and Napoleonic Wars of 1793–1815, soldiers' accounts began to privilege descriptions of experience over lengthy lists of facts about the battles in which they participated.[52] Ramsey labels these subaltern narratives 'affective eye-witness accounts', proposing that at this time the personal story of the soldier began to circulate as a mode of socio-cultural reflection upon war, inviting the public to share in the soldier's sufferings.[53] Through these cultural changes, the ordinary soldier-memoirist was granted a public voice in addition to an apparatus through which he could challenge both other representations of war and the authority of his social and military superiors. As The Veterans' Tale unfolds, the Second World War memoirists were not slow to take advantage of this well-established forum.

At the other end of the chronological scale, the development of modern technologies during the late twentieth and early twenty-first centuries has shaped the creation of soldiers' tales anew. The rise of the internet enabled autobiographical stories to be shared in online forums or posted on popular websites such as the BBC's 'WW2 People's War' webpage, an online archive allowing members of the public to post and read memories of people's experiences during the Second World War.[54] The use of helmet-cams attached to soldiers fighting in the recent conflicts in Afghanistan and Iraq has offered a somatic method of telling the combatant's battlefield story. Ascertaining what actually 'counts' as a war memoir in order to distinguish a genre with discrete rules has thus become a notoriously troublesome task, and in an essay indicatively titled 'No Genre's Land' Alex Vernon highlights persistent ambiguities in the war memoir's identity.[55] Much effort has been expended, particularly in the realm of auto/biographical studies, in trying to define exactly where memoirs fit into the spectrum of life-writing.[56] Arguably, devoting excessive attention to the complex wrangles over precisely where the latter should be located on the continuum of ego-documents does not much help to further understandings of the narratives themselves.

---

[52] Harari, Renaissance Military Memoirs, p. 67.
[53] Ramsey, The Military Memoir and Romantic Literary Culture, p. 10.
[54] Lucy Noakes, '"War on the Web": The BBC's "People's War" Website and Memories of Fear in Wartime in 21st Century Britain', in British Cultural Memory and the Second World War, (eds.), Lucy Noakes and Juliette Pattinson (London: Bloomsbury, 2013), pp. 60–76.
[55] Alex Vernon, 'No Genre's Land: The Problem of Genre in War Memoirs and Military Autobiographies', in Arms and the Self, pp. 1–40.
[56] Marcus, Auto/Biographical Discourses; Linda Anderson, Autobiography (London: Routledge, 2001); Pascal, Design and Truth in Autobiography.

As Harari acerbically but accurately remarks, 'From the perspective of military history, much of this debate is superfluous.'[57] Instead, he proffers a useful framework of identification, proposing that military memoirs may be diagnosed where they meet the following criteria:

1. They are synthetic narrative texts
2. They are written retrospectively
3. They are written to a considerable extent on the basis of personal memory
4. They deal with a considerable time-span
5. They have their authors appear as protagonists, and
6. They devote considerable attention to martial affairs in which their authors participated as combatants.[58]

To this might be added Hynes' driving criterion that a book constitutes a war memoir when it speaks with 'a voice that is stubbornly distinct, telling us what it was like, for *this* man, in *this* war.'[59] Abiding by these principles, *The Veterans' Tale* does not, therefore, include as veteran memoirs texts which stem from the extensive and nebulous hinterland of military life-writing. This includes co-authored narratives, personal testimony camouflaged as fiction, anthologies of testimony snipped from oral or published accounts, or chapters on the war that are contained within larger autobiographical works. Also excluded from this study are the wide and varied range of accounts that are often labelled as 'memoirs', constituting anything from a couple of hastily- typed pages to abrupt self-published accounts. By focusing on the cadre of Second World War memoirs that were brought out with more commercial publishing houses, it is possible to make use of the records which detail the communication between memoirist and publisher to probe in detail the intention and function of published veteran memoir. In particular, the recently catalogued archive of Leo Cooper, a renowned specialist publisher of military history, offers a veritable treasure trove for investigating the gestation process of published military memoir. Indeed, Cooper's efforts to grant former soldiers a voice, and to allow them 'to erect their own memorial' quietly underpin much of *The Veterans' Tale*, as many of the memoirs investigated in this book were either published by Cooper or under the Pen and Sword imprint which took over his backlist and catalogues during the 1990s.[60] A number of veteran-memoirists who were

---

[57] Harari, 'Military Memoirs', p. 290.
[58] Ibid., p. 290.
[59] Hynes, *Soldiers' Tale*, p. xv.
[60] Leo Cooper, *All My Friends Will Buy It: A Bottlefield Tour* (Staplehurst: Spellmount, 2005), p. 192.

ultimately published elsewhere also had some professional dealings with
Leo Cooper. The Leo Cooper Archive thus proffers a unique insight into
how what John Keegan calls the 'two worlds' of publishers and soldiers
have come together.[61]

Within the wider discussion of the history and identity of military life-
writing, the published Second World War military memoir has a distinctive history in its own right. Within this the identities of wartime and
post-war published narratives have acquired their own unique personae.
Official restrictions upon the wartime publication of military memoirs
lent these books a very different flavour to their post-war brethren. On
7 April 1942, a Cabinet decision was taken to impose a comprehensive
ban on the publication of service reminiscences. In some cases this ban
was relaxed, but these memoirs were required to pass through intense
official scrutiny to ensure that they did not compromise military personnel, equipment, locations, tactics, and (perhaps most importantly from
an official perspective) did not offer scathing opinions of the conduct
of the war. Heavily censored to ensure that they did not endanger public morale, wartime-published military memoirs frequently contained
hearty, if rather clumsy, messages of encouragement to the struggling
British nation. By November 1945, the ban was lifted, although procedures were put in place by each Service to ensure that personnel
were made aware of the provisions of the Official Secrets Acts. Soldiers
and naval personnel were advised to contact either the War Office or
the Admiralty should they wish to publish on matters arising from or
pertaining to their wartime service. The Air Ministry simply drew the
attention of airmen leaving the Service to the Official Secrets Acts.[62]
During the late 1940s and 1950s, some official safeguards against the
publication of information which might reveal wartime secrets remained
in place, but these operated on a much reduced scale. By the mid-1950s,
publishers were only required to submit the manuscript of a war memoir
for official vetting if the author was still a serving officer or had been
involved with intelligence work during the war. It remained vital to seek
official approval in the latter circumstance, as the memoirist might reveal
methods or identities of colleagues which could prejudice future intelligence operations in the event of another war. Other circumstances which
necessitated official permission to publish involved reference to any wartime secrets that the government wished to be kept secret, such as the
existence of ULTRA. During the 1950s, publishers or authors who were

[61] John Keegan, foreword, *All My Friends Will Buy It*, p. ix. This archive is currently held by
the University of Reading.
[62] The National Archives (hereafter TNA) /CAB 21/2683, Sir Henry Markham to
E. Bridges, 15 November 1945.

anxious or unsure about the regulations could apply to Admiral George
P. Thomson, Secretary of the Admiralty, War Office, Air Ministry and
Press Committee, for advice.[63]

Once the war ended and official restrictions began to lift, momentum
for publishing military memoirs gathered pace rapidly. Since the 1950s a
snowball effect occurred in the publication of memoirs of military veterans of the Second World War, with more appearing in each decade until
around 2010, when numbers began to sharply fall off as that generation
of veterans faded away. The years between 1945 and 1950 witnessed a
turbulent transition from a wartime to a peacetime publishing climate,
from which it is difficult to draw satisfactory conclusions about military
life-writing in the immediate post-war period. Until 1950, many publishing houses were cautious about commissioning too many war-related
titles. With the end of paper rationing in 1949, however, publishers' precious supplies of paper were no longer restricted to a relatively narrow
pool of titles deemed valuable to the nation's morale. Correspondingly,
publication lists gradually began to include an expanding variety of personal accounts which recounted experiences of war on many different
fronts, and from the perspective of a multifarious array of combatants.
This expansion was helped along by the new demand for cheap, mass
market paperbacks that had emerged from the late 1930s. However,
many of the combat narratives which appeared in the late 1940s were
frequently constructed in the same manner as the censored, and often
overtly propagandised, wartime-published texts, perhaps because they
too were often written during the war itself and left largely in their
wartime-edited forms. This especially tended to be the case with posthumous publications, such as Guy Gibson's *Enemy Coast Ahead* (1946)
and Keith Douglas's *Alamein to Zem Zem* (1946), but some living authors
such as Nicholas Monsarrat in his *Three Corvettes* (issued in October
1945) also did not revise the material they had drafted during the war,
although in some instances they did add new forewords.[64] Many combat narratives of the mid-to-late 1940s thus had a somewhat confused,
hybrid identity, and are difficult to integrate into discussions of the character of military memoir as it began to emerge with greater distance from
the war during the 1950s. The transition to the unique subjectivities

[63] Re-named the Services, Press and Broadcasting Committee in the 1960s, and re-titled
the Defence, Press and Broadcasting Advisory Committee in 1993. Despite the changes
of name, the committee remained constant in its provision of guidance to press and
publishers on subjects in which considerations of national security might be involved.
[64] Guy Gibson, *Enemy Coast Ahead* (London: Michael Joseph, 1946); Keith Douglas,
Alamein to Zem Zem (London: Editions Poetry, 1946); Nicholas Monsarrat, *Three
Corvettes*, 10th ed. (London: Mayflower, 1972).

which categorise the subgenre of veteran memoir first occurred around 1950. Correspondingly, this date, rather than 1945, constitutes the first bookend of *The Veterans' Tale*.

Within the history of the Second World War military memoir, it is virtually impossible to identify accurate statistics pertaining to the titles of war memoirs published. This is due to fluctuating classifications of 'memoirs' across the period, and inconsistencies within the British National Bibliography's (BNB) cataloguing system which date back to 1950. Nevertheless, a number of broad patterns and trends in the appearance of the veterans' tale are certainly traceable and proffer a valuable scaffolding for this research. The BNB catalogues indicate that during the 1950s, the tales of commandos, submariners, and prisoners-of-war were in especial demand. Unlike the POW memoirs published from the 1970s onwards, the narratives of the 1950s and early 1960s carried similar qualities of derring-do to the accounts penned by former members of elite special forces such as the Special Air Service and the Commandos. The POW narratives of this era are especially interesting, as they mostly fall into the category of 'escape and evasion' stories, rather than the tales of atrocity which later emerged from the narratives of surviving Far East Prisoners of War (FEPOWs). Since 1955, the appearance of war memoirs published by former army personnel including officers and other ranks has been relatively consistent. The naval war, however, was at its most prominent in military life-writing during the 1950s, with accounts written by both surface sailors and submariners appearing in the publishing lists. After 1960, the British submariner memoir rather faded away, and only a few accounts by surface sailors appeared after that. Royal Navy veteran-memoirs also remained predominantly written by officers. The fighter pilots' Battle of Britain narratives, too, were mostly authored by officer pilots. Only one of the large number of fighter aircrew memoirs published between 1956 and 2006 upon which this research draws was composed by a former sergeant pilot.[65] In contrast, the Bomber Command personal narratives were almost equally penned by sergeant and officer pilots alike. However until Miles Tripp's *The Eighth Passenger* appeared in 1969, the post-war testimonies of bomber aircrew remained virtually non-existent. Subsequently, throughout the late 1980s and early 1990s, Bomber Command veterans released a surge of personal narratives in order to 'set the record straight' about the controversial wartime strategic air campaign before it was too late.[66]

---

[65] Bill Rolls, *Spitfire Attack* (London: William Kimber, 1987).
[66] Frances Houghton, 'The "Missing Chapter": Bomber Command Aircrew Memoirs in the 1990s and 2000s', in *British Cultural Memory and the Second World War*, pp. 153–70.

The publishing climate for military memoirs changed significantly between 1950 and 2010. The 1950s and early 1960s were dominated by the narratives of senior commanders – particularly the former Desert Generals – who frequently used their memoirs to battle amongst themselves to justify strategic decisions, claim glory, and shift culpability. Although several memoirs of ordinary junior officers in the Army were also published during this period, the voice from the ranks was largely muffled until the end of the 1960s. Alex Bowlby's graphic and irreverent memoir of service in the Italian Campaign, *The Recollections of Rifleman Bowlby*, represented one of the very first published narratives to document the 'worm's eye' view of the Second World War. Having been rejected on seventeen occasions by publishing firms, it was not accepted for publication until 1969. Whilst this rejection was mostly (and not wholly unreasonably) wrapped up in publishers' fears of a libel suit, a broader social reason for the lack of memoirs published from ordinary soldiers was also apparent. When *Recollections* began to sell well under Leo Cooper's new imprint, that publisher offered Sphere the opportunity to bring the book out as a mass paperback edition. However, Sir Anthony Cheetham, the editor of Sphere, expressed regret that he could not accept the book for publication, explaining that he perceived little market for an ordinary, non-ranking soldier's tale. 'The reason', he asserted, 'is a simple sociological one. It has neither the weight and authority of a General's memoirs.'[67]

Once the 'Great Men' of the wartime British military had had their say, however, the 1970s proved something of a watershed in the production of war memoirs from the rank and file of the Army. The RAF, too, began to claim a greater share of attention as memoirs of former aircrew trickled out in steadily increasing numbers. A myriad of reasons may be attributed to the exponential swell in numbers of war memoirs entering publication since then. Since the war itself, the Second World War has formed an integral part of a well-embedded national 'pleasure-culture of war' in Britain.[68] Interest was intense among post-war generations of youngsters who remained fascinated by the conflict in which their fathers had fought, and lapped up tales of that war with enduring eagerness. This ready-made market for war stories meant that the memoirs of Second World War veterans increasingly offered an enormously attractive commercial prospect to publishers, who began to bring out more and more titles. Thanks also to seminal histories of battle such as John Keegan's

---

[67] University of Reading, Leo Cooper Archive (hereafter UoR LC/) A/2/79, Sir Antony Cheetham to Leo Cooper, 24 October 1969.
[68] Dawson, *Soldier Heroes*, p. 4.

The Face of Battle (1976) and Martin Middlebrook's series of books on Bomber Command, beginning with *The Nuremburg Raid* (1973), an 'experiential turn' in the history of warfare ensured that 'ordinary' servicemen's experiences of war also became a flourishing topic of interest within the scholarly domain. Other factors also influenced the emergence of veteran memoirs thirty years after the Second World War. From the late 1970s onwards, the veterans also began to reach middle-age and to think about retirement. For many, this life-stage offered the leisure and inclination to reflect upon their wartime experiences, and to think about making a record for their families and for posterity. After the Falklands War of 1982 re-ignited cultural memories of 'Britain's Finest Hour', the British nation also began to commemorate the Second World War with ever-increasing levels of pomp and circumstance, triggering a seemingly endless round of anniversaries and remembrance events. With renewed focus upon the commemoration of the Battle of Britain, RAF memoirs became particularly prevalent in the 1980s, but the numbers of accounts by armoured personnel and infantry also rose significantly. By the time of the great cycle of fiftieth anniversaries of the war in the 1990s, Leo Cooper was inundated with pleas to consider manuscripts. The impact of the commemorative cycles upon the production of these narratives from the 1990s onwards is indicated by the sheer number of veterans who sent their manuscript to Leo Cooper explaining that they thought the public interest in the war would generate sufficient sales to render publication commercially attractive to the publisher.[69] The hopes of making a little money from the publication of a war memoir undoubtedly prompted some veterans' decisions to try their luck and submit their manuscripts to publishing houses, but as *The Veterans' Tale* examines, the memoirists offered multiple other public and private explanations of their reasons for publishing a war memoir as well. The veterans' own stated reasons for writing and releasing a war memoir therefore particularly concern and inform this study.

The language and content of published veteran memoirs also underwent significant changes over the post-war decades. Throughout the 1950s and most of the 1960s, the war memoirs of junior officers and other ranks were written in the ubiquitous 'stiff upper lip' vein. The style was clipped and the veteran did not linger over descriptions of death and injury to the same graphic extent for which his later counterparts opted. Furthermore, until legislation governing what was acceptable and what was 'obscene' in publications was amended in 1959 and 1964, very little of a sexual or lurid nature found its way into

---

[69] See the Leo Cooper Archive held by the University of Reading.

veteran memoirs. 'Colourful' soldiers' language became more explicit in memoirs at the beginning of the 1970s, and by the end of the 2000s discussions of homosexuality had begun to appear far more openly in the veterans' tale. Veteran-memoirists also became more candid about emotional subjects, such as the experience of war neurosis and survivor's guilt. Nevertheless, there were also important continuities in the subgenre of post-war published veteran memoirs. Among the different services, experiences of battle tended to be represented in very similar ways between 1950 and 2010. Remarkably similar imagery, metaphors, and ideas consistently shaped the veterans' representations of their interactions with the landscape, weaponry, enemy, and comrades that comprised their battle experience.

The great range of military memoirs published by British veterans between 1950 and 2010 offers an overwhelming quantity of fruitful evidence about the diversity of frontline experiences. In order to enable some conclusions to be drawn about the nature of post-war published veteran memoir, a number of parameters necessarily restrain the scope of *The Veterans' Tale*. To streamline the source base, focus is firmly fixed on 'combatant' accounts of frontline service. An unapologetically purist definition of 'combatant' is employed here, centring upon accounts written by servicemen whose primary martial function was to confront the enemy directly in battle. *The Veterans' Tale* thus addresses those memoirs of former infantrymen, tank crew, aircrew, and sailors whose principal military task in wartime was to kill or be killed. Furthermore, for the sake of recovering and clarifying the 'ordinary' combatant's recollections of frontline experience, this study does not include narratives penned by 'extraordinary' personnel. Regrettably, special forces soldiers who fought with the Special Air Service, Special Boat Service, Long Range Desert Group, Commandos, or other irregular units such as 'Popski's Private Army', must await their own investigation. Nor does it focus upon the captivity memoirs of ex-POWs, or those who served in an intelligence capacity, as theirs are different types of collective tales yet again. Memoirs documenting the so-called 'forgotten' war in the Far East have also been excluded as the deeply racialized perceptions of the Japanese enemy that shape these texts render the veterans' representations of combat very different to those of their comrades who faced a German or Italian opponent. Nevertheless, in certain parts of the book, a small number of narratives from across these omitted categories are drawn upon to make illustrative comment upon the construction, intention, and function of veteran memoir.

There is, of course, a highly gendered dimension to reading these veteran memoirs which requires mention. John Tosh, Michael Roper, and

Martin Francis have rightfully articulated a need for historians of seemingly closed-off all-male institutions such as the British armed forces to bear in mind that it is problematic to remove women completely from the scene as if they had no impact whatsoever on male identity and experience.[70] RAF aircrew who participated in the Battle of Britain or Bomber Command's campaigns were stationed on domestic shores, with varying levels of access to military and civilian women. As Francis explains, the 'romantic distractions of the flyer ensured that the wartime RAF was never a closed homosocial world in which masculinity operated independently of a female presence.'[71] Relationships with women prominently studded the memoirs of aircrew veterans, but they were universally woven into all the other veteran narratives too. Women particularly maintained an emotional presence in these accounts of frontline experiences, with veterans recording that letters from wives and sweethearts had a significant impact upon their mood and feelings of ability to cope with war. The location of women in veteran memoirs is thus also unquestionably deserving of its own study. However, since *The Veterans' Tale* is ultimately concerned with the memoirists' representations of confronting the enemy in the field, and given that women were precluded from frontline combatant roles during the Second World War, this part of the tale must unfortunately also await another day.

This book thus maintains a firm focus on the memoirs of veterans who experienced 'the sharp end' of war as fighting men of junior or other rank, serving with the Royal Air Force's Fighter and Bomber Commands, armoured and infantry units within the British army, and the submarines and 'small ships' (destroyers, corvettes, and armed trawlers) of the Royal Navy. Among each of these branches of the armed services, veteran accounts most commonly clustered around specific wartime battles, campaigns, or theatres of war. For example, Fighter Command memoirs typically chronicled the Battle of Britain which took place in the summer and autumn of 1940, whereas Bomber Command narratives predominantly related the night-time strategic bombing campaign conducted by the crews of the 'heavy' four-engined Lancaster aircraft between 1942 and 1945. The Royal Navy's veteran-memoirists tended to relate tales of convoy escort duty and submarine wars in the northern waters of the North Sea, Atlantic, and Arctic Circle. Army narratives of former infantrymen and armoured crew typically recounted experiences of battle in key campaigns across North Africa between 1940 and 1943, Italy

---

[70] Michael Roper and John Tosh (eds.), *Manful Assertions: Masculinities in Britain since 1800* (London: Routledge, 1991), p. 3.
[71] Francis, *The Flyer*, p. 85.

between 1944 and 1945, and North-West Europe between 1944 and 1945. It is on these areas of common ground that *The Veterans' Tale* concentrates, exploring in detail similarities and differences in the veteran-memoirists' experience, understanding, and representation of these defining wartime events.

Important distinctions must also be drawn between wartime-published memoirs and their post-war counterparts. Although the former are naturally valuable in their own right, these books differed considerably to those published in peacetime because they lacked the temporal gap which shaped the unique reflective dimension of veteran memoir interrogated in this book. Nevertheless, it would be inappropriate to comment upon the post-war narratives without recognising the influence of their wartime antecedents. As Elizabeth Bruss observes, autobiography responds to what precedes and surrounds it at the time of writing.[72] Since post-war and wartime published memoirs form a distinct genre of military life-writing, some awareness of the latter is essential to a study of the former. For this reason, Richard Hillary's *The Last Enemy* (1942), Nicholas Monsarrat's *Three Corvettes* (1945), Keith Douglas' *Alamein to Zem Zem* (1946), and Guy Gibson's *Enemy Coast Ahead* (1946) are frequently drawn upon to explain or illustrate discussion of the post-war memoirs. Several of the post-war memoirists were clearly well-acquainted with these earlier well-known narratives. For example, Stuart Hills's *By Tank into Normandy* (2002) announced that the author had thoroughly enjoyed reading Douglas' book as it contained 'some marvellous pen portraits' of mutual acquaintances and fellow officers.[73] Former fighter pilot, Geoffrey Page, met Richard Hillary whilst they were both hospitalised and recovering from severe burns at East Grinstead during the war. In an amicable exchange of insults, Page confirmed that he had enjoyed reading *The Last Enemy*, although he described its author in less positive terms as a 'supercilious bastard'.[74] Such open acknowledgement of familiarity with the work of the wartime memoirists is rare in the post-war memoirs, but the presence of the earlier narratives lingers in the veterans' tale nonetheless.

Finally, the veteran-memoirists of the Second World War came from a mix of social backgrounds, but some trends in their publication of memoirs can be discerned. Veterans who recorded their experiences of

---

[72] Elizabeth Bruss, *Autobiographical Acts: The Changing Situation of a Literary Genre* (Baltimore: Johns Hopkins University Press, 1976), p. 166.

[73] Stuart Hills, *By Tank into Normandy* (London: Cassell, 2002), p. 54.

[74] Geoffrey Page, *Shot Down in Flames: A World War II Fighter Pilot's Remarkable Tale of Survival* (London: Grub Street, 1999), p. 116. Previously published as *Tale of a Guinea Pig* (London: Pelham Books, 1981).

holding commission in the Royal Navy were mostly drawn from the middle classes. Although the Second World War helped to rework some of the traditional class and rank hierarchies in the RN, naval officers between 1939 and 1945 were most likely to possess a middle-class background.[75] There was more social diversity among the army veterans, who ranged from Nicholas Mosley who was the son of British fascist leader Oswald Mosley and came from an aristocratic background and held junior rank in the 2nd Battalion, London Irish Rifles; through Alex Bowlby, who came from a middle-class background and had been privately educated at Radley, but who refused to take a commission and carried out his wartime service in the ranks of the 2nd Battalion of the Rifle Brigade; to John Kenneally, who was the illegitimate son of a prostitute and served time in a military prison before winning the Victoria Cross in Africa. Among the RAF, the dominant cultural representation of the Battle of Britain pilots as mainly consisting of well-off young boys wrenched out of university has been substantially challenged by research into the backgrounds of 'the Few'.[76] Admittedly, however, the memoirs of these aircrew do little to dispute the conventional popular impression of the socially privileged identity of the fighter pilot. The vast majority of the veteran-memoirists of 'the Few' were indeed drawn from a middle-class milieu and exposed to a specific range of cultural images which conditioned their expectations of war as a public-school-inspired adventure of sport, chivalry, and glory. Nevertheless, there are some difficulties in using social class as a tool with which to approach the post-war published veteran memoir. Should one deal with the class status of the memoirist at the outset of his wartime experiences, or the class into which he fell at the time of writing many years later? Disentangling these questions is not particularly straightforward. It is also problematic to attempt to discern if and how the memoirist's own subjective perception of his pre-war, wartime, and post-war class identities altered. British society changed so much before, during, and after the Second World War that using social class as a tool to illuminate aspects of the veterans' tale is of limited assistance. As such, questions of class have been addressed here mainly where the veteran himself seemed to feel it was relevant to his expectations, experiences, and recollections of combat.

In terms of the architecture of this book, Chapters 1–2 of *The Veterans' Tale* survey the provenance of the Second World War veteran memoirs.

---

[75] Penny Summerfield, 'Divisions at Sea: Class, Gender, Race, and Nation in Maritime Films of the Second World War, 1939–60', *Twentieth Century British History*, 22:3 (2011), 330–53.

[76] Tony Mansell, 'Flying start: educational and social factors in the recruitment of pilots of the Royal Air Force in the interwar years', *History of Education*, 26:1 (1997), 71–90.

Considering published war memoir as a unified genre, these chapters delve deep into the archives of major publishing houses to examine the veterans' stated reasons for producing and publicly distributing their war experiences in book form, and the physical processes of writing and publishing a military memoir in post-war Britain. Chapters 3–6 address the veterans' tale itself, analysing the narrative content of these military memoirs. Respectively focusing on themes of landscape, weaponry, the enemy, and comradeship, these four chapters probe the memoirists' literary representations of experience in the front line. Chapters 7–8 explore how ex-servicemen put their historical records to work both in private and public, assessing themes of self-fashioning and claiming agency over wartime experience in the veterans' tale.

1   Motive and the Veteran-Memoirist

> I was writing the book for [the dead], for those who were there, and
> for those who wanted to know what it was like – in that order. At the
> same time I was trying to forget the dead, to get shot of them.[1]

At the tender age of nine years old a little boy who would serve as a
Lancaster rear gunner a decade later in the Second World War painstakingly carved his initials into a tree. Many years later, the adult Jim
Davis was enchanted to discover that his childhood handiwork was still
clearly visible. Reflecting upon the longevity of his graffiti, he mused
that 'in this life I feel we all have to make an imprint and, if possible,
have to leave behind us a memory of ourselves, or something we have
accomplished in the minds of other people.'[2] As a veteran of the Second
World War, leaving behind a lasting 'imprint' of his and others' wartime
sacrifice for posterity was a responsibility Davis took very seriously.
Indeed, so strongly did he feel in the 1980s about the marked lack of
any kind of commemorative memorial to wartime bomber crews that
he became the driving force behind the erection of the International
Air Monument, dedicated to the Royal Air Force, Commonwealth and
Allied Air Forces, outside Plymouth. The veteran's publication of a war
memoir also manifested his evident desire to stamp his lifetime into
the consciousness of the nation. Like the tree and the monument, the
book operates as an inscription of Davis' presence in history, an explicit
statement which announces 'I was here'. More specifically, the memoir
also overtly testifies, to the former rear-gunner's self-reconstruction of
his identity as a combatant, whilst simultaneously enabling the wartime accomplishments of Davis and his crew to be propelled into the
public domain. The function of memoir as a monument to both private
wartime selves and former comrades, however, offers only one strand

---

[1] Alex Bowlby, *The Recollections of Rifleman Bowlby*, rev. ed. (London: Leo Cooper, 1989),
   p. 222.
[2] Jim Davis, *Winged Victory: The Story of a Bomber Command Air Gunner* (Ditton: R. J.
   Leach & Co, 1995), p. 85.

of the story behind the creation of the veterans' tale in post-war years. The veterans' desire to employ these books to 'make an imprint' was triggered by a wide number of other factors which were often bound together in a Gordian knot of motives. Yet by identifying key threads of common purpose it is possible to unravel the cords of veteran authorial intention. These men make abundantly clear that the published war memoir was not merely a passive statement of experience. On the contrary, memoirs offered the veteran a valuable conduit of active communication with a number of different audiences.

The epigraph which introduces this chapter is extracted from former rifleman Alex Bowlby's memoir, *The Recollections of Rifleman Bowlby* (1969), one of the more well-known narratives of wartime service with the British army. Educated unhappily at Radley, the ex-public schoolboy found himself serving with the predominantly Cockney 2nd Battalion of the Rifle Brigade, during its push through Italy from the spring of 1944. Unhindered by his social status as a Kipling-esque 'gentleman ranker', Bowlby developed a deep emotional attachment to his regiment and comrades which forms the central plank of his memoir. Seeking to explain why he chose to become a war memoirist, he made a valiant effort to classify three different audiences for whom he wrote *Recollections*. The most intimate of the trinity was a private communion with his own self: 'I was trying to forget the dead, to get shot of them'. The second audience was an external, civilian readership: 'those who wanted to know what it was like'. He hoped that his account would offer a glimpse into the sealed-off experiences of the frontline soldier for those who had no first-hand knowledge of what combat in Italy during the Second World War truly meant. The third – and in Bowlby's reckoning, the most important – audience was his erstwhile comrades from the battalion. Like Davis' memoir, *Recollections* was designed as a public tribute to a community of combatants which encompassed both the dead and the living. Bowlby's broad triumvirate of motives for the creation of a war memoir provides an effective framework within which to situate a more detailed assessment of private and public intention in the veterans' tale.

Audience of the Self

In the first instance, memoir had a special private value to veterans struggling to reconcile themselves to post-war civilian life. Numerous former servicemen discovered that their wartime experiences marred their ability to adapt to peacetime. Many of the veteran-memoirists in this study experienced a severe sense of disconnect upon their return to 'civvy

street'. Some found that this disjuncture prevailed for many decades and
their narratives testify to the lingering difficulties of readjustment from
combatant back to civilian. An odd dichotomy colours these literary recollections of combat. On the one hand, the war seemed to cast a far-
reaching taint over the veteran's efforts to build an existence for himself
away from the frontline. Physical and mental scars still tugged painfully
at unexpected moments. On the other hand, despite (or perhaps even
because of) the mélange of post-traumatic stress disorders, post-war
disillusionment, and failures to build lasting relationships which various
men carried forward through peacetime, the war was elevated to an apex
of memory which rested upon pride and satisfaction at a job well done.
For those who felt that peace had not delivered wartime promises of a
'New Jerusalem' in Britain the construction of a war memoir enabled the
veteran to process his combat experiences in a manner which afforded
personal succour in the post-war present.

Once the war was over, some servicemen were immediately able to slot
back into civilian life with comparative ease. Others found it more problematic, however, and a distinct anguish is voiced in multiple accounts of
adapting to peacetime in the mid-to-late 1940s. The first step on the path
back to 'civvy street' began with demobilisation. This brutally emphasised the soldier's disconnect, wrenching away a well-ordered existence
demarcated by the rigid hierarchy and familiar patterns of military life.
Despite the temporary dislocation experienced in the sights, sounds, and
smells of battle, each serviceman knew what was expected both of himself and others, and was able to locate with precision his own role in the
military machine. Being torn out of this familiar system through the process of demobilisation proved a humiliating and painful experience for
more than one former warrior. Ray Ward, a Scottish officer of the Argyll
and Sutherland regiment, was demobbed on 11 April 1946. At the store
where civilian clothing was handed out to the newly released soldiers, he
was disagreeably surprised to find that 'no distinction was made between
officers and other ranks. Officers received little deference and no favour-
itism was shown. On the contrary, some of the fellows dishing out the
clothes were bloody-minded enough to give the officers the shabbiest,
most ill-made and ill-fitting garments.'[3] The bewildered disenchantment
Ward displays in leaving behind the structure and hierarchy of his military existence was also echoed by Charles Potts, an officer who sombrely
identified a marked disjuncture between the infantry soldier's world on

---

[3] Ray Ward, *The Mirror of Monte Cavallara: An Eighth Army Story* (Edinburgh: Birlinn,
2006), p. 374.

the front line and the civilian life into which he was expected to slide back effortlessly:

> this man is the hardest used, and the least remunerated of all Englishmen in time of war. And when the war is over, and he is allowed to return to his loved ones, he finds that his suffering is far from finished. Those that have had the good fortune to remain at home, that have been able to save money, to rent houses at reasonable cost, to bring up families, have themselves so raised the rents, commandeered the markets, and 'walled-off' the comforts of life, that the returned soldier finds himself still excluded from all the simple things that had been the objects of his hopes and dreams during those times of deprivation. He cannot afford to buy or rent a home for himself at post war prices: he has missed his chances of working his way up in a job: his military experience is considered more detrimental than advantageous to his future: his health has been undermined by damp and fever: and his nerves are frayed. His prospects, in fact, are wholly depressing. Even if he goes into a shop to buy some simple commodity, he is greeted with the words, 'Sorry, but these are reserved for our regular customers.' How the devil, he asks himself, could they expect me to be a regular customer of any shop here, when I was fighting in the sands of Libya?[4]

An unmistakable tinge of bitterness at the returning soldiers' challenging material circumstances thus colours Potts' description of coming home. As Alan Allport notes, the relationship between the two wartime communities of civilians and soldiers was distinctly ambivalent in immediate post-war British society.[5] The British had fought a gruelling war on both the military and home fronts, and groups of demobilised servicemen and civilians took some time to reacclimatise to one another again. As the Potts extract indicates, for some returning servicemen home was not the place they had left behind, nor was it much like the place of which they had dreamed whilst fighting in far-distant corners of the world. Potts' unhappy perception of a financial and social gulf that had opened up between civilian and soldier during the mid-to-late 1940s also echoes a more widespread suspicion that Britons who had remained out of uniform had become ill-mannered, impatient, and grasping. For demobbed servicemen like Potts the return to civilian 'normality' became an experience for which some soldiers felt ill-fitted, finding homecoming an uncomfortable disappointment.[6]

The return to a civilian environment was also fraught with challenges for those who had conducted their war mainly from domestic shores. For men who had served in the RAF, the transition from wartime flyer to peacetime civilian was uniquely difficult to navigate. Echoes of

---

[4] Charles Potts, *Soldier in the Sand* (London: PRM Publishers, 1961), p. 69.
[5] Alan Allport, *Demobbed: Coming Home after the Second World War* (New Haven: Yale University Press, 2009), p. 11.
[6] Ibid., pp. 11–12.

distress at the prospect of leaving behind the intense joys and fears of aerial flight and battle frequently sound throughout these narratives. 'What on earth shall I find to do when I am not able to fly a Spit any more?' wondered Geoffrey Wellum.[7] His voice here is that of the twenty-year-old fighter pilot refracted through the middle-aged veteran but other fighter pilots prophesied as early as the first year of the war that it would be extremely difficult to readjust back into civilian life. In a letter written to his father in June 1940, Tony Bartley meditated that 'If I live through this war, I doubt I shall ever be able to settle down to a conventional life', while an extract from Hugh Dundas' wartime diary dated 11 November 1940 forecast that the 'dangers of forgetting the possibility of reverting to a normal life are enormous; it seems so incredibly remote.'[8] Many Bomber Command veterans also found it enormously difficult to return to 'civvy street'. Arthur White reported that 'Some managed to pick up the threads of their old, pre-war job but many others found that aircrew categories and a tour of ops were no qualifications for the jobs on offer in post war Britain and so they had to start again – at the bottom.'[9] Feeling short-changed by the new post-conflict order, he resentfully perceived an unwelcome new employment hierarchy in the post-war job market, in which the employability of ex-aircrew hinged upon their wartime military occupation. Military status was also identified as part of this system as pilots were more likely to have held rank than air gunners. Correspondingly there were, White complained, 'few opportunities in the post war world for pilots; fewer still for navigators and wireless operators and literally none for air bombers and air gunners.'[10] Former aircrew who were fortunate enough to secure a job after demobilisation also struggled to adapt back to the more conventional structures of civilian employment and time management. One of the luckier ones was former pilot Michael Renaut, who was offered his old job back at J Lyons & Co after being demobbed in June 1946. Yet he was wracked by unhappiness in his new employment: 'as time wore on I felt most unsettled and I missed the comparative freedom of the Services. My hours were 7 a.m. to 5 p.m. in a hot and busy factory for £15 per week and I hadn't really got the

[7] Geoffrey Wellum, *First Light* (London: Viking, 2002), p. 185.
[8] Tony Bartley, *Smoke Trails in the Sky*, rev. ed. (Wilmslow: Crecy Publishing, 1997), p. 19; Hugh Dundas, *Flying Start: A Fighter Pilot's War Years* (London: Stanley Paul and Co., 1988), p. 54.
[9] Arthur White, *Bread and Butter Bomber Boys* (Upton on Severn: Square One Publications, 1995), p. 12.
[10] Ibid., p.12.

confidence in my own ability to stay.'[11] Promoted to Manager of the French Pastry factory in 1949, Renaut explained that although he had won the DFC in wartime, during the post-war period his lack of self confidence remained a problem:

I was still unsure of my ability at twenty-six to run the place efficiently. After all, I had left Lyons at nineteen to join the RAF and all I could do well was fly an aeroplane! What good was this qualification to them? ... a lot of the work was beyond me; I simply hadn't got the experience and how could I have at twenty-six? In a way I still feared the sack and yet I'd burned my boats in the RAF by refusing a permanent commission and where could I turn to? Thousands of ex-servicemen must have gone through what I did and resettlement in peace-time was no easy matter.[12]

Renaut spent the remainder of his life crippled by war-induced anxiety which tormented both his personal and professional life. Later, upon transferring employment to the motor industry, he was unable to face the increased responsibility of his new position and suffered a succession of nervous breakdowns before his early death in January 1964.

The difficulties that some ex-servicemen experienced in slotting back into a civilian world which seemed disconcertingly unfamiliar cast a lengthy shadow down the decades following the war. Graeme Ogden wrote his naval memoir as 'an epitaph to those of us who, twenty years ago, set off to the wars and to those of us who returned sickened and dispirited by the futility of a now meaningless crusade.'[13] As this indicates, veteran resentment at the social status quo to which they returned was not necessarily restricted to the immediate post-war period. Several memoirists reflected upon a moment in time much farther down the line when each took stock of the changed world about them and found it woefully disappointing. In 1969 ex-bomb aimer Miles Tripp described conducting a search to contact his former Lancaster crew. He explained that he felt a desire to reconcile his wartime sacrifices with the new world order of the 1950s and 1960s:

I wondered whether, with the ever-present threat of nuclear holocaust and with race riots and civil disturbances everywhere, they thought our efforts, and the efforts of thousands like us, had been worth while. Or had our youth been as futile as an anonymous postcard addressed to nowhere and dropped unstamped into a disused letter-box.[14]

In 1989, Blenheim pilot Roger Peacock, writing under the pseudonym of 'Richard Passmore', was in no doubt at all about this question. He

---

[11] Michael Renaut, *Terror by Night: A Bomber Pilot's Story* (London: William Kimber, 1982), p. 181.
[12] Ibid., pp. 181–182.
[13] Ogden, *My Sea Lady*, p. 12.
[14] Miles Tripp, *The Eighth Passenger* (London: Heinemann, 1969), p. 119.

fashioned the dedication to his memoir to rail against contemporary society: 'to the men I am honoured to call my friends and comrades: air-crew on the day-bomber squadrons of the Royal Air Force between 1939 and 1945. I wish the Britain of today were worthy of their sacrifice.'[15] In some instances, a sense of disquiet at the fluctuations of the post-war world even extended into the new millennium. In 2007 a new edition of Edward Grace's memoir of serving throughout the North African and Italian campaigns reflected the disgruntlement of Ogden, Tripp, and Peacock. In the original edition, which was published in 1993, Grace concluded upon a relatively upbeat note:

I was able to look hopefully to the future, to the end of the war and to peace. The world after the war would surely have a new vision, free from strife. Then with Rupert Brooke I imagined:

    Honour has come back, as a King to earth,
    And paid his subjects with a royal wage;
    And Nobleness walks in our ways again;
    And we have come into our heritage.[16]

Significantly, this optimistic note was omitted from the post-9/11 2007 edition of *The Perilous Road to Rome*, which instead included a reflective and more detailed new epilogue. In this, Grace proffered a heavily revised description of his feelings upon learning that the war in the Far East was over in August 1945:

New ideas based on co-operation, conciliation and goodwill should ensure that never again could war threaten the destruction of the world. Hope was the watchword … Many years have now passed since that optimistic epoch. Perhaps Hope is still what we need and are depending on.[17]

As a consequence of this enduring disconnect and tone of disillusionment with 'civvy street' and the post-war world, many veteran narratives voice a clear longing to abdicate the memoirist's civilian identity and return to the sanctuary of an environment in which he had felt more comfortable and esteemed. Geoffrey Wellum began writing his memoir during the 1970s to remind himself that he had once been of enormous value to his country, returning to his beloved 92 Squadron in his imagination. As one of the youngest fighter pilots in the Battle of Britain, living for too long on strained nerves and adrenaline, Wellum had suffered badly

---

[15] Richard Passmore, *Blenheim Boy* (London: Thomas Harmsworth, 1981).
[16] Edward Grace, *The Perilous Road to Rome via Tunis* (Tunbridge Wells, Parapress, 1993), p. 161.
[17] Edward Grace, *The Perilous Road to Rome and Beyond: Fighting Through North Africa and Italy*, rev. ed. (Barnsley: Pen & Sword Military, 2007), p. 191.

when he was posted away from the squadron in the autumn of 1941. He felt bereft of both his identity and comrades and struggled against battle fatigue. After three years of operational flying, the pilot's health broke down whilst serving in Malta, and he suffered from acute sinus problems and a nasty operation which saw him invalided back to Britain. In his memoir, the reader hears the ring of agonising loss in his portrayal of his feelings about being posted for a rest: 'A has-been. No further use to anybody. Merely a survivor, my name no longer on the Order of Battle in the dispersal hut. A worn-out bloody fighter pilot at twenty years of age, merely left to live, or rather to exist, on memories, reduced to watching from the wings.'[18] Wellum began writing *First Light* at a time when, in his own words, his life was 'bouncing along at the bottom' at the end of a difficult period in his marriage and when his business went bust.[19] Explaining that he was at a particularly low ebb, he thought 'Well I have been of some use,' and so 'I sat down and wrote.'[20] An aching wistfulness to return to the military family and the veteran's wartime martial fraternity also lurks in other veteran memoirs. Of his return to Britain, former tank gunner Ken Tout recorded that 'If the Genie of the Lamp appeared now with all the promises of Arabia, I would barter my soul to be allowed to go back up the Vught road and report to Hank [his senior officer].'[21] Infantry officer Sydney Jary's memoir also expresses the same plaintive longing for the emotional comfort which he had once drawn from his old platoon. He first experienced this during the war when he was sent to Antwerp on leave for forty-eight hours:

I met a barrier. I had walked out of a world that I knew into one where I was desperately unsure of myself. Away from the battlefield, this world had no place for me ... I had wandered too far into dark and smoky battlefields across the Styx to find solace or comfort in the bright lights behind the blackout curtains of Antwerp. I longed to return to the Battalion and to 18 Platoon which, without my knowing it, had become my home.[22]

Jary freely admitted that he had struggled to adapt back to post-war civilian life, perceiving that war had unsuited him for employment in business as he had little patience with dealing with difficult clients and building superficial relationships with colleagues.[23] After fighting his way

[18] Wellum, *First Light*, p. 293.
[19] Andrew Pettie, 'Geoffrey Wellum: The terrible beauty of flying a Spitfire at the age of 18', *The Telegraph*, 10 September 2010.
[20] Christian House, 'The 89-year-old Boy', *The Spectator*, 17 July 2010.
[21] Ken Tout, *Tank!* (London: Robert Hale, 1985), p. 209.
[22] Sydney Jary, *18 Platoon*, rev. ed. (Winchester: Light Infantry Office, 2009), p. 90.
[23] Imperial War Museum (Hereafter IWM) Sound Archive, Sydney Jary, 18024.

through North-West Europe with his beloved 18 Platoon, he felt that the world of post-war business seemed comparatively shallow:

Antwerp had been a small taste of the real world and, as anyone who has served with good soldiers on grim battlefields will confirm, afterwards real life never seems real again ... there was no 18 Platoon to slink back to and without a loving wife it would have proved intolerable.[24]

Constructing a war memoir thus offered an opportunity to reconnect in some measure with memories of the veteran's wartime 'band of brothers'. In a letter to his publisher, tank veteran Donald Sutherland expressed pleasure that during the process of writing his manuscript, 'Lots of ghosts of old comrades have come fluttering round.'[25] The same sentiment was voiced by former fighter pilot, Bill Rolls, who commented that whilst writing his memoir 'I had some very pleasant times remembering people I had known and old pals whom I had lost ... I had many real ghosts helping me every time I sat down to the typewriter.'[26] Analysing his own compulsion to create a narrative of his service with the Rifle Brigade, Bowlby confirmed that evoking the unit which had meant so much to him granted an escape from the personal troubles he experienced in the 1950s:

As I discovered that peace can be a much more disturbing business than war and that the near-loss of one's own sense of self under pressure more terrifying than fear of death in battle I began retreating to memories of the war, and the happiness and security it had brought me.[27]

Writing a memoir thus performed an important function for the veteran during the post-war decades. In allowing the reincarnation of treasured bonds of wartime comradeship, military memoir could provide a vital solace to the veteran in the present day.

In his study of the impact of war and trauma on the memories of over 1,000 Second World War veterans in Britain, Nigel Hunt records that former combatants tended to discuss the immediate post-war years as a particular time of struggle to readjust. Frequently troubled by traumatic memories, many felt that they had received little psychological assistance to aid the process of healing. Additionally, servicemen had been told that these memories would simply fade over time, and their families were advised not to discuss the war with their menfolk in order to resume normal home life as soon as possible.[28] Upon being planted

---

[24] Jary, *18 Platoon*, p. 91.
[25] UoR, LC/ A/2/653, Donald Sutherland to Leo Cooper, 15 November 1984.
[26] Rolls, *Spitfire Attack*, p. 12.
[27] Bowlby, *Recollections*, p. 13.
[28] Hunt, *Memory, War and Trauma*, p. 150.

back into 'civvy street', therefore, many found that outlets for discussing their trauma were limited. This meant that the mental scars of war were given little chance to close and silver out. As a result, various veterans discovered that writing of their experiences offered a meaningful opportunity to ventilate traumatic memories and still-painful emotions. Former destroyer captain Roger Hill found the transition to peacetime almost insurmountable. Suffering frequent bouts of ill health brought on by the strain of the war, he took to 'retreating' into memories of the war as a kind of security blanket. Trapped in a dead end job as a 'seagull', or casual labourer, in a New Zealand dockyard, writing his memoir provided an escape. He notes that, having taken up his pen in 1965, 'I lived in two worlds, one the present of manual labour, eating and sleeping, and in the other I relived the war years and progressed from ship to ship and battle to battle in my mind'.[29] Writing his memoir certainly provided a measure of 'relief'. Quoting DH Lawrence, he remarked that 'A creative work may come out of inner stress or muddle or psychic illness; but if it is a good job well done, it heals both the doer and the receiver.' In essence, he reflected, 'One sheds one's sickness in books.'[30] Other veterans also turned to penning a memoir in the hope that it would provide a means of expunging lingering mental suffering. In particular, grief for lost friends could corrode a veteran's psychological equilibrium. Not all of the 'ghosts' of comrades past were entirely welcome visitors. Despite the pleasure Sutherland and Rolls obtained from awakening the shades of their former comrades, the spectres of Tony Spooner's loss assumed a far darker significance. Spooner operated as a Wellington pilot in Malta during the island's dark days under siege in 1942. When VJ day arrived in 1945, he was once again back on Malta:

Around me were ghosts and I knew that I could never again completely relax until those ghosts were exorcised. Perhaps in writing this book I will have exorcised some of them and removed for ever from the innermost corners of my mind the stamp of Malta GC.[31]

Guilt at surviving when so many comrades did not rendered the presence of the dead particularly intrusive for Ray Ward, who explained that he was partially prompted to write *The Mirror of Monte Cavallara* by 'the need to lay some ghosts to rest'.[32] The full extent of the lingering presence of these ghosts is revealed by his son Robin, who explained that his father was plagued by 'flashbacks' to his war days, returning to

---

[29] Roger Hill, *Destroyer Captain* (London: William Kimber, 1975), p. 11.
[30] Ibid., p .6.
[31] Tony Spooner, *In Full Flight*, rev. ed. (Canterbury: Wingham Press, 1991), p. 257.
[32] Ward, *The Mirror of Monte Cavallara*, p. 18.

the battlefield 'in dreams and nightmares ... Italy was where his wartime ghosts were and, for over fifty years, they visited him often and uninvited. Italy was where he saw his men die.'[33] In particular, according to his son, Ward remained haunted by one battle in the Allies' attempt to breach the Gothic Line in 1944 in which his A Company took 30 per cent casualties, but he 'scoffed at "the smothering care of compassionate counsellors and support groups"'.[34] Constructing a war memoir, however, allowed him to confront these 'ghosts' and to expend turbulent grief. Writing, as the veteran explained in a letter to Lieutenant Colonel Freddie Graham in 1966, thus functioned as an important 'safety valve!'[35]

The creation of a veteran's war memoir thus helped to draw the sting of traumatic loss. The act of fashioning a narrative enforced cohesion and context upon remembered experience, allowing the veteran to extract significant meaning from his combatant days. As Hunt recognises in his study, the development of a narrative of a traumatic event effects the assertion of individual control over that event.[36] This is apparent in Bowlby's construction of *Recollections*. The horror of his experiences in Italy, combined with an enduring sense of guilt at being in hospital when his unit sustained heavy losses during their attack on the hilltop town of Tossignano in December 1944, eventually resulted in the delayed psychological breakdown of Bowlby in 1955. Although the veteran had attempted to write a memoir since 1947, he dismissed the five or six drafts he had accumulated by 1954 as 'not much good'. Referring to his mental collapse in 1955, however, he wrote that 'As my world broke up I turned to the one thing I had left to hang on to – my book. I tried another draft.'[37] Describing himself as still 'earthed with grief' when he began the latest draft, he observed that crafting his account brought about a substantial shift in his relationship with the 'ghosts' of deceased comrades which enabled him to help to alleviate the enduring psychological torment.[38] He was surprised to find that 'As I scribbled [the words] down I thought of the dead. I owed them so much ... At the same time I was trying to forget the dead, to get shot of them.'[39] Bowlby remained deeply troubled by his war experiences for the rest of his life, recording that 'During the day-time depressions I often brooded about having missed the fight at Tossignano. I felt guilty about not having been with

[33] Ibid., p. 222.
[34] Ibid., p. 285; p. 11.
[35] Ibid., p. 389.
[36] Hunt and Robbins, 'Telling Stories of the War', p. 63.
[37] Bowlby, *Recollections*, p. 222.
[38] Ibid., p. 223.
[39] Ibid., p. 222.

the Company.'[40] Until his death in 2005, he suffered from depression, severe anxiety, sleeplessness nights, and neurosis, and as he informed his publisher, 'the dregs of the Sicilian fracas are always liable to become active again.'[41] Yet, like Ward, he discovered that writing his memoir functioned as a kind of emotional exorcism, proving sufficiently therapeutic that Bowlby could eventually find enormous pride and pleasure in both his service and his memoir.

It is clear from the veterans' tale that there was a self-defined 'right' time at which to write a war memoir. As Bowlby's multiple attempts to draft *Recollections* indicates, seizing the optimum moment in which writing of wartime experience would offer personal solace was an intensely private and individual affair. The wide range of dates during which these narratives were penned testifies to the different experiences of veterans in coming to terms with their wartime horrors. There was no prescribed limit upon the length of time it might take a veteran to decide that the moment was ripe to confront old memories. Denys Rayner was one of the earliest post-war naval memoirists to recount his exploits during the war at sea, publishing *Convoy Escort Commander* in 1956. Like most of the 1950s generation of war memoirists, his account is written in a laconic and terse style which does not dwell introspectively on wartime events. A valuable window into the psychological importance that the veteran ascribed to writing his book is granted by his friend Captain Stephen Roskill. Blending his own identities as a naval veteran of destroyers, official wartime historian of the Royal Navy, and editor of *Convoy Escort Commander*, Roskill penned a foreword to the book in which he explained the processes through which Rayner had arrived at his decision to tell his tale:

When men have lived through periods of great strain there often is, I fancy, a strong reluctance to commit their experiences to paper, at any rate until the passage of time has assimilated them into the whole pattern of their lives. The scars still then remain, but the wounds themselves are no longer raw, and by a process of healing relaxation the mind no longer shrinks from memories that for long could only hurt. It was at my suggestion that Commander Rayner began to write about the war at sea as he saw it, and it may have been mere chance that I made the proposal at the time when, at last, he felt able and prepared to record his experiences.[42]

Others took far longer to feel able to communicate their experiences and many did not begin their memoir until they were approaching the borders of old age. Frank Musgrove acknowledged that after the war it

---

[40] Ibid., p. 216.
[41] UoR, LC/ A/2/79, Alex Bowlby to Leo Cooper, dated only 'Tuesday'.
[42] Stephen Roskill, foreword to Denys Rayner, *Escort: The Battle of the Atlantic* (London: William Kimber, 1955), p. v.

took him nearly fifty years to feel able to talk about his war service as a navigator with Bomber Command, noting that he 'never mentioned this episode in my life even to closest friends.'[43] In his 2005 memoir, *Dresden and the Heavy Bombers*, he observed that 'It is only quite recently that I have felt able to mention these long-past events and this memoir is a product of this belated sense of release.'[44] In this respect, the veterans' tale shows some conformation to psychiatrist Robert Butler's renowned concept of the 'life review', a process whereby ageing people embark upon an evaluation of their lives, sifting through memory in order to tell a story that makes sense of their experiences.[45] Putting one's life in order before death is a psychological task that is natural to all ageing persons, yet it became charged with special significance for the veterans of the Second World War. Sometimes this review was triggered by retirement. Tank veteran Bill Bellamy, for instance, had kept a box filled with notes, maps, and photos of his wartime experiences tucked away in the loft ever since the war: 'For the first forty years or so, I didn't want to think about the war, but some time after I had retired the box came out of the attic and down to my office.'[46] Freed from employment as a voracious consumer of time, retirement granted the veteran the space and leisure in which to reminisce. 'For most,' reflected Arthur White, 'there comes a time in life when there is actually time for nostalgia.' Contemplating this new lifestyle, he mused that perhaps this moment arrived,

at the end of working life when the kids have grown up, the mortgage paid off, retirement looming ahead and there is time to think about the old days. This mental search could be sparked off by any one of a thousand things – for me it was sparked off by a Lancaster.[47]

In August 1980, White attended a Battle of Britain Memorial Flight over Dewsbury. Hearing the growl of the last surviving Lancaster's Merlin engines awoke old memories and he began to recall his wartime experiences, transcribing them onto paper.[48] Nostalgia and retirement were firmly interlinked in the veterans' decision to create a war memoir. It was not until late in life that Ray Ward became willing to face his wartime memories.[49] Post war association with his beloved Argylls was limited:

---

[43] Frank Musgrove, *Dresden and the Heavy Bombers: An RAF Navigator's Perspective* (Barnsley: Pen & Sword Aviation, 2005), p. 74.

[44] Ibid., p. 74.

[45] Robert Butler, 'The life review: an interpretation of reminiscence in the aged', *Psychiatry*, 26 (1963), 65–76.

[46] Bill Bellamy, *Troop Leader: A Tank Commander's Story* (Stroud: Sutton Publishing, 2005), p. xi.

[47] White, *Bread and Butter Bomber Boys*, pp. 12–13.

[48] Ibid., p. 16.

[49] Ward, *The Mirror of Monte Cavallara*, p. 222.

'contact was fitful and fleeting, motivated by bouts of nostalgia. The nostalgia became more evident after he retired.'[50] As Jean Freedman notes in her study of memory and culture of wartime London, nostalgia allows an individual to relive times of youthful danger from the vantage point of knowing that one safely survived the experience.[51] Retirement therefore granted some veterans vital leisureliness and emotional security to indulge in nostalgic narratives of a heady, exciting period when they were young, fit, and participating in a crusade against fascism.

Audiences of the Future

Despite the private value which many veterans reaped from the creation of these narratives, war memoirs were not necessarily written solely for an audience of the private self. Frequently they were also constructed with an eye to an external audience. Various narratives were cajoled into existence by the second of Bowlby's triumvirate of readerships, 'Those who wanted to know what it was like'. Family were firmly bracketed into this category, and more than one veteran found himself ushered into becoming a memoirist by close relatives. Former fighter pilot Geoffrey Page was consistently urged to write his memoir by his young bride. With characteristic modesty, he insisted that 'all credit' for the birth and subsequent popularity of his book must go to his wife.[52] For Arthur White, such a request came from his son, who reportedly urged him to 'Get it all down on paper'.[53] Memoir often functioned as a bridge between a veteran and his children. In a generation which was famously reticent about their war experiences, and tended to share only a few carefully selected anecdotes outside communities of other veterans, these narratives served as a portal into the past for the sons and daughters who lived with the impact of the war on their fathers. The importance of these books for both veteran and children is illustrated by the Ward and Ashton memoirs. Posthumously, the manuscripts of Ray Ward and former flight engineer Norman Ashton were lightly edited for publication by their respective sons Robin and Steve. After Ray's death in 1999, Robin discovered the manuscript of *The Mirror of Monte Cavallara* in an old Afrika Korps ammunition box in the cellar. Tied to it was a letter written by their father in 1995, addressed to Robin and his brother. In his epistle to his sons, Ward acknowledged that the narrative was partly a response

[50] Ibid., p. 11.
[51] Jean Freedman, *Whistling in the Dark: Memory and Culture in Wartime London* (Kentucky: University of Kentucky, 1999), p. 184.
[52] Page, *Shot Down in Flames*, p. 279.
[53] White, *Bread and Butter Bomber Boys*, p. 197.

to their persistent coaxing to put down on paper 'memories and impressions' of his wartime service with the Argyll and Sutherland regiment.[54] The prologue to *Monte Cavallara* was written by Robin, and explained how he felt that the process of gently editing the manuscript for publication, without drastically altering the style or content of the narrative, established a new connection with his deceased father.[55] This sentiment is also expressed by Steve Ashton, whose father, Norman, had penned an early draft of his memoir *Only Birds and Fools* shortly after the war. Like Robin Ward, Steve Ashton also edited his father's memoir for publication and he too resisted the temptation 'to make stylistic changes to bring the text into line with current trends. I felt it more important to preserve my father's manner of expression, which itself contributes to the historical record.'[56] Both men perceived that their father's war experiences indirectly shaped their own childhoods and understandings of the war. Steve Ashton, for example, reflected that,

I first heard the stories described in this book when I was a boy. Having tired of Goldilocks, I would listen spellbound to my father's tales of adventures with Reg Bunten, Bill Bailey and Corky Corcoran as they rode through the night sky inside a charger called W-William to wreak vengeance on Nazi Germany. Theirs was a world lit only by searchlights, tracer bullets and the green and red fairy lights of target indicators. A world shared with mischievous gremlins and goblinesque night-fighters. I was enthralled.[57]

Robin Ward also reflected on the indelible stories of his father's war service:

His life was marked by the war, and my brother Brian and I have been too by his experience of it. We grew up in the 1950s and 1960s ... Military-style discipline and eccentricities were not unknown in our house. Every day when he came home he would call out: 'Any news, mail, phone calls', as if still barking out questions to his lieutenants. For many years, he kept a pair of desert boots that were re-soled and re-heeled until the suede perished. When he put them on he would first shake them upside down, a desert army habit to expel scorpions. His glengarry and sporran hung in the hall. He was obsessed by the weather, another soldiering trait; when he went out he'd tap the barometer that hung by the front door. In the garden, he built dry-stone retaining walls, a skill he learned making sangars on the North African battlefields. If we criticised his driving, he'd say: 'What do you expect? I learned in the desert.'[58]

[54] Ward, *The Mirror of Monte Cavallara*, p. 13.
[55] Ibid., p. 18.
[56] Steve Ashton, preface to J. Norman Ashton, *Only Birds and Fools: Flight Engineer, Avro Lancaster, World War II* (Shrewsbury: Airlife, 2000).
[57] Ibid.
[58] Ward, *The Mirror of Monte Cavallara*, pp. 10–11.

Both men claimed that the respective memoirs gave them fresh insight into their fathers' characters:

After the war [Norman] returned to his home town and became a devoted father of five children. We have our own private memories of him during those years. Now, with the publication of this book, we also have a permanent record of a crucial earlier chapter in his life.[59]

Robin Ward expressed a similar sentiment, explaining that he felt he had retrieved a version of his father that he had never known:

His typescript was closely-spaced and frequently faint, as if to challenge me to read between the lines. I was not sure I ever really knew him or what I would find. He was an authoritarian figure, always rather remote, with his emotions well camouflaged. But in the memoir, he is an occasionally reckless, vulnerable and sensitive young man. That is how I see and begin to know him now.[60]

Outside the immediate familial category of 'Those who wanted to know what it was like', multiple memoirists widened their purview to inform all the generations who had not fought on the frontlines. As a professional historian of some renown during his later lifetime, former naval officer Norman Hampson cast a critical eye over his own motives for putting pen to paper. Despite swearing in 1944 that he would earn 'the gratitude of posterity' by becoming one of the few RNVR officers who did not publicise his experiences, some decades later he felt that the time was ripe to break this promise. Keeping a weather eye upon the changing tides of military history, by the late 1990s he thought that the new vogue for worm's eye studies of war might have created a new milieu of scholarly and popular interest in which his tale would be of interest and significance. There might, he hoped,

be a case for something that begins as 'history from below decks' and shows what it felt like to be swept up in a communal experience that must seem to the present generation almost as remote as the days of Hornblower.[61]

Some veterans optimistically hoped that publishing a narrative of combat during the Second World War might help the next generations to learn something from their experiences and perhaps prevent a similar global cataclysm. Battle of Britain pilot Bill Rolls went into hospital with heart problems in the autumn of 1980. He was surprised and delighted to be the subject of considerable attention from young doctors and

---

[59] Ashton, preface to *Only Birds and Fools*
[60] Ward, *The Mirror of Monte Cavallara*, p. 18.
[61] Norman Hampson, *Not Really What You'd Call a War* (Caithness: Whittles Publishing, 2001), p. vii.

nurses who all wanted to know what it was like to be a Spitfire pilot during 1940:

It was suggested that when I had recovered from the operation I should write a book about those days but to write it in language they could understand. [The doctor] said that most books on that period of history were too technical as far as the RAF were concerned and that I should write a book for the younger people to understand as they were interested to know what went on.[62]

A year later, Rolls' younger brother and son reiterated the request, informing him that he 'owed it to the younger generation to write down as much history as I could. There must be some lessons to be got from it.'[63] Another former flyer, John Wainwright, expressed a similar motivation for writing his memoir, remarking that 'It is also, deliberately, directed at another generation than my own ... A generation which (I hope) will have too much sense to permit World War III.'[64] So strongly did Wainwright feel the need to stress the horrors of his war that the concluding sentence of his memoir implored his readers 'For God's sake don't let it happen again'.[65] In the spirit of hoping to be of some use to subsequent generations, several veterans constructed their memoirs as a text of tactical reference for future combatants. Peter Dickens explained that upon being appointed as an unusually young man to command a Motor Torpedo Boat (MTB) Flotilla, he would have profited considerably from the availability of similar narratives of other MTB experiences. 'Being quite unprepared and untrained for the task I was avid to learn from anyone's experiences in World War I, but none had been recorded that I could find', he remarked ruefully.[66] In a similar vein, Group Captain Douglas Bader assured the future Air Vice Marshal 'Johnnie' Johnson that despite Bader's personal disagreement with Johnson's assessment of the efficacy of the wartime 'Big Wing' tactic, the latter's memoir was satisfactorily written 'in the tradition of our famous predecessors of World War I, Ball, McCudden, Mannock and Bishop.' 'Never let it be forgotten', continued Bader,

that our generation of fighter pilots learned the basic rules of air fighting from them. When I was a cadet at Cranwell I used to read their books time and time again and I never forgot them. I am sure this book of yours will be with the same enthusiasm by future generations of cadets. I commend it to them.[67]

[62] Rolls, *Spitfire Attack*, p. 12.
[63] Ibid., p. 12.
[64] Wainwright, *Tail-End Charlie*, p. 7.
[65] Ibid., p. 187.
[66] Peter Dickens, *Night Action: MTB Flotilla at War* (London: P. Davies, 1974), p. xi.
[67] Douglas Bader, foreword to J.E. 'Johnnie' Johnson, *Wing Leader* (London: Chatto & Windus, 1956).

Other veterans also took up their pens in the hope of being of some use to future generations of combatants. Peter Gretton explained that his main reason for telling his tale was the 'long apprenticeship' he had served in convoy work:

I believe therefore that although I have no special claim to skill in sinking submarines, I am well qualified to discuss the art of escorting convoys across the North Atlantic. Moreover, many of the lessons learnt at such cost in the last war are being forgotten, just as precisely the same lessons were forgotten after 1918 and after the Napoleonic wars. I hope this book will jog a few memories, for the facts are still important even in a nuclear age.[68]

As Gretton noted, despite significant geopolitical changes and technological developments since 1945, skills of seamanship and command would retain their value in the modern age. With the importance of off-shore oil fields to the British economy in the mid-1970s, Dickens believed it conceivable that small, fast craft might again be needed in order to defend the nation's interests. He felt that his role as memoirist was therefore to 'tell the story as accurately as possible so that our successors may pick out any lessons there may be for themselves, and history can usually provide such lessons to those with the wit to distinguish the principle from the transient.'[69] As in Gretton's account, the poignant wish of an old warrior to continue to serve his nation in some way in future battles can be detected in Dickens' desire to assist forthcoming crops of British servicemen.

As a generation of ex-servicemen to whom the idea of 'shooting a line' and boasting of one's exploits was cultural anathema, some Second World War veterans actively justified telling their story in public on the grounds that warriors of the future would draw comfort and learn valuable lessons from the human 'face of battle' recounted in their memoirs. Dickens referred to his perception that it was

presumptuous for someone as unimportant as I am to write about his own doings, and some attempt at an excuse is called for. To most people small, fast fighting craft were exciting and glamorous but ... now we have none. There seems a case therefore for trying to pass on some of the thrill, the delights and disappointments, failures and successes, problems and their solutions, experienced by a very young man in the enviable and uncommon job of Senior Officer of a Motor Torpedo-Boat Flotilla.[70]

Other veterans also reached out to communicate with new generations of combatants on an emotional level, seeking to provide quiet reassurance that it had all been done before and could be done again. George Macdonald

---

[68] Peter Gretton, *Convoy Escort Commander* (London: Cassell, 1964), p. xiv.
[69] Ibid., p. xi.
[70] Dickens, *Night Action*, p. xi.

Fraser's memoir of serving in Burma exemplifies this attitude particularly well. Through the medium of *Quartered Safe Out Here* (1993) he extended a paternalistic hand to British infantry in the 1990s:

[I]f any young soldiers of today should chance to read this book, they may understand that while the face of war may alter, some things have not changed since Joshua stood before Jericho and Xenophon marched to the sea. May they come safe to bedtime, and all well.[71]

Some memoirs became guides for future generations of servicemen almost by default. Sydney Jary's *18 Platoon*, an account of serving as a junior officer commanding 18 Platoon, 4th Battalion, Somerset Light Infantry, was greeted with such approbation in military circles that the book was officially launched at the Royal Military Academy of Sandhurst in May 1987. Jary maintained a lifelong connection to the officer training institution and *18 Platoon* became a staple teaching text in the Sandhurst library. Nevertheless, the veteran was astonished to find that his book was regarded as a textbook on low level military command.[72] So far as he was concerned, the book had been primarily written as an acknowledgement of the 'loyalty, courage and decency' of the men he commanded in his platoon, explaining that 'Written by a soldier, for soldiers, it has also been managed by soldiers. It has now been read by a great number of soldiers. It is indeed their book.'[73] The employment of Jary's excellent memoir as a teaching aid for successive generations of infantry is not quite as surprising as the veteran's innate modesty led him to suppose. To modern armed services, *18 Platoon* represented 'a classic account of small unit infantry action in full-scale war ... its insights into commanding men in battle have led to its being accepted as a *vade mecum* for those entering the profession of arms'.[74] Distributed among the British, Australian, New Zealand, United States, and Norwegian armies, Jary's narrative of human nature in the wartime infantry was praised most of all for 'the author's approach to command' which outlined the imperative of building relationships of mutual trust and regard between senior and lower ranks, and remained prized as highly relevant to modern military matters.[75]

---

[71] George Macdonald Fraser, *Quartered Safe Out Here: A Recollection of the War in Burma*, rev. ed. (London: Harper Collins, 2000), p. xxiv.
[72] Jary, *18 Platoon* , p. 133. One example of Jary's continued connection with Sandhurst is his participation in a Royal Military Battlefield Tour (2006) to Normandy, conducted to provide officer cadets with a practical understanding of real-life battlefield tactics and problems.
[73] Ibid., p. 134.
[74] Ibid., p. xxi.
[75] Ibid., p. xxi.

Audience of Comrades

When Jary wrote that *18 Platoon* was written 'by a soldier, for soldiers', he was also thinking of his own generation of combatants. His primary target readership was the same community of veterans that Bowlby identified as the third and most important audience for his own memoir. On the whole, these books were overwhelmingly created out of love and affinity for the veteran's former comrades and a desire to inscribe a permanent record of their martial fellowship for posterity. A considerable number of the memoirists in this study found themselves being urged to write their tale by friends who were themselves Second World War veterans. Jary mused that his book 'should have been written thirty years ago, but I was afraid that, over the years, I might have deluded myself about 18 Platoon and particularly about my relationship with it.'[76] At a reunion dinner in the early 1980s, however, a suggestion was aired that their former officer should author a book about their war experiences. Jary's fears that perhaps he had imagined the strength of his wartime relationship with his platoon were assuaged by a meeting with his former NCOs, with whom he had formed a very close bond during the war: 'The old magic was still there. It was real and had not faded over the years. I could now write with a clear conscience.'[77] Memoirists were sometimes urged to put pen to paper by former comrades who had written their own narratives and were keen for their pals to share in the experience. Bestselling author of *The Cruel Sea* (1951) Nicholas Monsarrat proved instrumental in the genesis of his wartime commanding officer's memoir. Visiting his old friend at his residence on the tiny island of Gozo, Sam Lombard-Hobson commented that,

naval contemporaries of mine were bullying me to put on record my varied experiences before they were lost to memory. 'Why not?', [Monsarrat] said; 'you've got a far better story to tell about the sea than ever I had. Have a go!' I roared with laughter, and told him that I would never dare to trespass on the sacred ground of others far more erudite than me. Anyhow, I was far too busy doing other things. A little later I was again confronted: 'For God's sake get on with it – I'll help you,' urged my one-time Number One.[78]

Not long after this conversation, Monsarrat succumbed to cancer and died in August 1979. 'As a gesture of affection and respect for my old friend and shipmate', wrote his former senior officer, 'I now accept his advice, to have a go and get on with the job.'[79]

---

[76] Ibid., p. xx.
[77] Ibid., p. xx.
[78] Sam Lombard-Hobson, *A Sailor's War* (London: Orbis Publishing, 1983), p. 10.
[79] Ibid., p. 10.

A veteran's erstwhile comrades thus often played an integral role in the decision to construct a narrative of the war, and the war memoirist assumed an important function as spokesman for his band of brothers. As Jary and Lombard-Hobson illustrate, some were appointed to the task by former comrades with whom intimate bonds had been forged during the war. A self-imposed sense of duty and responsibility to make a record of shared experiences compelled others to begin writing. John Horsfall, a former officer of the 1st Battalion, Royal Irish Fusiliers, declared that 'Many of our soldiers are still living, and having the records I owe it to them ... to set out for posterity what is perhaps an epic and which otherwise would for ever be lost.'[80] Whatever the individual circumstances of a memoir's origins, these narratives were intended to speak to and for a wide community of ex-servicemen, or as Charles Potts referred to this audience, all those 'who were themselves in the game'.[81] In their public assertion of the combat experience, war memoirs were regarded as a vital form of connection between physical and emotional communities of veterans in Britain precisely because they spoke so directly to the old soldier, sailor, or airman. By 1998, Hunt and Robbins note, a resurgence of Old Comrades' Associations had occurred in recent decades. The scholars attributed this to an increasing number of veterans' desires to discuss their experiences in a 'safe' situation.[82] Veterans turned to each other to reminisce in the knowledge that shared understandings of combat created specific codes of meaning which allowed empathy to be given and received, thus granting pleasurable and sad memories to be expressed in an emotionally secure environment. Crucially, as Jay Winter and Emmanuel Sivan posit, all written or oral soldiers' tales operate as expressions of shared codes among combatants, which are reinforced in the telling.[83] These memoirs fulfilled a similar function to the Old Comrades' Associations in that they created a space in which the reader could securely explore his own recollections in the knowledge that he was not alone. Some memoirs offered ex-serviceman a satisfying resolution of their own experiences, colouring in missing details from a particular battle. After *Recollections* was published in paperback in 1971, Alex Bowlby's publisher received a letter from a General Sir Horatius Murray, who wrote that he had found the memoir 'most interesting'. Murray explained that he had been the General in command of the 6th Armoured Division to which Bowlby's battalion had been attached.

---

[80] John Horsfall, *The Wild Geese are Flighting* (Kineton: The Roundwood Press, 1976), p. xiv.
[81] Potts, *Soldier in the Sand*, p. 1.
[82] Hunt and Robbins, 'Telling Stories of the War', p. 63.
[83] Winter and Sivan, 'Setting the Framework', p. 36.

Requesting Bowlby's address in order to 'congratulate him personally', Murray stated that 'I only know that it was of great importance that a book such as his should be published.'[84] Bowlby was also thrilled to inform his publisher that he had encountered an former tank recovery 'bloke' who had been captured in the desert and had adored reading *Recollections*. His response, as reported by Bowlby was encouraging: '"Right on the dot!" "I'm real chuffed by it!" etc etc.' Bowlby was further delighted that this veteran intended to pass his book along to a taxi driver he knew in York who had served in Burma.[85] War memoirs thus operated as an act of communion, reaching out to other veterans across the services. They ignited memory and allowed men to communicate their reminiscences within an environment of others who knew 'what it was like' to serve on the front line, even if they had never met personally or were not actively in old comrades' associations. In addition to allowing the reader to indulge in reminiscence or to discover further details of a battle in which they participated, war memoirs served as a voice for all those who were unable to tell their own wartime stories. Of Jim Bailey's memoir of serving with Fighter Command, Group Captain Peter Townsend commented that 'The best airmen are mostly simple people, who have been so overwhelmed by their love for flying that it has driven some of them to drink, others to silence, as great love often does.'[86] This memoirist, he thought, had written a book which spoke for all those airmen who could not or would not vocalise his experiences: 'every airman of our age who, reading your book, will feel you have given wings to his innermost thoughts.'[87]

War memoirs were intended to offer tribute to the community of veterans by publicly acknowledging the extent of the sacrifice they had made for the nation. Former air gunner John Bushby dedicated his memoir to an 'infinite army of young men for whom life was never quite the same again.'[88] Several memoirists expressed a firm belief that their former comrades' wartime achievements had been woefully unrewarded. Donald Macintyre intended his memoir to stand as a tribute to his many wartime naval companions, pointing out that sadly few of them had been rewarded with decorations for their efforts. He hoped that 'this account of the actions which we shared may to some degree compensate them.'[89]

---

[84] UoR, LC/ A/2/79, General Sir Horatius Murray to Leo Cooper, 26 April 1972.

[85] UoR, LC/ A/2/79, Alex Bowlby to Leo Cooper, dated only 'Tuesday'.

[86] Group Captain Peter Townsend, foreword to Jim Bailey, *The Sky Suspended: A Fighter Pilot's Story* (London: Bloomsbury, 2005), p. 5.

[87] Ibid., p. 6.

[88] John Busbhy, *Gunner's Moon: A Memoir of the RAF night assault on Germany* (London: Ian Allan, 1972).

[89] Donald Macintyre, *U-boat Killer* (London: Weidenfeld and Nicholson, 1956), p. xii.

Sydney Jary expressed considerable regret that his cherished NCOs, Owen Cheeseman, Doug Proctor, and Jim Kingston, had not been awarded any medals, explaining that this lack of public recognition comprised one of the main reasons why he wrote *18 Platoon*. Describing this motive as a 'sentimental explosion', he asked the Light Infantry Office at Taunton to sell his memoir, which he published through his own company, Sydney Jary Ltd. He anticipated that they might sell between 200–300 copies to 'the old and the bold' and that this would do justice to his NCOs. Amazed when he learned that the Regimental Secretary had rapidly sold £20,000 of books, Jary felt that his memoir had fulfilled its true purpose when his former comrade was invited to sign a copy of the book and asked if he was '*the* Jim Kingston' of whom Jary wrote with such admiration.[90] In this instance, the veteran-memoirist's quest for popular recognition of his wartime comrades was successful. Other armed services experienced particular problems in attaining the levels of public acknowledgement of their sacrifices to which their veterans felt entitled. Lack of military medals formed a pillar of especial resentment in the bomber aircrew narratives, due to a long-running and largely unsuccessful battle to obtain a campaign medal for Bomber Command veterans. At the close of the war, Sir Arthur Harris, Commander-in-Chief of Bomber Command since 1942, requested that a medal be granted to his air crews in recognition of their courageous wartime service. Instead, an unpopular distinction was made between those who had been operational before D-Day and those who had carried out their tours after this date. In memoirist Arthur White's view,

Bomber crews were snubbed by the Government's refusal to award a Bomber Command Campaign Medal in recognition of their efforts and sacrifices. In fact, crews embarking on their tours of operations after D-Day didn't even qualify for the Aircrew Europe Star but had to be content with the France and Germany Star.[91]

Jim Davis conveyed a particular sense of bitterness that this distinction had been drawn, noting that,

The France and Germany Star was given to all the soldiers and other personnel who crossed the Channel after D-Day and, of course, it was also given to those who actually crossed the Channel when the war was nearly over (a matter of a day or so). Every one came under the France and Germany medal. Surely then it would have been fair if all Air Crew who flew on operations against Germany at any time during the war should have been given the Air Crew Europe Star.[92]

[90] IWM Sound Archive, Sydney Jary, 18024.
[91] White, *Bread and Butter Bomber Boys*, p. 2.
[92] Davis, *Winged Victory*, p. 69.

With operational flying over Europe continuing to pose considerable risks to bomber crews for many months after D-Day, the division of entitlement to the coveted Aircrew Europe Star remained a contentious issue for Bomber Command, and many of this subgenre of war memoirs were published with the intention of drawing attention to this injustice.

It was not solely the living community of veterans with which the war memoirists were concerned, however. The dead were never far from their thoughts and various veterans felt a strong urge to tell their story on behalf of comrades who had not survived the war. The memoirs of former frontline combatants have been referred to as 'survivors' songs', a description which perfectly encapsulates the nature and function of these narratives as dual proclamations of mourning and celebration.[93] An epitome of the memoir as 'survivor's song' is provided by Alex Bowlby, who took the opportunity of the republication of *Recollections* in 1989 to add a new epilogue which self-assessed his motivations for penning the memoir in the first instance. He explained that during his service in Italy he had believed that his former corporal, 'Slim' Brandon, would be the person to write a book about the company:

I felt it wouldn't matter so much if most of us were killed. As long as Slim was around – and I was sure he always would be – he would see to it that we were not forgotten.[94]

'Slim', however, did not live to carry out this task, having been accidentally shot by his own Bren gunner long before the company returned to Britain. After his death, Bowlby explained, he perceived the task of recording the history of the unit must fall to him: 'the job I had earmarked for him was now mine.'[95] Reporting that the senior librarian at Sandhurst had informed his publisher that he thought *Recollections* would become a classic text for those studying the Italian campaign, Bowlby was told that this would grant the book 'a long life'. Patently thrilled by this praise, he expressed a sense of relief that his 'debt' to his former comrades was paid, rejoicing that 'The dead would live on in the book.'[96] Bowlby also revealed a deeper working of the memoir as 'survivor's song'. In the new 1989 edition, he explains that on Easter Sunday 1971, he journeyed to the battlefield at Arezzo where so many of his comrades had perished. He was taken aback to discover the existence of a military cemetery, as on a previous visit he had failed to find any permanent war graves, taking

---

[93] Mark Rawlinson, *British Writing of the Second World War* (Oxford: Oxford University Press, 2000), p. 43.
[94] Bowlby, *Recollections*, p. 222.
[95] Ibid., p. 222.
[96] Ibid., p. 226.

comfort in imagining the apparent lack of presence of the dead as part of Nature's healing process. His later memoir thus expressed some mental anguish:

Why hadn't I found out where their permanent ones were? Why hadn't I visited them? Because you didn't want to get too close to the dead, I thought. You wanted them buried alive in the book. They're rotting in their graves, chum. You've got to face them there. You've been dodging the column, running away from the pain and guilt of being alive when the best are dead, their lives wasted. Thrown away. For what? A botched civilization. A bitch gone in the teeth.[97]

The searing agony of the veteran-memoirist, who survived to write his tale where so many did not, is vividly outlined here. Bowlby's self-castigation for having, as he believed, 'buried alive' his former comrades in his narrative underscores a severe and damaging case of survivor's guilt. Indeed the function of memoir as tribute here is represented as something of a double-edged blade – for Bowlby, his literary memorial itself was a source of anguish as he believed that its construction allowed him to retreat from the reality that his friends were dead and so elide the 'pain and guilt' of the fact that he himself was still alive.

Nevertheless, Bowlby was a rarity among the memoirists of the Second World War. Most showed more self-compassion and did not employ their own narratives as a mechanism of flagellating themselves for survival. They wrote instead to fix an image of the fallen for eternity, a literary means of ensuring that their names lived for evermore. George Macdonald Fraser explained that one of his dominant reasons for writing a memoir of jungle warfare in the Far East was 'to make some kind of memorial' to his former comrades, many of whom were killed in action. He also explained that his comrades still seemed 'matchless' to him.[98] As this sentiment suggests, the creation and publication of a war memoir also allowed the veteran to sanctify his own memories of his comrades, placing their memory and sacrifice upon a public pedestal of remembrance. This commemoration extended far beyond the veteran's own immediate group of friends and comrades within his unit. Indeed, these narratives serve as tribute to a far broader, often faceless and unidentified martial fraternity with whom the memoirist expressed a bond of affection. Ex-fighter pilot Bobby Oxspring chose to craft his memoir as an accolade to the nameless majority of 'the Few', the 'unsung "average" pilots' whom he describes as performing 'Countless courageous acts' which 'remain unheralded'.[99] A precious letter received by

[97] Ibid., pp. 226–7.
[98] Macdonald Fraser, *Quartered Safe Out Here*, p. xviii.
[99] Bobby Oxspring, *Spitfire Command* (London: William Kimber, 1984), p. 16.

Alex Bowlby from the writer Arthur Koestler, who knew from first-hand experience just how difficult it was to write about friends killed in the war, also provides a revealing glimpse into the veteran's decision to write and publish his memoir. Comparing Richard Hillary's famous wartime memoir, *The Last Enemy* (1942), with Bowlby's recently released *The Recollections of Rifleman Bowlby*, Koestler wrote to Bowlby that 'Hillary's book deals with the tragedy of a small elite, yours with the plight of the Unknown Soldier; but you have certainly erected a monument to him.'[100] Bowlby was much pleased with this idea that his memoir represented not just a tribute to his own tight knit unit, but also a memorial to the unidentifiable remains of all who died in the Italian campaign. Testifying to this pleasure, a note scribbled across the bottom of Koestler's letter in Bowlby's handwriting proclaims simply 'A Monument to the Unknown Soldier' and this phrase subsequently appeared prominently on the dust jacket of the paperback edition.[101]

In creating these literary monuments to comrades known and unknown, the war memoirist hoped to prove himself worthy of their sacrifice and satisfy his own sense of honour. The best expression of this attitude, which continued to shape the post-war veteran memoirs, remains Richard Hillary's eulogy to his fellow 'long-haired boys': 'If I could do this thing, could tell a little of the lives of these men, I would have justified, at least in some measure, my right to fellowship with my dead'.[102] The possessiveness which rings throughout Hillary's reference to 'my dead' was echoed by Denys Rayner ten years later: 'If I were to include just one thing which did not happen I should be untrue to myself, and untrue to all those less fortunate than I who perished by wind, by wave, and by enemy action.'[103] Through the publication of a war memoir, the veteran thus exercised the right of the survivor to make a lasting 'imprint' of the wartime identity and sacrifice of others. Most of these narratives were not released with anything approaching the pomp and circumstance that accompanied the ceremonial unveiling of the International Air Monument outside Plymouth in 1989. Yet Davis' description of that occasion also serves to describe the collective mood of the war memoirists: 'I knew now that the monument was unveiled, nobody could prevent the truth from being known. It was now on public view for all to read for eternity.'[104]

---

[100] UoR, LC/ A/2/80/1, Arthur Koestler to Alex Bowlby, 12 April 1971.
[101] Ibid.
[102] Hillary, *The Last Enemy*, p. 178.
[103] Rayner, *Escort*, p. ix.
[104] Davis, *Winged Victory*, p. 105.

2   Penning and Publishing the Veteran's Tale

> [He] comes out fighting when journalists question his memory ...
> 'Are you trying to tell me that you can't understand how I can
> remember every detail? I can see it.'[1]

Once a veteran had decided to pen a record of his wartime experiences, he was faced with the complex task of assembling his memoir. The former serviceman's own memory constituted the predominant source used to construct his narrative, although most also opted to supplement private recollection with additional sources such as battalion or regimental war diaries, scholarly historical accounts, or their own wartime diaries and letters. It was clearly very important to the veteran that his audience should know how he was able to reconstruct his wartime experiences, and many memoirists foregrounded some word of explanation at the beginning of their narratives. Heavily stamping the concept of the military memoir as vital testimonial to the experience of war throughout these narratives, most veteran-memoirists insisted upon clarifying for their audience the exact measures undertaken to ensure accuracy and 'truthfulness' in their accounts. As the epigraph to this chapter – extracted from a journalist's interview with ex-fighter pilot Geoffrey Wellum in 2010 – illustrates, the narratives of Second World War veterans are notoriously vulnerable to charges of historical unreliability. This state of affairs is largely due to their reliance on the soldier's own remembrance of long-ago wartime events and the fragility of human memory. Collectively, therefore, as Wellum's antagonistic response to would-be detractors embodies, this genre of life writing displays a strong bent towards publicly legitimising the veteran's testimony of remembered combat experience. This chapter thus examines how the veterans sought to create an 'authentic' account of war. It also addresses a frequently tense relationship between veteran-memoirists and their publishers, focusing on a process of negotiation to ensure that the published memoir met both the veteran's desire to

[1] House, 'The 89-year-old Boy'.

recount the experience of war faithfully, and the commercial imperatives of the publishing house.

Writing Veteran Memoir

Inevitably, personal recollection represents a potentially problematic primary source of evidence in writing histories of warfare. Influences such as increased temporal distances and age can erode memory, whilst battle-induced trauma may also serve to destroy and fragment memory. As psychologist Nigel Hunt notes, memory itself is 'flexible', 'permeable', and 'changeable', and may be both consciously and unconsciously manipulated by the individual.[2] Consequently, a somewhat suspicious eye has been cast over published war memoirs from some scholarly quarters, suggesting that these documents are lacking in reliability and factually 'untrustworthy' as a historical source.[3] Perhaps predictably, any suggestion that their personal memories might constitute an 'obstacle to truth' received decidedly short shrift from the veterans in this study. Far from memories of their wartime experiences dimming as the veteran aged, some memoirists insisted that they were actually better able to recall specific events as they grew older. Former soldier John McManners was gratified to discover that 'Advancing years bring a sharp-focused clarity to the memory, just as the colours in a garden become deeper and more vivid as twilight falls.'[4] Others found that wartime experiences had been imprinted like a snapshot upon their mind's eye, as ex-infantryman Geoffrey Picot related of his battle experience:

Events had so scorched themselves on my mind that I could recall nearly every particular on a day-to-day basis. There was the move from that slit trench in one field to the other trench in a different field, this advance, that check, this tactical move sideways ... everything was crystal clear.[5]

Even in 1993, this veteran claimed, he was still able to know and portray 'exactly what it was like to be a front-line soldier' in the great Allied push through North West Europe after D-Day.[6] Similarly, despite the passage of some thirty years since he attacked enemy shipping in his Blenheim bomber, Ronald Gillman explained that 'the pictures still burn brightly in

---

[2] Hunt, *Memory, War and Trauma*, p. 2.

[3] Hynes, *Soldiers' Tale*, p. 23.

[4] John McManners, *Fusilier: Recollections and Reflections 1939–1945* (Norwich: Michael Russell, 2002), p. 9.

[5] Geoffrey Picot, *Accidental Warrior: In the Front Line from Normandy till Victory* (Lewes: The Book Guild, 1993), pp. 23–24.

[6] Ibid., p. 23.

my mind.[7] Both memoirists' choice of using imagery bound up with fire
to explain how they recalled war is striking. The associations this conveys
of intensity, violence, and passion suggest that these men believed their
experiences had been literally seared upon their memory, creating a kind
of mental photograph which could be reviewed throughout the post-war
decades. There is some evidence from within the field of neurosciences
to suggest that veterans did retain particularly vivid recollections of battlefield experiences. Personal memory focuses on and retains the 'more
salient features of life experience', particularly those which feature importance or uniqueness.[8] Where an experience had been insufficiently unique,
important, or dramatic enough to ensure life-long retention, minor stories
and recollections could easily slip the net of memory. As Jay Winter and
Emmanuel Sivan explain in their study of war and remembrance, most
experiences leave long-term memory traces which differ in weight. The
'density' of memory is shaped and enhanced by the dramatic or emotional
nature of the experience. Combat experience is especially 'dense' because
of the intense degree of emotional drama it involves; deeply affecting experiences further increase the density of the memory and so facilitate its
retention.[9] These veterans certainly perceived that specific memories of
sensational events had been etched into their minds and could be easily
retrieved. The recollections that McManners, Picot, and Gillman describe
fall into the category of 'flashbulb memories', a memory mechanism triggered by an event that was experienced as highly vivid, extremely positive, negative, or surprising, or personally important.[10] The existence of
emotional memory in coding, storing, and retrieving experience has been
widely been recognised in the field of neurosciences, which has coined
the term 'Emotional Enhancement of Memory' to describe the better
memory of highly emotional, rather than more mundane, events. When
measured after a delay between lived and remembered events, the tendency of human memory was to show a preferential consolidation of the
more emotionally experienced events.[11] Although psychologists Ulrike
Rimmele et al. have suggested that greater accuracy in contextual detail
is not necessarily ensured by higher levels of vividness of memory, they
do note that an individual experiences an increased subjective intensity
of an emotional memory, a greater impression of reliving the emotional

[7] Ronald Gillman, *The Shiphunters* (London: J. Murray, 1976), p. xiii.
[8] Hunt, *Memory, War and Trauma*, p. 118.
[9] Winter and Sivan, 'Setting the Framework', p. 12.
[10] Olivier Luminet and Antonietta Curci (eds.), *Flashbulb Memories: New Issues and New Perspectives* (New York: Psychology Press, 2009), pp. 1–2.
[11] Gemma Elizabeth Barnacle, 'Understanding Emotional Memory: Cognitive Factors' (Unpublished Thesis, University of Manchester, 2016).

event, and a higher confidence in the accuracy of the memory. It is thus evident that, to some extent, 'emotion enhances the subjective sense of remembering.'[12] Confidence in emotional memory was certainly exhibited by the veteran-memoirists. Geoffrey Wellum quite clearly viewed any suggestion that he might have forgotten or misremembered aspects of his combat experience as an impertinence: 'If you get an 18-year-old, you say, "There's a Spitfire, go and fly it and if you break it, there will be bloody hell to pay" ... Are you trying to tell me that you can't understand how I can remember every detail? I can see it.'[13] More succinctly, former fighter pilot Bobby Oxspring insisted that 'the memory of the more spectacular events will never fade.'[14] Inevitably, therefore, emotional aspects to remembering shaped the content of the narrative produced by the memoirist, even if only in so far as his assurance that he could indeed accurately remember the most exciting or dangerous moments. Unquestionably there are some problematic issues with the factual accuracy of the contextual detail of these 'flashbulb memories'. Yet since *The Veterans' Tale* is an enquiry into the emotional subjectivities of veteran recollections and records of wartime experience, the memoirists' confidence in their own memories of unique or distinctive emotive events serves as an important announcement of the veterans' desire to validate the 'authenticity' of their testimonials.

Nevertheless, despite this assertive confidence in the recollections of the 'more spectacular events', a revealing duality seeps into the veterans' self-confessed approach to assembling their narratives. Insistence that they could accurately recollect significant combat experiences operated alongside rueful acknowledgement of the inevitable limitations of human memory as a source of recall. Displayed alongside assurances that *particular* war experiences may be imprinted upon the mind of the combatant was a tacit acceptance that memory might pose some problems with the more general construction of the narrative. Former Lancaster pilot Jack Currie, for example, regretfully accepted that although he made every effort to remember his war experiences as precisely as possible, his memory 'after more than thirty years may not, I am afraid, be faultless', whilst fellow bomber veteran Norman Ashton mused that memory could certainly play 'strange tricks'.[15] In a revised edition of his war memoir, *Men at Arnhem*, published twenty-seven years after the book first appeared in 1976, Geoffrey Powell explored the 'strange tricks' of recollection in considerable detail. Intrigued by the divergent feedback he received about his

[12] Rimmele *et al.*, 'Emotion enhances the subjective feeling of remembering', p. 553.
[13] House, 'The 89-Year Old Boy'.
[14] Oxspring, *Spitfire Command*, p. 16.
[15] Jack Currie, *Lancaster Target*, 2nd ed. (London: Goodall Publications, 1981), p. 5; Ashton, preface to *Only Birds and Fools*.

memoir from other surviving veterans who had witnessed the narrated events, Powell recorded astonishment that his memory appeared to have been 'utterly mistaken' with regard to some incidents. In one instance, he was surprised to learn that, despite clearly remembering having witnessed the unit's doctor, John Buck, in the Breede Laan with his arms saturated in blood, Buck himself confirmed that he was not in fact the man Powell had seen. Memory, Powell was therefore forced to conclude, had in this instance 'been fallible.'[16] All the same, he remained defiantly convinced that his 'own reactions to the events, all etched in my mind, are accurate', a refrain which can be repeatedly heard throughout the veterans' tale. Thus, memoirists like Powell, despite having to accept that the exact details of their recollections might not be entirely factually correct in some circumstances, remained publicly adamant that their own recovered responses to the described events were fundamentally accurate.

Where veteran memory reached its limits it required something of a prod from external sources. Although asserting that old age had clarified some recollections, McManners allowed that 'the pattern is no longer continuous; the recollected details concern highly-selected, isolated incidents', acknowledging that, without access to the battalion's war diary to provide 'structure and coherence' he would have been unable to finish his narrative.[17] Indeed, despite frequent protestations of exact remembrance, nearly all of the memoirists in this study opted to draw upon additional sources to assist in the reconstruction of experience, offering this as evidence of their desire to produce an 'accurate' account. As the example of McManners highlights, a battalion war diary frequently proved a crucial aid to the memoirist in augmenting his own recollections, assisting the imposition of some form of order and sequence upon memory. Private diaries fulfilled the same function more efficiently as they contained greater levels of personal meaning for the veteran. Although Picot asserted that his experiences in advancing through North-West Europe had been 'scorched' upon his mind, part of his ability to recall these experiences so clearly in 1993 lay in the fact that, as soon as was possible, he had captured the incident upon paper:

I know now exactly what it was like because as soon as the guns stopped firing, while the details and the atmosphere of the fighting were still burning in my memory, I wrote it all down: what I had done, said, felt, seen, heard.[18]

Although the practice of keeping a diary was 'severely frowned upon' by the military hierarchy, many servicemen nevertheless chose to keep

[16] Geoffrey Powell, preface to *Men at Arnhem*, rev. ed. (Barnsley: Pen & Sword, 2003).
[17] McManners, *Fusilier*, p. 9.
[18] Picot, *Accidental Warrior*, p. 23.

58   The Veterans' Tale

surreptitious unofficial records of their experiences.[19] Like diaries, the
letters a serviceman sent home provided a precious cache of information
for the veteran seeking to construct an account of wartime experience
in the post-war decades. When ex-fighter pilot Tom Neil's father died in
1977, he discovered in the family home more than 600 of his own letters
which he had sent faithfully at least twice a week throughout his five
years at war. These letters formed the foundation of his war memoir, *Gun
Button to 'Fire'*, which was first published ten years after his discovery. He
explained that these documents had played an important role in assisting and enhancing memory, reflecting that 'on reading my own words
again – sometimes with great difficulty – I was reminded of many events
and incidents long since forgotten.'[20] Personal letters and diaries such as
those drawn upon by Picot and Neil thus represented an important tool
for the veteran seeking to pen a memoir of his wartime experiences. Their
function, however, extended far beyond merely providing details which
the memoirist could use as a framework for his narrative. They also acted
as a crucial window into the past for the veteran seeking to reconstruct
his wartime self. In a significant study which spans the diaries and correspondence of American service personnel from colonial conflicts to the
recent wars in Iraq, DC Gill views the motive for writing these types of
personal narrative as a kind of 'communion' which tethers individuals to
their pre-war sense of self and reality.[21] Her argument that creating a war
letter or diary 'allows soldiers a tenuous purchase on a world with which
they no longer have a sensory connection' may also be applied to a post-
war context.[22] If writing letters or diaries whilst on active service allowed
the combatant to invoke and explore his pre-war sense of identity, the
same argument holds true for the veteran looking back on his wartime
identity many years later in peacetime. In so far as diaries were written
for an internal audience – by the self for the self – they fulfilled a slightly
different purpose to the letters which a serviceman sent home to his family or friends. Although official and self-censorship meant that there were
some limitations to the information that wartime letters and diaries could
provide, these sources proved invaluable to the veteran who wanted to
resurrect his younger self for assessment. Hugh Dundas, for instance,
incorporated into his memoir two letters to his mother and brother which
describe in glowing terms the controversial 'BigWing' tactic championed

---

[19] Sandy Johnstone, *Enemy in the Sky: My 1940 Diary* (London: William Kimber, 1976),
p. 9.
[20] Tom Neil, *Gun Button to 'Fire'* (London: Kimber, 1987), p. 6.
[21] D. C. Gill, *How We Are Changed by War: a Study of Letters and Diaries from Colonial
Conflicts to Operation Iraqi Freedom* (NewYork: Routledge, 2010), p. 13.
[22] Ibid., p. 13.

by Douglas Bader. From the vantage point of some forty years later, Dundas remarked that the 'naïvety' of these letters 'brings a blush to my cheek.'[23] Although he winced at the opinions expressed by his youthful self, he used his correspondence to bring his past and present identities into coexistence in order to reconstruct for self-evaluation the ways in which he regarded his battle experience in 1940.

For airmen like Dundas, there was also another important source which could be used to supplement memory. All aircrew were required to keep diligently flying logbooks and operational records. Wishing to write about his service with Fighter Command, Bill Rolls felt that there 'was only one way to do it and that was by using my pilot's logbook as a reference and hope that it would jog memories.'[24] Many aircrew retained their logbooks after the war and subsequently used them to recover other memories of combat operations. For instance, although Oxspring asserted that 'the memory of the more spectacular events will never fade', he also admitted that he 'relied heavily' on copies of his combat reports and logbook entries to fill in the rest of the story.[25] Rolls, too, explained that, despite the brevity of the operational information contained within these sources, his logbook triggered memories which had long lain dormant when he produced *Spitfire Attack* in 1987:

I had not looked at the logbook for over thirty years and was surprised how readily the events in the logbook came to mind. It was like looking at a video of each entry, I could almost see every detail of those actions and people I had met during those times.[26]

For memoirists writing from the late 1960s onwards, additional sources of reference made the task of remembering and reconstructing experience somewhat simpler. In 1967, the Public Records Act of 1958 was amended to reduce the requisite 'fifty year rule' for the opening of public records to thirty years. From 1968 onwards, therefore, a backlog of material spanning some fifty years was released. For the Second World War veterans, this meant that virtually all the official records of 1939–45 became publicly accessible to peruse in the Public Record Office.[27] A wealth of previously unobtainable information about the operational aspects of war thus became available, of which veterans could make full use in their quest to jog memory and to ensure greater levels of accuracy in the details of their war services. For veterans who had already published their memoirs, the

---

[23] Dundas, *Flying Start*, p. 49.
[24] Rolls, *Spitfire Attack*, p. 12.
[25] Oxspring, *Spitfire Command*, p. 16.
[26] Rolls, *Spitfire Attack*, p. 12.
[27] Now The National Archives.

opening of the public records also afforded an opportunity to cross-check their own recollections against official records to ensure that they had produced a correct version of events, particularly if their narrative was to be republished. Some authors had to rethink matters when the records were opened. Tony Spooner, for instance, was dismayed to find that the original edition of his memoir, *In Full Flight* (1965), was 'slightly at variance in some details' to the sources newly made available in the Public Record Office. He decided, however, to leave the original text as it stood (albeit with one exception where he added in extra information about a Wing Commander Adrian Warburton), as he perceived that 'the discrepancies are small and the conveying of the overall atmosphere of the times is still here.'[28] Roy Conyers Nesbit, whose memoir of low level bombing operations was published in 1981, also noticed inconsistencies of detail with the official records. In his case, however, he argued that the official documents were themselves faulty, as there was no record of five of the sorties he made. Furthermore on two other operations the name of another navigator had been inserted in the place where his own should have been, whilst in yet another entry he was shown to have navigated a sortie on which he did not fly. Altogether, he claimed, 'Several incidents are recorded in the wrong sequence or are attributed to the wrong aircraft, and some episodes which might show the squadron in an unfavourable light have been conveniently left out.'[29] Charitably, he attributed these discrepancies to the third-hand nature of the information provided to the squadron intelligence officer and passed along to the squadron adjutant during trying circumstances on a fully operational frontline squadron, which was itself being subjected to enemy bombing raids at the time the data was collected and written up.[30] Nevertheless, Nesbit's tale strikes a resounding note of caution against assuming that any factual discordance in published memoirs must *de facto* be an error on the part of memory and memoirist.

A further great challenge in creating a war memoir was presented by the effort of recalling not just the details of combat, but also of the people with whom the veteran had shared his wartime service, whose characters and deeds had formed as much a part of his war experience as his own thoughts and actions. As a member of a fighting unit, whether as part of an infantry battalion or tank crew, fighter or bomber squadron, or ship's company, the serviceman's war experience and fate were tightly intertwined with his immediate comrades, officers, or those under his

[28] Spooner, *In Full Flight*, p. 15.
[29] Roy Conyers Nesbit, *Woe to the Unwary: A Memoir of Low Level Bombing Operations* (London: William Kimber, 1981), p. 12.
[30] Ibid., p. 12.

command if he had held wartime rank. The decisions, words, and actions of the veterans' wartime martial fraternity thus constituted an important thread in the weaving of any post-war narrative of combat experience, yet the recollection of former colleagues proved to be one of the key sticking points of personal memory. Whilst dates and incidents could be cross-referenced with other sources, it was less easy to remember and check the identities of comrades. In writing *Gun Button to 'Fire'*, Tom Neil found that some names 'faded into the mists' altogether.[31] Most veteran memoirs contained a note very similar to that incorporated in Norman Ashton's *Only Birds and Fools*. Although assuring his audience that every effort was made to ensure accuracy, Ashton proffered an apology if mistakes were unwittingly made: 'I apologise in advance and assure the offended that every story has been written with the best of intentions.'[32] It was not merely remembering and representing the identities of their fellow servicemen which caused difficulties for the memoirist, however, but also the issue of faithfully reconstructing dialogue decades after the war had ended. Eager to counter possible charges of inaccuracy, memoirists frequently deemed it important to explain how they recaptured the wartime speech with which they had been surrounded. In his *The Recollections of Rifleman Bowlby*, the eponymous author found it especially difficult to capture the conversation of his fellow infantrymen, writing five or six drafts that he felt were all unsatisfactory: 'The sentences were strung together and I couldn't remember any dialogue.'[33] Ironically, it was not until he suffered a nervous breakdown in 1955 that Bowlby felt he could faithfully reconstruct his comrades' speech: 'The dialogue came back. I saw the words in my head, just as they'd been spoken.'[34] Fortunately for other memoirists, the process of capturing discourse proved less tortuous, yet the question of how to accurately represent comrades' speech persistently troubled a number of veterans. Correspondingly, an acknowledgement of a certain degree of artistic license, alongside an apology and a justification, often appeared in these narratives, as illustrated in Jack Currie's *Lancaster Target* (1977): 'if I have attributed words or deeds to people who did not say or do them, I am sorry. The words, or something very like them, were said, and the deeds were done.'[35] John Bushby expressed a very similar sentiment in *Gunner's Moon* (1972), explaining that the 'dialogue, too is set down exactly as I remember it; and if it is thought indelicate in parts then I can only

---

[31] Neil, *Gun Button to 'Fire'*, p. 6.
[32] Ashton, preface to *Only Birds and Fools*.
[33] Bowlby, *Recollections*, p. 222.
[34] Ibid., p. 222.
[35] Currie, *Lancaster Target*, p. 5.

say it is how we spoke and the words are reproduced for accuracy not effect.'[36] In a variety of cases, the question of how accurately a serviceman's speech might be recreated without causing offence to the reader was to prove a thorny issue when the memoir entered the publisher's domain, in which the veteran-memoirist once again frequently found himself embroiled in battle.

Yet despite experiencing some self-acknowledged difficulties in remembering specific dates and details of places and people, the veterans remained adamant that the essence of their remembered emotional responses to wartime experience was accurate. Use of external sources such as diaries, letters, and official records lent structural support to these narratives of memory, and ought not to be interpreted as impairing the value of these memoirs as records that the veterans wished to make. Together, the veteran-memoirist's insistence upon the accuracy of emotional remembering, combined with a detailed explanation of the lengths to which he went in order to fill in any gaps of memory, is offered as a pledge of faithfulness in his authorial intention.[37] It was in that spirit of accepting that the memoirist had tried to fashion as authentic an account of wartime experience as possible that the veteran wanted his memoir to be read.

Publishing Veteran Memoir

The veteran's desire to construct as authentic a representation as possible of his war experiences, however, did not always interact smoothly with the commercial imperatives of the publication process. The publisher's agenda diverged from that of the memoirist on a regular basis. Frequently, the exigencies of creating a commercially appealing book came into open conflict with the desire to provide a historically authentic record of experience. The process of bringing a war memoir into publication invariably resembled a lengthy game of chess between veteran and publisher, with a complex set of moves incorporating advances and retreats on both sides. Battle lines of authenticity versus marketability were drawn up early on in the publishing process.

An initial stumbling block for many veteran-memoirists was the way in which the content and structure of their tale had to be remoulded and often pared down in order to meet the commercial requirements of the publisher. For the veteran, the period of training which he underwent

[36] Bushby, preface to *Gunner's Moon*.
[37] For further discussion of an 'autobiographical pact' between reader and author, see Philippe Lejeune, *On Autobiography* (Minneapolis: University of Minnesota Press, 1989).

before active duty often represented as integral a part of his wartime service as battle itself. From a commercial perspective, however, it was infinitely preferable to devote the bulk of the narrative to the combat experiences of the serviceman. Too much narrative focus on his training was regarded as an irritating hindrance to the 'real' story of killing and avoiding being killed. For instance, one anonymous would-be author in the mid-1990s received a letter from his agent that particularly highlighted this divergence of opinion between memoirist and publisher. Despite giving a glowing endorsement of the veteran's portrayal of battle scenes, the reader's report noted that there were certain flaws in the draft manuscript, provisionally titled *Time Seldom Wasted*. The veteran was informed that the descriptions of his period of training, which in all constituted about half the book, had 'been done before' and although interesting from a nostalgic point of view, was therefore 'hardly gripping stuff'.[38] By implication, the author's textual ratio of training to action would thus require serious revision in order to be accepted by a publisher. An editor's report on Donald Sutherland's manuscript for *Sutherland's War* in 1983 made remarkably similar stipulations, noting that 'Sutherland's war only really got interesting once he'd landed in Normandy – and since the first approx. 2/3 of the book is devoted to non-combatant carry-on-up-the-army stuff, perhaps a great opportunity has been missed.'[39] The insertion of technical details related to combat operations also proved a challenge in its own right for publishers. The editor of ex-fighter pilot Roger Hall's *Clouds of Fear* (1975) inserted a foreword to the book which outlined the difficult task he faced in reducing the manuscript to just over a third of its original length. Here, he explained how he tailored his editorial choices in order to both retain the integrity of Hall's narrative and also meet the tastes of the non-technically minded reader:

Some of the author's descriptions of aerial combat – which are among the most vivid I have ever read – had either to be pruned or completely omitted, but I have retained the text of those I consider to be quite outstanding. In any event I feel a certain justification in taking this course, since the accounts I have omitted were largely of a technical or repetitive nature, of more interest to wartime pilots than to the general reading public.[40]

The issue of characterisation in the narrative posed a further concern for editors. The reader's report on the manuscript of *Time Seldom Wasted* warned that if the human stories in these accounts were too dry, the book might read 'more like a regimental history'. From a commercial

---

[38] UoR, LC/ B/1/2/41/4, David Bolt to Jonathan Cave, 3 January 1996.
[39] UoR, LC/ A/2/653, Unidentified Editor to Leo Cooper, 28 November 1983.
[40] Roger Hall, *Clouds of Fear* (Folkestone: Bailey Brothers and Swinfen Ltd, 1975), p. 9.

perspective, this 'severely limits its appeal', and was thus deemed risky.[41] Therefore, in order successfully to harness the reader's empathy with the protagonists of the memoir, it was deemed vital for aspirant veteran-memoirists to develop characters in their book. This meant providing literary portraits of themselves in addition to those with whom their narrative of combat experience was studded. Despite the success of his Arnhem memoir, Geoffrey Powell experienced considerable difficulties in writing from such an intimate point of view. Noting that he found it 'too inhibiting' to describe his personal experiences of the battle, he and his publisher decided that the solution in his case was to mask his identity under the pseudonym of 'Tom Angus'. After this, he was relieved to find that his pen moved 'rather more freely.'[42]

Breathing life into the narrative in order to mitigate any appearance of a dry academic narrative of war, however, posed yet another set of challenges in the memoirist-publisher relationship. Enlarging on the more 'colourful' characters encountered by the veteran during his wartime service meant striking a balance between informing and entertaining the popular audience. The veteran-memoirist's desire for authenticity in his narrative often resulted in a clash between publisher and author. The coarseness of battlefield banter was not necessarily appropriate for a civilian readership, as demonstrated by the concerns of an editor at Leo Cooper's publishing house in 1983, who was worried that Donald Sutherland's memoir equated 'smut' with 'humour'.[43] The editor feared that 'the bawdiness went too far'. Although he himself was 'amused' by it, he was unsure that others would respond in the same fashion.[44] Indeed, the veterans' efforts to represent dialogue as faithfully as possible in their narratives was an area of frequent collision with editors, especially in the immediate post-war era. During this period, representations of the soldier's vocabulary appear to have been heavily censored in print, a state of affairs which in all likelihood contributed in no small measure to the dialogue in many 1950s war memoirs appearing improbably stilted. These narratives, for example, were characterised by considerable restraint in describing traumatic circumstances. In his *The Only Way Out* (1955), former infantryman Rex Wingfield referred in restrained terms to one battle as 'the biggest – up since Mons', whilst Robert Woollcombe's

[41] UoR, LC/ B/1/2/41/4, David Bolt to Jonathan Cave, 3 January 1996.
[42] Powell, preface to *Men at Arnhem*. This state of anonymity did not last for long, and subsequent editions of *Men at Arnhem* were published under Powell's real name. Leo Cooper also suggests that Powell's initial desire for anonymity was prompted by his continued work for the MoD, *All My Friends Will Buy It*, p. 173.
[43] UoR, LC/ A/2/653, Unidentified Editor to Leo Cooper, 28 November 1983.
[44] Ibid.

Lion Rampant (1955) simply announced that a barrage of 'unprintable' had landed upon a platoon.[45] However, in 1959 and 1964, reforms were made to the Obscene Publications Act which arguably did much to change a hidebound publishing climate. In his history of the British publishing industry, John Feather identifies the infamous prosecution of Penguin Books publishing company in 1960 as a turning point in this respect. An unsuccessful suit was brought against Penguin for printing DH Lawrence's formerly banned novel, *Lady Chatterley's Lover* (1928), and Feather argues that the 'virtual abandonment of literary censorship in Britain from about 1960 onwards certainly created a more liberal climate in which publishers could operate. Previously unmentionable subjects could be freely discussed in print'.[46] With more tolerant attitudes beginning to arise from the so-called new 'permissive society', the language used by war memoirists thus became markedly stronger by the end of the 1960s. Alex Bowlby's *The Recollections of Rifleman Bowlby* (1969), for example, was one of the first narratives to liberally incorporate the word 'fuck' – a term conspicuous by its absence in the memoirs of the 1950s.

Yet, within this new liberal climate, the war memoir industry remained fairly conservative. Some publishers continued to be wary of providing either legal or social offence through printing graphic 'barrack-room' language. For instance, although Bowlby's memoir delineated a marked shift in the memoirist's use of such soldiers' terms, he was forced to enter into strenuous negotiations with his publisher, Leo Cooper, in order to be allowed to make his language as 'authentic' as possible. Politely requested to make alterations to the swear words incorporated into early drafts of his manuscript, Bowlby replied with a list of his own, somewhat less polite, responses to the suggested revisions. For example, a suggestion was made that on page 167 he insert the word 'twat' instead of 'cunt'. Bowlby trenchantly explained to the publishing team that he felt the substitution of the word 'twat' was unsuitable in this context. He asserted that 'the word "cunt" can be used either as an aggressive insult or to express derision [whilst] the word "twat", in my experience, is used only to express derision.'[47] Similar scorn was poured on the suggestion that an epithet might be omitted in reference to the Regimental Sergeant Major. Bowlby sniped that he could not 'imagine anyone yelling for the

[45] R. M. Wingfield, *The Only Way Out: An Infantryman's Autobiography of the North-West Europe Campaign August 1944–February 1945* (London: Hutchinson, 1955), p. 157; Woollcombe, *Lion Rampant*, p. 44.
[46] John Feather, *A History of British Publishing*, 2nd ed. (Abingdon: Routledge, 2006), p. 205.
[47] UoR, LC/ A/2/79 Alex Bowlby's response to revisions for swearing, undated.

blood of an R.S.M without applying descriptive adjective. As actual objective used i.e. "fucking" has to be replaced to avoid repetition I stick to "sodding".[48] Even though agreement was eventually reached between author and publisher over these matters, Leo Cooper, Bowlby's normally stalwart champion, himself blanched at the language with which the former gentleman ranker flavoured his manuscript. Sending an advance copy of *Recollections* to Lieutenant-General Sir Richard Fyffe, formerly of the Rifle Brigade, in May 1969, Cooper expressed concern that the senior officer might not approve of the vocabulary: 'The only trepidation I have about sending you this book is that the language is too strong'. Ultimately, Cooper fretted unnecessarily. When *Recollections* finally appeared in the autumn of that year, praise for Bowlby's dialogue flowed from the *Times Literary Supplement*, which remarked that the soldiers' language was 'accurately recorded, and with less of a contrived air than usual.'[49] This was confirmed in higher circles. When the book was reprinted in 1989, Bowlby sent a copy to Professor Michael Howard, who had himself served in the Italian campaign. The historian's letter of thanks to Bowlby endorsed the authenticity of the language:

I know of it very well – many people have told me it is one of the best things written about the Italian campaign – but have never been able to get hold of it. Now I know they were right. You bring back those days with disturbing and convincing vividness. That is exactly the way that it was. The dialogue, in particular, you have got dead right.[50]

Although the likelihood of being prosecuted for printing 'obscene' material rescinded during the post-war decades, a perennial legal spectre still haunted the process of developing characterisation in the war memoir. In naming names, memoirist and publisher had to walk a very fine line between 'truth' and libel. Some of the more conscientious memoirists such as Robert Woollcombe took responsibility for avoiding libel upon themselves and scrupulously flagged up anecdotes to their publisher that they worried might cause legal difficulties. Others who wielded harsher pens or more grudging memories had to be brought tactfully but firmly into line by their publishers. For example, an editor of *Sutherland's War* enquired of the publisher whether it might 'not be sensible to ensure that the book is free from litigious matter – especially since many of the characters', shall we say "foibles", are highlighted?' In an effort to avoid litigation, he thus recommended that it might be 'a good idea' to place a note in the memoir's preliminary sections to assure the reader that, although

[48] Ibid.
[49] 'Mud and Larks', *Times Literary Supplement*, 13 November 1969.
[50] UoR, LC/ A/2/80/1, Sir Michael Howard to Alex Bowlby, 1 August 1989.

the characters in the book were 'real', the identities had been disguised.[51] On other occasions, a special coda was added to explain that the author had left out certain characters in the interests of avoiding offence. Tom Neil, for instance, notes in *Gun Button to 'Fire'* that of the names which he could remember, he had tactfully omitted some 'for reasons of delicacy'.[52] Others disguised rather than withheld identities in the manner of John Bushby, who explained that in two separate cases he had felt compelled to alter a name in order to 'avoid possible embarrassment'.[53]

The title of a published war memoir also proved a particular battleground between memoirist and publisher. Some of the fiercest wrangles took place over this issue. From the publisher's perspective, the choice of title for the memoir was much less personal and was underpinned to a far greater extent by a commercial agenda. For the memoirist, the title was intensely intimate as it codified his narrative. It communicated the emotional meanings that he attached to his narrative, and how he wanted that testimony to be interpreted by his audience. Bowlby was desperately eager to title his memoir *All Soldiers Run Away*, and exchanged much correspondence with his long-suffering publisher on the subject.[54] Derived from a quotation which is commonly attributed to the Duke of Wellington, Bowlby's preference indicated that his was not a 'gung-ho' memoir which narrated exaggerated and heroic tales of derring-do. Rather, his title reflected the memoir's main themes of passive endurance under heavy fire and unsavoury consequences of eroded morale such as desertion. His publisher, however, was less convinced that *All Soldiers Run Away* embodied quite the right message for a war memoir, and an eventual compromise was thrashed out by the inclusion on the title page of the Wellington quotation: 'All soldiers run away. It does not matter so long as their supports stand firm.' The other options which Bowlby put forward as possible titles are equally informative. His original choice of *Rifleman Bowlby Takes the Lid off War* was quickly disregarded by himself, as he felt that it struck 'too wacky a note'.[55] If he was not allowed to use *All Soldiers Run Away*, his second choice was to be *The Pity of War*. He explained that the latter 'has useful connotations with Vietnam, Biafra. It also carries the full meaning of the word pity, and is a half-line from

---

[51] UoR, LC/ A/2/653, Unidentified Editor to Leo Cooper, 28 November 1983.
[52] Neil, *Gun Button to 'Fire'*, p. 6.
[53] Bushby, preface to *Gunner's Moon*.
[54] Quotation originally attributed to the Duke of Wellington. Bowlby remained highly attached to this quotation as a title for a book, and attempted to use it for a forthcoming book on the battle of Cassino. Again, the title was rejected, and the book published under the more prosaic title of *Countdown to Cassino: The Battle of Mignano Gap* (London: Leo Cooper, 1995).
[55] UoR, LC/ A/2/79, Alex Bowlby to Leo Cooper, 17 December 1968.

Owen'.[56] This too was vetoed, and *The Recollections of Rifleman Bowlby* finally settled upon. As a nod to the renowned memoir of another former rifleman from the Peninsular Wars during the early nineteenth century, this implicitly situated Bowlby's memoir as another 'classic' account of war and satisfied honour all round.[57]

Negotiations between memoirist and publisher over new or revised editions of the veterans' tale are equally revealing. For some memoirists, the proposed release of new editions offered a welcome opportunity to refine certain elements of the original work. The issue of titles remained persistent. Alex Bowlby, for instance, took advantage of Leo Cooper's plan to reissue *Recollections* in 1989 to enquire plaintively again whether this title might not be switched to *All Soldiers Run Away*, perceiving that the proposed reissue seemed to 'offer the chance' of finally naming his memoir thus.[58] Again, Bowlby's suggestion was met with a kind but firm refusal from his publisher, who informed him that:

> The whole point of re-printing Recollections under its old title is that it was the very title under which it made its name. I have ascertained that, if the title were changed, the paperback company and the Book Club, to whom I have been talking, would not be interested any longer.[59]

The importance of the title of a war memoir in relation to the issue of commercial appeal is further reinforced by the various alterations made to the title of Tom Neil's Battle of Britain memoir. Originally published in 1987 as *Gun Button to 'Fire'*, a revised edition was issued in 2001 as *Fighter in my Sights*, before the original title was again revived in Amberley's 2010 edition. Neil noted that the title in the latter edition had been slightly amended because in its original form it had caused 'some confusion in the minds of some readers – in particular the ladies!' as there had been a gendered uncertainty over the meaning of the martial term 'Gun Button to Fire'.[60] In order to trigger the guns, the Hurricane or Spitfire pilot turned a button on his control column from the 'safe' position to 'fire', which was the last vital action performed by the pilot before entering combat.[61] An explanation had thus been incorporated which read *Gun Button to Fire: a Hurricane Pilot's Dramatic Story of the*

---

[56] Ibid. This refers to Wilfred Owen's famous lines, 'My subject is War, and the pity of War', quoted in *The Poems of Wilfred Owen*, (ed.) Owen Knowles (Ware: Wordsworth Editions, 2002), p. 101.

[57] The significance of this title is that recalls and invites comparison with the classic Peninsular War memoir, *The Recollections of Rifleman Harris*.

[58] UoR, LC/ A/2/80/1, Alex Bowlby to Leo Cooper, 3 August 1987.

[59] UoR, LC/ A/2/80/1, Leo Cooper to Alex Bowlby, 11 August 1987.

[60] Neil, *Gun Button to Fire* (Stroud: Amberley Publishing, 2010), p. 7.

[61] Ibid., p. 7.

Battle of Britain so that there could be no confusion as to what this memoir was about. Former bomb aimer Miles Tripp also suffered from a similar problem of misinterpretation. With the proposed reissue of *The Eighth Passenger* in 1993 he noted, incredulously, that two readers of the prior editions (1969 and 1985) had enquired who the 'eighth passenger' was; 'and I don't think they were pulling my leg.'[62] He therefore insisted that the blurb should specifically make it clear that the 'eighth passenger' on board the heavy bombers was 'fear'. The negotiations between Tripp and his editors over the reissue of his memoir also denote an important divergence in aims between memoirist and publisher. These discussions centred upon the issue of a blurb for the book. Tripp was sent a copy of the 'Advance Information Sheet', which contained a draft of the blurb, but he objected to some aspects of it. In particular, he did not appreciate the claim that the means by which the aircrew came through the ordeal was 'known only to God', 'not only because I am an agnostic but there are perfectly rational explanations of why most aircrew survived the strain. These include one's self-esteem, determination not to let one's comrades down, a very strong sense of duty, etc.'[63] In striving to achieve as authentic a representation of his combat experiences as possible, Tripp found the commercially driven hyperbole suggested by his editorial team distasteful.

Despite these clashing agendas, the aims of memoirist and publisher did converge with regard to the incorporation of a foreword to a memoir. It is an established feature of this genre that there tends to be some form of preliminary note inserted into the book. In its own right this lends an air of gravitas to the narrative but most importantly it again acts as a pledge of faithful intention. Like Tom Neil, some veterans opted to write their own foreword to provide context and explanation. Yet a popular trend was to employ other sources of authority to speak for their books. Arthur Gamble, a veteran of Bomber Command, was one of many authors who called upon former comrades to provide a few words to 'validate' the experiences portrayed in his memoir. In Gamble's case, the foreword to his memoir, *The Itinerant Airman* (2003), was written by his friend and former navigator, Arthur White, who had himself brought out a war memoir in 1995.[64] Former senior officers were frequently prevailed upon to provide an introductory note to a memoir, especially if they were both personal friends and household names. Douglas Bader wrote the foreword to his friend 'Johnnie' Johnson's memoir, *Wing Leader*,

[62] UoR, LC/ A/2/681, Miles Tripp to Georgina Harris, 5 May 1993.
[63] Ibid.
[64] Arthur White, foreword to *The Itinerant Airman*.

in 1956, announcing with expansive generosity that it constituted a 'splendid book'.[65] Prominent military historians were also prevailed upon to 'authenticate' the narrative. For example, in January 1988, Leo Cooper wrote to John Keegan, asking for his assistance in writing an introduction to the new edition of *The Recollections of Rifleman Bowlby* and 'placing the book firmly where it belongs – i.e. as a classic.'[66] As a reward for this 'brilliant introduction', Cooper promised to pay 'handsomely' in wine or cash.[67] Keegan subsequently delivered the required 'brilliant introduction', remarking that Bowlby possessed an 'acute ability to catch and transmit the quality of life in the regiment he belonged to.'[68] Some well-known scholars, however, could not be tempted into such recommendations, on the grounds that they had never fought themselves. In the mid-1990s, MP and controversial historian Alan Clark was invited to write a foreword to the reissue of Philip Stibbe's POW memoir, *Return via Rangoon*. He refused on the grounds that he was 'doubtful as to the propriety of non-combatants writing introductions to books by men who have actually been in action, and experienced the total stepchange in emotion, adrenalin, pain – and the rest – that go with that.'[69] The selection of a person who was in a position to comment with authority upon the veracity of the veteran-memoirist's tale was thus a business which was regarded very seriously by all concerned. In his foreword to Spellmount's revised edition of Peter Cochrane's *Charlie Company*, issued in 2007, leading military historian, Gary Sheffield, advised the reader that 'You are unlikely to find a better recreation of a regimental officer's experience of war.'[70] Such testimonial served to cement the veteran-memoirists' authorial pledge of faithful intention and accurate representation of wartime experience.

[65] Douglas Bader, foreword to *Wing Leader*.
[66] UoR, LC/ A/2/80/1, Leo Cooper to John Keegan, 5 January 1988.
[67] Ibid.
[68] John Keegan, foreword to *The Recollections of Rifleman Bowlby*, by Alex Bowlby (1989), p. 5.
[69] UoR, LC/ A/2/650, Alan Clark to Leo Cooper, undated.
[70] Gary Sheffield, foreword to Peter Cochrane, *Charlie Company: In Service with C Company, 2nd Queen's Own Cameron Highlanders 1940–44*, rev. ed. (Stroud: Spellmount, 2007), p. viii.

3   Landscape, Nature, and Battlefields

> [T]he emptiness and the space worked upon men's imaginations
> and so entered into their soldier's and sailor's tales.[1]

War, as Paul Fussell reminds in his investigation of First World War trench literature, takes place 'always within nature'.[2] A self-evident (and fairly fundamental) truth perhaps, but this observation provides a solid basis for exploring representations of environment in the memoirs of Second World War veterans. Fussell successfully encapsulates the concept of an irrevocable bind between the spatial boundaries of the natural world and human conflict, whilst also alluding to the fact that the latter is permanently sealed inside the former. Nature thus provides an immutable setting for the battles of mankind, yet the degree to which the twain was perceived by combatants as actively influencing each other requires further investigation. Well-established studies of combat experience in the Second World War have certainly recognised that a tangible relationship existed between a combatant and his natural surroundings, exploring the impact of terrain and weather upon his immediate physical and mental well-being.[3] Yet little scholarly attention has been directed towards the significance which combatants privately attached to these battlefields. Fussell's remark that war takes place 'always within nature' specifically referred to an intense symbolic significance that Western Front soldier-authors ascribed to a landscape of war that delineated the physical and psychological boundaries of their frontline experience between 1914 and 1918. The memoirs of Second World War veterans provide a similar insight into how the combatant imagined and relandscaped his old battle-grounds throughout decades of reflection after the war. Nature, in these narratives, is depicted as more than just a passive domain in which battle happened to take place. Instead, the natural environment is reconstructed

---

[1] Hynes, *Soldiers' Tale*, p. 116.
[2] Fussell, *The Great War and Modern Memory*, p. 231.
[3] Ellis' *The Sharp End of War* provides a classic example.

as a medium through which the veteran and his interpretations of war were shaped. Through an exploration of the memoirists' symbolic reconstructions of distinctive battle spaces in the elements of land, air, and sea, it is thus possible to gain an understanding of the intensely personal meanings veterans ascribed to their individual wars 'within' nature.

Unlike many Second World War battlegrounds, several zones of combat appeared to the combatant as a 'blank canvas' that was devoid of defining geographical features. Such landscapes were overlaid by the memoirists' own symbolism in order to interpret and represent the natural environment in which they fought. Three of Nature's 'blank canvases' particularly demonstrate the similarities and contrasts which soldiers, sailors, and aircrew projected onto their battle spaces. The Western Desert, the night skies above occupied Europe, and the northern waters of the Atlantic Ocean, North Sea and Arctic Ocean all represented isolated and barren arenas of conflict. The veterans' tale demonstrates a number of important ways in which the ex-serviceman sought to interpret and record the seemingly featureless combat environment that so critically shaped both his lived and remembered experience of war.

The Soldiers' Tale: The Army in North Africa, 1940–1943

The Italian invasion of Egypt in September 1940 marked the beginning of a bitter conflict that ebbed and flowed across the 1,400 miles separating Tripoli in Libya and Alexandria in Egypt. The intervening stretch of stony desert plain along the north Libyan coast and west of the Nile valley over which Allied and Axis forces galloped up and down for the next couple of years rapidly became one of the Second World War's most iconic battlefields, spawning a plethora of legendary military feats and personnel. Among all the theatres of war strung out across the globe, the desert war arguably attained top billing in the British public's memory.[4] The dominance of the desert war in British cultural memories of the Second World War has been well established by Mark Connelly, who notes that the desert campaign enshrined both a peculiarly British love of 'unequal struggles, last-man stands and successes despite the odds' and a deeply rooted cultural romance with natural wildernesses dating back to the nineteenth century.[5] Receiving a high profile in the wartime media, images of the desert as a landscape in which romance could be restored to warfare became widely broadcast, particularly after the decisive Allied victory at El Alamein in early November 1942, when over 100 British

4 Connelly, *We Can Take It!*, p. 207.
5 Ibid., p. 207.

and American war correspondents descended upon the desert and provided 'saturation coverage' of the campaign for their publics at home.[6] In March 1943 a British Ministry of Information-produced film, *Desert Victory*, documented the Allies' successful struggle against Field Marshal Erwin Rommel and his Afrika Korps, becoming the biggest box-office success of all British war documentaries.[7] At the heart of the nation's fascination with the North African campaign lay the desert itself: 'The Western Desert' intoned the narrator's opening lines in *Desert Victory*, 'is a place fit only for war.'[8] In part, it was the sheer emptiness of the Libyan, or 'Western', Desert that held such an intrinsic and enduring appeal for the nation, but the desert landscape also became legendary in its own right due to the way that its terrain and environment dictated the inimitable style, tempo, and character of 'pendulum' warfare along the North African coast.[9] An almost fabled appeal of this desert as an ideal battlespace has proved difficult to dislodge from scholarly, cultural, and literary discussions of the North African campaign, yet little has so far been said of the ways in which British veterans of the desert war imagined and symbolically reconstructed this environment in their tales and their reasons for so doing.[10] The memoirs of former British desert troops articulated a distinctive myth of this landscape, attesting that the Western Desert cast a strange spell upon combatants which held men in an arcane thrall that could endure throughout their lifetimes. Charged with intense personal meaning for its soldiers, as Christopher Bulteel's report of his first experience of fighting in the Western Desert illustrates, the desert environment often imprinted itself upon the recollections of veterans for many years after the war had ended. Fifty years after being sent with an advance party into the desert in 1943, Bulteel recorded that he could still remember 'the spiritual thrill of turning off into the desert' with exceptional clarity.[11]

[6] Jonathan Fennell, *Combat and Morale in the North African Campaign: The Eighth Army and the Path to El Alamein* (Cambridge: Cambridge University Press, 2011), p. 5.
[7] Released in March 1943, *Desert Victory* became the biggest box-office success of all British war documentaries, grossing an impressive £77,250 in the first 12 months; Ibid., p. 5.
[8] *Desert Victory*, directed by Roy Boulting (Army Film Unit, 1943).
[9] As Niall Barr explains, the nature of warfare in the Western Desert between 1940 and 1942 was characterised by such a state of flux that it acquired the soubriquet of 'pendulum war'. Niall Barr, *Pendulum of War: The Three Battles of El Alamein* (London: Jonathan Cape, 2004), p. xxxvii.
[10] Hynes, *The Soldiers' Tale*; Connelly, *We Can Take It!*; Rawlinson, *British Writing of the Second World War*; John Bierman and Colin Smith, *Alamein: War Without Hate* (London: Viking, 2002); Patrick Deer, *Culture in Camouflage: War, Empire, and Modern British Literature* (Oxford: Oxford University Press, 2009).
[11] Christopher Bulteel, *Something about a Soldier: The Wartime Memoirs of Christopher Bulteel M. C.* (Shrewsbury: Airlife, 2000), p. 61.

Bulteel was by no means alone in finding a certain spirituality in Nature's backdrop to war, and veterans' perceptions of experiencing a metaphysical connection to landscape were far from confined to the desert. However, the collective of meanings that were attached to the desert by military memoirists are unparalleled in other published personal narratives of the British army and the Second World War. These particular testimonies substantiate the claim made by Wilfred Thesiger in 1959, world famous explorer of deserts, that 'this cruel land can cast a spell which no temperate clime can match'.[12] In comparison to veterans' descriptions of other battle environments such as Italy or Normandy, the Western Desert stands out as infinitely more desirable, labelled by memoirist Ray Ward as the 'perfect battlefield'.[13] Experiences of fighting in the landscapes of European campaigns tend to be represented almost entirely in terms of witnessed carnage or physical discomfort, yet whilst these unsavoury aspects of war 'at the sharp end' are certainly visible in the memoirs of the desert troops, the desert veteran-memoirists invested their former surroundings with a distinctive symbolism which insisted that the combatant drew an active pleasure from fighting in this battle space. To Peter Cochrane the very name of the battleground he was about to enter enchanted him:

I enjoyed the fact that it was the Western Desert ... West has always been a conjurative word, from the Western Isles to ' Westren wind, when wilt thou blow?'; I should have disliked being in an Eastern Desert.[14]

The sheer enigma of the unknown desertscape cast out a lure to the newly enlisted. The soldiers who comprised the future war memoirists came from a generation of young men who had been offered tantalising images of the British empire via their education, literature, and cinema during the 1930s, yet opportunities to actually travel and comprehend these wonders for themselves were distinctly limited before the Second World War. For Ward and many others, overseas service with the wartime British army offered a welcome 'escape from humdrum lives at work or home. I was physically fit and romantically inclined. I looked forward to what seemed an exciting adventure'.[15] To youngsters like Ward who had seen little, if any, foreign travel, the desert landscape promised an exotic environment in which daring and glorious deeds must surely happen. Even for men who could claim to have seen something of the world, the desert's siren call enticed. In July 1941, Peter Roach so

---

[12] Wilfred Thesiger, *Arabian Sands*, rev. ed. (London: Penguin Books, 2007), p. 15.
[13] Ward, *The Mirror of Monte Cavallara*, p. 128.
[14] Cochrane, *Charlie Company*, p. 12.
[15] Ward, *The Mirror of Monte Cavallara*, p. 13.

envied his friends who were serving in more active branches of the armed forces, that he abandoned the merchant navy, which he described as that 'unglorious North Atlantic bus service', to begin training as tank crew.[16] Arriving in Cairo in 1942 with the rest of his draft, he was consumed by an overwhelming 'earnestness and eagerness to get up the desert', clearly construing 'the blue' as a space in which action and adventure seemed preordained.[17]

Upon arrival in the desert, several memoirists also remarked that their levels of anticipation and excitement were further boosted by the unexpected presence of a slightly incongruous signpost seemingly in the middle of nowhere, which instructed that the 'Western Desert' lay ahead whilst the Allied port of Alexandria lay seven kilometres behind. This signpost to adventure carried a marked significance for Bulteel, who explained that the act of turning away from Alexandria and following the sign to the desert constituted a 'symbolic moment' in his eyes, inspiring the 'spiritual thrill' with which he still associated with the desert fifty years later.[18] For Bulteel and Ward, passing the 'To the Western Desert' signpost marked the point at which their desert war began in earnest. Ward recalled that although the sign helpfully informed of the distance back to Alexandria, its lack of corresponding radius to the desert announced his immediate arrival: 'It was there. Vast and empty, except for drifting dust clouds that might be sandstorms, or stirred up by the jousting armies out there'.[19] With his physical arrival into the battle zone so obligingly inked out, Ward also suggested that the signpost indicated that a more profound inner journey was about to unfold for him. When his transport passed the signpost, he observed how 'Trucks packed with dead-eyed troops were retreating from the front and others, including mine, with wide-eyed innocents were heading for it.'[20] In August 1942 when Ward arrived in the desert, the Eighth Army was licking its wounds after heavy fighting during the First Battle of El Alamein in July, having suffered more than 13,000 casualties.[21] For Ward, this encounter with battle weary troops who had fought in the previous month's string of battles at the Western Desert signpost designated a symbolic landmark at which he believed his own identity as a soldier truly began. At the

---

[16] Peter Roach, *The 8.15 to War: Memoirs of a Desert Rat* (London: Leo Cooper, 1982), p. 22.
[17] Ibid., p. 39.
[18] Bulteel, *Something about a Soldier*, p. 60.
[19] Ward, *The Mirror of Monte Cavallara*, p. 121.
[20] Ibid., p. 121.
[21] The nomenclature of the string of clashes around El Alamein during the summer and autumn of 1942 is open to debate, but *The Veterans' Tale* follows Niall Barr's example in identifying the July battle as the 'First' battle of El Alamein, *Pendulum of War*, p. 184.

moment of passing the signpost, Bulteel too identified a personal inner change, reporting that he took considerable pleasure in the fact that he and his men were 'on our own now.'[22] Behind lay Alexandria and the civilised world: what lay ahead, he did not know, but at that moment he felt strong and resourceful at the prospect of entering the battle zone.

Bulteel's recorded pleasure at being 'on our own', thrown on the personal resources of himself and his men, underscores that collective veteran representations of the Western Desert as a seemingly 'perfect battlefield' are woven out of a core trope of isolation. The signpost which made such an impression on Ward and Bulteel also denoted a juncture which marked the sundering of this particular realm of battle from the rest of the world. A fundamental part of the desert's appeal as a battle space was that it was perceived to provide a self-limiting, tailor-made arena for war. Carved out of the North African littoral, the topography of the long coastal plateau, some 500 feet above sea level, which formed the greater area of battle, furnished combatants with a large and distinctively framed battlefield. In their narrations of military action within this landscape, desert veterans frequently opted to overlook their comparative proximity to coastal urban settlements such as Benghazi and Tobruk, despite these cities serving as key sites of battle during the North African campaign. If memoirists had seen action in these battles, their narratives display a marked tendency to regard them as separate from the rest of their war in the desert, compartmentalizing the interior of the Western Desert as a disassociated space in which opposing armies waged a private contest. This was the first time in history that armies had been able to fight, live, and work in the desert for lengthy periods of time, with the mechanisation of warfare allowing operations to be sustained within its interior for weeks and months on end. Ward's recollection that the desert army's reliance on wireless communication was frequently unpredictable because the weather and topography distorted signals further emphasises the troops' sense of insulation within this arena of war.[23] According to Ward, the fact that the fleshpots of Alexandria and Cairo lay only several hours away threw this concept of the desert as a segregated battle space into 'bizarre' relief.[24] Yet physical proximity to the civilian world did little to erode a highly prized perception of detachment from the rest of the war among the desert troops.

A sense of distinctiveness from the rest of the war pervades the myth of the desert in these memoirs. As Stephen Bungay points out in his history

[22] Bulteel, *Something about a Soldier*, p. 61.
[23] Ibid., p. 165.
[24] Ward, *The Mirror of Monte Cavallara*, p. 148.

of El Alamein, the desert war's 'significance grew out of all proportion to its scale' largely because for two years it was the only battle space which a British army was able to engage German troops with any success.[25] Until the Allied invasion of Sicily in mid-1943, the Continental battlefields remained all too visibly bogged down in dismal failure. Geographically remote from a string of ignominious British military defeats such as Dunkirk in 1940, followed by Greece and Crete in 1941, the image of the Western Desert as a 'perfect battlefield' became reinforced by the fact that, despite a number of setbacks such as the siege of Tobruk in 1941, victories in the desert were nevertheless occurring. Having joined up with the Eighth Army in the desert in early 1943, at a time when the British were advancing inexorably through North Africa and the pendulum of war was swinging heavily in the Allies' favour, Bulteel's memoir provides some indication of a new recruit's feelings about the prospect of participating in the desert war, conveying a palpable sense of excitement:

What has to be remembered is that, till that time, this was the only area in which we seemed able to wage successful war. We had had enough of the 'Dunkirk Spirit' in England. It was not only a couple of years out of date; but, splendid though it had been, no doubt, there was no blinking the fact that, by any military criterion, it had been a monumental defeat. Most of our soldiers had fled home to Britain with their tails between their legs, leaving their rifles behind for the Germans to collect as souvenirs. And this was not all. In North Africa, after a couple of years of careering wildly forward and backward across the desert, it really seemed that the campaign was near its end, and that we could win. We had been brought out of England to drive the enemy out of Africa, for good.[26]

A certain degree of contextualisation is required when addressing Bulteel's enthusiasm for joining the war in the desert realm, since he arrived at a distinct upturn in Allied military fortunes which undoubtedly conditioned his attitude towards this battle space. The memoirist had not experienced the long, arduous slog of 1940–2 in which the British desert force had suffered several bitter defeats and an alarming crisis of morale, but his allusion to this domain of battle as 'the only area in which we seemed able to wage successful war' pinpoints a need to closely address veteran perceptions of the unique effect of the Western Desert as an operating environment.

The desert campaign has been characterised as a war that returned an element of romance to battle because men found sheer joy in their ability to move freely about the battlefield.[27] The vastness of this battle space created the peculiarly fluid nature of the 'pendulum war'; as Barr's

[25] Stephen Bungay, *Alamein* (London: Aurum, 2002), p. 2.
[26] Bulteel, *Something about a Soldier*, p. 61.
[27] Hynes, *The Soldiers' Tale*, pp. 139–40.

eponymous history of the campaign notes, the distance between the Axis-held port of Tripoli at one end of the Western Desert and the home of the Royal Navy's Mediterranean fleet in Alexandria at the other end produced a law of diminishing returns which made continuous sustained advance by either side extremely difficult and resulted in the to-and-fro warfare of 1940–2.[28] Nevertheless, in representing the desert war, the veteran-memoirists did not wholly subscribe to the rose-tinted view of fighting in this environment that Hynes identifies in his study of war narratives.[29] For all the appeal of fighting in an exotic location, combat in the desert as it is related by the infantry veterans frequently bears a strong resemblance to the miseries of static trench warfare of the Western Front during the First World War. Ward ruefully recollected that 'My first duty in the desert I am sure every infantryman who served in the Eighth Army remembered: I dug trenches. Lots of them.'[30] Having arrived in mid-1942 when the British were still reeling from the battles of July, Ward was tasked with digging communications trenches and field gun positions behind a minefield in case the Afrika Korps should break through the Alamein line. A surprising quantity of recollections of mud also features in these narratives. For example, Lieutenant Charles Potts of the 1st Battalion, the Buffs, recollected that shortly after the Second Battle of El Alamein, a spell of hot dry weather was broken by rain which turned sand-encrusted men into 'a solid cake' of muddy matter.[31] This period of rain caused further problems during the great pursuit of Rommel's routed forces, as Ward narrated:

Desert tracks ploughed into furrows of loose sand during the initial chase turned to mud. Tanks and armoured cars speeding forward to cut off Jerry's retreat got stuck, or ran out of fuel. Wadis became swamps. We passed the flooded wreckage of the Afrika Korps ... Gun turrets lay upside-down in the mud.[32]

Furthermore, the isolation of the desert's interior which contributed to the fluidity of engagements between 1940 and 1942 also posed something of a double-edged blessing to combatants. The terrain seemed resistant to man's efforts to inscribe localised military cartography upon it and the bland vista posed 'one of the hazards of desert warfare: no one ever knew where this mythic "front line" was, except the men who were actually doing the shooting.'[33] Maps, reported Ward, were of very little use in this environment: 'apart from the coast road and a parallel

---

[28] Barr, *Pendulum of War*, p. 6.
[29] Hynes, *The Soldiers' Tale*, pp. 139–40.
[30] Ward, *The Mirror of Monte Cavallara*, p. 121.
[31] Potts, *Soldier in the Sand*, p. 20.
[32] Ward, *The Mirror of Monte Cavallara*, p. 177.
[33] Bulteel, *Something About a Soldier*, p. 97.

railway there was nothing on them except low ridges and wadis. The maps looked like Admiralty charts; indeed, sometimes we navigated like sailors, by the sun and stars.'[34] As a company commander, the dangers of irretrievably misplacing his troops in the desert occupied a good deal of Charles Potts' attention. Like Ward, he reverted to more traditional methods of navigation about the desertscape:

I was always careful to see that the men knew how to find the North Star, so that if ever they were hopelessly lost, they could walk towards it, keeping it always to their left. This north-easterly course would bring them eventually to the coast road, and prevent them from falling into enemy hands.[35]

Although the fluctuating nature of warfare in this battle space meant that the perils of battle ebbed and flowed for the desert soldier, he thus remained constantly at risk of being consumed by the landscape.

Oddly, however, the ever-present danger of vanishing into the maw of the desert seems to have heightened the desert troops' sense of fascination with this landscape. The veterans' tale suggests, in fact, that much of the Western Desert's power to captivate lay in its sheer size and emptiness. As a tank commander serving with 3rd Royal Tank Regiment who had first entered the desert in 1940, Bill Close reported that,

Space was the most awesome thing about the Western Desert. Whatever type of terrain was encountered, there was always plenty of it. The variety was infinite – soft dunes, stony flats, salt marsh, sand with boulders, sand with pebbles, pebbles with pebbles, miles and miles of flat plain, tortuous ravines or wadis, towering limestone escarpments – and hardly a sign that human beings had ever passed that way.[36]

This sense of the physical barrenness of the desert granted an opportunity to project martial fantasies onto the battlefield. The apparent lack of human presence alluded to by Close also formed a staple part of the desert myth as it is woven in these memoirs. In the same way as the veterans represent the desert war as spatially detached from the rest of the war, so too is the absence of non-combatants collectively insisted upon. With, as Ward explained, 'no civilian population to complicate the contest', the desert proffered a form of battle that was appealingly different from the mass industrialised warfare ripping Europe apart.[37] Whilst such portrayals of the desert as denuded of civilian presence are not entirely accurate, since the desert did contain odd villages and wandering tribespeople,

[34] Ward, *The Mirror of Monte Cavallara*, p. 126.
[35] Potts, *Soldier in the Sand*, p. 9.
[36] Bill Close, *Tank Commander: From the Fall of France to the Defeat of Germany*, rev. ed. (Barnsley: Pen & Sword Military, 2013), p. 57.
[37] Ward, *The Mirror of Monte Cavallara*, p. 128.

this landscape was comparatively uncluttered by the trappings of civilisation. Serving as an officer in the Royal Northumberland Fusiliers, John McManners had escaped from the German encirclement of Tobruk in mid-1941 and possessed first-hand experience of the brutality of war. He concurred with Ward's representation of the desert, however, praising the desolation of the landscape for offering 'a sort of arena for battle without killing women and children and flattening homes.'[38] By thus envisioning the desertscape as leached of civilian presence, the Western Desert could be understood as a 'clean' battleground in which warfare was distilled into its purest form.

In addition to stripping the civilian wreckage out of war, the desert environment was further represented in the veterans' tale as critically shaping the nature of the combatants who did battle there. The veterans' tale identified the Western Desert as a particularly significant landscape that transformed men into elite warriors. In its very hostility towards mankind, this environment was interpreted as uniquely stamping the soldier with prized martial qualities of independence, resourcefulness, toughness, and self-assurance. Peter Roach perceived that there was simply 'no room for pomposity with this brilliant hard heat beating on a land, severe and complete. Man was unnecessary here and seemed to feel it.'[39] This was not, as Close also reflected, a land which easily suffered fools:

No one could take liberties with this environment. The dry heat beat down fiercely during the day, while, in winter, the nights were bitterly cold ... The weather in this wilderness was unpredictable. Storms blew up out of nowhere and lasted for an hour or for days.[40]

In an environment in which both sides had to contend with extremes of temperature, fluctuations between drought and mud, fierce sandstorms, desert sores, and dangerous animal and insect life, active service in the desert was thus frequently represented as a battle on two fronts. As Potts remarked, 'It was not only a matter of fighting a human enemy, we had to fight the desert conditions also.'[41] Placing a slightly different emphasis on the relationship between combatant and landscape in the Western Desert, Ward opted to quote from the popular 1958 war film, *Ice Cold in Alex*: 'All against the desert, the greater enemy.'[42] Alongside its provision of a 'clean' battleground, the desert therefore also created an illusion of

[38] McManners, *Fusilier*, p. 71.
[39] Roach, *The 8.15 to War*, p. 42.
[40] Close, *Tank Commander*, p. 57.
[41] Potts, *Something about a Soldier*, p. 146.
[42] Ward, *The Mirror of Monte Cavallara*, p. 119.

placing both sides on an equal footing, appearing impartially hostile to all who fought within its borders. In its flatness and blankness, the desert terrain also seemed neutral, providing little by way of strategic value to any of the desert armies and offering armoured formations considerable possibilities for manoeuvre.[43] 'For men on both sides', wrote Ward, 'the desert seemed a greater enemy. It stripped everything to essentials.'[44] With both sides apparently suffering and benefitting from the desert environment in equal measure, a prominent aspect of the myth of the desert in the veterans' tale is that this 'perfect battlefield' facilitated a welcome renewal of medieval values of sportsmanship, gallantry, and mutual respect in battle. McManners discerned a 'veneer of chivalry which sometimes overlay the sheer cruelty of war in the desert' which Close's memoir corroborates. The latter reported that 'a certain spirit of 'live and let live' applied' in the desert:

it was considered 'bad form' to machine-gun a crew that managed to get out of a panzer or M-13. Once a tank had been disposed of, honour was satisfied. If anyone was lucky enough to escape from a 'flamer' or battered hulk, good luck to him.[45]

In Ward's memoir, this sense of chivalrous behaviour was attributed to an affinity with the enemy that was borne of the hostility and sterility of the desert landscape. He argued that the remote solitude of the desert created 'an odd intimacy with the enemy – the sense that in our isolated, lonely battlefield friend and foes shared a similar fate.'[46]

Perhaps surprisingly, despite the plethora of natural hazards posed by the desert realm, the memoirs of its veterans remain constant in their affection for this landscape. Ward recorded that his men retained a marked fondness for the desert even when they were transferred to Italy. For example, a move up to the Gustav Line in central Italy in February 1944 was distinctly unpopular with his Argylls, who did not appreciate the new terrain: 'Every man in the battalion would have given a year's pay to have been back in North Africa, footslogging through the hot dry, desert day.'[47] Importantly, this statement raises the issue that the reconstruction of the desert in these narratives was refracted through a prism of the veteran's other wartime experiences and post-war recollection.

[43] Barr, *Pendulum of War*, p. 182. It is worth noting, however, that by July 1942, the inexorable sowing of minefields by the Panzerarmee in the El Alamein area caused considerable problems for the Eighth Army, who found themselves unable to adopt the preferred desert tactic of simply bypassing strongly held positions.
[44] Ward, *The Mirror of Monte Cavallara*, p. 128.
[45] Close, *Tank Commander*, p. 2.
[46] Ward, *The Mirror of Monte Cavallara*, p. 119.
[47] Ibid., p. 229.

Bulteel's explanation of the anticipation he felt at being posted to the
desert in 1943, for instance, was conditioned by an awareness of the dismal defeat into which earlier battles on the Continent had disintegrated,
such as at Dunkirk, or in Greece and on Crete. Ward and Cochrane, on
the other hand, used their post-desert combat experiences in the Italian
campaign as a yardstick to relandscape this arena in their own recollections. Marching through Tuscany in July 1944, Ward was horrified by the
devastation wrought by the Allied and Axis armies upon the surrounding
countryside: 'Every few kilometres, we passed ruined villages – the calling cards left by the armies of both sides. Places that had existed peace-
fully for centuries had been abruptly visited by death and destruction'.[48]
For Cochrane, as another old desert hand, the carnage of the invasion of
Sicily and Italy also proved deeply distressing. He experienced considerable dismay upon landing at Taranto in January 1944: 'I realized with a
jolt that this was a different kind of war, one which involved civilians ...
here were poor folk whose houses had been smashed, their belongings
destroyed, fields unsown and animals killed'.[49]

Significantly, the power of the fantasy of the desert war concept as isolated from the charnel houses of the European battlegrounds extended
beyond the memoirs of North African veterans. For example, Donald
Sutherland, who served with his tank crew in the Normandy campaign,
also fantasised about an idealised form of combat in the desert. Musing
upon the scenes of devastation which he met in the immediate aftermath of the D-Day invasion in northern France, he cogitated that 'One
of the pleasanter aspects of the desert campaign must have been the
almost total absence of non-military objectives, whether they were cattle
or people and their possessions unfortunate enough to find themselves
in the path of war.'[50] Infantryman Sydney Jary expressed the same sentiment in his depiction of the Allied push through North-West Europe
in the winter of 1944–5. Upon setting up his platoon HQ in the village
of Schiefendahl on the Dutch-German border, he was distressed to witness the despair of a German civilian who was forced to evacuate her
cottage in order to make room for his men. 'It was at times like this',
Jary reflected, 'that I wished that we could fight our war in the desert.'[51]
At the crux of the desert fantasy woven into the veterans' tale, therefore,
stands the symbol of the desert as separate – physically and morally –
from the self-acknowledged degradation and revulsion of total war.

[48] Ibid., p. 262.
[49] Cochrane, *Charlie Company*, p. 110.
[50] Donald Sutherland, *Sutherland's War* (London: Leo Cooper, Secker & Warburg, 1984),
p. 125.
[51] Jary, *18 Platoon*, p. 94.

This is perhaps best illustrated by Cochrane, who asserted that in the desert 'the fighting went on without damaging anyone but soldiers, all the battles were in terrain that nobody had tried to inhabit: war was idiocy, but it was self-contained.'[52]

The Flyers' Tale: Bomber Command
and Occupied Europe, 1942–1945

Core tropes of isolation and blankness also shaped the ways in which former bomber aircrew reconstructed the sky as a battle space in their memoirs. From the winter of 1942–3, as the Allied strategic air offensive built up over occupied Europe, the majority of Bomber Command's operations were conducted nocturnally. At the same time, key changes were implemented to the ways in which the bombers utilised the night sky. Instead of planning attacks for moonlit nights, which left attacking forces vulnerable to Luftwaffe night fighters, the bombers now sought the cover of darkness. This change of tactics also coincided with increasing numbers of newly trained aircrew filtering into the Command. In the memoirs of surviving flyers, therefore, representations of raiding Germany between 1942 and 1945 primarily focus on the night sky as an arena of combat. As in the desert memoirs, the natural setting is portrayed as vast and empty, yet there is a sharp disjuncture between the interpretations that desert and bomber veterans placed upon their respective environments. Whereas the former portrayed nature as providing a 'perfect battlefield' designed to mould and complement combat, the latter construed the night sky as an inherently benign and protective space splintered by war, within which an artificially illuminated battle arena was branded into the darkness.

During the long and frequently tedious run to the target, aircrew, particularly pilots, gunners and bomb aimers, spent hours staring into monotonously featureless airspace. As Bomber Command's new offensive hinged, where possible, upon carrying out attacks on cloudy or moonless nights, the flyer's vision was invariably restricted to what John Bushby described as the 'immeasurable blackness of space'.[53] Yet, while Frank Musgrove embodied the feelings of many aircrew in his remark that flying through the night was a thoroughly 'boring business', a dominant theme in these narratives emphasises that the ex-bomber equated his lightless surroundings with safety.[54] Boredom, after all, was

---

[52] Cochrane, *Charlie Company*, p. 110.
[53] Bushby, *Gunner's Moon*, p. 81.
[54] Musgrove, *Dresden and the Heavy Bombers*, p. 32.

hardly life-threatening. Within the 'immeasurable blackness' of the night sky, the darkness itself became symbolically charged with protective qualities. Night was imagined as preserving the well-being of the crew as it appeared to offer a perception of isolation which many depicted as distinctly appealing. As in the desert, privacy was a quality the combatant prized in his natural surroundings. Yet, whilst desert troops employed tropes of isolation in order to imagine themselves as old-fashioned warriors bound together with their enemy by a semblance of equality wrought by landscape, bomber aircrew sought a more literal emptiness from their surrounds. Battle in the air was a more unequal experience for the men of Bomber Command than for their counterparts in the desert. The key airborne threat was Luftwaffe night fighters, which grew in force from 150 aircraft in 1940 to 1,250 by the end of 1944.[55] These German defenders were fast, manoeuvrable, and able stealthily to direct their fire into the bomber's most vulnerable spots in order to ignite its cargo of high explosives. The psychological impact of these aircraft upon the bomber crews is illustrated by Michael Renaut, who remarked that 'I had innumerable fears as a bomber pilot but none so horrific as those of attacks by night fighters. It was the knowledge that one was immediately at a disadvantage that frightened me.'[56] Even with the presence of rear-gunners to guard the aft of the Lancaster, it proved extremely difficult for bomber crews to defend themselves against this menace. An uneasy knowledge that their four-engined bombers remained more or less at the mercy of the Luftwaffe night fighters thus shaped aircrew perception of the darkness as a shield.

The Bomber Command veterans' tale suggests, therefore, that many aircrew cherished a fervent hope the darkness would render them invisible, allowing them to slink through the night undetected. Ron Smith, for instance, mused that there seemed a 'blessed' quality to the darkness, which he interpreted as a 'cloak that offered such welcome anonymity.'[57] Inconspicuousness was a treasured state to aircrew who knew that if they closed with the enemy the chances of survival were small. To this end, Bomber Command had already made an effort to ensure that individual aircraft would be veiled from sight of the German aerial and ground defences: 'Like wolves', memoirist Philip Gray explained, 'the big planes travelled in packs.'[58] The instigation of the bomber stream in

---

[55] Tony Iveson and Brian Milton, *Lancaster: The Biography* (London: Andre Deutsch, 2009), p. 110.
[56] Renaut, *Terror By Night*, p. 160.
[57] Ron Smith, *Rear Gunner Pathfinders* (London: Goodall Publications, 1987), p. 79.
[58] Philip Gray, *Ghosts of Targets Past: The Lives and Losses of a Lancaster Crew in 1944–45*, 3rd ed. (London: Grub Street, 2005), p. 41.

1942 was intended to confuse the defenders and afford the attacking force some protection. By concentrating aircraft *en masse* into a block which travelled together along common routes at meticulously designated heights and speeds, the objective was to blanket the enemy's radar so that lone bombers were more difficult to single out. Significantly, however, in these narratives, the veterans' claims of protection in the night sky are not attributed to the safety in numbers offered by the bomber stream. Indeed, quite the opposite seems to be true: any external security these men discerned during their mission was ascribed entirely to the natural shield of darkness. For example, Gray noted that the enveloping blackness encouraged an 'illusion that we were the only plane around', rendered invisible to enemy eyes by the obscurity of the night.[59] Although ruefully acknowledging that this was a 'ridiculous' notion, considering that his Lancaster was merely one of hundreds in the raiding bomber stream, like Smith, Gray insisted that the darkness bestowed a much-needed 'cosy' element to the experience, providing a salve to strained nerves.[60] The extent to which aircrew invested the darkness with protective qualities is further illustrated by Musgrove who, upon leaving the target area over Dortmund, plotted a course which took his aircraft north, out of the bomber stream, and forwards alone in the blackness. With hindsight, he reflected that

We were, in fact, making ourselves highly vulnerable. By detaching ourselves from the main bomber stream, we could be more easily picked off by fighters. But we did not feel more vulnerable; we felt safely enveloped by the dark night, blessedly distant from Dortmund's searchlights and flak.[61]

Musgrove's account of rerouting his Lancaster away from the target area underscores a dominant theme of light as a hazard in the Bomber Command veterans' tale. Significantly, despite knowing the dangers posed by night fighters to his lone aircraft, he concluded that the anti-aircraft defences of Dortmund represented a more immediate threat. His description of these defences as 'an apparently solid wall of searchlights and flak' positions light as the greater enemy in the target area.[62] Although the night fighter held the key to defensive success for Germany, from the winter of 1940–1 the Reich poured money into defences on the ground, using some 7,000 searchlights in support of the anti-aircraft batteries in Germany alone.[63] If an aircraft was unfortunate enough to be pinpointed

---

[59] Ibid., p. 132.
[60] Ibid., p. 132.
[61] Musgrove, *Dresden and the Heavy Bombers*, p. 26.
[62] Ibid., p. 26.
[63] Max Hastings, *Bomber Command*, 3rd ed. (London: Pan Books, 1999), p. 241.

86   The Veterans' Tale

by a radar-controlled searchlight, it was pinioned against the night sky by the beam, which was then rapidly joined by other searchlights until the plane was held in a cone of light. The sickening terror of being 'coned' in this fashion is one of the defining features of these memoirs: for each member of the crew this was remembered, as Musgrove noted, as 'a singularly desperate predicament'.[64] Peter Russell heartily concurred with this sentiment, explaining that 'It is a horrible feeling, dangerously close to hopelessness. For often we had seen an aircraft coned, seen it diving and turning, just as helpless as a wounded bird in a cat's clutches'.[65] The memoirist explained that the light in which the unfortunate crew were held was so bright that it actually had a physical impact on the body, which felt 'ice-cold as though your blood has frozen ... you cannot see your instruments. You hardly know which way up you are.'[66] Another ex-pilot, Peter Johnson, sought to convey the terrifying sense of imprisonment he experienced when his aircraft was 'coned' for the first time:

The near blindness induced by eight or ten of these very high-powered beams coming from every side produced a frightening sensation of being caged by light. No matter how you struggled, the dazzling beams would hold you and you lost all sense of movement. It was as if you were motionless in the sky, shells exploding all around you, waiting for the one which would destroy you.[67]

The relationship of these memoirists with the battalions of searchlights arrayed over occupied Europe represents just one aspect of a chillingly impersonal war. The bombers' war was an implacable game of cat and mouse, with the odds stacked high against the mouse. The constant threat posed by searchlights was not an enemy which could be defeated in a traditional manner in open engagement. As Johnson observed, 'we were not really fighting against them, we were simply trying to evade them.'[68]

Descriptions of these searchlights as a terrifying foe are revealing in that they portray light as an enemy in its own right, posing a formidable threat to the safety of the bomber. Emerging from the comparative security of the night sky, entrance to the arena of battle was abrupt, and the impact of the transition from benevolent darkness to aggressive luminosity was disorientating for aircrew. Indeed, these memoirs collectively depict an intense psychological disconnect between the flight through

[64] Musgrove, *Dresden and the Heavy Bombers*, p. 25.
[65] Peter Russell, *Flying in Defiance of the Reich: A Lancaster Pilot's Rites of Passage* (Barnsley: Pen & Sword Aviation, 2007), p. 150.
[66] Ibid., p.150.
[67] Peter Johnson, *The Withered Garland* (London: New European Publications, 1995), p. 175.
[68] Ibid., p.177.

the night sky and subsequent arrival in a target area which was staked out in multiple kinds of light. Johnson, for instance, recorded that he had enjoyed feeling cocooned in the relative safety of a 'black vacuum' on the flight to Essen, when the target area suddenly 'sprang into life':

[A] mass of searchlights, slowly, methodically, scanning the sky over a huge area. At the same time streams of tracer, some white, some coloured, followed the searchlight beams at quite low heights and lastly, at levels from well above our height to four or five thousand feet below came a dazzling display of twinkling stars, the Ruhr barrage of heavy ack-ack.[69]

The contrast between the benign night and the lights of war thus appeared chillingly stark. The tedium of the outbound journey was, as many of these memoirs illustrate, abruptly shattered by arrival upon the target. From deep inside the cavernous darkness, it seemed to these memoirists that they had been plunged into scenes from 'a living nightmare.'[70] Upon entering the concentrated space above the target, the velvet tranquillity of the night sky instantaneously morphed into a coruscation of intensive and lurid light displays in which large quantities of high explosives, coloured Target Indicators, fighter flares, photoflashes, and anti-aircraft searchlights jarred bewilderingly. The intense psychological impact on aircrew was documented by Smith who, upon arriving above Berlin in 1944, was loath to relinquish the perceived protection of the darkness in which his crew had travelled. He recorded that he was bewildered by the scenes outside his Perspex turret: 'suddenly we were over the Big City and I was petrified at the ghastly panorama all around. After the long hours of searching the night sky from the coast to be suddenly propelled into the brilliant hell over Berlin produced a freezing of the mind.'[71] Norman Ashton also documented the enormous shock of entering the skies above Duisberg: 'My mind was bludgeoned by the impact of it.'[72] The descriptions proffered in these narratives of the scenes of chaos amid which the bomber veterans suddenly found themselves resemble prose versions of Picasso's portrait of *Guernica*. Both literary and visual representations convey the same disturbing quality of jumbled agony: the familiar instantaneously displaced, reality rendered distorted and tormented. For the memoir's reader, as for Smith and Ashton, there is something of an assault on the senses in that there is almost too much to watch and comprehend. This is particularly illustrated in Frank Musgrove's vivid

---

[69] Ibid., p. 166.
[70] Gibson, *Enemy Coast Ahead*, p. 233.
[71] Smith, *Rear Gunner Pathfinders*, p. 23.
[72] Ashton, *Only Birds and Fools*, p. 15.

reconstruction of being intercepted by Focke-Wulf fighters above Witten on 12 December 1944:

The Lancaster just ahead of us was hit by cannon shells and exploded: bombs, fuel, aircraft and seven young men were suddenly a million incandescent fragments in the sky, a huge ball of fire, directly in our path. We flew through it and caught fire. Flames licked along our wings. But the fire had not taken firm hold and began to die down. Lancasters all around us seemed to be performing violent aerobatics, still carrying ten tons of bombs and a heavy load of fuel, to evade fighter attacks. One actually looped-the-loop. A crippled Lancaster with its port wing blown off cartwheeled down the sky alongside us and I saw crew members desperately trying to open escape hatches.[73]

Depictions of the airspace over a German city as a displaced space filled with mental torment dominate ex-aircrew memoirs. Against the dark backdrop of the night sky, it seemed to these veterans that out of the natural environment, the lights generated by combat had hewn a battle zone which was inherently unnatural. The fires of the target below added to the aura of apocalypse that framed this battle space. Arthur Gamble recorded that after sustaining an initial heavy daylight raid on 14 October 1944, by the time he and his crew returned on a follow-up raid that night, flying over Duisberg was 'like looking into the glowing coals of a huge blast furnace.' His representation of the stricken city as 'as near a picture of Hell as one could imagine', colours the scene with a distinctly fiendish aspect that is frequently rooted in the imagery of the bomber veterans' tale.[74] Smith's description of how he witnessed from his rear turret Berlin 'bubbling and boiling, splashes of fire opening out as the blockbusters pierced the terrible brew', paints the tortured city below as a dreadful fiery concoction, vibrant against the cauldron of the night.[75] As these extracts illustrate, bomber veteran-memoirists typically turned to discourses of the supernatural as the most efficacious mode of expressing the lurid chaos which dominated this setting. For example, Ashton's lexical choices in describing the target zone over Düsseldorf in May 1943 provide a typical representation of the scenes which aircrew witnessed at night:

The fierce red glow of bursting bombs, the white shimmering of incendiaries, the brilliant glare of target indicators, the blinding flashes of the photo flares, the red-gold strings of 'flaming onions', and the whole witches' cauldron of fire and belching smoke, was like hell let loose.[76]

[73] Musgrove, *Dresden and the Heavy Bombers*, p. 52.
[74] Arthur Gamble, *The Itinerant Airman* (Ilfracombe: Arthur H. Stockwell, 2003), p.117.
[75] Smith, *Rear Gunner*, p. 23.
[76] Ashton, *Only Birds and Fools*, p. 15.

This representation was mirrored in Russell's portrayal of the airspace above Essen in October 1944:

the scene below was fantastic. Fire raged over a large area, peppered with white explosions and lit every few seconds by a greater flash, obliterating in its vicinity all other sight of the red and orange conflagration as 4000-pounders, 'cookies', one from almost every aircraft, fell into the target area.[77]

Such was the impact of man-made light in this environment that Russell could only summarise the spectacle surrounding his aircraft as 'like an evil fairyland'.[78] Some explanation for the supernatural tropes with which these representations were invested is proffered by Gamble. Appalled by the scenes he witnessed over Duisberg in 1944, the memoirist insisted that the battle space appeared 'almost beyond description', indicating that suitable imagery to reproduce this tormented and alien setting was difficult to locate.[79] In order to reconstruct light's apparent perversion of the night sky convincingly, the veteran was clearly prompted to search for appropriately descriptive vocabulary outside the realm of the mundane and familiar.

In addition to the barrage of fiendish light spawned at the business end of the bombers' war, another pyrotechnic horror lurked in the night-marish world above German cities. Unquestionably the strangest aspect of the strategic air campaign in the veterans' tale is an almost unilateral insistence upon the legendary presence of enemy 'scarecrow' weapons at operational height in the target area. From 1943, alongside the barrage of flashes and bangs created by falling bombs and anti-aircraft defences, aircrew began to report being taken aback by great explosions in the immediate vicinity of their aircraft. Smith recorded that a strange 'mighty' detonation occurred just outside his turret. Shaken, he saw hanging in the air a 'large cloud of oily smoke with a flaming centre'.[80] Like many other aircrew, the memoirist remained convinced that this was not an actual aircraft going up in flames, but rather a 'spoof' shell sent up by the German ground defences to simulate an exploding Lancaster. Astonishingly detailed descriptions of these pyrotechnic contraptions are woven into the fabric of the veterans' tale. Gray, for example, explains that a spoof shell was,

[A] scare device which the ground defences mixed in with their regular shells. It was apparently a thinly encased projectile filled mostly with gunpowder and miscellaneous bits of wire, fabric, and other such factory rubbish. The spectacular

[77] Russell, *Flying in Defiance of the Reich*, p. 101.
[78] Ibid., p. 101.
[79] Gamble, *The Itinerant Airman*, p. 117.
[80] Smith, *Rear Gunner*, pp. 95–6.

explosion was relatively harmless, but it did appear remarkably like one of our own bombers blowing up...[81]

Miles Tripp was also sure that this 'terror weapon' had been cleverly designed to simulate pieces of an aircraft blowing apart, even to the extent of 'bits of wing descending from a flaming ball of oily black smoke.'[82] Firm conviction is thus frequently displayed in these narratives that the author had personally witnessed the use of 'scarecrow' shells amid the chaos of night time raiding.

There is, however, no proof that these shells ever actually existed. Researchers have laboured in vain to confirm that the Germans did deploy simulations of the destruction of a heavy bomber and the debate remains inconclusive.[83] Yet although no satisfactory evidence has to date been uncovered to prove the actual use of these weapons, the myth of the 'scarecrow' pervaded Bomber Command and many ex-aircrew recorded the phenomenon in their post-war memoirs as if it had indeed truly been unleashed in night skies above Germany. With the blackest of irony, the explosions which so thoroughly simulated a Lancaster's dying moments can most probably be attributed to the death throes of real aircraft. In the summer of 1943, the installation of *Schräge Musik*, 30-mm cannon which fired tracerless ammunition upward at a 15 degree angle, in Me.110 night fighters meant that the vulnerable underbelly of the bomber could be more easily targeted.[84] Even without this weapon, a single lucky hit on the bomb-bay, with its precious cargo of small 500- or 1,000-pound bombs and the thin-skinned 4,000-pound 'Cookie', spelt instantaneous fiery destruction for both crew and aircraft. The more puzzling aspect of all this is why so many RAF aircrew remained so steadfastly wedded to the existence of a mythical psychological projectile. The British press freely reported the use of 'scarecrows' as a dastardly German tactic, and in a report of April 1944 Bomber Command also seemingly officially confirmed that the Germans were indeed conducting psychological warfare by deploying special dummy flak shells with the aim of deterring RAF crews from approaching the target area.[85] There are also strong indications in many of the veteran memoirs that this information came to them from somewhere high up in officialdom, passed down to crews by squadron

[81] Gray, *Ghosts of Targets Past*, p.89.
[82] Tripp, *The Eighth Passenger*, p. 34.
[83] Martin Middlebrook, *The Nuremberg Raid, 30–31 March 1944* (London: Allen Lane, 1973); Tony Redding, *Life and Death in Bomber Command*, rev. ed. (Stroud: Fonthill Media, 2013); Hastings, *Bomber Command*; John Terraine, *The Right of the Line: The Royal Air Force in the European War 1939–1945* (London, Hodder & Stoughton, 1985).
[84] Terraine, *The Right of the Line*, p. 516.
[85] Middlebrook, *The Nuremberg Raid, 30–31 March 1944*, p. 179.

Intelligence Officers. Jack Currie described how, at the briefing for a raid on Cologne on 8 July 1943, the senior Intelligence Officer referred to the deployment of enemy spoofs during a previous raid on the city five nights earlier: 'A considerable number of scarecrow flares were employed by the enemy, but I don't believe anyone is going to be worried by these rather amateurish attempts at psychological warfare.'[86] Similar insistence that it was the Intelligence Officer who informed the crews of the existence of 'scarecrows' is also displayed in the narratives of Gamble and Jim Davis.[87] As Currie's narration of the Intelligence Officer's speech indicates, emphasising the awesome explosions as 'rather amateurish attempts at psychological warfare' robbed the sight of some of its terror. The sickening vision of a ball of oily smoke and fire bursting outside one's aircraft could be dismissed as a tawdry attempt to inspire terror in the RAF fliers. Even by 1995, when the whole thing had been largely debunked, some memoirists still accepted as fact that dummy shells had been deployed by the enemy's ground forces as a devious method of throwing the attacking bomber forces off track. Davis, for instance, darkly informed his reader that 'This was just one of the things that the Germans attempted to do to break the morale of Bomber Command.'[88] Gray provides a slightly more elaborate explanation of the subject, announcing that the enemy hoped these shells would 'panic the more inexperienced operators in the bomber stream, their alarm causing them to collide with another bomber close by.'[89] Demonstrating just how potent and deep-rooted the 'scarecrow' myth actually was for wartime and veteran bomber crew, Gray's memoir indicates that the rationale for this phenomenon was in some cases extended far beyond intent of simple scare tactics, with a whole sub-myth woven into the main fabrication in an effort to buttress morale.

Further credence to the theory that 'scarecrow' projectiles were accepted by Bomber Command as a means of masking the dreadful casualty rates of operational aircrew is granted by the accounts of a minority of crews who did not accept that these weapons existed. Nevertheless, their recorded reasons for this repudiation are instructive in their own right. On a raid to Cologne in March 1945, Gamble witnessed a Lancaster blowing up directly overhead. After this event, he openly refused to believe that 'scarecrows' were real:

After this Cologne raid I no longer swallowed this piece of hokum, for I KNEW that they were indeed direct hits, and what they had been telling us, and would

---

[86] Currie, *Lancaster Target*, p. 38.
[87] Gamble, *The Itinerant Airman*, p. 143; Davis, *Winged Victory*, p. 68.
[88] Davis, *Winged Victory*, p. 68.
[89] Gray, *Ghosts of Targets Past*, p. 89.

continue to tell us, was pure unadulterated 'bullshit'! I had been watching that Lancaster like a howk [sic] when it disintegrated before my eyes. One second it was there, the next second it had completely vanished.[90]

Whilst Gamble's voice deviates from the common belief of the existence of the 'scarecrow' shell, his account is revealing in so far as it suggests that Bomber Command crews were indeed consciously being encouraged by their intelligence officers to believe in these frightening devices. Testifying to the murky muddle of fact and fiction that the wartime British armed forces' rumour mill so frequently generated, Harry Yates evidently laboured under the impression that the Air Ministry had categorically denied the existence of these shells. Holding the key to this strange tale, he asserted that he and his crew were 'willing believers' in this 'mythical beast'.[91] Yates' memoir thus adds a critical further layer of understanding as to why so many aircrew apparently swallowed this myth. 'Psychological warfare', he wrote, 'was a lot friendlier than the real thing. If we had to get clobbered, we were only too pleased for it to be a spoof.'[92] In a demonic environment where the bomber crew were forced to press on regardless through fire, flak, and fiendish light displays, it is perhaps understandable that many aircrew found it infinitely preferable to imagine that the vivid explosions shaking their aircraft were simply an extension of unreality which could be dismissed as clumsy scare tactics.

In these memoirs, therefore, former aircrew interpreted the lights spawned by battle as a visual, actual, and psychological menace. Within the environment of the night sky, light was thus viewed as synonymous with danger whereas darkness became symbolised as merciful and protective. Daylight raids, as Yates noted, did not carry quite the same sense of fear inspired by the illumination of the night: 'Sunlight leached away much fieriness from bomb impacts and flakbursts and substituted quantities of dust and smoke. Everything became greyer and less pulsatingly dramatic.'[93] Russell concurred, commenting that in a daylight raid 'I was not forcibly made conscious of the fires and brilliant explosions on the ground, or even of the frightening pyrotechnics all around us in the air, or the waving arms of the searchlights, as I was at night.'[94] Yet while the night sky served to magnify the horror of the brightly lit target area, this amplification of the terror of the lights of battle further reinforced the construct of the darkness, outside the 'brilliant hell' of the target area, as a sanctuary for aircrew. Even inside the luminous parameters of this

[90] Gamble, The Itinerant Airman, p. 143.
[91] Harry Yates, Luck and a Lancaster (Shrewsbury: Airlife: 1999), p. 121.
[92] Ibid, p. 121.
[93] Ibid., p. 177.
[94] Russell, Flying in Defiance of the Reich, p. 127.

airspace, Gray posited, the darkness seemed able to rob flak bursts of the distress they induced in daylight. In the sunlight of a daytime raid over Gelsenkirchen, he found himself terrified by the lingering smoke puffs of exploding shells and flak bursts, 'hanging there in their hundreds like delegates of doom and disaster.'[95] By night, he claimed, the 'number one terror merchant during the day, was greatly subdued'.[96] Against the intense fear inspired by the lights of war that human conflict created, the night sky was thus interpreted as offering both safety and reassurance to the bomber crew. As in the desert memoirs, the isolation and sense of emptiness associated with these natural environments was craved by the combatant. The extent to which the bomber associated the blank canvas of the night sky with refuge may be deduced from the sheer sense of relief with which Musgrove described routing his aircraft away from Dortmund into 'blissfully black space'.[97]

The Sailors' Tale: The Royal Navy and the Northern Oceans, 1939–1945

Thousands of feet below the bombers' war, the Royal Navy's sailors found themselves operating in a battle space that only rarely lent itself to interpretations of its magnanimous protection of combatants. Although several scholars, such as Mark Connelly and Patrick Deer, have commented upon the somewhat lacklustre fashion in which the naval war entered British culture and remembrance of the Second World War, scholarly attention has yet to be really directed towards the interpretations that these sailors did place upon their watery operating environment.[98] To some extent this is perhaps due to what Connelly identifies as the British nation's cultural simplification of the war into chapters they find acceptable; invariably some aspects or chapters become a casualty left behind as the preserve of 'those interested enough to investigate the history more deeply.'[99] Significantly, Connelly and Deer both detect that, despite the success of wartime films such as David Lean's *In Which We Serve* (1942), the Royal Navy's war was never accorded prime place in the official war culture or popular imagination of the Second World War.[100] Despite the crucial work performed by the Royal Navy in keeping open the nation's arterial supply lines, a comparative scarcity of surface

[95] Gray, *Ghosts of Targets Past*, p. 88.
[96] Ibid., p. 132.
[97] Musgrove, *Dresden and the Heavy Bombers*, p. 26.
[98] Deer, *Culture in Camouflage*, p. 82; Connelly, *We Can Take It!*, p. 259.
[99] Connelly, *We Can Take It!*, p. 265.
[100] Deer, *Culture in Camouflage*, p. 82.

94   The Veterans' Tale

fleet engagements imbued the sailors' war with little of the dash and élan of the desert war nor the steadfast heroism of the strategic air campaign. As Connelly notes, the vital Battle of the Atlantic 'struggles to capture the imagination, lacking glamour and excitement.'[101] Deer also suspects that the 'remote seascapes, with their vast distance and long periods of seeming inactivity, did not seem to yield a sufficiently dynamic or cohesive iconography.'[102] Yet the naval veterans' tale does employ just such a collective symbolic representation of the northern oceans in which they served, thus proffering an important insight into the personal meanings that former sailors attached to the maritime environment in their remembered and recorded experiences of war.

The open stretches of the Atlantic and waters of the Arctic Circle formed a natural arena which, like the desert and the night sky, was also overlaid with discrete tropes of spatial isolation and interior vacancy. Like the desert troops, the sailors were all too aware of the natural dangers which characterised their battle space. Graeme Ogden's remark that operations in the North Atlantic consisted primarily of an intensely personal 'battle against the elements' underpins the extent to which the naval veteran contemplated his relationship with the natural environment in terms of a perennial struggle waged between man and sea.[103] Amid the vast and frequently storm-haunted expanses of northern waters sailors were acutely conscious that survival rested at least as much on the force and direction of wind and wave as upon defeating the German foe. 'A ship', wrote Donald Macintyre, 'is such a puny thing in the grip of the fury of the elements at sea.'[104] Having served for two winters on convoy escort duty through the North Atlantic, the memoirist recorded that the small ships and the crews who manned them all too frequently received 'a considerable beating' from the savagery of this environment.[105] Throughout the duration of the Second World War, this 'remorseless battle' was bitterly contested by sailors.[106] On 7 September 1939 outward bound ocean convoys commenced sailing and thus right from the very outset of the war the little ships of the Royal Navy were pitted against the twin foes of the Germans and the North Atlantic in a slogging match that lasted for over five years. During the early years of the war a dearth of available escort ships meant that merchant vessels could not be accompanied all the way

[101] Connelly, *We Can Take It!*, p. 259.
[102] Deer, *Culture in Camouflage*, p. 82.
[103] Ogden, *My Sea Lady*, p. 74.
[104] Donald Macintyre, *U-Boat Killer: Fighting the U-Boats in the Battle of the Atlantic*, rev. ed. (London: Cassell, 1999), p. 179.
[105] Ibid., 59.
[106] Ogden, *My Sea Lady*, p. 70.

across the Atlantic. In May 1940 the Royal Navy could only provide anti-submarine escort as far as longitude 12–15 degrees West, or some 200 miles to the west of Ireland.[107] Instead, incoming convoys were met in the Western Approaches by a naval escort which had just accompanied an outgoing convoy. Memoirist Peter Gretton recalled that bad weather and moonless nights rendered this task especially difficult for escorting destroyers such as his own command, HMS *Sabre*, in January 1941:

On a dark night it was by no means easy to keep in station; and it was not rare to find one or even two escorts adrift at dawn. In these circumstances the fear of enemy action receded into the background, and we had to concentrate on the purely domestic matters of keeping with the convoy and of avoiding weather damage.[108]

With the instigation in June 1941 of deep water convoy escorts all the way across the Atlantic, the hazards facing the accompanying naval crews also extended. At sea, a convoy of forty-five ships might cover five square miles of sea, which had to be patrolled by the escorts.[109] The merchant fleet itself was composed of a motley collection of tankers and freight ships of all sizes, ages, and conditions. The ferocity of oceanic weather meant that it was all too easy for escorts to become detached from their convoys, sometimes with fatal results. In poor weather, a merchant ship which was too old, too slow, or insufficiently watertight could not maintain convoy speed or position and so frequently fell out of line. As Gretton explained, one of the escorts would be detailed to locate the straggler and shepherd it back to the protection of the convoy. Yet in big seas, this duty could prove remarkably perilous, as Ogden discovered to his cost. The memoirist recounted how his anti-submarine trawler, HMS *Lady Madeleine*, turned back to search for a merchant ship which had become detached from his convoy in bad weather. Unluckily, upon setting out on this mission, the trawler immediately got into difficulties due to the depth of the swell. Well and truly lost in a running sea, Ogden as commander of the vessel faced an unenviable choice. If he increased the speed of his ship to outrun the storm, he would put a dangerous strain on his engines and steering gear. If, however, he maintained a slow pace, there was every risk that the heavy seas would pour down the smoke stack and put out the fires in the engine room. Describing this incident, he confessed that he was 'thoroughly frightened':

I had done the one thing that I had always dreaded, and we were in a position where we could easily lose our ship and our lives – but not in the face of enemy

[107] S. W. Roskill, *The War At Sea 1939–1945*, Vol. 1. (London: Her Majesty's Stationary Office, 1954), p. 343.
[108] Gretton, *Convoy Escort Commander*, pp. 50–1.
[109] Roskill, *The War At Sea*, Vol. 1., p. 464.

action. Small ships quite often disappeared in Atlantic gales, and nobody knew their fate. To fight one's ship and die in battle was one thing, but to be 'lost at sea', for the reason the captain didn't know his job, was an appalling thought.[110]

The risks sailors such as Gretton and Ogden faced in the desolation of the maritime setting were viewed as subject to oceanic caprice and these narratives suggest that the sailor understood his connection with his natural environment in the complex terms of a human relationship. Indeed, the symbolism which these men attached to the cold northern seas was often charged with an extraordinary level of emotional intimacy. Former RNVR officer Harry Foxcroft mused that seafarers shared 'a unique privilege':

That of living in daily contact with nature on the one timeless, unchanging, unspoilt element of all; the sea in all its moods of simple, often savage, beauty. The very element from which all life emanated.[111]

Foxcroft's personalisation of the sea as a temperamental being articulates the collective representation of the maritime setting throughout the naval veterans' tale. With all sectors of the northern oceans oscillating between periods of storm and calm, it was clearly tempting to imagine that the waters indulged in 'moods' that could be likened to those of a human female. In describing the Western Approaches, for instance, Jack Broome observed that the sailor was faced with a seascape which could, 'like a woman, be frightening, vicious, exhausting. Then, like the same woman it could be beautiful.'[112]

In northern waters, Nature is thus represented as an ever-present threat to man and machine. For all that Winston Churchill might declare in the House of Commons in September 1939 that the war at sea would be one of 'science and seamanship', in extreme conditions in open waters, neither of these could wholly guarantee the sailor's survival if the ocean appeared to be in an ill humour. In these memoirs, therefore, the ocean is represented as possessing an innately treacherous quality which was based upon an apparent capriciousness of environment. Intriguingly, this imagery particularly pervades the memoirs of submariners, who display an insistence that the sea could be fundamentally devious and malicious. For the most part during periods when their boats were submerged, the submariners' tale portrays a certain indifference to the surrounding sea. As Commander Edward Young observed, the tranquillity of the depths of the ocean led to a feeling that the submarine was relatively sheltered,

---

[110] Ogden, *My Sea Lady*, p. 90.
[111] Harry Foxcroft, *Hostilities Only 1940–1945* (Weymouth: Miller-Lee Books, 1999), p. 178.
[112] Jack Broome, *Convoy is to Scatter* (London: William Kimber, 1972), p. 76.

enveloped in a protective blanket of calmer waters, and he asserted that he 'always felt happier underwater'.[113] Yet, when they were obliged to surface, they were frequently astonished by the ferocity of conditions above and correspondingly display remarkably similar attitudes towards the sea as the men who crewed surface vessels. For instance, although submarine captain William King perceived something 'honest' about the long rolling swell to be found in the Atlantic, he wrote vividly of his intense dislike of the North Sea, whose comparatively shallow waters piled waves into 'ugly, steep, tumbling affairs'.[114] Throughout these texts the submariner's bewilderment at the apparent cunning and spite of the sea is evident. Young, for instance, was instructed to winter in the Arctic Circle and graphically described the misery of keeping watch on his surfaced submarine through the long, wild nights. He characterised his hours of watchkeeping on the bridge as a test of endurance, recollecting that the water 'leaps over the gun platform and springs up at you with seemingly deliberate malice.'[115] Similarly, Alistair Mars recorded being blown off course by a squall near the French coast whilst running only seven fathoms (thirteen metres) from the surface: 'It was an incredible situation. Despite all our learning, contraptions and gadgets, despite our technical knowledge, charts and machines, the sea had tricked us.'[116] Across all these narratives, the claim that the sea was a malicious element resounds assertively.

The sense of malevolence which the submariners identified in their environment also echoes throughout the accounts of their surface counterparts. Both sets of veterans insisted that the sea appeared to find an active and sadistic pleasure in inflicting torment upon seafarers and ships. Indeed, there is some suggestion in these memoirs that the sea's aggression posed a greater potential threat than the German enemy. For example, writing of the North Sea in the early months of the war, King remarked that,

The official naval prayer asks for 'deliverance from the dangers of the sea and the violence of the enemy.' ... this description became reversed. The enemy was only a small peril, as he would hardly be able to see or hear us, and his minefields had been dispersed by the lashing waves. The danger to pray against now was the sea![117]

Various sailors directed a special antipathy towards the perceived vengefulness of the northern seas. Macintyre recollected that 'sometimes a sea

---

[113] Edward Young, *One of Our Submarines* (London: Rupert Hart-Davis, 1952), p. 64.
[114] William King, *The Stick and the Stars* (London: Hutchinson, 1956), p. 35.
[115] Young, *One of Our Submarines*, p. 67.
[116] Alistair Mars, *Unbroken: The Story of a Submarine* (London: Frederick Muller, 1953), p. 55.
[117] King, *The Stick and the Stars*, p. 35.

would seem, without reason or warning, to rise up ... and hurl itself vin-
dictively down on the deck amidships', whilst Broome bluntly referred
to the unpredictable Atlantic as a 'bastard'.[118] Ogden perceived that his
beloved *Lady Madeleine* had been actively tortured by this ocean, recording that his trawler had spent three months on escort duty 'thrashing
about ... tormented by cruel seas and howling gales.'[119] Significantly,
this veteran's choice of adjective to demonise the sea was mirrored in
other naval memoirs. Former gunnery officer Robert Hughes provides
an illustration of this in his account of escorting Murmansk-bound convoys through the Arctic Circle. In his depiction of the destruction of the
SS *JLM Curry*, which cracked amidships, broke in half, and sank rapidly,
he wrote bitterly that 'the cruel sea swept over her grave'.[120] He employed
the same phrase to portray the sinking of the minesweeper HMS *Leda*,
'which had spent so much time in these cruel seas'.[121] Similarly, Broome
spent the first winter of the war providing an escort in the Channel and
Western Approaches. He recalled that 'the sea was teaching us in its
cruel way to be a crew – or else'.[122] Intriguingly, as the vocabulary of
these veterans suggests, much of the relandscaping of the sea in published war memoirs appears to draw upon a specific lexis laid down by
bestselling novelist, wartime memoirist, and RNVR officer Nicholas
Monsarrat. As an officer who served on convoy duty in the Atlantic and
on the East Coast runs between 1942 and 1945, in wartime Monsarrat
had published autobiographical accounts of his naval experiences before
releasing in 1951 a widely acclaimed novel which drew upon the same
material.[123] A tale of the convoy sailor's gruelling battle against the ocean,
The Cruel Sea became an instant and enduring bestseller, and in 1953
was turned into a popular film bearing the same name. As the title suggests, both novel and film employed an explicit frame of reference which
personified the sea as a sadistic enemy of the sailor. The adjective 'cruel'
was repeatedly stamped as a leitmotif throughout the book and the film
opened with a voiceover by Jack Hawkins, who played the lead role:

This is a story of the Battle of the Atlantic, the story of an ocean, two ships, and
a handful of men. The men are the heroes; the heroines are the ships. The only
villain is the sea, the cruel sea.[124]

---

[118] Macintyre, *U-Boat Killer*, p. 60; Broome, *Convoy is to Scatter*, p. 36.
[119] Ogden, *My Sea Lady*, p. 74.
[120] Robert Hughes, *Through the Waters: A Gunnery Officer in H. M. S. Scylla 1942–43*
(London: William Kimber, 1956), p. 143.
[121] Ibid., p. 67.
[122] Broome, *Convoy is to Scatter*, p. 32.
[123] Nicholas Monsarrat, *Three Corvettes* (London: Cassell, 1945); Nicholas Monsarrat, *The
Cruel Sea* (London: Cassell, 1951).
[124] *The Cruel Sea*, directed by Charles Frend (GDF, 1953).

Through Monsarrat, the phrase 'cruel sea' thus became established as highly recognisable in post-war British popular culture. In the second volume of his autobiography, *Life is a Four Letter Word* (1970), the title of his chapter on the war reinforced his belief that he had fairly captured the nature of the sea, reading simply, 'It *Was* Cruel' [memoirist's own italics].[125] As such, it is perhaps not wholly coincidental that memoirs of other naval veterans published after 1951 demonstrate a remarkable tendency to tap into an identical rhetoric of the sea as villain.

Whilst ascertaining the precise extent to which Monsarrat's work informed memoirists' reconstructions of their own wartime relationships with the sea is challenging in the extreme, it would be difficult to argue that his representation had not exerted at least some influence upon the ways in which other veterans wrote about the northern oceans since the epithet 'cruel' makes such a frequent appearance in their representations of the sea. Denys Rayner's memoir, published only two years after *The Cruel Sea* became the second-highest grossing film of 1953, records a fascinating irritation with such personification of the sea, which suggests that this veteran at least was well aware of the cultural power that Monsarrat's famous phrase wielded. Indeed, Rayner's *Escort*, first published in 1955, makes a concerted effort to steer representations of the wartime oceans away from such personalised language, stating firmly that 'I do not write of the sea, which has no personality of its own and does not change. The sea is neither cruel nor kind.'[126] Among the naval veteran-memoirists in this study, Rayner was alone in voicing this particular argument, but he was not the only author to challenge the 'cruel sea' construct. As Monsarrat's ex-commanding officer in HMS *Guillemot* on the East Coast convoys in 1941, and a close personal friend after the war, Sam Lombard-Hobson was ideally placed to comment in his own memoir upon his former lieutenant's representation of the sea:

Monsarrat's epic story of the U-boat war certainly describes ... every ocean crossing [as] a relentless struggle against the cruellest of cruel seas. In actual fact, taken over the whole period, the great majority of convoys got through without interference or mention; and the Atlantic, more often than not, is agreeably kind.[127]

Crucially, it was not Monsarrat's investment of the ocean with human qualities to which his former commander objected here; merely the charge that the sea possessed no redemptive characteristics. Both

---

[125] Nicholas Monsarrat, *Life is a Four Letter Word*, Vol. 2 (London: Cassell &Company, 1970), p. 1.
[126] Rayner, *Escort*, p. x.
[127] Lombard-Hobson, *A Sailor's War*, p. 54.

Lombard-Hobson and Rayner had something more in common than simple objection to the 'cruel' label pinned onto the sea, however. The latter explained that he contested such anthropomorphism because he believed it reduced the ocean's awe-inspiring supremacy:

Any apparent virtues it may have, and all its vices, are seen only in relation to the spirit of man who pits himself, in ships of his own building, against its insensate power. To conclude otherwise is to diminish its majesty.[128]

Lombard-Hobson also suggested that the epithets applied to the sea reveal more about the author's own personal responses to war than about the natural environment itself. In fact, Lombard-Hobson recorded that he remonstrated with Monsarrat after the war, informing the novelist that the ocean itself was not at fault: 'war was cruel, not the sea, and that only the ill-prepared or foolhardy, showing lack of respect for its power, regarded the sea as unkindly.'[129] He believed that his former junior officer's personal relationship with the sea had become tarnished by the brutality of battle he had witnessed, and his representation of the ocean as 'cruel' was simply 'the schizoid' nature of Monsarrat's own character:

I am sure, at the bottom of his heart, that Monsarrat must have had a love for the sea: he had been a yachtsman in his earlier days, and he was a born seaman. But war, which he loathed, was to drive him to write of the sea as cruel.[130]

According to Lombard-Hobson, Monsarrat had simply projected his own feelings of wartime bitterness onto the natural environment.[131] By this logic, therefore, it might well be argued that the commanding officer's own description of the Atlantic as 'agreeably kind' owed much to his own more tolerant personality and resilience to war. Other memoirists, too, represented the war as a kind of magic lantern which played out its images upon the screen of the sea. Ogden wrote of the 'moments of beauty' which had been part of his life in northern waters when under no immediate threat from submarines or aircraft:

In calm weather it was the utter silence of the new day which was so enthralling; the sea would be like milk beneath a lightening sky, then, when the sun began to creep over the horizon, the whole atmosphere became charged with luminous gold. If we were near the ice edge its pastel-blue peaks were tinted rose colour by the rising sun. At nights the northern lights illuminated the seascape with a weird, flickering brilliance.[132]

---

128 Rayner, *Escort*, p. x.
129 Lombard-Hobson, *A Sailor's War*, p. 135.
130 Ibid., p. 133.
131 Ibid., p. 135.
132 Ogden, *My Sea Lady*, p. 70.

Yet Hughes indicates that when enemy action threatened the surrounding seascape became invested with ominous portent. In the autumn of 1942, the memoirist sailed with convoy PQ18, bound for Murmansk. Of embarking on this voyage from the relative safety of Iceland, he recorded sailing over a 'red-splashed sea': 'I looked slowly around at the sky. Great blood-red streaks were slashed across the heavens, and we seemed to be headed straight into the bloodiest section.'[133] After the slaughter of the preceding convoy PQ17 in July it is perhaps small wonder that the memoirist presaged danger in these icy waters which appeared symbolically strewn with blood. The omens were fulfilled for Hughes as the convoy quickly came under fire from German aircraft along the Norwegian coast:

we painted in our pattern of war on the grey backcloth of the Barents Sea – the dirty black and yellow daubs of the shell-bursts, the vari-coloured arcs of the tracer, and the disturbed feathers of water as the bullets leaped low across the sea.[134]

These respective inscriptions of peace and battle upon the sea itself suggest that Lombard-Hobson was correct in judging that the former sailor projected his own responses to the naval war onto the blank canvas of the maritime setting. Like the desert, the northern oceans offered an unpredictable and frequently hostile operating environment in which a palpable sense of nature's power over mankind dominated. Unlike the desert, however, the question of nature's temperament became bound into the naval veterans' tale, with many memoirists attaching human characteristics of malice and trickery to the seascape. Despite Rayner's best efforts to mould cultural understandings of the sea away from this narrative of humanisation, Lombard-Hobson's insistence thirty years later that the Atlantic ought to be remembered as 'agreeably kind' suggests that naval memoirists found it difficult to relinquish anthropomorphised interpretations of the maritime environment.

Summary

Although former bomber aircrew, desert soldiers, and sailors imagined and reconstructed their battlegrounds using different choices of imagery and lexis, their representations nevertheless share a fundamental assumption that the natural environment played a dominant role in the definition and remembrance of combat experience. Whether the environment was imagined as remorselessly indifferent to human conflict, cunningly

---

[133] Hughes, *Through the Waters*, p.43.
[134] Ibid., p. 61.

malicious, or seen as a welcome shelter against man's battles, the natural world is relandscaped in these texts as far more than a simple domain within which war happened to occur. Landscape thus became invested with distinctive symbolism which allowed the veteran to make sense of his battle space, particularly in geographical locations which appeared to the combatant as something of a 'blank canvas'.

In order further to understand their relationship with the natural environment, several memoirists placed their own, and others', narrative reconstructions of battlegrounds under scrutiny. For example, Denys Rayner and Ray Ward both attempted to deconstruct the symbolism with which landscape was commonly reconstructed in war memoirs. Naval veteran Rayner displayed little patience with tropes which personified the northern waters. In his narrative, he declared that he had deliberately restricted his writing to ships and men alone, explaining that the sea 'is supremely indifferent, and wholly lacks sensibility.'[135] Published in 1955, only two years after the box office success of *The Cruel Sea*, his words might well be interpreted as an attempt to steer popular understandings and cultural representations away from the imagined malevolence of the ocean. If so, he failed singularly, as the anthropomorphisation of the sea flourished throughout the majority of memoirs which followed his own. In stark contrast to Rayner, former soldier Ward articulated a personal willingness to subscribe to the tropes through which the North African arena was understood, arguing that they posed a source of solace to the ex-combatant. Poignantly, he suggested that analogies of chivalric idealism which shaped the soldier's representations of the desert sprang from a conscious effort to draw a positive meaning from battle there, reflecting that 'many veterans of the fighting found the myths that embellish the campaign more comforting than the often grim reality.'[136] To an extent, therefore, the entire construct of the Western Desert as an isolated 'perfect battlefield', or indeed the night sky as 'blessed', may be understood as partly the product of the veteran's desire to detach himself from the human emotions of fear, pain, and loss which accompanied his combat experience.

---

[135] Rayner, *Escort*, p. x.
[136] Ward, *The Mirror of Monte Cavallara*, p. 128.

4   Machines, Weapons, and Protagonists

> Even this grey machinery of murder
>
> Holds beauty and the promise of a future.[1]

In 1942, Norman Hampson wrote the above lines whilst serving aboard HMS *Carnation*, a Flower-class corvette launched in 1940. They highlight this sailor's construction of a meaningful personal attachment to his ship as a source of alleviating the grim conditions of wartime operations at sea, and the post-war memoirs of Hampson and other seamen are punctuated with similarly expressive representations of the small ships of the Royal Navy. Like sailors, aircrew and tank crew also cast their weapons in a starring role in their accounts of frontline service to such an extent that several scholars suggest that martial technology has become overly prominent in a variety of representations. For instance, John Ellis comments that during the Second World War,

the machines came of age. Caterpillar tracks became a reasonably reliable form of advance, aircraft achieved ever-better performance figures, submarines posed a still more critical threat ... *Arma virumque cano* [I sing of arms and the man], announced Virgil. But in the popular epics fashioned out of the two world wars, the man dominates the First and the arms the Second.[2]

Similarly, in a recent popular history of the experiences of the wartime Royal Navy, Glyn Prysor complains that the sailor has been relegated to a marginal position in representations of the naval conflict:

The war at sea appears at first glance to have been somehow less human than other campaigns, shaped more by technology and intelligence, strategy and firepower, than by people. Much of the sailor's experience of war was unfamiliar: an array of complex machinery and novel technology ... All this has

---

[1] Norman Hampson, 'Corvette', reproduced in Brian Gardner, *The Terrible Rain: The War Poets 1939–1945* (London: Methuen, 1966), p. 117. Originally written aboard HMS *Carnation* in 1942.

[2] John Ellis, 'Reflections on the "Sharp End" of War', in *Time to Kill: The Soldier's Experience of War in the West 1939–1945*, (eds.) Paul Addison and Angus Calder (London: Pimlico, 1997), p. 15.

resulted in an almost unavoidable anthropomorphism: ships, not their sailors, are too often seen as the main characters. Yet ships were weapons, not protagonists.[3]

The veterans' tale is certainly riveted with tales of weapons, but the balance and nature of the relationship that Ellis and Prysor identify between man and machine in these accounts requires some repositioning. Whilst the narratives of British Second World War veterans are frequently loquacious in describing the tools of their various martial trades, claims that the tale of the man is subsumed into that of the machine are difficult to verify. Machines do indeed star in these narratives of combat experience, but they share the billing jointly with their crew. Indeed, in these memoirs, the men who operated ships, aircraft, and tanks fundamentally represent human and mechanical combatants as locked together into a cohesive battle unit, and it is this interdependent working partnership that takes centre stage in their accounts of war.

In his now-famous discussion of how to achieve a bond between an infantry soldier and his weapon, the American military theorist SLA Marshall noted in 1947 that 'fashioning the machine to man's use in battle was but half of the problem. The other half was conditioning man to the machine.'[4] On a grander scale, the same statement is equally relevant to the men who crewed ships, submarines, aircraft, and tanks. They too had to learn to adapt psychologically to their weapon. Representation of a rather symbiotic relationship between man and arms is therefore a dominant theme in these personal narratives. Like the memoirs of the naval personnel, the narratives of the men who served in Fighter Command during the Battle of Britain, and the crews of the armoured units that fought in Normandy in 1944, record that their authors also found ways of mentally acclimatising to their machines in order to form an efficient battle partnership. The veterans' tale thus suggests that some machines *were* regarded by the combatant as 'protagonists', if only because investing them with anthropomorphic qualities provided the human antagonist with a measure of comfort or hope. This chapter thus explores the representation of a variety of relationships that the former crews of aircraft, ships, and armour identified with their own 'grey machinery of murder'.

---

[3] Glyn Prysor, *Citizen Sailors: The Royal Navy in the Second World War* (London: Viking, 2011), p. 3.

[4] S. L. A. Marshall, *Men against Fire: The Problem of Battle Command*, rev. ed. (Oklahoma: University of Oklahoma Press, 2000), p. 22.

The Sailors' Tale: The Royal Navy and
the Northern Oceans, 1939–1945

'She was a damn fine little ship,' wrote former First Lieutenant William
Donald of his sloop HMS *Black Swan* 'and only a sailor knows what
those words really mean.'[5] As this statement illustrates, the emotional
meanings that naval veterans ascribed to their vessels were complex,
intense, and difficult to convey fully to non-mariners. Nevertheless, a
sense of powerful attachment to their vessels forms a central pillar of the
sailors' testimonies, offering an opportunity to understand the importance that the seaman attached to his ship as a fellow protagonist during the war. Recording the sailor's relationships with the Royal Navy's
'grey machinery of murder', the naval veteran-memoirists depict their
vessels as cherished feminine companions that could help to stave off
the feelings of isolation and fear which accompanied the war at sea, and
increased their hope of safe return.

Safe return was by no means guaranteed during the convoy escorts' war
at sea, particularly during the early years of the Second World War. When
the focus of battle shifted to the northern Atlantic by 1941 the ferocity
of gales in these waters caused inevitable wear and tear upon vessels,
adding to an existing shortage of escort ships. As Stephen Roskill, the
official naval historian and himself a veteran of the destroyers' war at sea,
remarked, the men who served on the 'little ships' during these months
acutely remembered 'the long-drawn strain of the Atlantic passages and
the constant frustration of trying to do too much with too little.'[6] During
the first year of the war, with only 101 destroyers and sloops to protect
some 3,000 ocean-going ships, the Royal Navy was very fortunate that
the U-boats had not yet reached their full strength in either numbers or
tactics.[7] Between 1940 and 1941, 137 Flower-class sloops, reclassified as
corvettes, entered service and rapidly became a naval byword for their
lack of suitability as ocean-going escorts.[8] Of serving in HMS *Carnation*,
Hampson recorded pertinently that 'You'd be rather more comfortable
in gaol and very much safer.'[9] At only 190 feet long, the corvettes
which constituted the workhorse of Atlantic escorts were designed for
coastal warfare rather than deep water service. A wartime aphorism that

---

[5] William Donald, *Stand By For Action: A Sailor's Story* (London: William Kimber, 1956),
p. 49.

[6] Roskill, *The War at Sea*, Vol. 1, p. 466.

[7] John Terraine, *Business in Great Waters: The U-Boat Wars, 1916–1945* (London: Leo
Cooper, 1989), p. 244.

[8] Corelli Barnett, *Engage the Enemy More Closely: The Royal Navy in the Second World War*
(London: Hodder & Stoughton, 1991), p. 256.

[9] Hampson, *Not Really What You'd Call a War*, p. 15.

a corvette would 'roll on wet grass' to forty-five degrees either side of upright hints at the misery that the poor sea-handling characteristics of these vessels imposed upon their unfortunate crew. Unsuited to the savage weather of the Atlantic, difficult to handle, and with a wide turning circle that impeded attacks upon U-boats, the early corvettes might have been fundamentally seaworthy, but they offered their crews a horrendously uncomfortable voyage.[10] Conditions aboard a wartime destroyer also left a lot to be desired. Indeed, Donald Macintyre insisted that his old V-and-W-class destroyer HMS *Walker* caused even more discomfort to the crew than a corvette:

[D]estroyers, with their corkscrew motion, the crash of their bows as they smacked down with each wave that passed under them and the whipping of the hull as their screws rose to the surface, were more wearing to the bodies and souls of their inhabitants. And they were wet![11]

In 1918, the author Rudyard Kipling gave an address to British junior naval officers in which he expressed a tongue-in-cheek sympathy for their future predicament in serving aboard 'that packet of assorted miseries which we call a Ship'.[12] The small ships that provided the bulk of convoy escorts throughout the Second World War proved equally befitting of that description. As the accounts of Hampson and Macintyre exemplify, the naval veterans' tale was thus quite frank in its detailed depiction of the 'miseries' of life at sea in wartime. Yet this only serves to highlight the peculiarly personalised relationship that these memoirists remembered experiencing with their vessels. Indeed, Robert Hughes voiced the sentiments of all the other naval memoirists in this study, when he reflected that the operational partnership between sailor and craft was underpinned by a 'strange affection for the ship herself.'[13]

As Hughes' choice of the adjective 'strange' to describe the sailor's mysterious affinity with his vessel indicates, supernatural beliefs exert some influence over these memoirists' identification and representation of an acute psychological bond between the Navy's men and machines during the Second World War. Their accounts indicate that seamen drew upon arcane maritime superstition as a buffer against an isolated and frequently hostile environment. Naval historian Brian Lavery posits that the appalling natural dangers of the maritime environment rendered conditions for the convoy sailor during the Battle of the

---

[10] By 1943 the design of corvettes had been modified to improve habitability for the crew and provide greater endurance and firepower.

[11] Macintyre, *U-Boat Killer*, p. 60.

[12] Rudyard Kipling, *A Book of Words: Selections from Speeches and Addresses Delivered Between 1906 and 1927* (London: Macmillan and Co., 1928), p. 157.

[13] Hughes, *Through the Waters*, p. 149.

Atlantic 'almost as horrific as on the Western Front in the First World War', whilst Churchill's doctor, Lord Moran, himself a survivor of the trenches, supposed that 'Life in a destroyer in northern seas in this war must be rather like trench warfare in a bad part of the line in the last war'.[14] This parallel between ocean and trench experience is an interesting one, as it suggests that naval personnel on escort duty might be viewed as 'sitting ducks' in much the same fashion as trench soldiers were often perceived as imprisoned in muddy passivity. Important developments in First World War historiography propose, however, that the soldier in the trenches was not quite as passive as the old 'lions led by donkeys' approach suggested. Alexander Watson's analysis of the formation of mental coping strategies on the Western Front offers a particularly useful insight into the modes of endurance constructed at sea during the Second World War. Watson found that the trench soldiers of the earlier conflict often subscribed to superstitious belief and ritual as a means of asserting personal control over their immediate environment.[15] In the veterans' tale of the Second World War, the sailors' representations of the 'strange affection' they felt for their ship may be viewed as part of a similar quest for individual security and reassurance amid a thoroughly frightening environment.

Because of all the discomforts, hazards, and uncertainties of service at sea, the naval memoirists collectively represent a personalised, intimate, and highly gendered relationship with their ships. A common denominator in all of these naval testimonies is that the machines of the sea were referred to as 'she' and invested with imagined qualities of sentience. As the gendered descriptions of Donald – 'she was a damn fine little ship' – and Hughes – 'strange affection for the ship herself' – illustrate, therefore, gendered personification lies at the heart of the naval veteran's representation of his relationship with his ship or submarine. This mode of personification drew upon centuries of seafaring tradition which locates a vessel as a cognisant female, and there are multiple explanations for why ships are feminised in this fashion, all of which are based upon folklore. Traditionally, superstition and sexism are offered as popular explanations of the prevalence of seafarers' discussion of ships as females. Pieter van der Merwe, a naval historian at the National Maritime Museum, explains a likelihood that the tradition 'relates to the idea of goddesses and mother figures

[14] Brian Lavery, *In Which They Served: The Royal Navy Officer Experience in the Second World War* (London: Conway, 2008), p. 70; Lord Moran, *The Anatomy of Courage*, rev. ed. (London: Constable & Robinson, 2007), p. 100.
[15] Alexander Watson, 'Self-Deception and Survival: Mental Coping Strategies on the Western Front, 1914–18', *Journal of Contemporary History*, 41:2 (2006), 260–1.

playing a protective role in looking after a ship and crew.'[16] Another popular theory suggests that sailors named their vessels in honour of their womenfolk whom they were leaving behind, as a way of taking their loved ones to sea with them, and an extensive body of salty jokes avows that a ship may be likened to a woman because of the high levels of maintenance and respect which both demand.[17] In any event, traditional sea lore holds that sailors embarking upon a long voyage invested their vessels with all the gendered qualities of a nurturing and loving, if occasionally unpredictable, spouse as a way of reassuring themselves that they were under the protection of a faithful and benevolent companion. Significantly, despite all the twentieth-century technology which modernised the Royal Navy's ships and submarines, the memoirs of its veterans suggest that they remained keen to subscribe to the old superstition that their vessel offered benevolent female companionship through the hazards of wartime sea-going. 'Who dares', demanded former stoker Sydney Hart, 'to say a ship is not a sentient thing.'[18] Attribution of a human disposition to these mechanical companions constitutes a core element of the naval veterans' tale. Donald avowed that a ship 'is not just a matter of steel and iron and wood, she has a personality of her own'; likewise, Hughes remarked that HMS *Scylla*, of which he privately thought as his 'Proud Lady', 'seemed to have a personality of her own'.[19] Intriguingly, despite his refusal to accept that the sea possessed a human character of its own, Denys Rayner identified in each of the six wartime ships in which he served 'a character as complex and as interesting as that of a woman.'[20] Like women, these memoirists mused, no two ships were exactly alike in temperament:

Loch Tulla was the diligent nursemaid, who would take me for a nice walk round the islands and bring me back for tea. *Verbena* the busy housewife. *Shikari* the rather raffish thoroughbred of whom my mother would have said 'A very nice girl, but (and you knew the sting was coming) just a little unreliable I always

---

[16] Pieter van der Merwe, 'Ask a Grown-Up: why are boats called she', *The Guardian*, 1 February 2014.

[17] Laurie Churchman suggests that the origins of this practice of referring to vessels in the feminine pronoun date back to ancient Greece. Laurie Churchman, *The Art of Boat Names: Inspiring Ideas for Names and Designs* (New York: International Marine/McGraw-Hill, 2009), p. 10. For further confirmation of the type of salty jokes in which some modern sailors continue to draw parallels between ships and women, see Rear Admiral Francis D. Foley, 'Why We Call A Ship A She', *Naval History*, 12:6 (1998), 43.

[18] Sydney Hart, *Discharged Dead: A True Story of Britain's Submarines at War* (London: Odhams Press, 1956), p. 207.

[19] Donald, *Stand By for Action*, p. 14; Hughes, *Through the Waters*, p. 149.

[20] Rayner, *Escort*, p. 234.

think.' *Warwick* the widowed lady who had once been a girl herself. *Highlander* the best-loved, in the prime of her life.[21]

Discernment of a 'personality' in a naval vessel was not confined to the memoirs of surface ships. Hart lovingly affirmed that his new submarine HMS *Thrasher* was 'As full of whims as a highly-strung woman'.[22] Furthermore, displaying a now familiar insistence that his submarine was 'almost human', former coxswain Charles Anscomb reflected at length on his relationship with HMS *Parthian*. One came to feel, he asserted, that 'she is alive ... with her good and bad humours, her tricks and her tantrums and her loyalty and strength too.'[23]

There is a fascinatingly esoteric suggestion in these narratives that sailors did not believe that a ship was born with her 'personality' inbuilt. Hughes, for example, perceived that HMS *Scylla* had acquired the 'strange quality' that ensnared his affections.[24] Similarly, while inspecting his new command HMS *Storm*, an S-boat in the basin at Cammell Laird shipyard, Edward Young visualised the development of his virgin submarine's persona in the months ahead:

By that time she would have acquired a past and a familiar personality of her own. Now she was still a composite of steel parts, inanimate and separate, not yet co-ordinated to a common purpose. History would not begin for her until the moment she moved in the water under her own power.[25]

These statements offer intriguing insights into how these seamen envisaged the formation of their ship's 'personality'. The verb 'to acquire' is often employed, inferring that an identifiable character was something which a vessel attained over time, rather than something that was specifically congenital. The belief that a ship retained a mortal identity is extended further into the supernatural by the insistence of several memoirists that their vessel possessed not only a persona, but a specific 'soul': an ephemeral core which renders a living entity human. 'I believe firmly', announced Hart, 'that ships have some quality that does not usually belong to inanimate things.'[26] Of being drafted to HMS *Triad*, a T-class submarine laid down in Barrow in 1939, and of the submarine's very first dive, the memoirist perceived that 'she seemed in some indefinable way to have acquired a soul.'[27] Importantly, however, like Young, he located

---

[21] Ibid., pp. 234–5.
[22] Hart, *Discharged Dead*, p. 138.
[23] Charles Anscomb, *Submariner* (London: William Kimber, 1957), p. 105.
[24] Hughes, *Through the Waters*, p. 149.
[25] Young, *One of Our Submarines*, p. 142.
[26] Hart, *Discharged Dead*, p. 206.
[27] Ibid., p. 29.

this development of a human spirit in the process of setting sail, once the vessel and her crew had commenced their professional partnership. The same concept also characterised representations of new surface ships gaining vitality through the unity of man and machine. Of *Scylla*'s Commissioning Day, Hughes wrote that 'The loudspeaker system came to life with the many orders to the ship's company, the bugle rang out at intervals, and the ship began to breathe.'[28]

Perceptions of this 'strange quality' of a human-like mortality were not solely reserved for newly commissioned vessels. Naval memoirists who had joined older ships also related the existence of a communion of spirits in which crew and craft became emotionally fused. Rayner speculated that the origins of his 'special bond' with his elderly V-and-W-class destroyer, HMS *Warwick*, had developed from an arcane connection between the ship and those who had formerly sailed in her. Embodying more than a telling hint of superstition, he wrote that:

the men who have lived in her leave behind either an aura of happiness or the gloom of unhappiness, either of which becomes as much a part of the ship as her own steel structure. *Warwick* had so happy an atmosphere as to be almost startling. As soon as your foot touched her deck you became aware of it. She radiated a human warmth from the whole of her slim figure.[29]

The suggestion here is that a ship drew its personality or 'soul' from the men who crewed her. Running alongside this, however, is also a view that, whilst every vessel was perceived as female, only particular ships retained a firm enough grip upon the memoirist's emotions to be invested with such tropes of humanity. In his perception that *Scylla* was endowed with 'that strange quality which some ships acquire', Hughes articulates that other vessels were unable to possess similar attributes.[30] Further narratives bear out this view. Hart perceived that HMS *Triad* had come to acquire a soul 'like every other ship found worthy', which implies that not every vessel was deemed sufficiently special to have developed this impression of humanity.[31] By these superstitious terms, if a ship carried a crew of men who were ill-fated, ill-disciplined, or simply 'unhappy', that 'strange affection for the ship' could not be forthcoming. These testimonies thus serve to reinforce the concept that a good relationship between a sailor and ship was founded upon equal partnership. If the crew were slack or miserable, they could not contribute to the upkeep and smooth

---

[28] Hughes, *Through the Waters*, p. 15.
[29] Rayner, *Escort*, p. 159.
[30] Hughes, *Through the Waters*, p. 149.
[31] Hart, *Discharged Dead*, p. 29.

running of their female companion, thus upsetting the delicate balance
of reciprocal responsibility for each other's well-being.

Pedantically, of course, any pairing of combatant and machine must
invariably be physically interdependent, yet where the fighter pilot tended
to veil this immutable fact in comforting affirmations of his own individual power, the seamen recognised their partnership as far more equally
weighted. As Noel Coward's character, 'Captain Kinross', in the naval
film, *In Which We Serve* (1942), informed his crew, a 'happy and efficient
ship' was central to the survival of all. Furthermore, he expounded, 'In
my experience, you can't have one without the other.'[32] A 'happy and efficient' relationship between sailor and ship was thus rooted in the acceptance that each was reliant upon the other for its safety. Fundamentally,
as Hampson pointed out, 'A warship at sea is a self-contained unit; you
cannot ring up headquarters for advice or instructions.'[33] Relating the
first night aboard his new command, the anti-submarine trawler *Lady
Madeleine*, Ogden reflected that 'perhaps in no other sphere of war were
men so dependent on one another and upon the ship in which they
served'. 'I did not realize then,' he announced, 'that a ship and her complement are bound together with the ties of life and death'.[34] Expanding
upon this sentiment, Hughes explained that sailors tended to perceive a
special bond with their ship because 'She had shared our dangers and
brought us safe to harbour. She was our home.'[35] As this remark highlights, whilst the connection forged between man and ship had a pragmatic basis in physical mutual reliance, from an emotional perspective
the vessel could be invested with traditionally prized feminine qualities of
nurturing and protecting, providing welcome physical and psychological
succour for the crew. In Kipling's early twentieth-century writings about
the Royal Navy, Mary Conley suggests that the author transformed the
ship into a site of female 'arousal in need of manly control.'[36] There is
little such overtly sexualised imagery in the Second World War naval
veterans' tale, however. Connotations of security and shelter therefore
served to amplify, and romanticise, the seaman's emotional response to
his ship into something which resembles the bonds of reciprocal love
that knot together successful matrimony, testifying to the old naval saw
that seamen were 'married' to their vessels due to the length of time
they spent together and the experiences they shared on their voyage.

[32] *In Which We Serve*, directed by Noel Coward and David Lean (British Lion Film, 1942).
[33] Hampson, *Not Really What You'd Call a War*, p. 31.
[34] Ogden, *My Sea Lady*, p. 19.
[35] Hughes, *Through the Waters*, p. 149
[36] Mary A. Conley, *From Jack Tar to Union Jack: Representing Naval Manhood in the British
Empire*, 1870–1918 (Manchester: Manchester University Press, 2009), p. 148.

Mutual respect, rather than sexual domination, is the key image in these memoirs. Indeed, the ways in which these men tapped into centuries of seafaring folklore and invoked the reassuring qualities of protectiveness, nurturing, and love which might be found in a good spouse suggest that the naval veteran viewed the unique partnership with his machine as something akin to a treasured romantic affair. Several memoirists even discussed being parted from their ship in a manner which is more akin to the ending of a love affair. For example, Hart described leaving HMS *Truant* as 'like having a leg cut off. Only a man who has grown deeply attached to a ship can understand the loneliness of a separation from her.'[37] Similarly, separated from his beloved HMS *Parthian*, Anscomb was singularly unimpressed when he joined HMS *Tempest* in October 1941, noting bitterly that 'my old love had died hard.'[38] A curious form of spiritual romance is thus woven into the seaman's narrative representations of his wartime relationship with his ship. Whilst not all ships engendered the same levels of 'strange affection' in their crew, the intimate connection that many sailors experienced with their vessels is revealingly depicted in a romantic mixture of superstitious and affectionate tropes. Macintyre's description of HMS *Hearty* in January 1940 encapsulates the naval memoirists' romanticisation of the partnership between man and machine. This, he announced, was 'the ship that I knew I could lose my heart to.'[39]

The Flyers' Tale: Fighter Command and the Battle of Britain, 1940

High above the unforgiving waters of the 'cruel sea', a somewhat different, albeit equally romanticised, relationship unfolded between the airmen and their machines. By the beginning of July 1940, 754 British Hawker Hurricanes and Supermarine Spitfires were pitted against 1,464 Luftwaffe fighter aircraft and 1,808 bombers.[40] Fought over the south-east of England during the summer of 1940, the Battle of Britain was etched into British culture and remembrance as an iconic event in the military narrative of the Second World War. The aircraft of Fighter Command became almost as adored national treasures as their highly fêted pilots. Rarely have the machines of war been so entrenched in the affections of combatant and public alike, and the British public's love

[37] Hart, *Discharged Dead*, p. 128.
[38] Anscomb, *Submariner*, p. 106.
[39] Macintyre, *U-Boat Killer*, p. 10. Later renamed HMS *Hesperus*.
[40] Stephen Bungay, *The Most Dangerous Enemy: A History of the Battle of Britain* (London: Aurum Press, 2000), p. 107.

affair with the Hurricane and the Spitfire continued for another seventy years. The devotion these machines inspired in their aircrew proved equally enduring. Indeed, the intensity of fondness which the Hurricane and Spitfire unleashed in 'the Few' compelled Richard Hillary's so-called 'inarticulate' breed of aerial warriors to lyricize about their aeroplanes in an intimate discourse which irradiates their memoirs.[41] Strikingly, the relationship forged between these aircraft and their flyers does not appear in any other type of fighter narratives. For example, one Beaufighter Mark II pilot described his machine as 'downright evil', noting that it 'seemed to breathe an air of malevolence'.[42] Similarly, Richard Hough, a Battle of Britain veteran who wove his personal recollections throughout a scholarly account of 1940, described his later experiences of flying the Typhoon in less than glowing terms: 'I never loved her ... One reached an armed truce, an understanding brought about by a balance of terror.'[43] In his history of the Battle of Britain, Stephen Bungay supposes that the peculiar bond of 'the Few' with their aircraft was forged out of 'the power eros'.[44] Yet the love of the fighter pilot for his machine, as it is mediated through these narratives, appears forged less by sensual sentiment than by a somewhat egocentric desire for personal possession and control. Thus far, some scholars have demonstrated an understandable tendency to focus upon the ways in which aircrew – Spitfire pilots in particular – represented their aircraft in gendered terms of beauty and femininity.[45] Such identification of a gendered element to the flyer's rapport with his aircraft, however, constitutes only a minor element of the complex relationship between Fighter Command's men and machines during Britain's 'finest hour'.

The physical connection of man and machine provided a basis for the development of an intense emotional bond. For example, due to the 'snugness' of the cockpit, WGG Duncan Smith remarked that he felt 'part of the Spitfire, a oneness that was intimate.'[46] For tall, broadly built men like Tim Vigors and 'Johnnie' Johnson, the sensation of physical closeness to their machine was further increased by their shoulders rubbing up against the fuselage.[47] Although Hurricane pilots benefitted

[41] Richard Hillary, The Last Enemy, rev. ed. (London: Pimlico, 1997), p. 43.
[42] Graham White, The Long Road to the Sky: Night Fighter over Germany (Barnsley: Pen & Sword Aviation, 2006), p. 6.
[43] Richard Hough and Denis Richards, The Battle of Britain: The Jubilee History (London: Hodder & Stoughton, 1989), p. 96.
[44] Bungay, The Most Dangerous Enemy, p. 82.
[45] Francis, The Flyer; Bungay, The Most Dangerous Enemy.
[46] W. G. G. Duncan Smith, Spitfire into Battle, rev. ed. (London: John Murray, 2002), p. 22.
[47] Tim Vigors, Life's Too Short to Cry: The Compelling Memoir of a Battle of Britain Ace (London: Grub Street, 2006), p. 136; Johnson, Wing Leader, p. 26.

from a more spacious cockpit, a similar sense of literal fusion between man and machine was also apparent. Drawing upon a survey of various fictional and non-fictional literary sources which documented this affinity, Martin Francis's study of the RAF and wartime British culture recognises a strong 'sense of flyer and aircraft becoming a single, merged entity.'[48] His interpretation of this unified 'entity' suggests that the man became subsumed by the machine: 'the mechanization of the flyer's body appeared so advanced that human presence in the aircraft had been erased completely'.[49] Yet the corpus of fighter pilot memoirs reviewed here testifies that the opposite was true and that some delicate resetting of this viewpoint is required. The case for this adjustment is made by Smith's claim that 'you buckled the Spitfire on', an observation also made by former sergeant pilot Bill Rolls, who noted that the aircraft felt 'as though you had it strapped on you'.[50] Rather than the body of the flyer becoming 'mechanised', therefore, these men thought that the balance of power in fact lay the other way around, perceiving the aircraft as an appendage of the pilot. Indeed, Smith's remark that 'the Spitfire became an integral part and an extension of one's own sensitivity' highlights the fact that the flyer's relationship with his aeroplane was shaped by dynamics of power, and both he and Rolls proffer a delicate reminder that, ultimately, the machine was responsive to the pilot's own will.[51]

It was, however, a common aircrew perception that their aircraft harboured animate qualities, and like the naval authors, flyer memoirists often insisted outright upon the sentience of their machines. Tom Neil, for example, roundly declared that his aircraft was 'alive!'[52] Investing 92 Squadron's Spitfires with the mortal essence of human beings, Geoffrey Wellum announced that they 'live just like the rest of us, they understand.'[53] Others conveyed their machine's imagined vitality through the conference of personal pronouns and stereotypical gender roles upon their aircraft. The Spitfire, in particular, was commonly envisaged as ineffably female. With its fluid lines, narrow fuselage, elliptical wing, and the jaunty angle of its nose, the aircraft seemed to Hough 'essentially a feminine machine, dainty, provocative, not always predictable.'[54] Merton Naydler, a Spitfire pilot who flew with the Desert Air Force in North Africa, concurred, observing that this aircraft was 'a feminine-looking

[48] Francis, *The Flyer*, p. 166.
[49] Ibid., p. 166.
[50] Smith, *Spitfire into Battle*, p. 86; Rolls, Spitfire Attack, p. 22.
[51] Smith, *Spitfire into Battle*, p. 86.
[52] Neil, *Gun Button to Fire*, p. 40.
[53] Wellum, *First Light*, p. 145.
[54] Hough and Richards, *The Battle of Britain*, p. 92.

little plane, and as deadly as any female of the species.'[55] Notably, these testimonies are based upon its performance in addition to its appearance. Hubert Allen, for instance, ruminated that 'In certain of her mannerisms she was nearly as awful a bitch as the loveliest woman I ever met.'[56] Through this lexis, the design faults of the early models of Spitfires, such as overly sensitive controls, poor vision to the rear, and an inadequate battery of weaponry, could be disguised as quirks of a distinctive character, lending further weight to the illusion that the aircraft possessed cognisance.

The full nature of the fighter pilot's emotional connection to his aircraft is, however, illustrated less through gendered symbolism than by a distinctive iconography which cemented the notion of the aircraft as a living creature. The majority of Battle of Britain memoirists turned to the animal kingdom in search of suitable imagery to craft this representation. Perhaps surprisingly, obvious ornithological sources of inspiration were little tapped. Smith's allusion to his Spitfire as a 'golden eagle' provides almost the sole example of a flyer likening his aircraft to the birds of the air.[57] Instead, these pilots typically imagined their machines in either equine or canine terms. Innate differences in aesthetics and combat performance between the Spitfire and Hurricane, however, resulted in a marked disparity in the type of breeds to which these machines were likened. The two types of aircraft were frequently compared against each other, with the veteran drawing upon these animal references as a device for parading the comparative attributes of each type of machine. Allen, for example, acerbically announced that the Spitfire represented 'a race-horse where the Hurricane was a hack.'[58] Naturally, Allen was a Spitfire pilot. Pilots of the 'Hurry', however, were just as quick to praise their aircraft. Geoffrey Page, who had been transferred from a Spitfire squadron to fly Hurricanes in the Battle of Britain, commented that 'whereas the Spitfire had all the speed and grace of the greyhound in its sleek appearance, the Hurricane portrayed the excellent qualities of the bulldog, being slower but much more solidly built than the other.'[59] Similarly, when his squadron was refitted with Hurricanes in June 1940, Neil was placed in a prime position to compare his new machine with his

---

[55] Merton Naydler, *Young Man You'll Never Die* (Barnsley: Pen & Sword Aviation, 2005), p. 24.
[56] H. R. Allen, *Battle for Britain: The Recollections of H. R. 'Dizzy' Allen DFC* (London: Arthur Barker Ltd, 1973), p. 11.
[57] Smith, *Spitfire into Battle*, p. 10.
[58] Allen, *Battle for Britain*, p. 11.
[59] Page, *Shot Down in Flames*, p. 30.

former Spitfire. In general, he mused, 'we were not disappointed. While it may not have had the refinements of a Spit, our recent acquisition was rock-solid and possessed of an obvious ruggedness and strength. No shrinking violet, this!'[60] With its thickset structure, the Hurricane provided a steady gun platform and Neil correspondingly perceived that in the air its pilot detected a 'feeling of steadiness' in his aircraft, a 'no-nonsense' manner, which the Spitfire lacked.[61] This led him to affectionately describe 'the old Hurricane' as 'strong as a carthorse' in low altitude clashes with bombers, where the fighter operated at its best at around 15,000 feet.[62]

The Spitfire, however, so its pilots asserted, was simply 'in a different class.'[63] If the Hurricane constituted the workhorse of Fighter Command, the Spitfire was bred for speed and pleasure. After learning to fly on cumbersome training aircraft, Tony Bartley was agreeably surprised by the speed of the Spitfire, drawing the same analogy as Allen that this aircraft constituted a 'racehorse' whereas other aircraft, including the Hurricane, were firmly relegated to the 'hack' category.[64] In terms of eye-catching aesthetics and the responsiveness of the way it handled in combat, the Spitfire appeared to embody high-class bloodlines. Indeed, Johnson, Vigors, and Wellum articulated a firm opinion that the aircraft manifested all the attributes of a 'thoroughbred', with the latter positing that his Spitfire waited for take-off 'trembling' like a pedigree racehorse 'at the start of the Derby.'[65] In some respects, the Spitfire narratives read almost like a personal bloodsport between elite British and German fighter aircraft in 1940. As Alfred Price notes in his history of the Spitfire, differences in performance and handling between the top British and German machines were marginal, and in combat it was frequently the pilot's own grasp of tactical considerations that normally dictated survival.[66] A pilot's survival largely depended upon a detailed knowledge of how both types of plane would react in combat situations. For instance, although machine guns synchronised to fire through the propeller arcs made it a formidable adversary when met in head-on combat, or dived upon, the dangerous Messerschmitt Bf.109 (Me. 109) had a particular weakness. Hampered by higher wing loadings, this aircraft could be out-turned by the Spitfire Mark I, the predominant model of 1940, which

[60] Neil, *Gun Button to 'Fire'*, p. 40.
[61] Ibid., p. 39.
[62] Ibid., p. 86.
[63] Allen, *Battle for Britain*, p. 11.
[64] Bartley, *Smoke Trails in the Sky*, p. 9; Allen, *Battle for Britain*, p. 11.
[65] Wellum, *First Light*, p. 138.
[66] Alfred Price, *The Spitfire Story*, rev. ed. (London: Arms and Armour, 1999), p. 78.

was particularly suited to tight evasive manoeuvres. The superior aerodynamics of its elliptical wing, and the sensitivity of its controls, meant that the Spitfire possessed the ability to confront the lethal German fighter on more or less equal terms, with good odds of victory. This state of affairs is consequently reflected in the choice of simile which the Spitfire pilots selected to represent their machine, as the connection of this aircraft to thoroughbreds and greyhounds, bred for the specific purpose of winning, irrevocably bound the Spitfire up with key associations of being a champion.

Greyhounds or bulldogs, thoroughbreds or carthorses, these allusions all combine to produce a discrete discourse with which the fighter pilot memoirist deliberately invested his aircraft. With the whole spectrum of the animal kingdom available to choose comparisons from, it is notable that the majority of these authors opted for dogs or horses. Since both of these animals are traditionally faithful companions of man, the decision to represent their aircraft in these terms indicates that the memoirists viewed their machines in much the same light. Hough, for instance, described the rapport with his Hurricane as like a 'man-and-working-dog relationship.'[67] Further illumination upon the depth of this connection is cast by Neil, who reflected that 'I felt about aircraft much as I had done about my old dog... a combination of loyalty and love. Silly, really, but it was a genuine and deep-seated emotion.'[68] These choices of imagery to communicate the fashioning of this bond might be further explained as evidence of the flyer's unceasing struggle to dampen ubiquitous combat fears. On the ground, a fighter squadron was, as Neil wrote, 'very much a close-knit family affair', yet the fighter pilot's experience as a combatant was largely solitary.[69] Although members of a squadron endeavoured to protect each other in the air as far as possible, Roger Hall explained that, 'In the middle of an aerial fight you were really your own master'.[70] Once in the cockpit, therefore, the flyer's spatial detachment from his fellow pilots meant that self-reliance was the key to survival, a fact which elicited trepidation as well as excitement in the fighter pilot. When his squadron was scrambled, Smith explained that 'for all the nearness each one of them was as remote as a star.'[71] Bartley also declared that 'One of the unique and most alarming experiences in one's life must surely be to find oneself alone in an aeroplane for the very first time, completely dependent

[67] Hough and Richards, *The Battle of Britain*, p. 84.
[68] Neil, *Gun Button to 'Fire'*, p. 145.
[69] Ibid., p. 28.
[70] Hall, *Clouds of Fear*, p. 40.
[71] Smith, *Spitfire into Battle*, p. 46.

upon oneself to get back to mother earth.'[72] He too reflected at length that the airborne pilot experienced intense feelings of isolation: 'Air combat was a personal, individual challenge, because we fought alone... We had no comrades marching shoulder to shoulder. No pipes or drums, and the loneliness was sometimes more frightening than the bullets.'[73] In these accounts the investment of aircraft with stereotypical equine and canine qualities implies, therefore, that the author interpreted his machine as a vital source of companionship when he was airborne.

Furthermore, the flyers' choice of imagery to represent their aircraft also underlines an entrenched desire for individual control over all aspects of combat. To this end, the selection of dogs and horses as symbols of their aeroplanes underscores a significant imbalance in the dynamics of power in this relationship between man and machine. By imagining the aircraft as a working animal, the flyer could invest it with the reassuring character and responsiveness of a living companion. By the same token, however, the flyer could establish himself as the superior partner in this relationship. Tethered to the canine and equine tropes – in particular the latter – is an overt lexis of private control which articulates the pilot's urge to exert a sense of personal dominance over his machine. Depictions of the fighter pilot becoming the 'master' of his 'mettlesome' aerial mount abound in these narratives.[74] For example, Wellum remarked of his Spitfire that it appeared to have the demeanour of a 'horse watching the approach of a new and unknown rider and wondering just how far to try it on and generally be bloody minded.'[75] Similarly, Neil mused that his aircraft seemed to be 'pulling hard like a wayward horse' which he subsequently 'reined in'.[76] Johnson too explained that upon taking off 'it was time to take a firm hand with this little thoroughbred, for so far she had been the dominant partner in our enterprise.'[77] These assertions of the fighter pilot's supremacy over his machine might be construed as a further response to the fears generated by combat. Among aircrew of both Fighter and Bomber Command, it has been recognised that such fears 'often had more to do with the presence or absence of personal agency than with an objectively defined degree of danger.'[78] The memoirs of the former

---

[72] Bartley, *Smoke Trails in the Sky*, p. 9.
[73] Ibid., p. 59.
[74] Neil, *Gun Button to 'Fire'*, p. 33.
[75] Wellum, *First Light*, p. 101.
[76] Neil, *Gun Button to 'Fire'*, p. 32.
[77] Johnson, *Wing Leader*, p. 27.
[78] Francis, *The Flyer*, p. 113.

certainly suggest that their isolated position in sole command of fast, manoeuvrable aircraft allowed them to subscribe to a heartening myth that they were in full control of their own fate. In particular, the frequent depiction of aeroplanes as horses in these narratives echoes DH Lawrence's description of that animal as 'the symbol of surging potency and power of movement, of action, in man.'[79] In representing his relationship with his aircraft in such terms of dominance, therefore, the former fighter pilot's expressions of determination to 'master' his mechanical mount might be interpreted as assertions of 'personal agency' that helped to calm his anxieties about battle.

The fighter pilot's emotional attachment to his aircraft, as it is reconstructed in the veterans' tale, was thus founded upon a blend of intimate tactical mastery of the machine that varnished a valuable veneer of individual agency over his performance in combat. Yet like the sailors, these veterans remained cognisant that their beloved machine could instantaneously morph into a death trap. The greatest fear of the fighter pilot was always the risk of fire in the air. Spitfire and Hurricane pilots sat behind eighty-five gallons of 100 octane fuel, which ignited to thousands of degrees within a few seconds.[80] The latter were especially vulnerable, since the Hurricane's reserve fuel tank was housed directly in front of the dashboard. As Neil recorded, these aircraft could also catch fire particularly quickly due to a lack of 'blanking plates' between the wings and the fuselage, meaning that the natural draught pattern therefore speedily drew the blazing fuel from a ruptured wing tank into the cockpit.[81] The veteran recounted that 'lurid tales of dashboards melting and running like treacle' were in constant circulation around his squadron.[82] Upon catching fire, the pilot only had seconds to bale out of the conflagration that rapidly consumed the cockpit. Yet opening the cockpit hood to escape could have the fatal effect of sucking the flames back into the pilot's face. Pilots were ill-equipped to face such ferocious infernos, lacking flame-retardant suits, and being provided with goggles whose rubber straps easily melted.[83] Hillary provides the most famous example of a pilot who suffered the effects of the latter in a particularly horrific fashion. His oxygen mask was a variant on a Type D mask made with a fabric outer and a chamois lining. Because this mask did not form a seal to his face, when he inhaled, the continuous flow of oxygen drew

---

[79] D. H. Lawrence, *Apocalypse and the Writings on Revelation*, (ed.) Mara Kalnins (Cambridge: Cambridge University Press, 2002), p. 102.
[80] Bungay, *The Most Dangerous Enemy*, pp. 176-7.
[81] Neil, *Gun-Button to 'Fire'*, p. 92.
[82] Ibid., p. 92.
[83] Bungay, *The Most Dangerous Enemy*, pp. 176-7.

the flames inexorably inwards.[84] Page was also badly burnt during the Battle of Britain when he received a direct shot to his engine. Surprise gave way to terror when the fuel tank blew up and the cockpit of his Hurricane ignited into flames: 'the bare skin of my hands gripping the throttle and control column shrivelled up like burnt parchment under the intensity of the blast furnace temperature.'[85] Both memoirists were hospitalised for many months undergoing painful reconstructive surgery. Pilots who were fortunate enough to avoid this experience retained an equally strong terror of fire, partially sustained by the dreadful evidence of the injuries sustained by fellow aircrew. After meeting Hillary at East Grinstead Hospital, Smith reflected that 'to be wounded is one thing, but to be burnt to a frazzle is a sacrifice that cannot ever be repaired.'[86] During the war an estimated 4,500 allied airmen suffered serious burns.[87] Although the majority of these were bomber aircrew who sustained injuries in the latter years of the war, the veterans' tale indicates that the prospect of fire haunted the fighter pilot's experience and memories of combat.

Nevertheless, witnessing or experiencing these horrors did not dent the ex-fighter pilot's staunch affection for his aircraft. It stands testament to the strength of the emotional bond between man and machine in this context that such joy in the experience of flying the Hurricane and Spitfire still pours out of the veterans' memoirs. Significantly, KW Mackenzie referred to the Hurricanes of 501 Squadron as 'trusty steeds', a description which conveys all the qualities of faithfulness, reliability, and personal control that the flyer clearly sought from his machine.[88] This phrase, however, also serves to inject a spice of chivalric romance into the heated aerial clashes of 1940. On the whole, the 'Knights of the Air' discourse which has become so attached to popular and some scholarly understandings of 'the Few', is conspicuous by its absence in Battle of Britain personal memoirs. Yet, as Mackenzie's association of the term 'steeds' with Fighter Command's aircraft illustrates, it is through the flyer's relationship with his machine that a faint tint of knightly combat colours these literary representations of battle. Samuel Hynes, perhaps speaking in his own capacity as veteran combat pilot-turned-literary-critic-turned-war memoirist, recognises in the

---

[84] David Ross, *Richard Hillary: The Definitive Biography of a Battle of Britain Fighter Pilot and Author of the 'The Last Enemy'* (London: Grub Street, 2000), p. 125.
[85] Page, *Shot Down in Flames*, p. 74.
[86] Smith, *Spitfire into Battle*, p. 55.
[87] Francis, *The Flyer*, p. 138.
[88] K. W. Mackenzie, *Hurricane Combat: The Nine Lives of a Fighter Pilot* (London: William Kimber, 1987), p. 57.

relationship a flyer developed with his aircraft an irresistible allure of finding ancient martial romance. After the industrialised mass slaughter of the Western Front during the First World War, he claims, an individual's ability to control his movements in battle 'restored' the combatant's enjoyment of war.[89] This, however, is quite a generalisation, and the narratives of 'the Few' actually show very little inclination to romanticise their battles, as the following chapter's discussion of their uneasy representations of killing demonstrates. But it is certainly fair to state that these texts corroborate to some extent Hynes' declaration that, in these machines, 'men could once more take pleasure in the dangers they faced, because they could choose what action they took against them.'[90] Arguably, therefore, the nature of the loyal and companionable working partnership constructed between aircraft and pilot allowed the latter a rare chance to indulge in an element of rose-tinted self-deception. By imagining his aeroplane as a 'trusty steed', he could harness a nostalgic glimmer of romance to his battles as one of the nation's airborne champions.

The Tanks' Tale: Armour and the Normandy Campaign, 1944

In his military history of six armies doing battle in Normandy during the summer of 1944, John Keegan mused that some armour crews thought 'with gratitude of the tank as an old friend' which had absorbed considerable punishment on their behalf and survived.[91] The veterans' tale of armour during the Normandy campaign tells a wholly different story, however, in which if such instances of affection for the tank had indeed existed, they were excised from the collective published narrative. Amid the rubble of the pulverised northern French landscape, the relationship of tank and 'tankie' is depicted as sour and singularly lacking in pretensions to romance of any kind. The combined natures of the tactical operating environment and the machines themselves served to strip the tanks' war of any claim to martial romance during the push to reclaim Europe after D-Day. Lacking the reassuring fantasy that characterised the emotive relationships of sailors and ships or fighter pilots and aircrew, the dominant representation of the armoured combatant's mood towards his machine is one of dour pragmatism. Some indication of the overall joylessness of this relationship is proffered by tank commander

---

[89] Hynes, *The Soldiers' Tale*, p. 123.
[90] Ibid., p. 123.
[91] John Keegan, *Six Armies in Normandy: From D-Day to the Liberation of Paris June 6th–August 25th, 1944* (London: Jonathan Cape, 1982), p. 199.

Ken Tout, who described the sensation of dropping through the hatch into his Sherman M4 as becoming suddenly 'subterranean. Death beetles inside a steel wall. Mobile troglodytes.'[92] Immediately, the experience of tank crew is set up as dark, primitive, and somewhat hapless, a notion to which Tout's fellow veteran-memoirists wholeheartedly subscribed. Devoid of the individual myths of personal agency which comforted the fighter pilots, or the superstitious, tender co-dependency that underpinned the sailor's connection with his ship, the tale of the tank thus reveals an entirely different facet of the partnership of men and machines during the Second World War.

The high attrition rate of armour and crews throughout the fighting in Normandy between June and September 1944 provides some explanation of why these veterans did not represent the tank in the same fond terminology as their counterparts in Fighter Command or the Navy. Collectively, narratives of the tank war in Normandy relate a story in which casualties and shortages resulted in the constant reshuffling of crews and vehicles. The general interchangeability of armoured men and machines was illustrated by Bill Close, who had his eleventh tank destroyed underneath him three weeks before the end of the war in Europe. Similarly, Tout arrived with the 1st Northamptonshire Yeomanry in Normandy on 15 June as commander of a light Stuart tank. Within a fortnight he was appointed as gunner to the crew of a Sherman, and by early August had been transferred again, this time as a specialist gunner to operate the 17-pound gun of a Sherman Firefly. That such itinerancy offered little time to bond with a machine is further suggested by the veterans' revealing overall lack of attachment of names or personal pronouns to their descriptions of going into action with their tanks. Armoured vehicles did generally carry names although tank naming conventions depended upon individual battalions. Within a battalion, each squadron was assigned a letter of the alphabet. The names of individual tanks within a squadron's troops were then grouped around a specific theme such as geographical features or places. For example, the tanks of 3 Troop, C Squadron, 1st Northamptonshire Yeomanry, were named after towns in Northamptonshire that began with the letter 'H'. Accordingly, the troop leader's machine was named 'Helmdon', whilst Tout's tank bore the name of 'Hellidon'.[93] Throughout all the editions of Tout's narrative, however, this is the only mention of the fact that his vehicle even possessed a name. Mostly, he refers to his machines

---

[92] Tout, *Tank!*, p. 43.
[93] Ken Tout, *By Tank: D to VE Days* (London: Robert Hale, 2010), p. 16. This is the third, revised, edition of *Tank!*, first published in 1985. In action, however, his tank was referred to only by its wireless code name of '3 Baker.'

impersonally as 'the tank' or 'the Sherman'. This follows a distinctive pattern in the memoirs of former tank crew, in which we are often granted a glimpse of the tank's identity during the veteran's relation of the commencement of landing in Normandy, but thereafter the machine tends to be referred to as simply 'the tank' or 'the Churchill', etc. One has to scrutinise their narratives very closely to learn that Bill Bellamy's Cromwell was named 'Abbot of Chantry', or that Stuart Hills' Sherman bore the unusual appellation of 'Bardin Collos'.[94] According to Hills' co-driver, 'Bardin Collos' translated as an Arabic term that suggested the tank would inevitably become a casualty. Ultimately it drowned whilst attempting to land on the beaches of Normandy. Given this tank's watery fate, its name carried some prescience. The untimely demise of 'Bardin Collos' certainly explains why this machine disappears from the narrative, but it is significant that thereafter Hills does not refer to his replacement tank by name. Like Tout, his vehicle simply becomes 'the Sherman'. This pattern suggests that, whilst the assigned names of tanks seemed important at the outset of the memoirist's war experiences, by the time he had joined battle the personal meaning derived from the name attached to the tank became less significant as the imperatives of survival began to dominate the martial partnership of man and armour in Normandy. Indeed, John Foley's memoir of commanding 5 Troop, A Squadron, 5th Battalion, King's Own Royal Regiment of Lancashire, which comprised of three Churchills named *Avenger*, *Alert*, and *Angler*, offers further insight into the lack of significance ascribed to the names attached to tanks. Shortly after landing, he received a number of visitors from other armoured regiments who were quick to point out the dangers of serving in a tank that had its identity emblazoned on its hull:

They explained with relish just how easily a German 88 millimeter gun could penetrate the front of a Churchill, and they dictatorially advised us to paint out the names on our tanks.[95]

Whilst deploring what he interpreted as his visitors' 'air of pompous superiority', Foley reluctantly acknowledged that in hindsight this advice had been correct:

Looking back on it they were quite right, of course. Our tank names were painted in large, yellow letters bright enough to be seen ten miles away by any enemy gunner whose pay book wasn't in Braille.[96]

---

[94] Bill Bellamy, *Troop Leader: A Tank Commander's Story* (Stroud: Sutton Publishing, 2005), p. 71; Hills, *By Tank into Normandy*, p. 73.
[95] Cedric John Foley, *Mailed Fist: With A Tank Troop Through Europe* (London: Panther Books, 1957), p. 51.
[96] Ibid., pp. 51–2.

Although he remained unhappy about removing these individual mark-
ers of identity from his vehicle – there 'seemed to be something slightly
shameful about painting out those names; rather like "casting away
his arms in the face of the enemy"' – his account of this affair underscores that depersonalisation of the tank had a pragmatic basis in sheer
survival.[97]

The distinct lack of fondness with which tanks in Normandy are represented in the veteran memoirs was also critically moulded by several
other factors. To some extent, the brittle relationship of tank crew and
armour may be interpreted as a product of the unsatisfactory combat
setting in which these men found themselves. Frequently, the desert war
is invoked in these narratives as a golden era of tank warfare, thanks to
its provision of seemingly limitless space in which armour could move
with speed, independence, and grace. By 1941, British cavalry regiments
had all been mechanised, but associations with the ethos and lineage
of elite horsed regiments lent armour in the desert a similar lustre of
knightly romance to that with which the fighter pilots' performance in
the Battle of Britain was glossed. Ray Ward, who was appointed to serve
on Montgomery's bodyguard for three months, recalled that even in late
1942, tank commanders 'still tended to be the types who spoke the lingo of
the Light Brigade', recalling that Montgomery's personal tank was always
referred to as 'the army commander's charger'.[98] As one of the earliest,
and best-known, memoirists of the tank war in the desert, Keith Douglas
represented his own senior officers of the Nottinghamshire Sherwood
Rangers Yeomanry in the mould of the class of gentleman officers who
had led British horsed regiments for centuries.[99] Such depictions of tank
crew as a modern generation of armoured horsemen are notably lacking,
however, in the veterans' tale of armour in Normandy, 1944. Similarly,
descriptions of manoeuvres that echo Douglas' portrayal of a return to
traditional cavalry tactics in the Western Desert – the regiment 'wheeled
and halted' and 'We continued to move across the plain at top speed,
and in high glee, elated with all the excitement of the hunt' – find no
place in the memoirs of Normandy.[100] Nor, to be just, do they find much
expression in other narratives of desert veterans, who eschewed any
such shades of martial romance in their portrayal of armoured warfare
between 1940 and 1943. For example, Bill Close, Rea Leakey, and Peter
Roach relate an infinitely more pragmatic tale of dust, heat, sand sores,
flies, sand storms, fuel shortages, and the horrors of burnt-out tanks, all

---

[97] Ibid., p. 52.
[98] Ward, *The Mirror of Monte Cavallara*, p. 167.
[99] Keith Douglas, *Alamein to Zem Zem* (London: Editions Poetry, 1946), p. 156.
[100] Ibid., p. 45; p. 60.

of which were mitigated in Douglas' memoir by his undimmed enthusiasm for soldiering. According to Hynes' interpretation of *Alamein to Zem Zem*, martial romance was restored to the mechanised war in the desert in response to a clear 'joy in the freedom of movement' in a battle space that allowed armies the liberty to 'manoeuvre, charge and withdraw'.[101] Again, however, 'this charging business' as one diarist of the desert war sardonically referred to the tactic of throwing armour at an enemy position, was actually met with considerable scepticism by tank crews in North Africa.[102] As historian David French points out, the propensity of armoured regiments to 'charge' German positions and anti-tank guns in the desert actually owed little to commanding officers of armour fancying themselves as modern-day incarnations of the horsed cavalry, and everything to interwar doctrine that placed excessive reliance upon tanks alone to mount inadequately supported attacks on German anti-tank screens.[103] The impalement, and subsequent disembowelment, of the tanks of the 2nd, 4th, and 22nd Armoured Brigades under just such circumstances in June 1942, effectively removed any illusions of glory that could be attached to the tanks' desert war.[104] Tellingly, despite his own subscription to the myth of the desert war, upon being shown around the inside of a Grant tank, Ward was repelled by the cramped, dark interior: 'They were death-traps when hit. I envied the tankies' courage but not their occupation. If this was how the modern cavalry went to war, it was not romantic. After that, I never complained about joining an infantry regiment.'[105]

Nevertheless, despite the fact that memoirists of tank warfare in the desert generally showed little inclination to perceive themselves as armoured knights, armoured veterans of Normandy clearly imagined the desert war as the heyday of the tank, invoking the myth of the desert as a means of magnifying the miseries of their own operating environment in 1944. Peter Roach's memoir set up a revealing tension between the prized 'privacy' of the desert and the comparative lack of seclusion in Normandy:

Fighting a war on the threshold of Europe and a stone's throw from England was horrible. No longer could we get quietly on with the job, governed by the dictates of war, but now there was a constant pressure brought by the hordes of

---

[101] Hynes, *The Soldiers' Tale*, p. 140; p. 141.
[102] George Forty (ed.), *Tanks Across the Desert: The War Diary of Jake Wardrop*, rev. ed. (Stroud: Sutton Publishing, 2003), pp. 33–4.
[103] David French, *Raising Churchill's Army: The British Army and the War against Germany 1919–1945* (Oxford: Oxford University Press, 2000), p. 222.
[104] Ibid., p. 222.
[105] Ward, *The Mirror of Monte Cavallara*, pp. 167–8.

journalists, politicians and hangers-on which distorted the job. To ask men to go and die is accepted as reasonable if a country feels itself seriously threatened, but to ask them to die in public is nothing short of barbaric.[106]

Another memoirist of both campaigns, Bill Close, recorded that the confined countryside in Normandy caused much perturbation, not least to his own troop sergeant: 'Like many desert veterans, Geordie felt uneasy in this land of small fields and wooded areas'.[107] Commissioned into the Nottinghamshire Sherwood Rangers Yeomanry in January 1944, Stuart Hills had no personal experience of action in the desert with which to compare service in Normandy, but he too observed:

How some of our desert veterans longed for the open spaces of Libya and Tunisia, where tanks could manoeuvre and fight an altogether different type of battle to this close-range slugging match of attrition in which they were now involved, but we had little option and had to endure in our turn … In rolling desert, where attacking or defending tanks remained hull-down and invisible in small depressions, there were advantages for both sides.[108]

As Hills further noted, the landscape thus granted no favours whatsoever to the attacking British: 'The bocage could be turned into a veritable fortress, and indeed it was.'[109]

British armour found itself fighting in the close terrain of Normandy for far longer than had been anticipated, with dreadful consequences.[110] Plans for the invasion of Normandy had hinged upon deep thrusts by Allied armoured columns which would strike south to capture and secure Caen by 10 June. The Germans took advantage of the Allies' inability to carry out this plan within the allotted time, digging their defensive positions deep into the Normandy countryside. Rather than the swift, deadly strike anticipated, therefore, the campaign in Normandy became a crushing war of attrition conducted at close quarters. The seams of hedges and sunken lanes that criss-crossed the landscape robbed the tank of its speed and mobility. Frequently, tanks suffered the indignity and vulnerability of becoming hedgebound, stuck in ditches, or wedged in tight lanes. This problematic terrain did little to endear tank warfare to armour crews, who waged a continuous struggle against landscape. On paper, Charles Farrell of the 3rd Battalion, Scots Guards, thought that it ought to be possible to deploy the Churchill's cross-country abilities to position it in places where it could not easily be seen by the enemy, such

---

[106] Roach, *The 8.15 to War*, pp. 142–3.
[107] Close, *Tank Commander*, p. 109.
[108] Hills, *By Tank into Normandy*, p. 102.
[109] Ibid., p. 100.
[110] John Buckley, *British Armour in the Normandy Campaign 1944* (New York: Routledge, 2004), p. 86.

as up against the side of a barn or haystack, or at the junction of a high hedge. In reality, he reflected, this tactic was 'easy to preach' but 'fiendishly difficult to put into practice in battle.'[111] Hills, too, noted that the bocage therefore posed 'unfamiliar and disconcerting problems, even for the most experienced crews', and armour was painfully forced to learn a whole new set of operating lessons.[112]

The terrain in Normandy also bestowed a further indignity that illuminates the tank veterans' lack of fondness for their machines. The enforced close fighting of the bocage left tanks highly vulnerable to marauding German infantrymen. Hidden behind the numerous hedgerows or in the thick woodlands of this countryside, a single well-placed enemy soldier carrying an anti-tank weapon could skulk in wait for the tanks, which could rarely prevent or even detect his presence until it was too late. The German Panzerfaust posed a considerable threat, as it was both cheap to produce and easy for a single soldier to carry.[113] Although historian John Buckley has suggested that the Panzerfaust did not cause an especially high proportion of British casualties in Normandy, accounting for only about 6 per cent, this is not the tale the veterans, who attach considerable psychological significance to this weapon, relate.[114] Close explained that his troop sergeant's uneasiness at serving in a different environment to the desert was largely the result of the fact that the encompassing ditches and hedgerows were 'ideal ambush positions for bazooka men.'[115] Equally, Hills rather bitterly mused that in the desert, there had been 'no danger of an infantryman with a hand-held Panzerfaust suddenly popping up from nowhere to fire at close quarters.'[116] Fear that every hedge might conceal death at the hands of a lone infantryman therefore underpinned the intense vulnerability of tanks in the bocage, particularly since they were often unable to move fast enough to get out of range. With tanks thus pinned down and blinded by the Normandy terrain, new operational relationships between men and machines were developed. As infantryman Sydney Jary recorded, since the advent of the Panzerfaust, 'the grim lesson to learn ... was never to let your supporting armour stray too far from close infantry protection.'[117] By 1943, the essential value of close cooperation between infantry and armour had been officially recognised and it was a virtual precept that infantry were required to

[111] Charles Farrell, *Reflections 1939–1945: A Scots Guards Officer in Training and War* (Bishop Auckland: The Pentland Press, 2000), p. 75.
[112] Hills, *By Tank into Normandy*, p. 102.
[113] Ellis, *The Sharp End of War*, p. 129.
[114] Buckley, *British Armour in the Normandy Campaign*, p. 89.
[115] Close, *Tank Commander*, p. 109.
[116] Hills, *By Tank into Normandy*, p. 102.
[117] Jary, *18 Platoon*, p. 19.

secure the forward progression of the tanks. Despite the might and fire-power of the tanks, therefore, these armoured behemoths largely relied for protection upon infantrymen operating outside the shield of a steel shell, a fact which did not help to endear their machines to the tank crews. All of this meant that the autonomy of the tank was considerably lessened after D-Day. This combination of the adverse Normandy terrain, the ever-present threat of the Panzerfaust, and official partnership with the infantry served to rob tank crews of the fundamental freedom of movement requisite to illusions of martial romance. From the start of the Normandy campaign, therefore, tank men were not granted much opportunity to form any semblance of romantic attachment to their machines.

Landscape, therefore, clearly constituted one major factor that shaped the veterans' representation of his relationship with his tank. A second source of the tankie's portrayal of little affection in this partnership was an uncomfortable awareness of an apparent inferiority of British armour in comparison to the German tanks and anti-tank guns.[118] 'Tiger-phobia', an overbearing fear of the German Tiger tank (often accompanied by its mobile, heavily armoured, and powerfully gunned comrade, the Panther) was a source of some concern among the Allied high command in 1944, since Allied tank crews remained stubbornly convinced of the innate superiority of German armour.[119] That Shermans, Churchills, and Cromwells were hopelessly outclassed by the Tiger and its dreaded 88-mm gun is presented as doctrine in the memoirs of British tank veterans.[120] In the spring of 1944, Peter Roach and 1st Royal Tank Regiment returned to England to prepare for the forthcoming invasion. Upon learning that the regiment was to be refitted with the new Cromwell cruiser tanks, the memoirist records that 'There was gloom' among the men.[121] In a vehicle recognition class, Roach and his comrades quizzed the Officer Commanding about the relative thickness of armour, weight of projectile, and muzzle velocity of the British and German tanks: 'He was an honest man and when he had finished there was silence. Each sat quietly brooding.'[122] Equipped with a similar performance 75-mm

---

[118] John Buckley's *British Armour in the Normandy Campaign* provides an excellent detailed assessment of the comparative merits of British and German armour in Normandy.

[119] Ibid., p. 106.

[120] A long-running debate in the military historiography of Normandy enquires into whether German armour was indeed significantly superior to British tanks. In a revisionist study, Buckley suggests that it was less the case that the Tiger had better armour than that the British tanks only had, at best, 75-mm guns which failed to punch a hole in the Tiger. Buckley, *British Armour in the Normandy Campaign*, p. 129.

[121] Roach, *The 8.15 to War*, p. 129.

[122] Ibid., p. 129.

gun to the Sherman, the Cromwell suffered from the same inability to punch through the armour of Tigers and Panthers. Others articulated almost identical fears, based on the belief of the inferiority of British armour. Donald Sutherland related that when attacking Cromwells ran into a force of Tigers, 'the Great Umpire in the Sky waved his stick and all the Cromwells fell down.'[123] Ken Tout, too, took pains to record the fear that the Tiger inspired: 'those 54-ton Tiger tanks, with their high-velocity guns and impenetrable armour, smash down the walls of the mind and set my Sherman blazing on the instant.'[124] Andrew Wilson's memoir of serving in a Crocodile – a Churchill adapted as a flame-throwing unit – with 141st Regiment, Royal Armoured Corps, has provided a much-quoted account of a conversation between himself as a newly arrived young officer being welcomed by a more senior officer:

What do the Germans have most of?
Panthers. Panthers can slice through a Churchill like butter from a mile away.
And how does a Churchill get a Panther?
It creeps up on it. When it reaches close quarters the gunner tries to bounce a shot off the underside of the Panther's gun mantlet. If he's lucky, it goes through a thin piece of armour above the driver's head.
Has anybody ever done it?
Yes. Davis in C Squadron. He's back with headquarters now, trying to recover his nerve.
How does a Churchill get a Tiger?
It's supposed to get within two hundred yards and put a shot through the periscope.
Has anyone ever done it?
No.[125]

Although Wilson's 'little catechism of British and German armour' carries a somewhat apocryphal whiff, like Roach, Sutherland, and Tout, he makes a firm point that British tank crews felt at a distinct disadvantage in terms of armour and firepower. Whilst the British had to approach from a dangerous closeness, and preferably from a flank, to damage German armour, the latter could quite comfortably knock out the British at a range of 1,500 yards.[126] Furthermore, the Germans only required an average of 1.62 shells to kill a Sherman tank, but the British had to hit a Panther with 2.55 shells, and a Tiger with 4.2.[127] These were not odds to inspire great faith among the tank crews of the British army.

[123] Sutherland, *Sutherland's War*, p. 126.
[124] Tout, *By Tank*, p. 67.
[125] Andrew Wilson, *Flamethrower* (London: William Kimber and Co, 1956), p. 54.
[126] French, *Raising Churchill's Army*, p. 102.
[127] Ibid., p. 105.

To this perception of the inadequacy of British armour was added the disagreeable knowledge that combat survivability once the machine had been hit was not promising. In the pitiless slang of the British army, two thirds of all Allied tanks were said to have 'brewed up', or burst violently into flame, upon being hit.[128] As Tout explained, the Sherman tank in particular was 'susceptible to several methods of instant destruction. The most feared and frequent event is a shot into the engine, which inevitably produces an instantaneous inferno.'[129] The flammability of the Sherman was notorious – of forty five Shermans knocked out between 6 June and 10 July 1944, thirty seven 'brewed up'.[130] Such was its propensity to ignite that it was given the labels of 'Ronson', after the famous cigarette lighter, by the British, and 'Tommy cooker' by the Germans. Fire, a number of veterans agreed, constituted an ever-present terror for armour crews. Close explained that 'one of the worst fears a tank man has is of being trapped in a burning tank', whilst Hills added that 'The biggest fear ... was a direct hit. Most of us experienced one at some time or another, and it was largely a matter of luck whether you emerged alive.'[131] With only one or two seconds to get out, those fortunate enough to survive were still likely to suffer horrific burns, a fact to which Roach attributed his distaste for the Cromwell, which had insufficient hatches to enable the driver to escape with alacrity. With laudable understatement, he remarked that 'to men who had watched their friends incinerated this was depressing.'[132] New hatches were devised and fitted, but Roach failed to indicate whether this exponentially increased his love for the Cromwell. The veterans' tale of tank warfare in Normandy thus provides little sense of scope for the establishment of a positive psychological connection between man and machine. Instead, this partnership is depicted as essentially unhappy in both a physical and mental sense.

Tank crews lived with the knowledge that their machine possessed a dual nature as preserver and destroyer.[133] The veterans' tale records that the thick steel walls of the tank were regarded with equal measures of hope and dread by armour crew. On the one hand, the tank's solid hull provided a reassuring physical buffer against the enemy. As tank commander, Bellamy's task was to ride in the turret of his Cromwell,

[128] Terry Copp, "'If this war isn't over, and pretty and damn soon, there'll be nobody left, in this old platoon ...'": First Canadian Army, February-March 1945', in *Time to Kill*, p. 153.
[129] Tout, *Tank!*, p.58.
[130] Buckley, *British Armour in the Normandy Campaign*, p. 127.
[131] Close, *Tank Commander*, p. 111; Hills, *By Tank into Normandy*, p. 167.
[132] Roach, *The 8.15 to War*, p. 129.
[133] Keegan, *Six Armies in Normandy*, p. 199.

passing directions to the crew inside and keeping a sharp lookout for signs of the enemy. Recollecting that he would infinitely have preferred to travel inside the machine, he wrote of a 'terrible feeling of vulnerability that one has in a tank turret. It is very high and thus seems visible to all for miles around.'[134] Participating in Operation *Totalise*, an Allied offensive in August 1944 which deployed massed tanks to breach the enemy's position at Caen, Tout's squadron advanced rapidly through the night. Much to his unhappiness, in order to further speed progress, he was ordered to get out and help his tank to find a way through the dense countryside on foot. Denuded of his machine, he felt distinctly uneasy:

A few pedestrians like myself emphatically wave fag-ends to keep the monsters away from crushing flesh and blood. We are not at ease out here on our feet, treading the dangerous earth. We are not infantrymen. We inhabit a different element, as different as are sea and air.[135]

The duality in the tank's nature was well summed up by Tout:

But we are safe if we stay inside, safe from the unmentionable hordes that people the darkness, safe ... until a mine explodes underneath us or an 88mm erupts in sudden anger out of the darkness and smashes through the turret wall, lighting the instant cremation pyre.[136]

Yet it could also prove counter-productive to rely too much on the protection offered by the 'steel wall' of the tank. Such dangers were highlighted by the plight of Hills' gunner, whose nerve cracked and was consequently forcibly removed from the front line by ambulance:

Nobody quite knew what had happened, but for some reason he would not come out of the tank. He slept in it, ate in it, refused the opportunity even of a game of football, which he loved. Sam speculated that he had become 'armour-conscious', needing to feel that he had that security of being inside the tank all the time.[137]

Whereas the fighter pilot and seamen experienced some degree of pleasure in their machines, therefore, the tank is predominantly represented by its veterans with an indelible sense of menace. Tout recounted an anecdote in which his Sherman passed by a very frightened stray German soldier. Attempting to envisage how his tank appeared to the petrified youngster, he wrote that 'I realize what we look like to him: thirty tons of crushing steel, fifty feet of churning iron track swaying towards him like a diabolic mincing machine. And our great gun, yawning steel-black,

---

[134] Bellamy, *Troop Leader*, p. 62.
[135] Tout, *Tank!*, p. 60.
[136] Tout, *By Tank*, p. 65.
[137] Hills, *By Tank into Normandy*, p. 130.

probing down, straight at his head.'[138] The tank also posed a 'diabolic' threat to the wellbeing of its own crew, even in the most innocuous of circumstances. Several of these narratives articulate a common myth which circulated among front line crews during 1944 and 1945. Bellamy related that when he was at rest during the night, he deliberately parked his tank alongside his sleeping trench. Others, however, were tempted to make different arrangements:

Some of the crews had thought to dig trenches and then run the tank over the top as a shelter but I had been told that in another regiment one of the crews did this and the tank then settled in the mud, slowly asphyxiating them.[139]

The view from the interior of the tank was also heavily laden with menace. Perhaps more so than other memoirists in this study, fear of being trapped within the metal structure haunted the thoughts of these men. As Hills observed, when under mortar fire, tank crews suffered agonies of mind:

The impact on a tank, which might resolve itself in physical concussion or, at worst, incineration, could lead to near panic and a shattering of morale. We cowered in our compartments under the intensity of these bombardments, knowing full well that there was no safer area to which we could try to move. Claustrophobia and the inability to escape from it were an added strain on our nerves – one felt literally hemmed in by the prospect of death or serious wounding and quite unable to end the onslaught. It was understandable, therefore, that such conditions led to some men becoming 'bomb-happy'.[140]

The 'protection' offered by this armour could turn in an instant against the men it sheltered: 'In a moment our mobile home can be transformed into a self-igniting crematorium ... a self-sealing mausoleum ... or a self-detonating bomb, its own walls shattering into lethal shards of sharp steel projected in wild ricochets, back and forth through the confined space.'[141] Tout's repetition of 'self' here serves as a brutal emphasis of the machine's capacity to transform into a tomb for its crew.

A cornerstone of the tank veterans' tale in Normandy was a morbid connection of the machine with what Tout labelled as 'a murdered and mutilated countryside.'[142] Whereas the fighter pilots and seamen had the advantage of fighting in comparatively 'blank canvases' of landscape which granted space and liberty for imagination to roam and construct comforting beliefs, the operating environment of Normandy was cruelly

---

[138] Tout, *Tank!*, p. 67.
[139] Bellamy, *Troop Leader*, p. 87.
[140] Hills, *By Tank into Normandy*, p. 131.
[141] Tout, *Tank!*, p. 13.
[142] Tout, *By Tank*, p. 49.

different. One of the most disconcerting aspects of the Normandy countryside was that its sylvan rurality appeared almost English.[143] A sense of
shock at the destruction wrought upon this normally pleasant landscape
studs the veterans' tale. Having left behind the noise and confusion of
'the bugger's muddle' of the beachhead, Sutherland noted that the scene
confronting him was 'not quite as pastoral as it had first appeared.'[144]
Extensive collateral damage to human and animal life amid the bucolic
landscape made a stark impression upon newly landed British troops.
With considerable distaste, Hills narrated:

> We set out in our spanking new Sherman through roads and fields littered
> with the bloated corpses of dead cattle, besieged by flies and by now stinking
> to high heaven. Here and there were the unburied bodies of soldiers of both
> sides, grotesque waxwork figures which seemingly had no connection with
> reality.[145]

For Sutherland, as he passed through the carnage of the Falaise pocket
at the end of August, the horrors continued:

> This was to prove a horrific experience. There was not a copse, not a thicket,
> which did not house its quota of mangled dead. The roadsides were lined with
> them and in the fields the grotesquely bloated bodies of farm animals, their
> stiffened legs pointing to the sky, lay like children's toys thrown carelessly
> aside.[146]

Such descriptions of moving through Normandy are tainted with a sense
of monstrosity, shifted into a frightening realm of inversion dominated
by anti-pastoralism and macabre surrealism. The litter of grisly remains
that covered Normandy meant that it was very difficult for tank crew
to remain physically or psychologically detached from the surrounding
devastation, and the tank itself is represented as especially bound up
with this cadaverous environment. Hills, for example, commented that
in the narrow lanes, tank crews had to exercise great care not to run over
the dead.[147] Stopping for a brief respite and a brew, Tout's men found
the mangled remains of a German soldier in the tank tracks.[148] Whereas
combatants in other services and battle spaces were arguably granted
a valuable boost to their morale by the mobility of their machine, in
this context, the inexorable propulsion through Normandy thus posed

---

[143] Gary Sheffield, 'Dead Cows and Tigers: Some Aspects of the Experience of the British
    Soldier in Normandy, 1944', in *The Normandy Campaign 1944: Sixty Years On*, (ed.)
    John Buckley (London: Routledge, 2006), p. 120.
[144] Sutherland, *Sutherland's War*, p. 125.
[145] Hills, *By Tank into Normandy*, p. 90.
[146] Sutherland, *Sutherland's War*, p. 132.
[147] Hills, *By Tank into Normandy*, p. 90.
[148] Tout, *Tank!*, p. 94.

little comfort to tank crews, littered as it was with grotesque portentous reminders of lurking nemesis. Sutherland mused that:

[I]t was impossible to avoid seeing the dead, their bodies and faces caught in the grotesque posturing of broken puppets. To glance with professional interest at a 'brewed-up' Tiger or Panther tank in order to assess the manner of its disablement was to see the torso of the driver half out of his escape hatch or the mangled remains of the commander sprawled on top of the turret.[149]

For Hills, the close proximity to the decaying shells of men and tanks 'brought home to me with a trembling horror what I was now going to face and perhaps suffer. I knew then that more scenes of carnage would inevitably follow'.[150] Inauspiciousness was woven into the fabric of the landscape. Having landed in France, Roach's reconnaissance troop spent some time encamped in one spot in order to retrain and acclimatise to the new terrain. Every time the troop left its designated field, Roach recalled, 'we had to pass two knocked-out tanks of a sister unit as grisly reminders.'[151] Similarly, as he drew near the front line, Foley observed ominously that 'The trees gradually became leafless skeletons, turning bare, shattered arms towards the darkening sky. Rusty, burned-out tanks dotted the flattened cornfields as sombre reminders of what might lay in store for us.'[152] These narratives therefore suggest that, to the tank crew, their machine appeared inextricably woven into a macabre tableau of present and future destruction.

Amid the tangled Normandy bocage, machines thus categorically failed to invest combat, and recollections of combat, with any air of romance for their crew. Indeed, as the testimony of Tout proclaims, going to war in a tank in 1944 actively stripped battle of any shreds of pretension to romance:

Shorn of the glamour of lances and pennants and galloping horses and trumpets ... for all the armour and weaponry, the internal husk, myself, is a frail human being, able, in a fraction of a second, to transmute into a screaming maniac or a heap of blood-stained khaki tatters with a stripe on its sleeve. Or an evil-smelling cinder.[153]

During the early stages of the Allies' attempt to reclaim Europe, therefore, it is clear that the partnership between man and machine offered little joy to armour crews. Instead, the tankie was simply forced to endure

[149] Sutherland, *Sutherland's War*, p. 132.
[150] Hills, *By Tank into Normandy*, pp. 90–1.
[151] Roach, *The 8.15 to War*, p. 140.
[152] Foley, *Mailed Fist*, p. 56.
[153] Ken Tout, *Tanks, Advance! Normandy to the Netherlands, 1944* (London: Robert Hale, 1987), p. 119.

this grimly functional relationship as best he could, and it was this sense of bleak fortitude which shaped the tank veterans' narrative depictions of this machine.

Summary

It is evident that many factors influenced the ways in which a combatant interpreted, and represented, a relationship with his machine. The natural setting clearly played a dominant role in determining the imagery and discourses in which these memoirists chose to imagine their mechanical partner, as did the specific nature of the fighting, and the type of machine in which they served. Yet several veterans also reflected that the personality of the serviceman himself was integral to the forging of a successful combat partnership with his aircraft, tank, ship, or submarine. They argued that some types of disposition were simply unsuited to particular machines. For example, Peter Russell, who served as a pilot with both Coastal and Bomber Commands remarked that he felt his personality would not have been apposite for fighter aircraft: 'There were many whose ambition it was to be a fighter pilot. Certainly, it appealed to the more extrovert. Nobody could call me that.'[154] Charles Anscomb suspected that a man's natural disposition dictated his aptness for a seafaring role: 'A true sailor is a natural man, with a surge of heart too big to be explained. His is no trade. It is a calling.'[155] Insisting that the requisite character traits, or 'symptoms', for a sailor were akin to 'those of a great passion', he thus provides some explanation for the former seafarer's sentimental romanticisation of his relationship with maritime vessels.[156]

From a more expansive perspective, the multiple discourses used by these memoirists to depict a combatant's connection to his mechanical companion offer important insights into this alliance. Whether these tropes assert the individual power and control of martial romance, or the reassurance and optimism of a superstitious, romantic bond, or simply a grim, pragmatic fatalism, they combine to reinforce the centrality of the human experience at the heart of these 'epics'. The veterans' choices of lexis and imagery to represent their relationships with these machines serve as a persistent reminder that at the core of the latter stood at least one man pumping life and action throughout hull and fuselage. Thus, even though machines suffuse these narratives of war experience, it

[154] Russell, *Flying in Defiance of the Reich*, p. 20.
[155] Anscomb, *Submariner*, p. 11.
[156] Ibid., p. 12.

cannot be concluded that they 'dominate' to the exclusion of the human combatant. Rather, what emerges from these memoirs is an insight into the variety of modes through which the veterans understood and ascribed importance to the soldering together of man and machine in martial partnership. As the next chapter explores, the meanings which memoirists attached to this partnership between human combatants and the machines of war also shaped their representations of destroying the enemy.

5 'Distance', Killing, and the Enemy

> [W]hile technology was used to facilitate mass human destruction, it did very little to reduce the awareness that dead human beings were the end product. What is striking is the extent to which combatants insisted upon emotional relationships and responsibility, despite the distancing effect of much technology.[1] [Emphasis my own]

Joanna Bourke's study of killing in twentieth century warfare offers a profitable starting point from which to examine how the veterans' tale recorded deeds of violence on the battlefield between 1939 and 1945. Endorsing Bourke's recognition that 'from the moment of killing, the event entered into the imagination and began to be interpreted, elaborated, restructured', these narratives of human behaviour during the Second World War provide a unique insight into the ways in which veterans identified wartime relationships with their enemy and how these men thought they had brought themselves to kill.[2] The ongoing challenges for military historians seeking to formulate a theory about what makes soldiers perform the ultimate act of destruction have been well outlined by John Keegan, whilst Lieutenant-Colonel Dave Grossman's thought-provoking exploration of the psychology of the act of slaying stresses that training men to kill has posed a perennial problem which contemporary military establishments still struggle to overcome.[3] Although Grossman's work in pioneering the field of 'killology' – 'the scholarly study of the destructive act' – is not without its critics, like Bourke he rightfully places a heavy emphasis upon the role of technology in psychologically facilitating killing in combat.[4] Grossman suggests that the

---

[1] Joanna Bourke, *An Intimate History of Killing: Face-to-Face Killing in Twentieth-Century Warfare* (London: Granta Books, 1999), p. 7.

[2] Ibid., p. 10.

[3] John Keegan, 'Towards a Theory of Combat Motivation', in *Time to Kill*, pp. 3–11; Dave Grossman, *On Killing*, rev. ed. (New York: Back Bay Books, 2009).

[4] 'Killology' as defined by Grossman on his website www.killology.com. Robert Engen's critique of Grossman's core theory that man possess an innate resistance to killing identifies a number of methodological flaws with *On Killing*, in 'Killing For Their

progressive mechanisation of battle by the mid-twentieth century was highly influential in helping the combatant to overcome natural inhibitions to slaying, as martial technologies facilitated important levels of mechanical, psychological, emotional, moral, cultural, or social 'distance' between killer and victim.[5] If a target was rendered faceless in the serviceman's imagination, it could be perceived as somehow less human and he could emotionally disassociate himself from the act of killing. The memoirs of British Second World War veterans affirm the necessity of attaining this psychological and emotional detachment in order to kill, and Grossman's theory of critical perceptions of 'distance' from the enemy broadly frames the veterans' representations of their grisly role in the 'teeth arms' of the wartime services.

Pushing aside the role of more formalised processes of military training in committing the act of killing, the veterans' tale proposes that the serviceman took responsibility into his own hands for crafting personal psychological mechanisms that enabled him to kill. The veterans' tale privileges the importance of the serviceman's own imagination in shaping his physical and psychological responses to combat. These memoirs indicate that each service constructed different fantasies about the enemy upon which they drew to help them negotiate their own acts of killing. Probing the question of how servicemen carried out extremes of violence in modern warfare, Bourke identifies 'numbed consciences' and 'agentic modes' as two critical processes.[6] In the former instance, men simply damped down moral cognisance and emotionally shut themselves off from the consequences of their actions; in the latter, combatants claimed a sense of authority over their deeds in order to subscribe to reassuring beliefs that they were masters of their own fates. These two processes can be clearly identified in the testimonies of sailors and aircrew. Yet strangely they do not appear at all in the narratives of soldiers. In the soldiers' tale a resolute silence is walled around discussions of the killing act across the battlefields of Europe and North Africa between 1939 and 1945. Unlike the sailor or fighter pilot, who fashioned his narrative upon the process of how he brought himself to kill and how he responded to the death of his target, the soldier-memoirist opted instead to recount other aspects of his dealings with the enemy's body, narrating particular feelings of affinity with German infantry, prisoners of war, and the dead. In muffling their tales

Country: A New Look at "Killology"', *Canadian Military Journal*, 9:2 (2008), 120–8. See also Grossman's rejoinder, 'S. L. A Marshall Revisited ... ?', *Canadian Military Journal*, 9:4 (2008), 112–3.

[5] Grossman, *On Killing*, p. 57.

[6] Bourke, *An Intimate History of Killing*, p. 5.

of killing, the soldiers' memoirs thus tell a markedly different story of combat relations in which they intensively personalise images of their enemy and insist that emotional closeness existed between opponents.[7] In many ways, therefore, the veterans' tale as a collective testifies to the role of martial technology in making the killing process more mechanical. Nevertheless, in exhibiting a revealing range of complex emotional reactions to committing acts of violence these memoirs also embody Bourke's argument that personalisation of the foe remained an integral part of the lived and remembered experience of killing in battle.

The Sailors' Tale: The Royal Navy and the Northern Oceans, 1939–1945

'In all the long history of sea warfare', wrote the official historian of the naval war, 'there has been no parallel to this battle, whose field was thousands of square miles of ocean, and to which no limits of time or space could be set.'[8] The naval veterans' tale relates that throughout the bitter contest to control both Britain's vital supply lines, fought out in the desolate wastes of the north Atlantic, and to keep open the convoy routes to Russia through the icy northern waters of the Arctic, this sense of spatial and mechanical 'distance' critically shaped the sailor's responses to killing and his enemy. Convoy escorts on the deep water runs waged a different kind of war to their counterparts on the coastal convoys. To some extent, they were perhaps comparatively fortunate in that out in the Atlantic or Arctic oceans, they were not constantly surrounded by grim reminders of the terror of death at sea. Far out at sea, there were certainly vivid moments of especial horror – a burning tanker immolating its crew, a merchant vessel hissing down into oblivion within seconds, a life-raft filled with the skeletal corpses of an unfortunate ships' company – yet the sea rapidly claimed the dead and the war moved on. Out in deep waters, Robert Hughes explains, the sea is

a clean battlefield. The stricken ships slide into the deep, and the floating wreckage is soon dispersed by the ceaseless wash of the waves. You see no shattered buildings, no rotting corpses, nothing but the eternal sea and sky.[9]

In contrast, the tale of battle along the 'tramlines' of Britain's east coast convoy routes or in the shallow waters of the English Channel during the D-Day invasion unfolds a different story in which the sea as a 'veritable

---

[7] No such relationship between enemies is depicted in the memoirs of former Far East personnel, in which the Japanese are portrayed in highly racialized terms of deepest loathing.
[8] Roskill, The War at Sea, Vol. 2, p. 335.
[9] Hughes, Through the Waters, p. 91.

graveyard of sunken ships' acquired a particularly visible, grim identity.[10] As naval and merchant casualties of German E-boats and aircraft along the swept channels between the Forth and the Thames mounted, the waters became increasingly hazardous to shipping due to the number of wrecks that piled up. The pitiful fate of unlucky vessels was all too clear, since the masts and funnels of many remained above water level, and those completely submerged were marked by warning lights, causing memoirist William Donald to remark that at night the tombs along the channels became an eerie 'Piccadilly Circus of flashing green lights.'[11] For those in action in the English Channel during the latter stages of the war, like Donald Macintyre, matters were hardly better since the comparatively shallow waters housed the remains of shipwrecks from many centuries of war. Among these graves, it was possible for U-boats to camouflage themselves away from the locating 'ping' of the Royal Navy's sonar, presenting their hunters with a new set of challenges in destroying the enemy. On the other hand, the very desolation and physical distance of the northern oceans as a battle space seemed to magnify the sailor's ability to adopt the 'numbed conscience' as a mechanism of killing. The performance of violence in this operating environment was lent a unique emotional detachment which Norman Hampson mused accounted for 'one of the reasons why I had opted for the navy: you didn't even see the men whom you killed, or who killed you.'[12] Broadly speaking, therefore, because of the mechanical distances at which the war out at sea was conducted, it was possible for the British mariner to know on an intellectual level that he was fighting a human enemy, but to deny emotionally that he was killing real men, should he so wish.[13] With the visible results of violent acts swiftly hidden by the ocean's shroud, it was comparatively straightforward for the seamen to convince themselves that they were killing machines rather than men. This led Hampson to muse that killing in the Royal Navy was 'perhaps less brutalizing than close combat in the army, but it tended to leave you insensible, even if it did not make you sadistic.'[14]

The submariners' tale indicates a particular subscription to the 'numbed conscience' as a means of killing. On the whole, the British submariners' memoirs exemplify the 'insensible' nature described by Hampson, portraying a cold and mechanical approach in which the destruction of U-boats and ships is conducted with a calm dispassion

[10] Lombard-Hobson, *A Sailor's War*, p. 113.
[11] Donald, *Stand By for Action*, p. 64.
[12] Hampson, *Not Really What You'd Call a War*, p. 56.
[13] Grossman, *On Killing*, p. 58.
[14] Hampson, *Not Really What You'd Call a War*, p. 56.

that borders on indifference. A scaffold of unimaginative aloofness surrounds the submariners' depicted feelings about killing enemy ships and men in these narratives, and Hart's description of destroying a target off Norway provides an example of the emotionally detached language in which the submariners' kills are typically represented. The simplicity of his assertion that his boat now had 'at least one sinking to our credit' illustrates a distinct lack of concern about the fate of the German crew.[15] The dead ship is never mentioned – once the torpedoes hit home, it simply disappears from the submariner's thoughts. To some extent, the sheer physical distance between a submarine and its target may be held accountable for this psychological remoteness. As William King remarked, 'Submarines are seldom able to confirm their successes by observation.'[16] It was very unlikely that a boat would linger to watch the aftermath of its actions; even should it do so, as Hughes pointed out, wreckage was rapidly claimed by the waves. Hart provides further insight into the submariner's emotional detachment from the killing act, reporting an attack on a schooner off the African coast which he surmised contained supplies of ammunition for Rommel: 'she was a mass of potential death for our hard-fighting, hard-pressed, fellow-countrymen.'[17] Underpinning the memoirist's detached attitude is therefore a conviction that he was not a killer of 'innocent' ships. Subsequent corroboration of this is offered by Hart's laconic description of torpedoing another enemy ship: 'we heard that ominous dull knocking sound that signified success, and the Axis lacked a sizeable ship. Just how her crew felt about it wasn't our business – little we cared.'[18] Hart's clarification of the process by which submariners sank enemy vessels provides further explanation of how these men managed to retain cognitive remoteness from their role as agents of death. From underwater, the killing act seemed to lend itself to an emotionless state:

I would like to explain that to torpedo a ship travelling ... at a speed of over twenty knots is not the work of a bullet-headed, death-or-glory, boaster. It is a job for a cool, highly-trained technician ... It demands a scientific calculation that can cause two objects to meet at a distance of over a mile, one travelling at one speed at right angles to the track of another travelling at quite a different one.[19]

There was, he asserted, certainly no room for any element of 'By Guess and By God' about the operation.[20] Destroying targets from underwater

[15] Hart, *Discharged Dead*, p. 5.
[16] King, *The Stick and the Stars*, p. 66.
[17] Hart, *Discharged Dead*, p. 91.
[18] Ibid., p. 94.
[19] Ibid., pp. 149–150.
[20] Ibid., p. 150.

142   The Veterans' Tale

at long-range via an intricate web of dials and machinery inevitably created a psychological barrier between submariner and victim. Killing, as
Hart indicates, was for the submariner an innately scientific process of
velocities, depths, and angles, which correspondingly had a mechanising
effect on the crews' emotional responses to the enemy in their sights.

For the submariner's counterparts 'up top', the killing process was
equally reliant upon technology, with the development of HF/DF (high
frequency direction finding equipment), new weapons such as the
'Hedgehog' forward-throwing spigot mortar, and the Leigh Light com-
bining with further innovations in sonar and use of the larger, deeper
depth charge patterns to create a highly effective system of anti-submarine
warfare by 1943. As U-boat slaying technology developed, the war out
at sea began to swing in Britain's favour, but during the years before
1943, when the Battle of the Atlantic reached its most vicious peaks, and
the Russian convoys fell frequent prey to slaughter, the convoy war was
always hazardous and always under threat from U-boats.[21] The strategy
and technology of neutralising this threat has been well documented elsewhere, but the sailors' attitude towards their enemies has been the subject of rather less discussion.[22] During the Second World War, German
submarines were regarded with what historian John Terraine identifies
as an 'almost superstitious dread'.[23] On the deep-water Atlantic and
Arctic convoys, actual ship-to-ship engagements were rare, and when
Winston Churchill famously chronicled in his own memoirs that 'the
only thing that ever really frightened me during the war was the U-boat
peril', he voiced not only comment upon the ability of these vessels to
cut Britain's vital supply lines, but also a deep-rooted cultural fear of
the submarine in Britain.[24] This anxiety can be traced back to the role
of submarine warfare during the First World War. Such was the cultural
impact generated by this new form of warfare during the earlier conflict
that Denys Rayner recorded how 'as an inky schoolboy eight years of age,
I first seriously considered sinking U-Boats', sketching a crude outline
of a submarine-killing petrol bomb in his geometry book.[25] Associations

[21] Terraine, *Business in Great Waters*, p. 286. Although as the historian and a number of
memoirists point out, the actual danger from U-boats was rather less at certain times
than is often supposed. For some months after October 1940, for instance, the Atlantic
virtually emptied out of U-boats as they returned to Germany due to shortages, training,
and refitting, returning only some months later. Again, by May 1943, the U-boat packs
had been driven out of the Atlantic and between June and September of that year, only
one ship was lost in convoy.
[22] Roskill, *The War at Sea*, Vol. 1; Barnett, *Engage the Enemy More Closely*; Terraine, *Business in Great Waters*.
[23] Terraine, *Business in Great Waters*, p. 673.
[24] Winston Churchill, *Their Finest Hour* (London: HoughtonMifflin, 1949), p. 529.
[25] Rayner, *Escort*, p.17.

of *Schrecklichkeit*, or 'frightfulness', attached to the U-boat war between 1914 and 1918 carried over into the Second World War.[26] Even without manifestations of deliberate atrocity, the very nature of the submarine's war between 1939 and 1945 was perceived as underhand due to the lack of warning targets received before they were torpedoed. It was within this historical context, and having further witnessed at first hand the abrupt sinking of friendly ships, that the sailors of the 1939–45 war constructed and later recorded meaning around the German submarines. In their memoirs, the very term 'U-boat' is charged with special meaning, imbued with connotations of treachery, black cunning, and malevolence. This machine represented 'the devil'.[27] The disparity between the naval memoirists' references to British 'submarines' and German 'U-boats' is, as Nicholas Monsarrat observed in his autobiography, indicative of the singular hatred that British seamen directed towards the enemy machines:

[Depth charges] didn't really kill people; they just sank U-boats, metal objects which were trying to kill *us*. The convention that whereas we had submarines (noble and skilful), the hated Hun actually used U-boats (wicked and treacherous), was still a persistent gloss on history.[28]

The sheer level of British naval abhorrence of these machines is further illustrated by the specific verb that was used to describe their demise. The act of despatching a U-boat was given its own special terminology. Aircraft and tanks are represented as being 'destroyed' in the wider veterans' tale, but the U-boat was 'killed'.[29] The employment of this particular verb in the Navy's wartime lexicon, and subsequently in the narratives of its veterans, suggests that the German submarines were viewed much as malignant creatures of the deep, to be tracked down and deprived of life. In this context, the verb 'to kill' carries a depth of satisfaction at a job well done; the sailor's sense of fulfilment in eliminating a German submarine is exemplified by Macintyre, who wrote that the 'hunt for, the stalking of, and the final killing of a U-boat had always seemed to me to be the perfect expression of a fighting sailor's art'.[30] Indeed, Macintyre found such gratification in destroying these vessels that he titled his memoir *U-Boat Killer*.

An enduring sense of hatred was also reserved for the other machine that posed a severe threat to Allied shipping during the Second World War. Enemy aeroplanes are also despised throughout the naval veterans' tale.

---

[26] Deliberate policy of intimidating civilian population by iron-handed behaviour in order to prevent any interference with military movements. Terraine, *Business in Great Waters*, p. 44.

[27] Ogden, *My Sea Lady*, p. 101.

[28] Monsarrat, *Life*, p. 27.

[29] Broome, *Convoy is to Scatter*, p. 25; Macintyre, *U-Boat Killer*, p. 16.

[30] Macintyre, *U-Boat Killer*, p. 16.

During the early years of the war, as Germany occupied the French and Norwegian coastlines, the air threat to British shipping steadily increased as airfields were taken over or newly built in order to lengthen the Luftwaffe's reach. The primary German airbase at Banak in northern Norway particularly menaced Russian-bound convoys along the rim of the Arctic Circle. In the first instance, the Luftwaffe was deployed to pinpoint the mass of ships and vector other German aircraft and submarines to the location, before participating in the actual destruction of the convoy. Correspondingly, naval memoirists who served on these icy voyages vociferously aired their condemnation of this airborne enemy. Sailing for Murmansk with convoy PQ18 in 1942, Hughes recollected that he 'hated aircraft with a deadly hatred, and fired at them with a cold fury'.[31] Two convoys earlier, Ogden had also reached the same state of abhorrence of this foe, and he vividly depicted the mental torment suffered by surface crew when one of the German planes appeared overhead. On this occasion, the memoirist and his anti-submarine trawler provided part of the escort for PQ16 in May 1942, which was only marginally more fortunate than its ill-starred successor, PQ17. Ogden recorded that PQ16's fate was sealed when a single reconnaissance aircraft was sighted in the sky on 24 May, causing him a 'sickening feeling':

this solitary enemy aircraft was the messenger of death and disaster for P.Q.16. From now onwards the convoy's fate would be held in the retina of a German pilot's eye. Its struggle to avoid destruction by twisting and turning would now be of no avail. There could be no escape. The barbed harpoon had been plunged into the whale's side, not to be withdrawn until its captors had killed it and its blood had turned the pale Arctic sea to crimson.[32]

Roger Hill reported experiencing an almost identical sensation in his destroyer HMS *Ledbury* only weeks later when a Blohm and Voss scout sighted PQ17 and began to shadow the convoy. Hill's simple description of the aircraft as 'evil' offers deeper insight in the levels of fear and detestation with which escort sailors regarded this enemy.[33] To Ogden, the unceasing presence of their airborne tracker represented a malevolent omen:

As I watched this evil shadow through my glasses, I thought of it as a gigantic bat, a *fledermaus*, a spectre consorting with a butcher, a Schlachter. I knew for certain that P.Q.16 was under sentence of death; it was now only a question of how many of our ships and their crews were going to perish in the icy waters of the Arctic seas.[34]

[31] Hughes, *Through the Waters*, p. 119.
[32] Ogden, *My Sea Lady*, p. 114.
[33] Hill, *Destroyer Captain*, p. 42.
[34] Ogden, *My Sea Lady*, p. 115.

To a considerable degree, the label of 'evil' which was affixed to these German planes was born of an intense feeling of helplessness which the very appearance of these machines generated. On summertime Arctic convoys there was 'no darkness in which to hide in those northern latitudes and we were under observation by our executioners for twenty-four hours a day.'[35] The searing awareness of vulnerability which these sailors experienced was not diminished when the time came for Action Stations against the aircraft. Hampson felt that his role of relaying the captain's orders to the guns was too passive to promote any reassuring sense of personal agency:

> When we were in action against a submarine, it did not occur to me that this was any different from our exercises off Tobermory and that this one might bite. Air attacks were a very different matter, since all I had to do was to watch the enemy coming at us. That petrified – or, to be more accurate, jellified me.[36]

Perhaps unsurprisingly, therefore, there is a marked sense of psychological 'distance' between these memoirists and the crew of the enemy aircraft. In these narratives, it is the machine itself onto which the combatant projects his emotional response and the 'numbed conscience' is clearly manifested. In an anecdote which detailed his experiences of escorting a convoy under fire from dive bombers and torpedo bombers in May 1943, Hampson voices the sailors' indifferent attitude towards the fate of German aircrew: 'It was said that several of the torpedo bombers had been shot down but no one ever asked what had become of their crews.'[37] This former sailor's dismissive report of the onslaught was typical of the naval memoirists' dispassionate tales of killing German aircrew.

Yet for all that the British naval memoirists clearly despised the submarines and aircraft against which they fought, their narratives display a number of occasions in which the carefully cultivated 'numbed conscience' succumbed to recognition of the human qualities of their enemy. Luftwaffe aircrew were regarded as synonymous with their despised machines. Intriguingly, however, the naval memoirists exhibit a clear inclination to separate the actions of the U-boat from its human crew in their representations of battling these submarines. Indeed, whilst sailors were unquestionably granted an opportunity to emotionally deny that they were killing men as well as machines, the veterans' tale suggests that those engaged in anti-submarine warfare did frequently personalise their enemies. In the war at sea the roles of hunter and hunted could switch rapidly. Whilst the sailors' memoirs certainly attribute much of

[35] Ibid., p. 115.
[36] Hampson, *Not Really What You'd Call a War*, p. 46.
[37] Ibid., p. 56.

their success to new technological developments in anti-submarine warfare, the theme of applauding good 'seamanship' on both sides occupies
a tellingly prominent place in their narratives. During the dark winter
nights of 1940, Rayner reported, a U-boat was able to surface and attack
with virtual impunity, 'until we could detect his presence with radar we
fought him with our eyes, with seamanship, and with bluff.'[38] Macintyre
also documented that he had longed to join the anti-submarine effort
because 'contact with the enemy would be at close quarters, and the
fight would develop finally into personal combat in which good seamanship might well decide the issue.'[39] Acknowledgement of the enemy's skill
and courage is correspondingly a key feature in these narratives, and
Jack Broome explained that some satisfaction could be found in pitting
one's 'seamanship' against that of the enemy. As a thirty-eight-year-old
pre-war submarine commander in the Royal Navy, he had been bitterly
disappointed to find himself on the wrong side of the Admiralty's ruling
that wartime submariners must be under thirty-five years in age upon the
outbreak of war in 1939. Like a handful of what he described wryly as
'doddering' former submarine commanders, he was appointed to an aged
destroyer in the hopes that his specialist knowledge would prove useful
in the anti-submarine war. His private view of this role was described as
setting 'Thieves to catch thieves'.[40] To his own surprise, he enjoyed his
new duties: 'I instinctively saw the attacking problems of U-boat skippers
probably much the same as they did, which often gave me a chance to
upset their tactics.'[41] Despite witnessing the mauling of convoy PQ16 in
May 1942, Graeme Ogden even went so far as to proclaim that he was
moved by a feeling of 'admiration' for U-boat sailors, insisting that these
machines were 'clearly manned by brave determined crews ... one day
I should like to talk to a U-boat commander and learn his side of the
picture.'[42] Evidently, therefore, the fact that the German submariners
also belonged to a community of seafarers struck a resounding emotional
chord with these memoirists, who collectively attest that it was possible
to applaud the courage and ability of this enemy whilst simultaneously
deploring his work. Recognition of the U-boat crews as talented seamen
in their own right thus underpins the surface sailors' representations of
battle, granting the German submariner a face and acknowledgement
of his seafaring talent in this contest of wits and skill that was notably
lacking in relation to his Luftwaffe counterpart.

[38] Rayner, *Escort*, p. 74.
[39] Macintyre, *U-Boat Killer*, p. 16.
[40] Broome, *Convoy is to Scatter*, p. 30.
[41] Ibid., p. 25.
[42] Ogden, *My Sea Lady*, p. 101.

To suggest therefore, as Grossman does, that naval personnel did not suffer psychological trauma from their violent actions because 'most of them don't have to kill anyone directly, and no one is trying to specifically, personally, kill them' is to grossly oversimplify the complex human relationship of enemies at sea during the Second World War.[43] As the naval veterans' tale relates, in many ways the war at sea was an intimate war, with mechanical adversaries to be hunted and terminated, and skilful human foes to be outwitted. Furthermore, it was not unknown for the sailor, in particular those serving as convoy escorts, to be confronted with the physical body of his enemy. The Royal Navy preferred not to leave German submariners to drown and attempted rescue if at all possible.[44] Having sunk *U 99* in March 1941, Macintyre took its surviving crew prisoner, including its commander, the famous U-boat ace Otto Kretschmer. The memoirist recorded his surprise at finding that the German commander was 'far from being the fanatical Hitlerite we had half-expected': 'as a professional naval officer and a most skilful one, he had much the same attitude to politics as we had ourselves'.[45] Despite his indifference to the fate of downed German aircrew, Hampson recorded experiencing a sense of outrage when his captain in HMS *Easton* proposed to abandon the crew of the scuttled Italian submarine *Asteria* in 1943: 'I was utterly horrified. He did not even have the miserable pretext of wanting to avenge our casualties since the submarine had not done either of us any harm.'[46] Fortunately, the commanding officer of a fellow destroyer was senior to his own captain, and insisted upon retrieving the stricken crew, much to Hampson's private relief: 'Since my rather difficult objective was to help to win the war without doing anything to kill anybody, this could be considered at least a partial success.' In light of a rather ghoulish Admiralty policy which refused to accept confirmation of a U-boat 'kill' without physical evidence, British sailors on deck could also physically encounter the dead body of the German submariner, or at least what was left of it. Royal Naval debriefing officers required a bucketful of bodily evidence to prove that a U-boat had truly been eliminated. Having killed *U186* in HMS *Hesperus*, Macintyre and his crew dutifully picked up 'a few specimens of evidence, on one of which was found a gruesome piece of flesh' before returning to their convoy.[47]

Further personalisation of the seagoing enemy can also be found in the submariners' tale. In these narratives minor breaches of the 'numbed

[43] Grossman, *On Killing*, p. 59.
[44] Although under circumstances which endangered the ship this was clearly impossible.
[45] Macintyre, *U-Boat Killer*, p. 43.
[46] Hampson, *Not Really What You'd Call a War*, p. 49.
[47] Macintyre, *U-Boat Killer*, p. 131.

148   The Veterans' Tale

consciences' of these men can infrequently be glimpsed. Significantly however, where these are voiced, they further reveal the submariner's peculiar desire and ability to clamp down upon his emotions. Hart attempted to predict what the result of his submarine's torpedoes might be by visualising the scene aboard his target:

as likely as not the crash of an exploding torpedo was the first indication of danger that our targets received. Just how did those bewildered enemy seamen feel when that devastating blow-up occurred?... Was there wild, hysterical panic, for instance? Or was there the cool, fatalistic acceptance of emergency that, God be thanked, usually follows disaster under British ensigns – White or Red? It was easy for an imaginative man to picture the scene as destruction came – the surge of panic, the frenzied efforts to preserve life; the screeching grind of torn metal ripped to shreds; the stench of death – phew![48]

Similarly, Alistair Mars admitted to experiencing a rare 'moment of pity' for the crew of an Italian merchant ship off Genoa, musing that they were 'doubtless sleeping off their vino and garlic lunch'.[49] Nevertheless, the fact that both men recoursed to racial caricatures to describe this fleeting connection with their targets suggests that the impulse to empathise with the doomed men was kept under firm control by reducing the enemy to two-dimensional stereotyped figures. Edward Young's experience of rescuing the signalman of a U-boat 'killed' by his submarine, HMS *Saracen*, provided an unusually personal encounter with the foe. He recorded being somewhat disturbed when the German 'became conscious for a brief moment, long enough to open his eyes and look straight at me with an appalling expression of despair and hatred'.[50] Significantly, however, the former British officer abides by the veterans' collective tacit refusal to dwell upon the submariner's role as agent in the destruction of others. He simply recounts this anecdote and moves on with his narrative, firmly shuttering the window of reflection it proffers.

Collectively, these narratives suggest that although the Royal Navy's sailors were granted an opportunity to remain mechanically, spatially, and consequently emotionally detached from their enemies, this protective sense of psychological 'distance' was not immune to fracture. The surface sailors' distinction between human and mechanical combatants was rooted in a sense of passivity that was instilled by the ability of German aircraft and submarines to arrive, kill, and depart with relative stealth and impunity, but even though the U-boat is represented as an abominable menace, some element of fellow feeling for enemy submarine crews is

[48] Hart, *Discharged Dead*, pp. 90-1.
[49] Mars, *Unbroken*, p. 67.
[50] Young, *One of Our Submarines*, p. 92.

clearly regarded as important in these veterans' tales. Despite the fact that the Navy's own submariners remained resistant to any inclination to empathise with the foe, the fact that they record fleeting instances of wondering about their human enemy suggests not that they were more heartless than their comrades 'up top', but that imagination had to be more firmly leashed as a means of psychological self-protection in the crushing depths of the ocean. As Torpedo Officer aboard HMS *Sealion*, Young observed that his captain was 'more sensitive than most naval officers' and never managed to acquire the submariner's desirable 'crust of emotional indifference towards his targets'. 'It was not', reflected the memoirist,

that he was blind to the necessity of inflicting destruction and loss of life in the merciless struggle in which we were all engaged, but I believe that when one of his torpedoes scored a hit on a target he could not help picturing vividly in his imagination the twisted steel, the torn flesh, the inrush of water, the choking lungs.[51]

For precisely this reason, Hart remained resolutely convinced that the hallmark of a 'good submariner' was the firm repression of imagination in order to concentrate on the business at hand.[52] According to the collective naval veterans' tale, therefore, whether consciously or subconsciously, the Royal Navy's targets were often not entirely as dehumanised or 'faceless' as might be supposed. Whilst the war at sea might well have produced an environment in which combatants could become 'insensible' to the performance of violence towards their enemy, the nuances and complexities of human relations in battle throughout the naval veterans' tale testifies to the acuteness of Bourke's claim that 'combatants insisted upon emotional relationships and responsibility, *despite* the distancing effect of much technology.'[53]

The Flyers' Tale: Fighter Command and the Battle of Britain, 1940

Imagining the consequences of their violent deeds also proved potentially psychologically destructive for the aircrew of Fighter Command in 1940. Their memoirs suggest that Battle of Britain pilots attempted to adopt a curious mixture of 'numbed consciences' and 'agentic modes' as a means of killing. In 1942 Richard Hillary claimed that the fighter pilot was 'lucky' because he possessed neither the 'personalised' emotions of the soldier 'handed a rifle and bayonet and told to charge' on

---

[51] Ibid., p. 76.
[52] Hart, *Discharged Dead*, p. 105.
[53] Bourke, *An Intimate History of Killing*, p. 7.

the battlefield, nor the 'dangerous' emotions of bomber crew revelling in structural destruction.[54] The fighter pilot, thought Hillary, was in fact 'privileged to kill well' because his emotions were those of 'the duellist – cool, precise, impersonal.'[55] Again, the importance that fighter aircrew attached to feeling in control of their environment, actions, and emotions is made plain. Hillary's words display an evident subscription to the eternal 'Knights of the Air' discourse which culturally enveloped – and still surrounds – 'the Few', yet the numerous post-war memoirs of his comrades demonstrate that this idealised ability to kill 'well' in 1940 proved rather more difficult to sustain than *The Last Enemy* implied.

Faint traces of Hillary's fantasy of the flyer as a 'duellist' who fought coldly and impersonally can certainly be identified in these narratives, which frequently bear a passing resemblance to those of the submariner. Both sets of memoirists allowed themselves to fantasise that machines, rather than men, were skilfully fought and clinically dispatched. Although the fighter pilots fought at considerably closer quarters than the submariners, KW Mackenzie's summary of aerial battle as 'a challenge, impersonal, machine against machine' mirrors the attitudes expressed throughout the naval memoirs.[56] Echoing Hart's idealisation of the 'good' submariner, Roger Hall supposed that the ideal fighter pilot must sever all emotion in battle, becoming 'callous and cold and ruthless'. Scrutinising his initial instinctive horror to witnessing the fiery demise of a Junkers 88, he sternly perceived that his response was inadequate: 'I felt that I should be quite useless as a fighter pilot if I couldn't control my thoughts and imagination.'[57] Tim Vigors, on the other hand, was rather pleased that he seemed to have achieved this prized state of emotional detachment from the enemy when downing a German aircraft over Dunkirk: 'I was aware that I had killed a fellow human being and was surprised not to feel remorse'.[58] 'Johnnie' Johnson further affirmed that 'when the Messerschmitts hit the ground and burst apart, we had no thought for the fellow inside.'[59] Similarly, Tom Neil reflected that Fighter Command aircrew were becoming 'impervious' to the daily business of death and injury, wondering 'Was it because we did not actually see the crashed aircraft, the terrible burns, or the gory remains? Probably be different if we did.'[60]

---

[54] Hillary, *The Last Enemy*, p. 97.
[55] Ibid., p. 97.
[56] Mackenzie, *Hurricane Combat*, pp. 45–6.
[57] Hall, *Clouds of Fear*, p. 57.
[58] Vigors, *Life's Too Short to Cry*, p. 163.
[59] Johnson, *Wing Leader*, p. 302.
[60] Neil, *Gun Button to 'Fire'*, p. 117.

His surmise proved correct. Their narratives suggest that it was virtually impossible for the flyer to remain wholly devoid of 'personalised'
emotions throughout the Battle of Britain. These books are littered with
accounts of moments of especial clarity when compassion and vivid
horror broke through the fighter pilot's assumed shield of psychological
remoteness from the killing act. On occasion, the impact of battle upon
the enemy flyer's body was rendered disturbingly visible, as Neil himself
discovered when destroying a Dornier:

two large objects detached themselves from the fuselage and came in my direction, so quickly, in fact, that I had no time to evade. Comprehension barely
keeping pace with events, I suddenly recognized spreadeagled arms and legs
as two bodies flew past my head, heavy with the bulges that were undeveloped
parachutes.[61]

Struggling to deflect a Me. 109, Tony Bartley was rescued by his flight
commander, who dispatched the German machine with a long burst
of fire: 'The aircraft flick rolled, then spewed out its pilot. I was close
enough to see his helmet fly off, a white face and blond hair streaming
grotesquely. He didn't pull the rip cord.'[62] Even in dogfights where the
body of the enemy was not immediately visible, hidden from sight inside
the disintegrating aircraft, some victories were equally fraught with horror for the British flyer. Geoffrey Page was especially upset by a brief
tussle with a Stuka, which he reduced to 'a flaming inferno'. He recorded
that this incident shook him to his core: 'Somehow it had been different
in all the other fights ... Then it had been a completely impersonal affair
and I hadn't witnessed the death throes of the doomed plane.'[63] In the
sharp ferocity of battle, the fighter pilot was not often granted the leisure
to observe or reflect upon his results, yet in the rare instance that he did
not immediately have to turn his attention towards another enemy, a
dreadful cognisance of his actions sometimes took hold. 'Sitting dazed
in the cockpit', Page 'flew the aircraft home mechanically', his thoughts
lingering upon the 'horror' of 'destroying two other human beings'.[64] A
similar response to a kill was documented by Geoffrey Wellum, who shot
down a German plane and watched it fall into the sea, 'a horrible and
lonely place in which to die.'[65] Like Page, on the flight home he was
surprised by the depth of his reaction to the act: 'What a world. Geoff,
you've just killed a bloke, a fellow fighter pilot.'[66]

[61] Ibid., pp. 94–5.
[62] Bartley, *Smoke Trails in the Sky*, pp. 11-12.
[63] Page, *Shot Down in Flames*, p. 63.
[64] Ibid., p. 63.
[65] Wellum, *First Light*, p. 209.
[66] Ibid., p. 207.

As these two memoirs indicate, some flyers found it difficult to over-come normative social taboos surrounding killing. Killing in wartime, and especially during the threat of invasion of Britain's shores in the summer of 1940, was naturally sanctioned at the highest levels of official-dom. Yet upon experiencing such moments of horror at meting out such violence, several authors wondered if their actions were really morally acceptable. Experiencing some compassion for the German pilot he had consigned to the sea, Wellum reflected his deed was 'just about as callous and as calculating as you can get, just plain cold-blooded murder. The bloke didn't even know what had hit him.'[67] The emotive term 'murder' also found its way into the narrative of Page, who remained unsure as to whether he was returning to the airfield 'a bloodied fighter pilot, or was it a murderer hiding behind the shield of official approval?'[68] As Wellum and Page demonstrate, killing as a fighter pilot was not necessarily a remote and impersonal affair, and raised moral questions which clearly haunted Fighter Command veterans for many years afterwards.

As close-range witnesses to the death of the enemy, these fighter-memoirists thus display precisely the kind of 'personalised' emotions which Hillary deplored. At the same time, however, the so-called 'danger-ous' emotions that he associated with bomber crew – 'who night after night must experience that childhood longing for smashing things' – also find an outlet in their memoirs.[69] Having made his first kill above Dunkirk, Vigors recorded that he experienced 'that same satisfaction that I had known in Ireland when out pigeon shooting on a summer's evening.'[70] Wellum's accounts of attacking a Heinkel 111 – 'This is looking good. I think he's going. Yes, I've got him. And since you're going, take that for luck, you bloody son of the bloody Fatherland', and the 'take that you sod' feeling he experienced in destroying German planes – transmit a similar sense of bloodlust.[71] Strong fears of becoming too attached to killing echo through-out a number of the flyer narratives. Page was appalled to realise that when he incinerated a Stuka he registered not only 'horror' but also 'fascination' at his act.[72] So powerfully did this mixture of emotions affect him that he penned a letter to his friend, Michael Maw, in an effort to rid himself of the anguish they caused. The honesty in this letter is searing:

Maybe I am a bit sorry for myself at this moment, but, and it's a great big but, I enjoy killing. It fascinates me beyond belief to see my bullets striking home and

[67] Ibid., p. 207.
[68] Page, Shot Down in Flames, p. 63.
[69] Hillary, The Last Enemy, p. 97.
[70] Vigors, Life's Too Short to Cry, p. 163.
[71] Wellum, First Light, p. 151; p. 181.
[72] Page, Shot Down in Flames, p. 63.

then to see the Hun blow up before me. It also makes me feel sick. Where are we going and how will it all end? I feel as if I'm selling my soul to the Devil. If only you were here. I need someone to talk to who isn't tied up in this game of legalized murder.[73]

Significantly, in writing this soul-baring correspondence Page was attempting to communicate with a friend who had died some months previously. This dialogue with the dead conveys an impression that the flyer was sufficiently bewildered and disturbed by his guilty pleasure in killing that he dared not express his fears to the living for fear of judgement at breaking the taboo. Had the stiff-upper lip of the wartime RAF not dictated otherwise, he might have learned that others shared his discomfort.

In the midst of all the discussions on killing in these narratives, the question of chivalry in aerial battle forms a staple feature. Whilst actually embroiled in combat, there was decidedly little room for acts of chivalry. As Stephen Bungay notes in his history of the Battle of Britain, the 'Knights of the Air' often fought 'more like medieval foot soldiers peering through a visor and slashing with an axe at anyone they thought might be on the other side.'[74] Nevertheless, elements of a 'live and let live' system were claimed to characterise a combatant's approach towards enemy aircrew once they were forced to bail out, or 'take to the silk' in RAF parlance. Johnson avowed that the following tacit rules of air combat applied:

When you sent a Messerschmitt spinning down out of control, the pilot either got out or he didn't. If he baled out, then the rule which we followed throughout the war was that he should be allowed to drift down to earth without being riddled with cannon fire. It was an act of chivalry which we had inherited from our forebears of the previous war; and despite accounts to the contrary, I never knew of a pilot who was shot at as he drifted helplessly to the ground.[75]

Neil insisted that these 'rules' applied to both sides. Relating the tale of a member of his own squadron, whose parachute inexplicably collapsed at 1,000 feet, he commented that it was 'rumoured that a Hun had shot at him on the way down but we did not believe that; no self-respecting airman, friend or foe, would do such a thing.'[76] Others, however, were less sure. Officially documented instances of men being gunned down in their parachutes may well be 'isolated examples', but several memoirists resolutely maintained that the possibility constituted a distinct threat.[77]

[73] Ibid., p. 64.
[74] Bungay, *The Most Dangerous Enemy*, p. 242.
[75] Johnson, *Wing Leader*, p. 302.
[76] Neil, *Gun Button to 'Fire'*, p. 57.
[77] Bungay, *The Most Dangerous Enemy*, p. 166.

Having sustained direct hits to his oil and glycol tanks, Bartley initially made preparations to evacuate his stricken Spitfire and then changed his mind:

I saw my enemy preparing for another attack, and knew it meant suicide to jump with him around. Escaping airmen over their own territory were fair game in some combatants' log book, and a friend of mine had been shot down in his parachute.[78]

He got back into his cockpit and nursed his plane into a crash landing instead. Hall wrote a particularly graphic account of witnessing a Hurricane pilot bailing out, only to receive bursts of fire from two marauding enemy aircraft:

I saw the tracers and the cannon shells pierce the centre of his body, which folded like a jack-knife closing, like a blade of grass which bends towards the blade of the advancing scythe. I was too far away to interfere and now was too late to be of any assistance … the red I could see was that of the pilot's blood as it gushed from all the quarters of his body. I expected to see the lower part of his body fall away to reveal the entrails dangling in mid-air but by some miracle his body held together. His hands, but a second before clinging to the safety of the shroud lines, were now relaxed and hung limp at his sides.[79]

Hall's tale is particularly interesting, as it is subsequently presented to the reader as a dream experienced by the memoirist. It is never made explicit whether or not he truly witnessed the demise of the Hurricane pilot, or whether the image was the product of a brain under excessive strain at the height of the battle. The former explanation seems most likely, due to a strange foreword written by Hall's editor in which he attempted to forestall a possible adverse public reaction to this murderous tale:

It is to be hoped that this will not rekindle a hatred of the Germans that has been allowed to smoulder and die down over the past twenty-five years or so. After all, as the author takes pains to explain, men who fly in combat are often driven by sheer fright into a state of subhumanity.[80]

Here, the episode assumes an air of mystery. If the tale of the slaughter of the unfortunate Hurricane pilot was only ever a dream, it might be enquired just why the editor was so concerned that its telling might spark an anti-German backlash. The very fact that such a placatory statement was deemed necessary reinforces the gravity with which the issue of shooting at parachutists was regarded among the RAF. Either way, the entire dispute over whether mutual chivalry in refusing to fire upon

[78] Bartley, *Smoke Trails in the Sky*, p. 37.
[79] Hall, *Clouds of Fear*, pp. 120–1.
[80] Ibid., p. 10.

aircrew who had taken to the silk truly existed suggests a deeper desire to extract vestiges of honour from the frenzy of bloodletting in aerial combat. This need to identify at least some elements of chivalrous behaviour in battle thus provided a balm for the fighter pilot's anxieties about taking pleasure in brutality, as it bolstered their identity as a military elite fighting a 'clean' war.

Ultimately, therefore, these memoirs of the so-called 'Knights of the Air' do not, in fact, bear out Hillary's triumphant claim that the fighter pilot's approach to his enemy was that of a 'duellist'. Rather, they portray a rapid breakdown of the cool, impersonal emotional distance which these men imagined as the martial hallmark of the flyer and strove to attain. In their displays of the fighter pilot's simultaneous 'horror' and 'fascination' at killing, the narratives of 'the Few' lay bare the psychological torment which dogged many aircrew. The highest praise that Hugh Dundas could bestow upon his great friend and comrade, 'Johnnie' Johnson, as the highest-scoring Allied ace, was that 'he never became a desiccated killer-machine, which was the way with some other outstanding fighter leaders. He was always warmly human and his emotions were generous and earthy.'[81] Becoming an 'outstanding' fighter pilot was thus clearly associated with the surrender of normative, balanced emotions, but the painstaking efforts documented by these memoirists to resist both the numbing brutality and homicidal pleasures of aerial warfare thus testify that these men felt that in reality they were far from being privileged to 'kill well'.

The Soldiers' Tale: The Army in Europe and North Africa, 1939–1945

Although Hillary's assumption of the 'privilege' of the fighter pilot as killer is not entirely borne out by the veterans' tale, he was much nearer the mark when he wrote of the soldier's attitude towards killing as characterised by peculiarly 'personalised' emotions. Indeed, the narratives of soldiers serving in the campaigns across North Africa, Italy, and North-West Europe unfold a tale in which their attitudes towards killing and the enemy appear as 'personalised' to such an extent that a thick silence is cast over the individual's performance of violence. Throughout these battlefield accounts, there is little trace of the carefully cultivated insensibility with which the seamen and aircrew sought to represent their killing, nor is there any real acknowledgement of bloodlust. Wartime senior officers were puzzled by the ordinary British soldier's apparent lack of enthusiasm for killing, and in a much-quoted letter after the decisive second

---

[81] Dundas, *Flying Start*, p. 79.

156   The Veterans' Tale

battle of El Alamein in November 1942, General Bernard Montgomery was moved to ruminate that 'The trouble with our British lads is that they are not killers by nature; they have to be so inspired that they will want to kill.'[82] This quotation has become embedded in military historiography of the British army, particularly during the campaigns in North-West Europe after D-Day, throughout which low morale is frequently suggested as a reason for poor performance on the battlefield. Yet, as military historian David French observes, the British soldier's lack of relish in killing ought not to be confused with poor morale.[83] Attesting to the veracity of French's argument that the main objective of this largely conscript force was to defeat – rather than exterminate – the enemy and then return home, memoirist Peter Roach also detected a sense of prevailing temperate pragmatism among the British army:

Reared on the cynicism following the First World War we would not allow ourselves any patriotic fervour, Nordic mysticism or bravado. The drain was blocked so we rolled up our sleeves, took a deep breath and plunged our arm in to the limits.[84]

Charles Potts also explained that he lacked any visceral belligerence towards his enemies:

I could never feel any animosity towards the Germans or Italians whom we were fighting. I considered that to fight them was a painful duty, like beating a criminal, or spanking a naughty boy. I believed the enemy's cause and their intentions to be wholly bad, and that it was my duty to obstruct them with all the power that lay in me; that in this I was merely an instrument of justice; and that the only way to make Jerry behave was to knock him down.[85]

The 'pleasures of imaginative violence' remain unvoiced in representations of closing with the enemy in the narratives of either tank or infantry veterans relating the great Allied push to reclaim Europe.[86] Nevertheless, some insight into the soldier's lived and remembered experience of killing in North-West Europe after D-Day can be gleaned by drawing a brief comparison between the differing accounts of tank crew and infantry personnel. Like the sailors, the tank veterans refracted their accounts of

---

[82] Frequently quoted in historiography. For example, see Stephen Brooks, *Montgomery and the Eighth Army: a selection from the diaries, correspondence and other papers of Field Marshal the Viscount Montgomery of Alamein, August 1942 to December 1943* (London: Bodley Head for the Army Records Society, 1991), p. 90; Michael Snape, *God and the British Soldier: Religion and the British Army in the First and Second World Wars* (London: Routledge, 2005), p. 131.
[83] French, *Raising Churchill's Army*, p. 122.
[84] Roach, *The 8.15 to War*, p. 57.
[85] Potts, *Soldier in the Sand*, pp. 109–110.
[86] Bourke, *An Intimate History of Killing*, p. 30.

killing through the protective sense of mechanical 'distance' granted by their machines. Rather sardonically, Ken Tout explained that

In a tank one does not so often see people die. The tank is a nice, clean, hygienic and civilized method of slaughter. Press a button and the enemy drops out of sight, but undoubtedly safely dead. You don't even have to wipe your bayonet or wash your hands. A kind of 'humane killer' device which causes no pain at all – to the killer.[87]

The tank memoirists were unquestionably more candid and business-like about the fact that they killed, although it is notable that their descriptions of performing acts of violence mostly tended to be bound up in a theme of revenge for deceased friends or self-preservation rather than active rancour towards the Germans. Bill Bellamy took pains to explain that 'I never gained any satisfaction from the act of killing. I acted more in the spirit of self-preservation than in a determined effort to kill the enemy.'[88] Bill Close also reported that an instinctive tendency to protect himself motivated his destruction of the enemy, especially during the closing stages of the campaign in North-West Europe. Somewhere near the Dortmund-Ems Canal in the spring of 1945, a 'determined but misguided' German hit Close's tank with a Panzerfaust, then attempted to surrender. Having eliminated the soldier, the memoirist rationalised his murderous act by explaining that the 'unknown hero with the bazooka was dealing with a lot of worried, anxious men.'[89]

The fact that the tank veterans exhibited such frankness about the act of killing serves to highlight the odd silence that marks accounts of closing with the enemy upon the same battlefields in the accounts of former foot soldiers. From a purely practical perspective, it has been enquired whether Second World War infantry killed as frequently as might be supposed. Questions about the numbers of soldiers who actually brought their weapons to bear in action during the Second World War were raised in a startling – and still hotly debated – study by the American military theorist SLA Marshall in 1947 which claimed that only one in four men in battle had fired at enemy personnel.[90] Such controversial doubts regarding the subject of fire ratios under combat have no place, however, in this qualitative enquiry into how veterans understood and recorded their approach to the enemy in action, since they can only result in fruitless (and potentially insulting) speculation. Perhaps a slightly more useful theory with which to partially explain the lack of recorded violence

[87] Tout, *Tank!*, p. 63.
[88] Bellamy, *Troop Leader*, p. 172.
[89] Close, *Tank Commander*, p. 3.
[90] Marshall, *Men Against Fire*, p. 50.

in the soldiers' memoirs is the 'empty battlefield phenomenon.' Since 1870, dispersion of troops on the battlefield had become increasingly less dense, and by the Second World War, troop density had decreased to roughly one man per 27,500 square metres.[91] This phenomenon has been used to explain the battlefield dynamics that simultaneously generated increasing weapon lethality and decreasing casualties, and implies that it was not beyond the bounds of possibility that individual soldiers may never have despatched the enemy face-to-face in the melee of combat. Yet this too is to wander dangerously close to the edge of unproductive assumption; all too often whether the author engaged in the ultimate act of destroying another human life is obscured in these veteran memoirs. What is more productive is to probe the ways in which he did record his responses to his adversary when, unlike his counterparts in the other services, he was denied even the protective semblance of self-shielding mechanical 'distance' on the battlefield.

Rather than describing the actual act of slaughter, the soldier-memoirists opted to focus upon portraying a more intimate familiarity with, and personalisation of, the body of the enemy in its specific forms of corpse and prisoner of war, as well as still-active combatant. In these corporeal forms, British contact with the enemy often elicited recognition and even a strange feeling of fellowship. According to former platoon commander Sydney Jary, a unique reciprocal empathy between combatants sprang from battle. He claimed that opposing forces of infantry 'are joined by a bond of mutual compassion which few but the aristocracy of the battlefield can understand.'[92] Rex Wingfield, an infantryman who served in the push through North-West Europe in 1944, provides a particularly instructive representation of the British soldier's relationship with the body of the enemy. Advancing upon a slit trench, he observed two Germans cowering in it. He perceived one of them to be 'wearily asleep'. The memoirist reported that he and his comrades were aghast when a British officer directed fire from his Sten gun at the comatose German, who simply folded to the bottom of the trench. Crying with exhaustion, the surviving German – who Wingfield described with rough sympathy as 'all in' – informed them that his mate had already been dead before the British officer opened fire. The incident evidently struck a nerve with Wingfield, who reported a strong sense of revulsion at the entire episode:

We looked at the officer with hate in our eyes. He had been a failure in carriers, mortars and anti-tanks, and now he was foisted on to us. This was his first day

[91] James J. Schneider, 'The Theory of the Empty Battlefield', *Military Science*, 132:3 (1987), 37.
[92] Jary, *18 Platoon*, p. 117.

with us, and in our eyes he was guilty of desecrating the dead. The dead of both sides were sacred.[93]

This anecdote reveals much about the author's attitude towards the enemy, both dead and living. In the first instance, Wingfield's condemnation of the British officer, echoes Jary's claim that infantrymen from both sides were bound together by certain unspoken rules which this officer clearly ignored. Secondly, this tale points towards the sanctification of the dead. Removed of their status as a threat, they are deemed 'out of play' and are consequently governed by different conventions. Yet the British officer did not know when he loosed off his Sten at the 'sleeping' German that the man was already deceased; his intention, it is implied here, was simply to kill a live, helpless enemy. Consequently, Wingfield's outrage at the 'desecration of the dead' was evidently also conditioned by notions of a fair fight and respect for the defeated enemy.

Aside from their differences in recounting the act of killing, the memoirs of tank and infantry veterans relate a very similar tale of psychologically responding to the enemy. Both sets of servicemen encountered at first hand the shambolic wreckage to which men on the battlefield were reduced. In both sets of memoirs, therefore, considerable attention is given to representation of responding to the enemy in the aftermath of battle. British soldiers acquired a degree of intimacy with the habits and character of their enemy which was denied to the sailors and airmen who might, under rare circumstances, just about be afforded a passing glimpse of their opponents. Often, the close proximity between opposing forces meant that frontline troops were able to gain a sensory familiarity with the very anatomy of their foe. Tank commander Ken Tout provides a valuable illustration of how he and his fellow combatants were able to acquire an intimate knowledge of the enemy's person before they even laid eyes on him:

we have, since landing, invaded his shelters and his dug-outs after he has retreated. We have picked up his letters and tried to decipher the strange Gothic script. We have seen him surrender in his baggy, field-grey uniform and his easily recognizable pudding-basin helmet. We have also heard his guttural language and smelled his strange, animal smell, a foul odour acquired from chemically treated clothing (we also carry that smell on our khaki), constant proximity to putrefying flesh and consumption of rancid food.[94]

Because death was frequently bound into the very landscape in which they operated, it was frequently impossible to avoid coming into contact with the enemy's body, whether it was alive or dead. Familiarity

[93] Wingfield, The Only Way Out, p. 97.
[94] Tout, Tank!, p. 63.

with the enemy's body thus underpins these veterans' interpretations and representations of battlefield relations. The smell of the enemy cadavers invoked particularly intense responses. Outside a Normandy village, Robert Woollcombe stumbled across a chalk pit of which he recollected that German corpses 'littered it like flies. Many must have been accounted for by artillery fire. Every yard there were bodies. The faint musty odour still comes back to one's nostrils in any weather.'[95] In the woods of Normandy, Tout described being sickened by a lingering 'putrid, sickly sweet smell, leaving a loathsome aftertaste on the palate, like the taint of a rotting orange.'[96] This stench of death was traced to the rotting bodies of several German soldiers. For several memoirists, their first face-to-face confrontations with the enemy were with corpses. Shortly after the great battle of Monte Cassino in Italy, Alex Bowlby found himself travelling in convoy through the ruined outskirts of the town:

A row of black crosses, topped with coal-scuttle helmets, snatched our pity. The smell – the sour-sweet stench of rotting flesh – cut it short. Instinctively I realised I was smelling my own kind, and not animals. I understood what they must feel in a slaughter-house. These dead were under the rubble. If we could have seen their bodies it would have helped. The unseen, unconsecrated dead assumed a most terrifying power. Their protest filled the truck.[97]

To Bowlby, the malodour of rotting flesh forcibly brought home a sense of recognition that the corpses were those of men like himself. Yet it was not the fact *per se* that these bodies were deceased that lent the decaying cadavers terror, it was their invisibility that daunted Bowlby. Again, imagination is portrayed as a severe handicap to the combatant. Unable to rationalise the dead by witnessing their faces, horror-filled fantasies about what they might look like terrified this memoirist. In contrast, he narrates moving through a 'backwash' of fallen enemy soldiers who had been caught in an artillery barrage. 'What had been man was now a bundle of rags ... yet the bodies seemed curiously remote ... They had none of the horror of the unseen dead.'[98] For this veteran, once the body of the dead foe was rendered recognisable, displaying at least the remnants of human form and face, its power to strike fear was drawn.

Others found that it was more difficult to detach themselves emotionally from the dead enemy. Unlike Bowlby and Woollcombe, several memoirists insist that becoming acquainted with the decomposing

[95] Woollcombe, *Lion Rampant*, p. 63.
[96] Tout, *By Tank*, p. 13.
[97] Bowlby, *Recollections*, p. 20.
[98] Ibid., p. 33.

anatomy of the enemy prompted a surge of emotions which variously included empathy, pity, and respect. In Tunisia John Kenneally encountered the corpses of German infantry whose attack on his position had been beaten off by the Irish Guards. Fresh from the horrors of fighting through burning Tunisian cornfields, in which many of his comrades lay dead or wounded, he did not expect to feel moved by scenes of carnage among the enemy: 'They had done much worse to my dead and wounded comrades'.[99] Nevertheless, he reflected,

It struck me forcibly as I wandered amongst them that these guys were just the same as us; they suffered as we suffered, they died as we died or were going to die and the only difference between us was our uniforms. I respected them.[100]

Similarly unanticipated emotion was experienced by Ray Ward during the great Allied pursuit of the Axis forces through North Africa after the Second Battle of El Alamein in the autumn of 1942. Thanks to severe rain storms, the desert route rapidly became a sea of mud littered with the human flotsam and jetsam of Rommel's retreat and 'Makeshift German cemeteries appeared like islands in the quagmire' whilst 'Sodden bundles of fabric turned out to be corpses'.[101] Ward reflected that he was unexpectedly surprised to feel 'saddened' by these sights: 'Odd that I should have felt that in some way the dead Jerries were comrades too.'[102]

The veterans' tale suggests that preconceived images of the German soldier as an inhuman 'Hun' often dissolved upon first contact. Various memoirists found that the captive body of the enemy inspired at least as strong an emotional response as his corpse, and some, like John Foley, were surprised to find that prisoners-of-war bore little resemblance to caricatured images in the British media. Upon landing shortly after D-Day, his first sight of the enemy arrived in the form of a group of captured Germans. He was astonished to find that they appeared 'just ordinary', 'rather scruffy' soldiers. 'So this was the *Herrenvolk*! But where', he enquired, 'were the blond and arrogant supermen we had heard so much about?'[103] For others, making the visual acquaintance of a captured enemy transformed uncompromising imagined knowledge of the foe into unanticipated sympathy for his plight. Woollcombe experienced an unforeseen sense of connection with a prisoner who was 'clutching my legs and pleading for his life. One did not blame him for

---

[99] John Kenneally, *The Honour and the Shame* (London: Headline Review, 2007), p. 75.
[100] Ibid., p. 84.
[101] Ward, *The Mirror of Monte Cavallara*, p. 177.
[102] Ibid., p. 177.
[103] Foley, *Mailed Fist*, p. 12.

his terror.'[104] Through the extension of such empathy, the body of the captive enemy operated as a point of reference against which the British soldier could measure his own fears. As Tout recalled,

We have simply waved at them, frightened, grey-faced men, frequently much older or younger than any of us, often shocked into incontinence, indoctrinated with a fear of being shot on surrender. We have waved at them in a rather sympathetic manner and have pointed them back towards the rear.[105]

Wingfield's memoir demonstrates a particular sympathy towards the enemy prisoners, as he saw in them a reflection of his own identity as both man and soldier. Whilst his unit received a group of Germans into their care, a shell landed nearby. Without pausing for thought, Wingfield grabbed the nearest prisoner and together they tumbled into the shelter of ditch:

We clung to each other, trembling. The shell burst. The stark lunacy of war hit us both at the same time. Ten minutes ago we'd have cheerfully killed each other if it had come to that, and yet here we were instinctively protecting our mate – only the two mates happened to be wearing different uniforms.[106]

His rationalisation of his actions offers a valuable window into a carefully constructed fantasy of a special brotherhood amongst infantrymen:

Our prisoners were Infantry and we received them as comrades. These blokes had been going through it just like us, only they'd had our Artillery thrown in as well. We knew what that meant. We'd had some. Regardless of race or uniform, we 'flatties' were a people apart from, and superior to, other human beings. These Germans were men like us and they'd had a hell of a time since D-Day, shelled all day and denied sleep at night because they were retreating and being harried by the Allied Air Forces. We passed them food and cigarettes. It wasn't charity or pity, but understanding and comradeship. They understood too.[107]

It is worth noting the memoirist's specific insistence that he did not pity these captives. As an emotion, pity is loaded with connotations of charity or superiority. For Wingfield this was a connection between equals of a singular breed and worthy of special honour.

Wingfield's discourses of 'understanding and comradeship' particularly stud the narratives of combat in North Africa. Amid the fighting in Tunisia, John Horsfall noted, 'we came to have a considerable professional regard and respect' for Walter Koch's 5th Parachute Regiment: 'Dangerous as enemies they fought a clean war, and pleasantries were

---

[104] Woollcombe, *Lion Rampant*, p. 56.
[105] Tout, *Tank!*, p. 63.
[106] Wingfield, *The Only Way Out*, pp. 72–3 .
[107] Ibid., p. 73.

passed whenever the circumstances permitted.'[108] Once again the 'myth of the desert' was invoked as a campaign peculiarly lacking in rancour or atrocity, and a special bond was imagined between antagonists in the desert war. Rea Leakey, who saw action with 1st Royal Tank Regiment at Tobruk in 1941, insisted that with only one exception,

I never witnessed or heard of a case of foul fighting by the German Afrika Korps. On the whole, they fought very hard, but they fought clean and they treated prisoners and wounded well.[109]

Ray Ward expressed a firm conviction that the status of the desert as a 'perfect battlefield' generated a unique connection between British and German soldiers. He declared that the desert armies shared a bond of professional respect which translated into warm mutual regard signified by their nicknames for each other: 'We didn't call Rommel or his men Nazis – just "Jerries". They called us "Tommies" or "Jocks".'[110] Battlefield relations in the desert thus rapidly became woven into the myth of a 'clean' war, which was seemingly accepted on both sides. Rommel's own war memoir, titled *Krieg ohne Hass* (*War without Hate*), epitomises what one study of this arena describes as 'a bizarre comradeship of antagonists'.[111] The notion of a 'war without hate' in North Africa has been rightfully been disputed by Barr, but the salient point here is that these memoirists clearly subscribed to the myth of a 'clean' war in the desert. Applauded for his decision to abide by the Geneva Convention, Rommel was remembered as

probably the Eighth Army's most popular general. I certainly felt that our morale and self-esteem were boosted by the knowledge that we were fighting a daring and honourable enemy. He had a reputation for 'fair play'. That virtually guaranteed him the respect of the British officer class. Perhaps we forgot about the regime he served.[112]

Ironically, Rommel became the poster-boy for the British soldier's fantasy of what battlefield relations ought to be in all theatres of war. In Europe, for example, Rex Wingfield recorded that he drank a toast to the German commander upon his death in 1944, explaining that 'Rommel was not a man, but a god to both sides'.[113] Indeed, Wingfield's simple tribute stands as the epitome of many of his fellow memoirists' emotional responses to the enemy, whether as living combatant, dead body, or captive: 'He was one of us.'[114]

[108] Horsfall, *The Wild Geese are Flighting*, p. 45.
[109] Rea Leakey, *Leakey's Luck: A Tank Commander with Nine Lives* (Stroud: Sutton Publishing Ltd, 1999), p. 67.
[110] Ward, *The Mirror of Monte Cavallara*, p. 128.
[111] Bierman and Smith, *Alamein: War Without Hate*, p. 1; Barr, *Pendulum of War*.
[112] Ward, *The Mirror of Monte Cavallara*, pp. 127–8.
[113] Wingfield, *The Only Way Out*, p. 94.
[114] Ibid., p. 95.

By no means, however, does the veterans' tale comprehensively wrap depictions of their responses towards the enemy in a blanket of reasonable goodwill. Although Montgomery lamented that the British soldier lacked visceral belligerence, these memoirs suggest that there were indeed circumstances under which combatants could well be 'so inspired that they will want to kill'. Snipers are openly detested in these accounts because, as Rex Wingfield explained, 'Ordinary Infantry were doing a job, like us, but snipers were low, nasty, mean fighters' who could 'hold us up out of all proportion to their numbers.'[115] It was felt that snipers did not play by the rules of open face-to-face combat. Instead they conducted what Kenneally described venomously as 'bloody guerrilla warfare', explaining that 'every soldier hates snipers; the odds are always with them'.[116] With their long record of cruelty, the Waffen-SS were also universally hated, and are portrayed in these memoirs as utterly exempt from the honour and fellow-feeling extended towards the ordinary German soldier. Ken Tout recorded that the mere thought of this particular enemy had the power to terrify him: 'Within my skull lurk horrific hordes of murderous SS fanatics and thugs, who, when I open the door of my mind, rush forward and occupy and terrorize my entire being.'[117] Both Robert Woollcombe and Bill Bellamy also perceived that this was a despicable enemy who deserved little sympathetic treatment. The prisoner with whom Woollcombe earlier documented experiencing an unanticipated flash of understanding had served with the 12th SS Panzer Division, which had committed a number of atrocities during the early days of Operation *Overlord*. Manned by enthusiastic former members of the HitlerJugend, these men were ardent subscribers to the Nazi cause. On 7 June 1944, the division shot twenty-three Canadian prisoners just outside of Caen, and carried out a policy of reprisals against further prisoners and French villagers throughout the Normandy campaign.[118] After the war, a number of members of the division stood trial for war crimes. Realisation of to which unit his prisoner belonged clearly coloured Woollcombe's response to the captive's plight: 'this Nazi ... was one of the "Herrenvolk."' Consequently, he explained, 'One felt no compassion.'[119] Similarly, despite Bellamy's stated lack of 'satisfaction from the act of killing', he reflected that

The only time when I had felt a strong urge to kill was when we faced the SS Panzer divisions, who behaved so wickedly at the time of the breakout from France.[120]

[115] Wingfield, *The Only Way Out*, p. 62.
[116] Kenneally, *The Honour and the Shame*, p. 152.
[117] Tout, *By Tank*, p. 67.
[118] Robin Neillands, *The Battle of Normandy* (London: Cassell, 2003), p. 81.
[119] Woollcombe, *Lion Rampant*, p. 56.
[120] Bellamy, *Troop Leader*, p. 172.

Broadly speaking, aside from displaying a clear antagonism towards those units of the enemy who were deemed as despicable opponents such as snipers, the Waffen-SS, and Panzerfaust-wielders, the memoirs of tank and infantry veterans suggest that the British veteran did not seek to consciously dehumanise the opposition on the battlefield. As French suggests, the wartime army failed to indoctrinate its soldiers with the kind of ideological fervour that might have imbued them with the desire to close with the enemy and embrace the act of killing at close quarters.[121] Nor were the British armed forces subject to the kind of sadistic disciplinary system that inculcated brutalism in the German troops.[122] The use of the death penalty in the respective armies provides an excellent case in point here. In 1930 the British Army Council revoked the death penalty for cowardice and desertion on active service, and no men were executed for the latter offence during the Second World War.[123] The German army retained the death penalty for a wide range of military offences, executing between 13,000 and 15,000 men between 1939 and 1945.[124] Unlike the German regime, the British military authorities largely did not prime their soldiers to kill by brutalising their soldiers to the extent that they took out their aggression upon those weaker than themselves, nor did they inculcate the British troops to believe their enemies to be subhuman and therefore fit only for extermination.[125]

In 1945 social anxieties about the return of a generation of servicemen mentally warped by wartime active service circulated in Britain. Concerns about the potential brutalisation of the 'People's Army' identified the demobbed soldier as a particular impending social problem. The army in particular was frequently popularly construed as a 'debased institution' with the power to corrupt the soldier through continuous exposure to violence.[126] Among the British soldiers' memoirs, therefore, the substitution of descriptions of how the combatant experienced and understood the killing act with representations of a peculiar form of kinship with the enemy perhaps becomes more explicable. Although the tank memoirist frankly acknowledged his own role in the performance of violence, the infantry memoirist preferred instead to discuss engagements with the enemy through a prism of affinity with the German soldier, insisting upon the existence of a reciprocal battlefield fellowship

[121] French, *Raising Churchill's Army*, p. 122.
[122] Ibid., p. 134; p. 154.
[123] David French, 'Discipline and the Death Penalty in the British Army in the War against Germany during the Second World War', *Journal of Contemporary History* 33:4 (1998), 544.
[124] French, *Raising Churchill's Army*, p. 153.
[125] Ibid., p. 153.
[126] Allport, *Demobbed*, p. 11.

between honourable equals. These accounts thus assert that the British infantryman and his enemy were bound together in what Jary describes as 'mutual compassion', which brought a reassuring degree of humanity to the battlefield. Regarding the question of whether battle had coarsened his beloved platoon, Jary insisted emphatically that 'War developed in 18 Platoon consideration for comrades and humanity towards civilians and prisoners-of-war.' 'Certainly', he insisted, 'no soldier of mine was made brutal, rather the opposite.'[127] Testifying to Montgomery's remark about the British soldier not being a 'natural' killer, Charles Potts recorded that 'I was much happier when [the enemy] gave himself up as a prisoner, and saved us the indecent task of having to shoot him.'[128] The sense of emotional closeness to the personalised living, captured, and dead enemy upon which these combatants insisted is explained with striking simplicity by Ward's plaintive reflection that 'most of us wanted to believe that some decency could survive the absurdity, chaos and cruelty of war'.[129]

Summary

Among the different branches of Britain's armed forces, there were clear differences in the type of fantasy that combatants projected onto their opposition. The accounts of the war at sea and in the air collectively testify that it was far easier to carry out acts of extreme violence when the foe was in some manner dehumanised and mechanised in their imaginations. Sailors and airmen were perhaps more fortunate than the soldiers in that they were granted an opportunity to employ what Norman Hampson labelled the 'grey machinery of murder' as a kind of psychological shield from behind which they could elide moral responsibility for their actions, and express professional satisfaction in a job well done. Yet as Bourke observes, 'technology still failed to render the dead completely faceless' in the Second World War.[130] Despite the best efforts of machine-bound combatants to achieve a psychological remoteness from their target, they often found themselves willingly or unwillingly extending an emotive bond towards their opposition. These memoirs further attest that the protagonists experienced moments when their defensive mechanisms of 'distance' fractured and they forged a fleeting emotive bond with the dead and living foe. Arguably, a reluctant recognition of the enemy's identity as a human being in these moments bestows upon

---

[127] Jary, *18 Platoon*, p. 89.
[128] Potts, *Soldier in the Sand*, pp. 109–110.
[129] Ward, *The Mirror of Monte Cavallara*, p. 128.
[130] Bourke, *An Intimate History of Killing*, p. 6.

the naval and aircrew memoirs an often uneasy tension with the author's designated martial function as a killer.

A similar anxiety stalks the infantry memoirs. Prose reconstructions of confronting the enemy allowed a veteran to assess his own wartime identity as a killer. Ward's assertion that he and other soldiers needed the reassurance of believing in ideals of humane compassion among the bloody tatters of the battlefield suggests that these veterans keenly sought to identify themselves as 'decent' men when it was all over and they returned to a civic culture that deplored violence. The ex-soldiers' odd silence over the actual act of killing may perhaps partially be attributed to an understandable personal reluctance to recollect or discuss distressing graphic details of driving a bayonet into another man's guts or obliterating him at close quarters. Given that these memoirs were often constructed with a specific audience of the veteran's family in mind, it is also unlikely that these men would have wanted their wives or children to read that they had taken visceral pleasure in killing a man face-to-face. Among these carefully shrouded representations of violence, by substituting scenes of second-hand slaughter for first-hand execution, the veteran tacitly asserts a lack of personal responsibility for the killing. In effect, he distances himself from the horrors of battlefield. The searing exactitude of Bourke's comment that twentieth-century soldiers rarely confessed to finding professional gratification in their engagements with the enemy because to 'describe combat as enjoyable was like admitting to being a blood-thirsty brute' is borne out by Nicholas Mosley's reflection on the difficulties of writing an accurate war memoir about the Second World War. There was, he mused, 'a whiff of immature triumphalism in stories about successful killing – unless one has paid the price of being killed oneself.'[131] Unable to hide behind the 'grey machinery of murder', the removal of cultural and emotional 'distance' from the enemy in their reconstructions of the battlefield perhaps allowed infantry veterans to reassure themselves that their own status as 'good' human beings fighting a just war remained intact.

The ways in which these memoirists interpreted, elaborated, restructured, or muffled extremes of violence in their narratives thus reveal not only how they thought they reconciled themselves to killing during the war, but also how they felt about their murderous actions decades afterwards. The core tropes in which the memoirists couched their representations of engaging with the enemy may be explained in the following terms: 'chivalry was evoked to stifle fears of senseless violence; intimacy was substituted for confusing anonymity; skilfulness was

[131] Nicholas Mosley, *Time at War* (London: Weinfeld and Nicholson, 2006), p. ix.

imposed to dispel numbing monotony.'[132] Respectively, the veteran-memoirists of Fighter Command, the Army, and the Royal Navy injected these discourses into their accounts of facing the foe in order to reassure themselves and their readers that they had not become brutalised by the wartime killing enterprise. These are not the narratives of automaton-like killing machines who exterminated ruthlessly. The extent to which memoirists from all three armed services insist upon emotional relationships with the enemy thus offers important comment on the creation of these documents as historical records. Several historians have noted the tendency of the British soldier – and arguably by extension naval personnel and aircrew – to regard the war as an unpleasant but necessary job that had to be finished so that everyone could return to their jobs and families.[133] That these veterans wove into their narratives multiple instances where they recognised the human identity of their opposition suggests that they wanted to be remembered as finishing the job in a decisive but decent manner.

Nevertheless, combat was a lonely act. Even when technology provided mechanical and psychological distance from the enemy, combatants forged elements of an emotional relationship with the enemy. Linked to this desire to personalise relations with the enemy to varying degree, was the enormous psychological importance memoirists attached to personal relationships within their own services. As Marshall noted, 'On the field of fire it is the touch of human nature which gives men courage and enables them to make proper use of their weapons.'[134] The next chapter thus interrogates the veterans' understandings and representations of human relations within their own units as a crucial mechanism of motivation and endurance in combat.

---

[132] Bourke, *An Intimate History of Killing*, p. 68.
[133] French, *Raising Churchill's Army*, p. 122; Sheffield, 'Dead Cows and Tigers', p. 127.
[134] Marshall, *Men Against Fire*, p. 41.

6   Comradeship, Leadership, and Martial Fraternity

> The heart of the matter is to relate the man to his fellow soldier as
> he will find him on the field of combat, to condition him to human
> nature as he will learn to depend on it when the ground offers him
> no comfort and weapons fail.[1]

Despite the best efforts of military theorists, historians, and psychiatrists, there exists no universal explanation of what makes men fight or why they break down in battle. Merging these discussions in 2006, Simon Wessely, professor in psychiatric medicine at King's College London, identified a fundamental relationship between combat motivation and demotivation, suggesting that the bridging element was the key role of the small group in combat.[2] After the Second World War new views on combat motivation emerged as a result of several surveys sponsored by the US War Department, including SLA Marshall's study of American soldiers fighting in the Pacific. This led to the enshrinement of 'primary group' theory in Western military doctrine.[3] The primary group was regarded as the core motivation for fighting and the key to preventing breakdown in battle.[4] Marshall's work is not without its critics, and more recent studies have commented upon the limitations of using small group theory as a one-size-fits-all approach to twentieth-century combat motivation. As Hew Strachan notes, 'primary group' theory is all too frequently inflated to such an extent that it does not allow for calculations of the importance of training, the impact of high casualties, increased flow of replacements, or 'misfits' in a unit.[5] Bruce Newsome also warns of a need to distinguish

---

[1] Marshall, *Men Against Fire*, p. 38.
[2] Simon Wessely, 'Twentieth-Century Theories on Combat Motivation and Breakdown', *Journal of Contemporary History*, 41:2 (2006), 269.
[3] Samuel Stouffer (ed.), *The American Soldier: Combat and Its Aftermath* (Princeton: NJ, 1949); Edward Shils and Morris Janowitz, 'Cohesion and Disintegration in the Wehrmacht in World War II', *Public Opinion Quarterly*, 12 (1948).
[4] Wessely, 'Twentieth-Century Theories on Combat Motivation and Breakdown', 278.
[5] Hew Strachan, 'Training, Morale and Modern War', *Journal of Contemporary History* 41:2 (2006), 212.

between 'intrinsic' (genetic, cultural, or social) and 'extrinsic' (derived from military socialisation, training, and other conditioning) combat motivations.[6] In undertaking any study of what makes men fight and what keeps them fighting, it is imperative to bear in mind that a wide and complex range of factors, including underlying differences between coercion and discipline imposed by the military as a means of personnel management, as opposed to innate qualities of self-discipline in the soldier, serve to condition combat motivation and demotivation.

Nevertheless, the British veterans' tale of combat during the Second World War foregrounded personal relationships within their units as the ultimate spur in battle. The memoirs of British veterans share and articulate a core theme of placing a premium on the social-emotional relationships forged between fighting men within a small unit. The term 'small' is fluidly interpreted throughout these memoirs. Among the army memoirists, 'small' could mean anything from regiment down to platoon level; in the Royal Navy the company of a 'little' ship or submarine was regarded as a discrete combat unit; Bomber Command regarded the individual Lancaster crew as a seven-man fighting unit. Reflecting Marshall's insistence that combatants ideally needed to be conditioned to 'human nature' so that they could draw strength from each other in battle, the memoirists frequently turned to Shakespeare's *Henry V* for inspiration in order to communicate the intense value that combatants attached to their comrades. The playwright's immortal lines, 'We few, we happy few, we band of brothers:/ For he today that sheds his blood with me/ Shall be my brother' particularly resonate throughout the veterans' tale.[7] During the Second World War, *Henry V* became irrevocably connected to the British war effort as the play served as a national parable of British tenacity in the face of overwhelming odds. The 'band of brothers' excerpt from King Henry's famous 'Crispin Crispian' speech was memorably invoked in 1940 when Churchill alluded to the Battle of Britain pilots as 'the Few'. In 1942, Laurence Olivier's stirring declamation of this speech on a radio programme entitled 'Into Battle' served as 'a patriotic call to arms for embattled Britain', and was followed up two years later by that actor's immensely popular production of *Henry V*.[8] Given the wartime parallels drawn between *Henry V* and the British war effort, perhaps it is unsurprising that a number of veterans of the Second World War invested Shakespeare's immortal lines with an almost talismanic status in their own representations of that war, adopting the phrase 'band of brothers'

[6] Bruce Newsome, 'The Myth of Intrinsic Combat Motivation', *Journal of Strategic Studies*, 26:4 (2003), 24.
[7] Shakespeare, *Henry V*, in *William Shakespeare*, (ed.) W. J. Craig, p. 491.
[8] Marjorie Garber, *Shakespeare After All* (New York: Anchor Books, 2004), p. 36.

to portray an idealised image of a close-knit martial fraternity in their memoirs. Several infantry veterans also invoked important scenes from the play to convey their own experiences on the front line. Ray Ward reminisced that some of his fellow officers would gather in his dugout during off-duty evenings in the desert to read *Henry V*, recording that they especially enjoyed the dialogue of the four captains: 'We identified with their thoughts on war, and the play's themes of brotherhood, bravery and honourable old age. We were responsive to its stirring rhetoric and the fact that the play does not shy away from the horrors of war.'[9] Shakespeare's famous scene depicting the battle of Agincourt held particular personal meaning for several memoirists. Edward Grace wrote that the evening before a big offensive in North Africa, 'the Commanding Officer walked around with encouraging words, rather like Henry V before Agincourt. We were all outwardly cheerful, making jokes and pretending the night was for adventure.'[10] Similarly, in his description of the prelude to the opening up of the Second Front, Robert Woollcombe quoted the Crispin's Day speech as means of conveying the excitement and pride of the troops.[11] Thus, *Henry V* frequently became employed as a touchstone for veterans' own interpretations of the battle experience. The 'band of brothers' tag itself was also explicitly referred to in several memoirs of former Royal Navy and RAF personnel.[12] Even where this tag is not directly evoked in the narratives, the sense of martial 'brotherhood' it embodied, and the core themes of leadership, courage, and morale with which the playwright knitted together his 'band of brothers' also form central pillars of these veterans' discussions of relationships within their own combat units.

The Soldiers' Tale: The Army in Europe and North Africa, 1939–1945

'Without being over-sentimental,' asserted John Kenneally, 'men can love each other.' Reflecting on the nature of this affection, he identified the emotional relationships of men within a military unit as 'born of mutual suffering, hardships shared, dangers encountered, mutual experiences. It is a spiritual love and it is even stronger than brotherly love. It is called comradeship'.[13] This regard for the soldier's fellow fighting

---

[9] Ward, *The Mirror of Monte Cavallara* , p. 148.
[10] Grace, *The Perilous Road to Rome*, p. 16.
[11] Woollcombe, *Lion Rampant*, p. 39.
[12] For example, see Hart, *Discharged Dead*, p. 38; Mars, *Unbroken*, p. 14; Johnson, *The Withered Garland*, p. 197.
[13] Kenneally, *The Honour and the Shame*, p. 54.

man forms a staple theme in the memoirs of former British infantrymen, throughout which the 'band of brothers' concept runs as a prominent leitmotif. Binding their identities irrevocably to those of their comrades, these writers assessed their own value as combatants in the light of their place among this martial fraternity. Several memoirists perceived that the nature of the infantryman's war helped to weave the soldier into a 'unique, almost tribal fellowship'.[14] Ray Ward thought that infantry became emotionally linked by a commonality of specific experiences: 'All of us were ordinary men, of all types, cast in extraordinary roles, having to exist in the extraordinary conditions of the "poor bloody infantry" at the "sharp end of war".'[15] Geoffrey Picot insisted with some pride that the infantryman was the 'king of warriors' because he did not have the protection of heavy machinery, and confronted the enemy on a far more intimate basis than any other form of combatant. The soldier could thus spend his much of his time in 'almost continuous crisis. Lacking the psychological comfort of a large gun, vehicle, ship or similar equipment, he can cling only to his pals, and they to him.'[16]

In lieu of a machine upon which to lavish affection and imagine as a source of comfort in battle, these memoirs document that the infantryman cherished his comrades as a stimulus to his own morale. A lynchpin of private, internalised morale was simple determination not to let one's pals down by giving way to terror. Picot recorded how, in North-West Europe, he was shocked to discover that an 'insidious' fear was beginning to gnaw at his powers of endurance. When he took stock of how many of the men who had accompanied him in the D-Day landings had been killed, he realised that he was now one of the longest-serving men in the unit. Grimly calculating the law of averages, he assumed that he too would soon be killed, and found that his self-control began to unravel. 'It was then', he noted, 'that a subtle military factor rescued my morale':

I could see that most men were absorbing the strain reasonably well, so I decided that I had better try to look as if I was. Only later did I learn that all were frightened and most took pains to conceal their fear. Nearly all of us played this concealment game. Thus, a man pretending to be brave gave bravery to his comrades; as they, with their pretence, likewise gave bravery to him.[17]

It is striking that Picot identified the upswing in his resolve as triggered by his comrades to be a 'military factor'. Martial discipline and coercion are other factors that force the soldier to overcome fear, yet

---

[14] Ward, *The Mirror of Monte Cavallara*, p. 17.
[15] Ibid., p. 17.
[16] Picot, *Accidental Warrior*, p. 282.
[17] Ibid., p. 28.

they leave little trace in these memoirs, which collectively recount a tale of self-discipline as motivation in combat. Peter Cochrane devoted some thought to the question of what kept men fighting, drawing the conclusion that 'cowed, unthinking obedience quite unfits a soldier for the modern battlefield.'[18] He asserted that military discipline in the Second World War was in the final analysis an internal affair, 'in a curious way, self-imposed'.[19] Advancing towards Hill 270 in the Avellino valley in southern Italy, Christopher Bulteel was spurred on by the near presence of others in his unit: 'To hesitate now would be treason.'[20] All three men display a conviction that the bedrock of discipline in battle was the soldier's own resolution and determination to continue in order not to let his comrades down, cementing Richard Holmes's observation that 'the bonds of mateship tied men willingly to the altar of battle.'[21]

This sense of comradeship extended beyond the front line. As a young gentleman ranker, Alex Bowlby became so absorbed into his predominantly Cockney 'band of brothers' in the 2nd Battalion of the Rifle Brigade that he sought the shelter of their company even when the unit was resting. Rather than visit Assisi on his own, he chose to go to see Bob Hope and Bing Crosby with his comrades because their company made him feel 'safe'. He recorded that

So far I'd coped with fighting better than I'd hoped. I didn't want to meet anything that might weaken me. Putting it another way I was afraid of anything coming between me and the Company, afraid of losing the love and support I had found there.[22]

Bowlby's attachment to his fellow riflemen demonstrates that employing the unit as a source of private morale was a two-way process. Whilst he did not want to 'weaken' his input to the collective deposit of morale, he was also able to withdraw sufficient funds to keep himself afloat. Conversely, men who boosted their own spirits by contributing to raising those of their comrades found that the resolution and rough affection of their fellows provided ballast for their own abilities to cope. Ward, for example, wrote that he drew private strength from the 'almost superhuman powers of endurance' of his Jocks, in whom he found 'a quiet determination to stick it out to the end, and more often than not a cheerful courage and fortitude that lifted my spirits'.[23] As Bowlby's account illustrates, the military unit itself represented an important source of morale for the

[18] Cochrane, *Charlie Company*, p. 119.
[19] Ibid., p. 119.
[20] Bulteel, *Something About a Soldier*, p. 199.
[21] Richard Holmes, 'The Italian Job: Five Armies in Italy, 1943–45', in *Time to Kill*, p. 210.
[22] Bowlby, *Recollections*, p. 89.
[23] Ward, *The Mirror of Monte Cavallara*, p. 289.

soldier, regardless of the personal relationships he formed with individuals within it. One of the key flaws in the 'primary group' theory is that the ebb and flow of casualties and replacements naturally eroded the small group loyalties of soldiers, and Holmes warns that historians must not get 'too misty-eyed about the pulling-power of the regiment'.[24] Yet these memoirists avow that the 'band' was equally as important as the 'brothers' in providing motivation on the battlefield. Bowlby explained that, as the unit moved up through Italy in 1944, he became 'afraid of straying too far away from the Company ... I had grown less dependent on individuals but, paradoxically enough, more dependent on the Company. It had given me the only real sense of security I had ever had.'[25] Similarly, when Cochrane bade farewell to his beloved C Company four years after joining it in 1940, he recalled that 'Like an old knife that has had three new blades and two new handles, it was and it wasn't by then the same company.' Whilst the men who served under him had changed countless times, he insisted that 'Charlie Company' still retained its identity as a unit.[26] The British regimental system steeped recruits in the martial ethos and traditions of a regiment as a mechanism of binding soldiers together in a structure of mutual loyalty, care, and pride. The success of this stratagem is evident from the importance that the veterans' tale attached importance to 'the regiment' as a source of physical and psychological support on the battlefield. Bulteel recorded that during the invasion of Salerno, his unit was tasked with taking an enemy-held hill crest. As he climbed through streams of Spandau fire, he reported 'wondering all the time why I was charging at all':

Was it for my king and country? Was it for freedom? Was it for my family, my neighbours, for the women and children with whom I'd been brought up? Was it for personal glory? No, no to all of these, a thousand times no.

It came to me in a blinding flash: I was fighting with my men, my comrades. I was charging with my regiment ... The Coldstream Guards were going to get to the top of this hill; and I was with them. I could not let the Regiment down.[27]

'Band' and 'brothers' were thus synthesised as equally integral to the soldier's private sense of resolve. A rare glimpse into this phenomenon on a mass scale is provided by Kenneally's account of being awarded his Victoria Cross in 1943. Upon returning to the battalion at Tunis:

I had a wonderful reception. Guys stopped what they were doing and crowded round to slap me on the back and shake my hand, shouting congratulations; it

[24] Holmes, 'The Italian Job', p. 211.
[25] Bowlby, Recollections, p. 169.
[26] Cochrane, Charlie Company, p. 1.
[27] Bulteel, Something About a Soldier, p. 199.

was a rare moment. We shared the honour and the glory of the Victoria Cross as we had shared the suffering, hardship and bloody murder of the *Bou*. There was no envy – infantrymen know better than that. It was not I who had won the medal: it was an Irish Guardsman. We were all Irish Guardsmen and we had all played a part.[28]

The sublimation of the individual soldier's identity to that of his unit thus provided a measure of support for the former combatants in this study. Nevertheless, they also recognised that others were less fortunate in their relationships with the fellowship. In Wessely's identification of the 'primary group' as both the reason why men fought and why they broke down in battle, he sagely notes that 'If soldiers fought for the primary group, then, the argument goes, soldiers ceased to fight when the primary group failed them.'[29] The veterans' remarkably frank discussion of disruption in group solidarity on the battlefield demonstrates an acute awareness of the fragility of reliance upon the 'band of brothers' ideal as a sheet anchor of combat morale. Collectively, these narratives are careful not to portray an overtly romanticised representation of human nature on the battlefield. Discussing relationships between members of a frontline unit, Ward admitted:

Not all were heroes or paragons of military virtue. We were human enough to prefer comfort and safety to discomfort and danger. We had a natural instinct for self-preservation. Most units – and mine was no exception – had their fair share of misfits, scoundrels and shirkers.[30]

Given the vast numbers of men drafted into Britain's largely conscript army, there were invariably one or two 'licensed croakers' in every unit.[31] Fortunately for Cochrane, the other members of his company found the relentlessly gloomy prognostications of such men a source of hilarity, and the memoirist drew the conclusion that 'they were useful because they got out into the open the forebodings any sensible fellow would have, forebodings much less oppressive when given an airing by somebody else.' Grumblers, however, could only be tolerated under one specific circumstance. They must have proven themselves good soldiers when the unit went into battle. Otherwise, 'If he were a bad one, he would just be a malcontent, and must go.'[32]

Cochrane was cognisant of the damage that soldiers who could not, or would not, adjust to group life could cause to the unit as a whole.

---

[28] Kenneally, *The Honour and the Shame*, p. 111.
[29] Wessely, 'Twentieth-Century Theories on Combat Motivation and Breakdown', p. 278.
[30] Ward, *The Mirror of Monte Cavallara*, p. 17.
[31] Cochrane, *Charlie Company*, p. 144.
[32] Ibid., p. 145.

Yet these individuals also failed to benefit from the protective psychological shield offered by the 'band of brothers'. When the self-control of such men snapped, they sometimes simply ran from battle. Significantly, in these memoirs only a fine line is drawn between 'battle fatigue' and desertion. The fact that the one frequently stemmed from the other posed distinct problems for officers such as Potts, required in moments of crisis to determine whether a 'coward' in battle was genuinely suffering from war neurosis, or temporary pusillanimity. 'A genuine case of shell-shock is a pitiful sight', he mused. 'I have seen a man, starkly crazy, frothing at the lips and biting mouthfuls of sand from the ground.'[33] Nevertheless, differentiation between 'the lunatic' and 'the deserter' proved difficult for this officer:

The other cases are what the troops call 'bomb-happiness', which is another name for unconcealed cowardice. Few men like to show their fear before others; but there are exceptions; there are some who will go to any lengths to escape the danger of remaining under shell-fire; who will unashamedly feign illness, pretend to be shell-shocked, or even inflict a wound on themselves; anything to get away to safety. Fortunately these cases are rare, but I suppose that every battalion has one or two of them.[34]

His method of dealing with such recalcitrants was short and sharp:

It was fatal to show sympathy with such men, for self-pity is the root of their trouble, and sympathy increases their self-pity. The best treatment is stern discipline. By scolding them, by cursing them, or even by shaking them and shouting at them, one may frighten them back into sense.[35]

There is an indicative whiff of First World War military thinking here, which viewed victims of psychiatric breakdown as the product of a hereditary weakness of character that rendered them unsuited to war. Thus, this argument ran, men broke down in battle because of existing weaknesses of character which predated experience of war-related trauma. Among military command and psychiatrists this degenerative explanation of combat demotivation began to erode during the Second World War, but its manifestation in this context provides a revealing comment on the informal value systems that operated at troop level among the army and its veterans. Lack of sympathy for men who cracked in the manner that Potts describes was often predicated upon a utilitarian awareness that one man's refusal of battle increased the risk to others in the group. Horsfall explained that,

[33] Potts, *Soldier in the Sand*, p. 37.
[34] Ibid., p. 37.
[35] Ibid., p. 37.

Our men did not like deserters. It is not hard to understand why, and their crime with its overtone of cowardice was bitterly resented. There was the feeling of being let down and that they were deserting them, their friends and comrades – like the case of one of our mortar crews where the number one found himself without his mate or his ammunition. He said sadly that he had been personally deserted.[36]

'Doing one's bit' on the field is thus invested with enormous importance in the veterans' tale, as Kenneally exemplifies in his account of experiencing compassion for a forlorn group of men he encountered at a North African Casualty Clearing Station after a ferocious battle in the desert. Observing that the soldiers looked 'much the same as us, covered in dust, scorched clothing and unshaven', he asked a medic corporal why they were receiving no medical attention. The NCO's reply that the men had run from battle and so would be last to be treated aroused Kenneally's ire:

I looked at the corporal: his trousers still retained a crease, his shirt was pressed and he was well shaven. It was obvious that the nearest he'd been to a battle was in bed with a reluctant girlfriend. 'What the fuck do you know about it?' I said. I grabbed the tea dixie from him and limped over to them. Bill took sandwiches and others followed suit. Frightened and wild-eyed, one or two had the shakes, obviously suffering from shell-shock, and could hardly drink the tea.

There was bound to be the odd malingerer amongst them, but they had all been there at the thick end, and who were those bastards to judge them? Most soldiers develop resilience, but there were some who would never acquire it. Such men were these. We were all disgusted at their treatment.[37]

Although desertion continued to pose a problem at senior command level throughout the Second World War, the veterans' tale acknowledged that the 'band of brothers' could only sustain individual endurance in combat so far. They thus tend to view the crime of desertion through rather more nuanced eyes than the generals, who repeatedly bayed for the reinstatement of the death penalty for this offence. This attitude stemmed from identification of two serious crises of morale which occurred in North Africa 1941–2 and Italy 1944–5.[38] In 1941, desertion rates in North Africa peaked at 10.5 per 1,000.[39] Furthermore, between January 1944 and January 1945 over 22,000 men were tried for desertion during the Italian campaign – indeed Bowlby recorded inflated wartime rumours that 30,000 soldiers were 'on the trot' whilst he was in Italy.[40]

[36] Horsfall, The Wild Geese are Flighting, pp. 90–1.
[37] Kenneally, The Honour and the Shame, p. 97.
[38] French, 'Discipline and the Death Penalty in the British Army', 532.
[39] Strachan, 'Training, Morale and Modern War', 223.
[40] French, 'Discipline and the Death Penalty in the British Army', 540; Bowlby, Recollections, p. 177.

Throughout the veterans' tale, understanding was extended towards the soldier who had repeatedly proven himself in battle, only to find that he had exceeded his overdraft in terms of endurance. In the desert in 1942, Ward was forced to place one of his sergeants under close arrest because the man had refused to patrol, claiming that he was overworked. The memoirist wrote that he had some sympathy with the NCO:

He had won an MM on Crete, so may well have been justified in thinking he'd done his bit. But he wouldn't change his mind, despite pleas and threats... Perhaps he had simply had enough – of the shelling, the Stukas, the frightful noise. If so, his was not the only case of battle fatigue I had seen, or would see.[41]

Others expressed identical views to a War Office report on morale in Italy in 1944, which concluded that most desertion of duty or unit was 'involuntary' and could be prevented by prompt treatment at rest centres before men succumbed to the impulse to run.[42] Horsfall had already drawn the same conclusion a year or so previously, and recorded that, on occasion, he was willing to overlook these lapses:

Occasionally there were cases which had our sympathy, where a fusilier simply aberrated after previous stouthearted service, perhaps due to a bad letter from home or temporary loss of nerve, or even through fatigue. But these cases rarely reached courts martial, not in good regiments anyway, where everyone knew each other.[43]

A temporary change of scene such as a week or two spent with the mule columns well behind the lines usually sorted these men out. Afterwards 'they would be only too delighted to be safely back with their friends in the line.'[44] Desertion was only one manner of opting out of the unit, however. Others deliberately chose to inflict wounds upon their body in the hope that they would be sent back from the frontline to the comparative safety of a casualty clearing station, or even discharged home. Such men attracted no sympathy from the veterans and Horsfall referred to two cases of self-inflicted wounds in his unit as 'perhaps worse' than the deserters.[45] Yet despite the memoirists' condemnation of men who betrayed the fraternity of comrades by seeking such dubious escape routes, several were all too aware that the mind could seductively and treacherously entreat an individual to break with the fellowship. Bowlby recorded awakening one morning at the end of May 1944 to find that several men including his own section-commander had deserted overnight.

[41] Ward, *The Mirror of Monte Cavallara*, p. 156.
[42] Ben Shephard, *A War of Nerves* (London: Jonathan Cape, 2000), p. 239.
[43] Horsfall, *The Wild Geese are Flighting*, p. 91.
[44] Ibid., p. 91.
[45] Ibid., p. 65.

The incident reminded Bowlby of the times when he had been fortunate enough to avoid a beating at school whilst his classmates had not: 'I had the same guilty feeling of excitement. The ethics of desertion had a deeper pull. They were so unexpected.'[46] He was to experience the same temptation to remove himself from battle during a moment of crisis in an attack on the summit of Monte Orlando when a bomb landed only six feet away. Bowlby found himself looking straight at it when it exploded:

The reds of the explosion were clamped on my retina. For several minutes I could see nothing else. This plus the blast plus the fact that we couldn't dig in reduced me to jelly. Desert. Desert. Desert. The next time, I promised myself. The next time I will. Before the attack. A court martial's better than this.[47]

A similar 'pull' to absent himself from the battlefield was also experienced by Nicholas Mosley, who recorded that in early 1945 he 'began to fantasise about how one might get out of this futile situation by a discreet self-inflicted accident'. Would this, he wondered,

be more or less reprehensible now that I had got an MC? I imagined I might fall from my hayloft onto the concrete floor below with one leg tucked under the other in a yoga position: might this not give me a not-too-badly broken leg which would get me back to hospital?[48]

The temptation to succumb to the lure of relinquishing the subordination of fear often stalked the combatant. It was this constant battle with the self that Potts identified as triggering his anger with one of his soldiers who turned tail at Alamein:

'Bomb-happy' men made me lose my temper, or perhaps it would be truer to say that they aroused me to great anger. I have sometimes wondered why they made me so angry. I think that it was probably because I, too, was terribly frightened, and I did not see why they should be allowed to show their fear whilst I had to bottle up mine. My anger may have been a form of hysteria.[49]

According to these memoirs, the 'band of brothers' concept thus proved something of a double-edged blade in the British Army's psychological armoury. For some individuals, set apart by nature or circumstance, the small group could never function as a source of combat motivation. For other soldiers who found their reserves of endurance wearing perilously thin, martial fraternity could only reinforce their crumbling nerve so far. In their recognition that men fight in groups but that if a group is left in the field for so long that it becomes combat-ineffective, the infantry

---

[46] Bowlby, *Recollections*, p. 17.
[47] Ibid., p. 183.
[48] Mosley, *Time at War*, p. 126.
[49] Potts, *Soldier in the Sand*, pp. 37–8.

memoirs thus bear witness to the eternal paradox of the 'primary group' as both source of combat motivation and demotivation on the field of battle.[50]

The Sailors' Tale: The Royal Navy and the Northern Oceans, 1939–1945

A similar paradox is woven into the naval veterans' tale. Within the Royal Navy, special meaning had long been attached to the rhetoric of a 'band of brothers'. After the Battle of the Nile in 1798 this phrase was employed on several occasions by Admiral Horatio Nelson in reference to the group of captains under his command.[51] Significantly, Nelson's use of the 'band of brothers' label was reserved for his senior officers alone, removing the egalitarianism with which Shakespeare charged the original speech and emphasising rank as the touchstone of this elite martial fellowship.[52] Reflecting both the importance ascribed by the Admiral to relationships between naval officers in battle and the fact that this cadre of RN memoirs were primarily written by the officers themselves, the Second World War naval veterans' tale focuses mainly on the personal dynamics of the 'upper deck' and the captain's responsibilities for ensuring effective discipline and harmonious working relations throughout the ship. At their core, these narratives outline the process by which the commanders created the type of harmonious ship's company that could bolster the individual and collective morale of the crew, yet they also recount that too much personal investment in the 'primary group' exacted a terrible psychological toll on officers.

'Ships' companies are invariably genuine, first-rate material; the only thing that can ruin them is their officers', declared Jack Broome.[53] As a former commander of both submarines and destroyers, he was well-placed to reflect that naval warfare during the Second World War was 'a human rather than a technological way of life'.[54] Heavy emphasis is placed in the memoirs of Broome and others on the importance of creating a 'happy ship'. Although rather a nebulous concept and difficult to quantify, the official history of the New Zealand armed forces during the

---

[50] Wessely, 'Twentieth-Century Theories on Combat Motivation and Breakdown', 279.
[51] Alfred Thayer Mahan, *Types of Naval Officers Drawn from the History of the British Navy: With Some Account of the Conditions of Naval Warfare at the Beginning of the Eighteenth Century, and of Its Subsequent Development During the Sail Period* (London: Sampson Low, Marston & Company, 1902), p. 379.
[52] 'For he to-day that sheds his blood with me/ Shall be my brother; be he ne'er so vile': Shakespeare, *Henry V*, p. 491.
[53] Broome, *Convoy is to Scatter*, p. 82.
[54] Ibid., p. 24.

Second World War provides a useful framework for understanding the 'happy ship' trope. Medical officers in the New Zealand navy observed key variations in instances of neurosis among the companies of different ships, which a subsequent study of wartime psychiatric disorders among naval personnel attributed partially to whether or not the crews felt themselves part of such a 'happy' ship. They found that this concept was charged with intense meaning, broadly signifying a company in which there was 'mutual trust and respect between officers and men, and dependent to a great extent on officers and senior ratings who not only knew their jobs but who also had a sympathetic understanding of the men under them and could get the best out of them.'[55] The same view emerges from the memoirs of British naval veterans, who testify that careful handling of the ship's company created men who were able to continue their endeavours despite considerable strain, discomfort, and danger. Several commanders even implied that when the strange chemistry of a 'happy ship' was in operation, the crew seemed to flourish when conditions at sea worsened. Peter Gretton reported that relations between his officers, petty officers, senior ratings, and crew aboard the destroyer, HMS *Sabre*, were heartening: 'the worse the weather and the filthier the conditions on the mess decks, the cheerier the sailors became. They were never depressed, and were the finest ship's company I have ever met.'[56] Similarly, Donald Macintyre mused that conditions in the ferocious winter weather of the North Atlantic should have provided a perfect recipe for dissension among the crews of the convoy escorts. With poor weather conditions frequently continuing for weeks on end, he perceived that the adversities of wartime service in the Atlantic were conducive to friction among all aboard:

Depression follows depression with monotonous regularity giving no respite to dry out clothes or the ship between one screaming gale and the next. It would not have been surprising if morale had dropped, petty irritations grown into flaming rows, dislikes into hatred – in fact, if all the symptoms of an unhappy ship had developed. But I heard of few such cases. Somehow the miseries shared welded ships' companies as a rule into happy teams.[57]

The same trope also sounds strongly among the memoirs of underwater crew. Due to the exceptionally confined nature of submarine warfare, veterans of 'the Trade' insisted that good dynamics between members of the crew were imperative in order to form an effective combat team.

[55] T. Stout and M. Duncan, 'War Surgery and Medicine', in *Official History of New Zealand in the Second World War* (Wellington: Historical Publications Branch, 1954), pp. 646–647.
[56] Gretton, *Convoy Escort Commander*, p .47.
[57] Macintyre, *U-Boat Killer*, pp. 60–61.

Sydney Hart asserted that 'In all my sea-going years I have never found happier ships than those whose main work lay under water'.[58] He based this attitude on a claim that submariners were,

the most cheeriest of all sea-going men; it would have been fatal to enrol the grousing type, since we were so closely packed and so dependent on one another's good humour, that a dissentient element might have made for downright confusion and, indeed, a rot.[59]

The process of welding together individual sailors into a crew who would be sufficiently cohesive and proficient to fight the ship through months of hostile weather and enemy attacks was of paramount concern for those at sea. Correspondingly, this persistent anxiety forms a core theme in the sailors' personal narratives. When William Donald wrote that 'a ship is not just a matter of steel and iron and wood, she has a personality of her own', he insisted that this 'personality' was granted by the nature of the relationship between captain, officers and ship's company.[60] If there was a sour note in this finely balanced tripartite relationship, the ship itself might function less effectively as a unit. Denys Rayner recorded his dismay at joining his new command HMS *Highlander*, an H-class destroyer commissioned in 1940. Upon making his first round of the ship at Troon, he became 'a little worried at the atmosphere' he encountered, since none of the crew he had met were particularly forthcoming or interested in their new captain.[61] He was horrified to discover that in addition to a defaulters' list 'as long as your arm', there were more than twenty requests to change to another ship.[62] Reporting a speech that he made to the mustered ship's company, he informed the crew that he was accustomed to having 'a happy ship. There's something wrong in this one ... I want to see you chaps with smiles on your faces. I haven't seen one since I came aboard.'[63] Later, he suggested that the trouble stemmed from *Highlander*'s former use as a senior officer's ship carrying a senior officer's staff who spared little time for the men.[64] In private, he discussed this state of affairs with his First Lieutenant and Engineer Officer:

I think it's just something that's been allowed to grow up between the officers and the men. They are thoroughly 'browned off'. After all the poor beast has had a new Captain almost every quarter. You can hardly expect her to be a happy ship.[65]

[58] Hart, *Discharged Dead*, p. 187.
[59] Ibid., p. 183.
[60] Donald, *Stand By For Action*, p. 14.
[61] Rayner, *Escort*. p. 181.
[62] Ibid., p. 184.
[63] Ibid., p. 184.
[64] Ibid., pp. 185–6.
[65] Ibid., p. 184.

Upon tearing up the defaulters' list to start afresh and addressing the existing muddles over pay, medals, and lack of promotion which had caused the bad feeling among the ship's crew, Rayner documented that the atmosphere aboard *Highlander* improved to a vast extent. Indeed, the coxswain, who was previously overworked due to the high numbers of defaulters, came to possess such an abundance of free time that he was put in charge of organising the ship's concert.

The necessity of officers displaying concern for the well-being of their crew is thus presented as of paramount importance in the naval veterans' tale. Before obtaining a commission two years into the war, Herbert Messer served below decks as an able seaman. He recorded experiencing a sense of shock when he joined up, noting that 'those on the lower deck were each in their own individual pit and dependent on the goodwill and moods of their officers.'[66] Serving as a Commission Warrant rating below decks for three months aboard HMS *Carnation*, Norman Hampson also discerned that very little of the type of pleasurable close-knit relationship between crew and officers that ensured a 'happy ship' existed in this corvette. It is evident from his memoir that poor leadership and lack of concern for those below decks did not create good relationships between the crew, who found themselves operating in conditions that did not make,

for good humour, mutual tolerance or social harmony. We were not jolly sailorboys, united by the brotherhood of the sea. I remember a particularly evil occasion when some of his messmates taunted Len Bowen in the hope that he could be goaded into hitting one of them, which would have allowed them to get him stripped of his leading seaman's rank, pay and pension. Len was perfectly aware of what they were trying to do and he refused to play their game, but this manifestation of raw hatred was something not easily forgotten. It was more or less a matter of luck whether the crew directed their outbreaks of temper against the sea, the navy or each other. No one ever referred to the Germans. I got the impression that the general feeling was that they were up against it in the same way as us.[67]

Hampson identified the first lieutenant as the weak link on the upper decks, insinuating that he did not act in the best interests of the crew. 'On the whole', he thought, 'the crews accepted ... danger and discomfort with no more than routine grumbling. What made them almost homicidal was being made to sacrifice their scanty leisure time for fatuous reasons of officiousness or display.'[68] In naval jargon, 'pusser' was the label applied to such 'fatuous' modes of regulation, a derogatory term which carried all the venom of a foul epithet. Indeed, Hampson noted

[66] Herbert J. Messer, *Able Seaman RNVR* (Braunton: Merlin, 1989), p. 25.
[67] Hampson, *Not Really What You'd Call a War*, pp. 19–20.
[68] Ibid., p. 15.

that among *Carnation*'s crew, 'pusserdom' was greeted with 'hatred and dread', and he darkly indicted his unpopular first lieutenant as 'pusser'.[69] As a corruption of the rank of 'purser', the term signified an excess of bureaucratic detail and adherence to the letter of regulations generally rumoured to be found in the 'battlewagons', or 'big ships', which were commonly assumed to be bastions of rigidly enforced protocol that was both comprehensive and invasive. Here, a crucial distinction is drawn between the 'big' and 'small' ships of the Royal Navy, with a number of memoirists asserting there was a prized flexible, or 'human', quality to life aboard sloops, corvettes, destroyers, anti-submarine trawlers and submarines. In a small ship in wartime that was continually at sea, Hampson proudly asserted, there was neither time nor inclination to carry out this level of 'spit and polish'.[70] Carried to excess, 'pusserdom' could threaten the morale and safety of the operational crew, as this memoirist learned when his despised first lieutenant ordered the hinged scuppers on the bulwark to be welded shut because he felt that they detracted aesthetically from the smooth lines of the ship. When a gale at sea trapped vast quantities of water on the upper deck, the ship was almost fatally flooded in direct consequence. With the corvette's proclivity for rolling viciously, and the disturbance to its centre of gravity, the affair might easily have ended in tragedy.

The 'pusser' trope highlights the fragility of relations between crew and officers in the smaller ships, and 'small ship' discipline is thus represented in these memoirs as something of an art-form. The worst excesses of an overly zealous officer's 'pusser' micromanagement of the ship are illustrated in Hampson's narrative, yet all of the naval memoirists – including the two non-ranking submariners Charles Anscomb and Sydney Hart – testify that strict discipline remained essential to rivet together a ship's company. When Sam Lombard-Hobson was first given his own command, he recalled the 'wise advice' of his former captain: 'relax discipline one iota when things are good, and you have lost control when they are not'.[71] Achieving an optimum level of naval regulation which ensured high morale and good working relationships throughout a ship was clearly a tricky and delicate task, however, which was rendered more complex by the ambiguity of what actually constituted 'good' discipline. Perplexing twin statements issued by Anscomb suggest that officers could find themselves placed in a confusing situation with regard to enforcing regulations. On the one hand, the former coxswain

---

[69] Ibid., p. 14.
[70] Ibid., p. 14.
[71] Lombard-Hobson, *A Sailor's War*, p. 146.

expressed a liking for the 'Captain Blighs' of the Royal Navy, observing that 'Nothing at sea is more vitally necessary than discipline and a taut ship.'[72] On the other hand, he also claimed that if a seaman was 'a pirate by nature', he was best suited to service aboard a destroyer or submarine in which discipline was more relaxed.[73] According to this experienced petty officer, therefore, the ideal balance of command and control over a ship's company was strict enough to ensure efficiency, but not so rigid as to fracture morale. Lombard-Hobson wrote of the particular difficulties faced by the captain in striking this balance of discipline:

A pit-fall which had to be watched by young commanding officers ... was that of letting up on discipline. After a ship had been in commission for a year, and its company been through some testing times of war and weather, it was tempting for the captain to show some leniency in the strict observance of standards of dress, personal appearance and punctuality, especially when the ship was operating on its own, and away from the critical eye of higher authority.[74]

Concerned that he was possibly being too hard on his men by asserting his own firm resolution to maintain strictest discipline on board at all times, he sought out a highly respected senior lower-deck rating for advice. The reply, he wrote, 'impressed and convinced me': 'You will not have a happy ship's company if you *ever* let up on discipline [Italics memoirist's own].'[75]

The naval veterans' tale thus posited that good relations between crew and officers in the 'small ships' of the Royal Navy depended upon a strict but humane kind of discipline which took stock of an individual's character and skills in order to coax maximum efforts from him and make him feel valued. Submariner Edward Young noted that by the time his new command had been at sea for ten weeks, the period of living and working in such close proximity had 'given the crew every chance of shaking down together':

Each man gradually revealed his strength and weakness. We learnt where we could safely put our trust and where further supervision would be needed. At the same time *Storm* was developing a corporate identity of which the men were dimly aware and already a little proud.[76]

Young's account, like those of his fellow maritime memoirists, indicates that morale in the Navy was anchored by a dominant strain of paternalism which filtered down directly from the bridge.[77] These narratives

[72] Anscomb, *Submariner*, p. 17.
[73] Ibid., p. 23.
[74] Lombard-Hobson, *A Sailor's War*, pp. 153–4.
[75] Ibid., p. 154.
[76] Young, *One of Our Submarines*, p. 162.
[77] G. D. Sheffield, *Leadership in the Trenches: Officer-Man Relations, Morale and Discipline in the British Army in the Era of the First World War* (Basingstoke: Macmillan, 2000), p. 81.

demonstrate that the blend of fatherly authoritarianism and concern for the well-being of the troops which Gary Sheffield identifies among British officers on the Western Front between 1914 and 1918 was also prevalent among the Royal Navy's 'small ship' officers between 1939 and 1945. The institutionalisation of a similar 'bureaucracy of paternalism' is primarily represented as the responsibility of the vessel's captain, who is often portrayed in these memoirs as a patriarchal figure. William Donald, former officer of the sloop HMS *Black Swan*, recorded that his captain was 'very like a father to the rest of us: which, I suppose, is what the Captain of a ship should be.'[78] Hughes, too, expressed fulsome praise for his commander, emphasising the importance of his role in uniting the company into a 'happy ship':

On looking back it seemed miraculous that the motley looking crew who had stared resentfully at *Scylla* in the shipyard at Greenock could have been welded into such a great body of men ... the strongest bond was loyalty to the Captain and supreme confidence in him as a leader. Defaulters were few and we lived happily, confident in each other, sharing our jokes, and taking part in all the little activities and associations aboard.[79]

The need for punitive discipline rarely features in these memoirs, which tend to corroborate Macintyre's declaration that it was 'hardly ever necessary to punish wrongdoers' as commander of HMS *Hesperus*.[80] On the rare occasion when it was necessary, he employed his own methods of ensuring good behaviour:

All that was required was to let the culprit know that he would be drafted away from the ship if he could not reform and nearly always this was enough. Occasionally we carried out our threat and the rest of the ship's company were the happier for their loss.[81]

According to these narratives, the senior officer also had a duty to ensure that relations on the upper deck ran smoothly and harmoniously. The relationship between a captain and his first lieutenant is depicted as especially important, as it was through the latter that the interplay of human relationships within the company was supervised. Responsible for ensuring that the captain's orders were carried out promptly and efficiently, the 'Jimmy' played a vital role in maintaining discipline and morale at sea. In this way, a good first lieutenant could either make or break a ship's company. In HMS *Verbena*, Rayner was not immediately allocated a first lieutenant when he took command of the corvette. He thus had to

---

[78] Donald, *Stand By For Action*, p. 15.
[79] Hughes, *Through the Waters*, p. 138.
[80] Macintyre, *U-boat Killer*, p. 115.
[81] Ibid., p. 115.

combine this role with his own duties as captain, a task which he found immensely wearing:

The Captain and the First Lieutenant are complementary to one another. However good the former may be, his ship cannot be a success unless the latter is efficient. If the Captain is responsible for the ship's body, to the First Lieutenant falls the charge of her soul. He is at once the translator of the Captain's authority to the men and their own ambassador at the court of that authority. In many ways it is more difficult to be a good First Lieutenant than a good Commanding Officer, for the Captain only looks one way, while Number One must look both fore and aft.[82]

When Rayner was finally given a new first lieutenant named Jack Hunter, he perceived that the mood of the entire ship lifted and the men achieved a new degree of unity. He believed that his new 'Number One's' charisma and sense of humour functioned as a 'catalyst which changed the parts into one corporate whole, so that anything which affected anyone of us was felt by all.'[83] Clashes of personality between a captain and his officers were inevitable on occasion and could have serious implications for the ship. A disagreement between Alistair Mars and his 'Number One', a man he identified as 'Taylor', about proceeding at speed in heavy weather caused an unpleasant spat. Upon being accused by his first lieutenant of courting the risk of breaking the boat up by running her at high speed, Mars was furious that his authority was challenged in such a manner. He was especially disgruntled by what he considered Taylor's 'confounded cheek ... I was particularly upset because this was not the first difference we had had, and even the suggestion of bad feeling is fatal among a small group of men living in such proximity as we were.'[84] He was subsequently forced to request a transfer for this officer:

I could not get away from the fact that Taylor and myself had certain incompatibilities of temperament. Such differences might pass unnoticed in a big ship, but they are exaggerated and distorted in the emotional confinement of a small submarine. Taylor, I decided, must be replaced. It was no reflection on him as a man or as a sailor. It was simply that our temperaments did not allow us to serve together.[85]

Disharmony on the upper deck could make life equally unpleasant for more junior officers. When Hampson passed his board of selection to receive a commission as sub-lieutenant in 1942, he was transferred to the destroyer HMS *Easton*. Significantly, his relationship with his new captain was so bad that he refused to identify either ship or captain in

---

[82] Rayner, *Escort*, p. 65.
[83] Ibid., p. 89.
[84] Mars, *Unbroken*, p. 51.
[85] Ibid., p. 82.

his narrative. His transition from lower deck to wardroom was rendered problematic by his perception of his new commander as an inefficient officer and deeply disagreeable man:

I diagnosed him at the time as 'a tin god with an inferiority complex'. If things did not work out as he would have wished, he took it for granted that this was due to the incompetence of his subordinates.[86]

Eventually, relations became so strained that Hampson left the wardroom if the captain was present and subsequently requested a transfer as liaison officer to a Free French sloop.

The view from the bridge, however, poignantly reveals the weight of the burden of authority borne by wartime naval commanders. As Sheffield observes, in war, 'the leader's role is Janus-faced: to exercise paternal care for his men; but also to ensure that they risk their lives by fighting.'[87] The conflict between these two roles is particularly prominent in these naval narratives. Like Henry V on the eve of Agincourt, these memoirists convey psychological torment at exerting such responsibility over the lives of all their men. With keen insight, Hampson later identified his troublesome captain as a man deeply riven with insecurity and anxiety about his position as commander of a destroyer:

[He] was in a job for which nature had not intended him. His inclination to be affable and easy-going was at odds with the kind of authority that he had been trained to think he ought to exercise, and as soon as he was at sea he became an entirely different man. I think he may have suffered from a kind of permanent identity crisis, convinced of the merits of strong and confident leadership without having the qualities that would have allowed him to exercise them.[88]

The old adage about the loneliness of command also tolls desolately throughout a number of other narratives. Hart, for instance, expressed considerable sympathy for his submarine commander, musing that the rank 'must be almost indescribably lonely' as the captain had no superior to apply to when in doubt or difficulty.[89] Broome suggested that the same predicament applied to all commanders equally, noting that there were 'times when skippers feel a bit shut off and lonely. You can't discuss things critically and openly with your own officers.'[90] This state of affairs was not helped by a naval tradition that the captain could only enter the officers' wardroom by invitation, which further enforced the aloofness and isolation of the rank.

[86] Hampson, *Not Really What You'd Call a War*, p. 36.
[87] Gary Sheffield, 'Dead cows and Tigers', p. 126.
[88] Hampson, *Not Really What You'd Call a War*, p. 35.
[89] Hart, *Discharged Dead*, p. 70.
[90] Broome, *Convoy is to Scatter*, p. 208.

The paternalistic discipline which ensured a 'happy and efficient' ship thus came at a heavy personal cost to the captain, especially when there were awkward dilemmas to resolve. In June 1940, Donald found himself faced with an awkward predicament. Many of his crew came from the West Country and were uneasy about their families' proximity to France during the invasion threat. Numerous requests were put in for compassionate leave, which left him with an agonising decision:

much as I sympathised with each request from the personal point of view, I had to steel myself to be hard-hearted from the national point of view. A man's absence from his ship, and particularly a key rating, meant a loss of efficiency which we could not afford just then. The ship had to come first and foremost.[91]

There were also moments of self-doubt. Young was most perturbed to find a case of desertion on his hands, in the form of an able seaman who was unable to form good relationships with the rest of the crew, and absconded whilst the submarine was berthed at Arrochar:

I was very depressed all day by the desertion. It disturbed my complacent belief that *Storm* was developing into a reasonably happy ship's company. I felt that it must in some way be my fault, and that I should have realised something was up with the lad.[92]

Significantly, he felt that he had failed in his own ability to weld together his crew, even though the deserter had been a natural social 'misfit'.

Furthermore, responsibility for the safety of the vessel and all on board added another heavy psychological burden. From the moment the engines first started turning until he could ring off upon return to harbour, the commander's ceaseless awareness that he carried the ship took a heavy psychological toll. Submarine commander William King was the only memoirist who perceived that this duty placed the captain in a relatively fortunate position among the company, as he benefitted from 'the spur of ultimate responsibility'.[93] The others refuted this view, documenting in grim detail the grinding pressures of the captain's eternal responsibility with no respite. As Donald noted:

The slightest error of judgement on your part and the whole lot can be lost. And even when you are off the bridge – since everyone is human and must sleep now and then – the ship is still yours. If the Officer of the Watch makes a mistake, it is your mistake; and, by golly, it was easy to make them on the East coast in war-time.[94]

[91] Donald, *Stand By For Action*, p. 40.
[92] Young, *One of Our Submarines*, p. 159.
[93] King, *The Stick and the Stars*, p. 6.
[94] Donald, *Stand By For Action*, p. 53.

For the commanding officers of escorts on the deep water Atlantic and Arctic runs, or submarines conducting long spells of sea time, these anxieties were rendered even more acute. For men like Donald who served on the East Coast convoys, the voyage only lasted around three days. On the longer convoys sleep became a serious problem for captains, yet fear of relinquishing temporary control of the ship to officers of the watch is frequently voiced. Broome recounted that 'What we dreaded was an inexperienced officer-of-the-watch allowing us to sleep on – either through compassion, or fear of our wrath at being disturbed – when he should have roused us'.[95] Similarly, Young wrote that:

I never lost an opportunity of impressing on my officers that I would prefer to be called to the bridge a hundred times in the night, no matter how trivial the occasion, rather than be called too late. There were times in later patrols, especially after a succession of anxious nights, when I found it difficult to live up to my own precepts; to be called out on a false alarm just after I had dropped into a sleep for which my brain had been screaming for forty-eight hours was absolute torture, and it was often as much as I could do to tell the officer-of-the-watch that he had been right to call me.[96]

According to these memoirs, such a perpetual state of heightened alertness and responsibility invariably took its toll on the commanding officer's physical and mental health. Surprisingly few statistics of psychiatric breakdown at sea survive, but by 1943 the Admiralty had recognised that a number of captains of small escort ships had been left in command beyond the point that they were effective leaders.[97] Echoing Lord Moran's famous study of the nature of courage, former destroyer captain Roger Hill believed that a man began the war with a certain number of 'points' which represented as much as he could personally stand, and these became used up by living on one's nerves. For the captain, he felt that this presented especial problems: 'If you are going to be taut and react instantly to every emergency on the bridge of a destroyer, you are going to have a reaction and crack quicker than a man in a quieter job.'[98] Ideally, he argued, leave or a spell of duty in a more restful job ashore could replenish these vital 'points', yet he also posited with some bitterness that the only real rest a destroyer captain received was

[95] Broome, *Convoy is to Scatter*, p. 77.
[96] Young, *One of Our Submarines*, p. 177.
[97] Edgar Jones and Neil Greenberg, 'Royal Naval Psychiatry: Organization, Methods and Outcomes, 1900–1945', *The Mariner's Mirror*, 92:2 (2006), 8.
[98] Hill, *Destroyer Captain*, p. 153. Moran believed that a combatant's resolve to keep fighting was analogous to possessing credit in a bank account: 'Courage is will-power, whereof no man has an unlimited stock; and when in war it is used up, he is finished. A man's courage is his capital and he is always spending.' *The Anatomy of Courage*, p. xxii.

when his ship was sunk or damaged.[99] Ironically, the captain's official and self-imposed duties reached a point where they began to work to the detriment of the crew. After four years at sea, Hill began to feel the strain mounting unbearably and reported that he inevitably vented this on his crew and officers: 'as a captain more nearly approached a breakdown, or operational fatigue as it was called, so he became increasingly impossible to serve and live with.'[100] Similarly, in early 1942 Macintyre was feeling the pressure of two years at sea and related that 'I was near the cracking point.' Approaching harbour in Newfoundland, his signals staff made a small error in exchanging recognition signals with the port, and he shouted at the Yeoman of Signals. Later, he realised that his attitude was 'entirely unreasonable and unjustified and resolved to try to control myself better in future, but at the same time I began to wonder whether I was heading for that psychological condition known as "operational fatigue".'[101] By mid-1943 he felt that he had been worn down past the point of being able to command competently: 'Freshness and a never-wearying alertness were essential to come out on top in this game and I knew I was losing them. It was time for me to go.'[102] According to these memoirs, therefore, when a commander reached this stage, the decision to leave his men is portrayed as the final act of duty to them. As in the soldiers' tale, the paradox of psychologically investing too heavily in the 'primary group' is again made apparent.

The Flyers' Tale: Bomber Command and Occupied Europe, 1942–1945

Within the confines of a heavy bomber, the interplay of human relationships bore a resemblance to the crews of submarines and small surface vessels. Both sets of combatants inhabited an intimate, closed-off, little world in which each man's virtues and vices were known to all. The question of leadership, however, provides a pivotal difference between aircrew and naval personnel. Inside the ships of the Royal Navy, each sailor formed a link in a well-defined chain of command that stretched all the way up to the vessel's captain, providing the ship's company with a safety-net of officially appointed paternalism. Max Hastings claims that a similar sense of reassurance was also conveyed to aircrew by the hierarchy of rank on a bomber squadron, positing that 'the decisive factor in the

---

[99] Hill, *Destroyer Captain*, p. 154.
[100] Ibid., p. 154.
[101] Macintyre, *U-boat Killer*, p. 61.
[102] Ibid., p. 171.

morale of bomber aircrew, like that of all fighting men, was leadership.'[103] However, the memoirs of Bomber Command veterans militate to suggest that this was not in fact the case. Frank Musgrove's narrative witheringly condemns Hastings's view as 'Public School nonsense', arguing that a squadron bore more resemblance to 'a peace-time airport than an Army regiment'.[104] He dismissed Hastings's argument that the chain of command which characterised the other services also strengthened aircrew, explaining that from top to bottom in Bomber Command, 'leadership' of any kind was 'largely invisible'.[105] 'At briefing', he wrote caustically, 'we were not sent off into battle with a stirring oration like that of Henry V before Agincourt. At the most, we had a "Good Luck, chaps" from the CO (who probably wasn't going anyway).'[106] Peter Russell also reflected that good discipline in Bomber Command was more than simple

leadership by one man, it was something very different from the sort of eagerness to follow (or perhaps readiness to go out in front) such as a man like the Duke of Wellington was said to be able to get from his 'scum of the earth'.[107]

What was required, he argued, was 'something more subtle'.

Having roundly condemned Hastings's explanation of military authority as the foundation of morale among aircrew, Musgrove expressed approval for John Terraine's history of the RAF, praising its 'far more intelligent grasp of the subtle realities of flying'.[108] In his study, Terraine recognises that the RAF was unique among the services, as it was not an officer-function to lead the troops into battle. Certainly this historian's argument that external military norms of 'command' were not really applicable to a bomber squadron – inside an aircraft 'all that was required from the crew was exceptionally high morale and sense of duty and an ability to conquer fear' – finds repeated confirmation among the memoirists of Bomber Command.[109]

In Musgrove's view, Bomber Command's system of tours of operations was 'an inspired structural invention which sustained most crews … a crew simply got on with it.'[110] Norman Ashton concurred that the tour system provided statistical elements of consolation. After four trips, he was granted home leave and 'went home feeling quite a veteran. It was a common saying in Bomber Command that any

[103] Hastings, *Bomber Command*, p. 216.
[104] Musgrove, *Dresden and the Heavy Bombers*, p. 59.
[105] Ibid., p. 61.
[106] Ibid., p. 60.
[107] Russell, *Flying in Defiance of the Reich*, p. 130.
[108] Musgrove, *Dresden and the Heavy Bombers*, p. 59.
[109] Terraine, *The Right of the Line*, p. 466.
[110] Musgrove, *Dresden and the Heavy Bombers*, p. 63.

crew completing four operations had an even chance of finishing their tour.'[111] Nevertheless, the importance of the tour system should not be overstated as the construct could work to the detriment of aircrew. After a bad operation, the prospect of completing the rest of the tour could seem insurmountable, or as Jack Currie disclosed, could inspire treacherous false confidence:

Some of the old hands thought that there were two particularly perilous phases in the tour. One was during the first half dozen missions before you knew the ropes, and the other occurred at about the twenty-sortie mark, when a spurious euphoria might lure a crew into contributing by carelessness to their own destruction.[112]

Based on such testimony, it is difficult to explain the source of aircrew morale purely on a basis of the 'strong mathematical regularity' which the tour system enshrined.[113]

Instead, among these RAF narratives, the 'touch of human nature' emerges again as key to the cohesiveness of the bomber 'band of brothers'. Unlike in the Army, however, operational units were wholly comprised of volunteers. Discipline among each seven-man bomber crew thus acquired a markedly different character which Russell argued represented 'discipline by consent':

I realised that these bomber aircrew would do anything they were called upon to do. It was the opinion of their fellow aircrew that mattered. In order to keep their esteem they would keep pressing on regardless, even when they themselves knew that they were dangerously tired.[114]

From the beginning of their service with Bomber Command, the interplay of human relationships was characterised by a uniquely consensual nature. The RAF endorsed this by allowing men to select their own crew members, which Jim Davis thought 'the finest plan that Bomber Command ever devised.'[115] The element of choice allowed aircrew to believe that they were exerting a modicum of control over their own fate. Raw instinct was the key criterion on which these memoirists based their selection. Davis, for example, paired up with another gunner and wandered around a cricket pitch filled with hundreds of other flyers searching for a crew: 'we passed many pilots but rather like a lady trying on hat after hat in a store, we both decided we would move on until we

[111] Ashton, *Only Birds and Fools*, p. 16.
[112] Currie, *Lancaster Target*, p. 93.
[113] Musgrove, *Dresden and the Heavy Bombers*, p. 63.
[114] Russell, *Flying in Defiance of the Reich*, p. 130.
[115] Davis, *Winged Victory*, p. 31.

both felt the same about the pilot we were seeking.'[116] A skilled pilot was viewed as integral to increasing the chances of one's survival. Yet Frank Broome's account of teaming up with a pilot reveals that crewing-up was not necessarily straightforward, and casts some light on the deliberations of aircrew during this process. Upon meeting a Flight Lieutenant looking for a crew, he observed that the pilot had a stern face and had the look of a disciplinarian:

We didn't know how far that went, it could be too late to back out on that score if we were to have any misgivings. The fellow might be a real bind. He might even be a real 'basket'. Maybe he would expect a lot from his crew. Maybe Peter and I would not be good enough. Perhaps he wanted really 'shit-hot' air gunners. Well, we would like a 'shit-hot' pilot and captain too.[117]

Broome placed considerable importance in 'the idea of a friendly sort of crew. I thought it was highly desirable, if not essential!'[118] Miles Tripp concurred that achieving a suitable balance of temperaments from the outset was vital, noting that:

This arbitrary collision of strangers was basically a marriage market and yet the choice of a good flying partner was far more important that a good wife. You couldn't divorce your crew, and you could die if one of them wasn't up to his job at a critical moment.[119]

John Bushby agreed that crewing-up was a 'decisive moment':

A bomber crew is a small fighting team; each a specialist and each depending on the others. It is vital that men so put together shall be in harmony on the ground as in the air. There is no room for clash of personalities on a run-up to the target. Even some small off-duty bickering or unpleasantness can fatally detract from the concentration and instant communication essential in the air.[120]

Despite the unique and unprecedented degree of choice granted to the flyers in the selection of their military crew mates, they were well aware that this choice marked only the beginning of their combat relationship. It was impossible to be sure how one's fellow aircrew would stand up during an operation. Davis clearly considered himself fortunate in his choice of crew, and wrote a positively lyrical account of the relationships he cultivated with the other six members, proudly declaring that 'my

---

[116] Ibid., p. 31.
[117] Frank Broome, *Dead Before Dawn: A Heavy Bomber Tail Gunner in World War II* (Barnsley: Pen & Sword Aviation, 2008), p. 140.
[118] Ibid., p. 140.
[119] Tripp, *The Eighth Passenger*, p. 9.
[120] Bushby, *Gunner's Moon*, p. 84.

crew mates were the cat's whiskers to me'.[121] He insisted that such a bond required careful cultivation and nourishment:

You had to gain confidence in each other, you would feel that confidence grow only when you witnessed the abilities of your crew mates. You would learn to love them, eat with them, sleep with them, go out with them, you would gradually all blend with each other so that in the end you would feel like brothers. The bond between you would become so tight that it would never break and the brotherly feeling would remain for the rest of your life.[122]

Within this developing brotherhood, there were distinctive social conventions. Alongside a period of training, the alchemy between a crew also took place on the ground, with the men of each unit eating, sleeping and socialising together so far as the official distinctions of rank permitted.[123] Jack Currie explained that,

Crews usually kept their own company, but it was considered all right for the pilot of one crew to associate with the pilot of another on occasion, or indeed one navigator with another, and so on. But for, say a gunner to be in company with the pilot of another crew more than once or twice would be thought unnatural and disloyal.[124]

In this manner, a crew became yoked together and learned to function as a team both on the ground and in the air. Ideally, as Macintosh noted, aircraft and aircrew would consequently become 'honed into a sharp and deadly weapon'.[125] However, any disruption to the painstakingly crafted and finely balanced operational unity of the crew was ill-received, as the issue of replacements demonstrates. As part of the training process in Bomber Command, aircraft were often required to carry trainee 'second dickies' (second pilots) to help them learn their trade. Equally, if an operational crew was a man short for any reason, a replacement 'spare bod' could be temporarily drafted in from a crew who was not on the duty roster that night. Arthur Gamble wrote that the majority of aircrew 'detested' these substitutions, whether they were losing one of their own team for the sortie, or flying with a trainee second pilot.[126] His justification for this attitude grants an insight into the finely tuned nature of the combatant relationships in a heavy bomber:

Each crew was a closely-knit unit which had been welded together through long weeks of intensive training. Their survival through the first three or four

---

[121] Davis, *Winged Victory*, p. 51.
[122] Ibid., p. 32.
[123] There were separate messes and sleeping quarters for flight officers and flight sergeants.
[124] Currie, *Lancaster Target*, p. 11.
[125] Don Macintosh, *Bomber Pilot* (London: Browsebooks, 2006), p. 204.
[126] Gamble, *The Itinerant Airman*, p. 118.

operations on the squadron, developed a bond between them and a routine particularly suited to that crew as a whole. Although the training for each crew was exactly the same, the seven individual personalities making up each crew interpreted the information each received in a manner peculiarly suited to themselves. Therefore the sum of these seven different personalities ensured that each seven-man crew would be uniquely different, and would adopt a different routine and attitude from its neighbours.[127]

If, as Macintosh articulated, aircraft and aircrew were tempered into a unique 'weapon', the introduction of an alien personality was akin to expecting a gun to fire when loaded with the wrong calibre of ammunition. With the safety of hindsight, Broome acknowledged a 'silly' popular belief that aircraft carrying 'spare bods' and 'second dickies' were jinxed, a theory that was seemingly granted credence by the number of aircraft that went missing when carrying a different or extra crew member.[128] Gamble attributed this superstitious belief to the flyer's engrained view of 'any deviation from the normal routine as an omen of impending ill fortune.'[129] Superstition aside, it is tempting to wonder whether the loss of these aircraft with replacement or additional crew members might have been caused to some degree by an imbalance of the human chemistry inside the machine.

Despite the lyricism of Davis, most memoirists acknowledged some flaws in the seven-way aircrew relationship. One particular subject of grievance was the disparity in status among the crew. Rear gunners were paid considerably less than the others. In October 1944, a Committee on the Composition of Air Crew found that whilst pilot officers were all paid a standard 14/6 per week regardless of their trade, there were considerable discrepancies between the rates of pay among non-ranking aircrew. For example, a sergeant pilot could earn 13/6, whilst an air gunner only drew wages of 8/–.[130] Although Davis himself was a rear gunner, and insisted that these men never mentioned nor grumbled about this wage differential, it still lurked as a potential hairline fracture in the crew relationship. Tripp, for example, recorded that the financial discrepancy created 'an unacknowledged but undeniable status distinction.'[131] The trade of bomb aimers also attracts some scorn in these memoirs. Macintosh asserted that 'due to them being failed pilots and the fact that they did not appreciably affect the survival value of a crew, [they]

---

[127] Ibid., p. 119.
[128] Broome, *Dead Before Dawn*, p. 271.
[129] Gamble, *The Itinerant Airman*, p. 119.
[130] TNA/AIR 14/1011 Committee on the Composition of Air Crew Present range of Air crew categories and rates of pay, October 1944.
[131] Tripp, *The Eighth Passenger*, p. 9.

were deemed to be fairly low coin in the crewing market.'[132] Musgrove concurred, reporting that he was 'delighted' to have been selected for navigator training: 'I should have been bitterly disappointed to be a bomb-aimer, which I always considered a non-job and held in complete contempt. And still do.'[133]

Additional invisible and potentially lethal tensions could result from issues of rank. Most Lancaster crews were a mixed bag of senior NCOs and junior officers. On the ground, this demarcation was made plain by the segregation of the ranks into separate messes. On the other hand, rank distinctions amongst a crew when airborne were considerably more jumbled, as rank did not necessarily signify a pilot, yet pilots assumed command of the aircraft. From a detached perspective, this appears a situation tailor-made for resentments and misunderstandings, yet the memoirists were quick to insist that the strange fluctuating dichotomy of rigid versus haphazard rank distinctions did not in itself cause problems. Trouble loomed, however, if these distinctions started to change among a crew due to promotion. The memoirs of Gamble and Arthur White illustrate how the seams of crew relationships could be strained to near breaking point when hitherto satisfactory crew dynamics were suddenly shattered by changes in rank. Both men were members of the same crew, yet White and two others were commissioned part-way through their tour and moved into the officers' quarters to join their two crew members who were already commissioned. White perceived that when this transition was made, it 'did seem to isolate Ronnie and Poker [respectively the other crew mate and Gamble] and I think they felt it. After all, we were the same team and had shared the same experiences – both good and bad.'[134] Gamble's memoir confirms White's suspicion that he and 'Ronnie' were unhappy that their efforts appeared to have been overlooked by the RAF authorities:

we felt a little bit aggrieved at this, wondering what sort of misdemeanour we had committed that we had been left on the sidelines, not to be considered of the same value as the rest of the crew ... it left us with an underlying sense of resentment at the unfairness of it all. We therefore agreed to adopt the attitude, 'Who wants to be a bloody officer, anyway,' whenever the subject was broached by the rest of the lads.[135]

Nevertheless, these memoirs testify that, despite tensions and rifts within the crew's interlocking relationships, every effort was made when aloft

---

[132] Macintosh, *Bomber Pilot*, p. 58.
[133] Musgrove, *Dresden and the Heavy Bombers*, p. 13.
[134] White, *Bread and Butter Bomber Boys*, p. 153.
[135] Gamble, *The Itinerant Airman*, pp. 145–6.

to place differences aside in order to maintain essential levels of concentration and communication. Although Gamble felt sore about being passed over for promotion, he insisted that relations with the newly commissioned crew members remained intact: 'this in no way affected our relationship with them ... we were genuinely pleased at their promotion. We were still "Skipper, Mo, Art, Monty, Gibby, Ronnie and Poker" to each other, and a highly proficient unit to boot!'[136]

A similar tale of enforced unity in the air emerges from accounts of clashing personalities among aircrew. Ultimate responsibility for the aircraft rested with the pilot, who correspondingly assumed an unofficial oversight of crew dynamics. If the formalised leadership of Hastings's argument is virtually undetectable in these narratives, faint traces of a more fraternal mode of leadership are certainly discernible. Lancaster bomb aimer, Tripp, for instance, dwelt at length upon the divergent temperaments, backgrounds, and character traits of his crew. Unafraid to acknowledge their frequent differences of opinion, he portrayed their relationships as becoming increasingly strained as they worked their way through their tour. He attributed the mounting disharmony to the cumulative stress of three months' operational service: 'tempers were becoming short, and mutual insults were intended to wound rather than amuse.'[137] As each member of the crew increasingly suffered from fatigue, personal characteristics became increasing irritants: 'George developed the habit of addressing everyone as "Kiddie" and whereas he had once been phlegmatic his moods began to fluctuate between facetiousness and despondency. Ray and I could barely speak to each other without quarrelling'.[138] Significantly, however, it is Tripp's pilot, 'Dig', who is represented as holding the crew together. He is characterised as 'more of a leader than an equal' in the crew pecking order, as he would not hesitate to order backbiting crew members to 'belt up' in the air.[139] Yet rather than remaining aloof from the bickering of his crew 'Dig' added his own contribution, deliberately using the phrase 'you'd whinge if your arse was on fire' purely because he knew it irritated Tripp. Macintosh, a Lancaster pilot, also recounted strained circumstances. Reflecting on his crew, he recorded that 'Sometimes they didn't like me, and occasionally, in discussions which I fostered, said I was overbearing and didn't always muck in like the skippers of other crews.'[140] Yet he would not let this affect operations: 'I never allowed any arguments in the air, which

[136] Ibid., p. 146.
[137] Tripp, *The Eighth Passenger*, p. 71.
[138] Ibid., p. 71.
[139] Ibid., p. 103; p. 31.
[140] Macintosh, *Bomber Pilot*, p. 204.

happened occasionally on other crews.'[141] If the seven-man bomber crew
may be likened to a 'band of brothers', these memoirs suggest that the
pilot, teasing, chastising, and responsible by turns, fulfilled the role of
supervisory eldest sibling.

Among these memoirs, the subject of fear and endurance among aircrew provides a particularly valuable insight into the interplay of human
relationships in Bomber Command. On 22 April 1940 the Air Member
for Personnel had become so concerned about the rising rates of psychiatric casualties among flyers that a set of regulations was circulated,
stipulating that aircrew who stated an intent not to fly without a medical reason would be deemed 'Lacking in Moral Fibre' and removed
from the RAF.[142] Aircrew who no longer felt psychologically able to face
the demands of operational flying thus risked being administratively
stamped with the term 'Lack of Moral Fibre', stripped of rank, and igno-
miniously posted away from the squadron to assessment centres, often
to spend the rest of the war digging latrines. Russell's description of the
flyer's response to the cracking of a man's nerve epitomises the general
approach towards the subject in these veteran narratives: 'It was probably
an occurrence that any member of aircrew could contemplate happen-
ing, but the prospect of it filled him with horror.'[143] In his study of official
justification for this initiative, Edgar Jones observes that the RAF's crude
stigmatisation of the term was calculated to lend force to the policy of
deterring aircrew from refusing to fly.[144] Such was the impact of this
policy that the disgrace and humiliation deliberately invested in the label
'LMF' leaves a visible imprint in the majority of the bomber veteran
memoirs. It is notoriously difficult to retrieve statistics of how many aircrew were branded as LMF, mostly because the wartime RAF remained
extremely concerned that 'cowardice' might spread infectiously through
aircrew and Lack of Moral Fibre cases were dealt with harshly but as
quietly as possible. The memoirists invariably denied knowing anyone
who was so designated. Beneath this blanket refutation, however, lurks a
collective story in which accounts of cracked nerves and inability to cope
are common. Although the official secrecy which shrouded the entire
issue might well have rendered their expressed ignorance of LMF processes and statistical data technically accurate, most of the memoirists
report encountering aircrew who were physically and mentally unfit to

---

[141] Ibid., p. 204.
[142] John McCarthy, 'Aircrew and "Lack of Moral Fibre" in the Second World War', *War and Society*, 2:2 (1984), 87.
[143] Russell, *Flying in Defiance of the Reich*, p. 135.
[144] Edgar Jones, '"LMF": The Use of Psychiatric Stigma in the Royal Air Force during the Second World War', *The Journal of Military History*, 70 (2006), 440.

keep flying. Bushby, for example, recounted a tale of a young rear gunner whose plane was shot up by a German night fighter upon landing after a raid. The sole survivor, the gunner was found dragging the headless body of the navigator out of the flaming wreckage. Afterwards he did 'the sensible and courageous thing' and reported to the CO to explain that the sight of an aircraft brought the horror back to him and he felt he was a menace to his new crew. Bushby's empathy with the plight of the young gunner is made very clear to his reader, and in this instance the airman was treated kindly by the RAF: 'I believe some officious "trick cyclist" temporary medical officer did try to attach the "LMF" label to his case but was over-ruled after a sympathetic senior officer at Group had been told the facts.'[145]

Yet a different anecdote in Bushby's memoir reveals the limits set upon the flyer's sympathy for aircrew who lost control of themselves. Despite his compassion for the young gunner, Bushby was scathing when his own bomb aimer's nerve snapped during an attack on Bremen. On this particular raid in 1942, conditions above the city were daunting, with thick flak and multiple searchlights in action. On the run over the target, the bomb aimer failed to confirm that the bomb load had been dropped, and it was not until the aircraft reached the outer perimeter of the target area that he informed the rest of the crew that he had forgotten to push the master switch to release the explosives. Grimly, Bushby's pilot refused to accept this explanation at face value and insisted upon another, more successful, run. The veteran's account of this episode is relentlessly unsympathetic:

There was no doubt about it. Our bomb-aimer had been scared, almost to the point of fear. Now there was nothing wrong in that. Any man who was not scared to go on ops was either a freak or a liar. But our bomb-aimer had committed the unpardonable crime of showing it. This was the real courage of aircrew. Not in being unafraid, but in keeping one's fear to oneself, in making a moral effort to protect the rest of the crew from infection.[146]

After the Bremen raid, he never saw the bomb aimer again: 'Whatever had been done, had been done quietly and without fuss. He was near the end of a tour anyway and a posting, maybe administrative, maybe instructional, had been quickly arranged no doubt to his satisfaction as well as ours.'[147] This observation about the quiet reassignment of the airman being to the crew's 'satisfaction', as well as presumably the unfortunate

[145] Bushby, *Gunner's Moon*, p. 143.
[146] Ibid., p. 142.
[147] Ibid., pp. 142–143.

bomb aimer's, demarcates the point at which sympathy for one man had to be weighed against the lives of others.

A number of other memoirists agreed that an open display of fear in the air posed an immediate threat to the entire unit, as it could lead to crew relations unravelling with frightening speed. Lancaster pilot Harry Yates acknowledged that LMF was harsh but in some circumstances necessary to save other lives:

There must be many alive still for whom the passing years have not erased the pain of those cruel words. But better even this than that these people should get as far as the Ruhr or the main German cities. Fear there was unavoidable, death always close. No crew could afford one of their number to snap on board and plunge everything into hysteria and chaos.[148]

Macintosh corroborated this, explaining how if terror was allowed to show, it could destroy the poise of a whole crew:

Fear, like a trickle in the wall of a dyke, quickly became a flood, breaching the barriers of the mind and stomach and communicating itself to the whole crew. Expecting trouble, their already taught [sic] nerves stretched to every bang and flash, drastically lowering their efficiency.[149]

Clear expectations of aircrew behaviour when suffering from fear and combat fatigue are thus stapled into these veterans' representations. It is important to recognise, however, that these memoirists censured 'cowards' only for showing fear, not for experiencing it. There is a strong trace of the sentiment 'There but for the Grace of God go I' in these narratives, and the authors' approaches towards fear are sanguine in their tacit acceptance that no man was immune. Philip Gray observed that 'even heroes have a break-down point. Honour and moral fibre are variables. Like pain, the threshold is different in each one of us.'[150] John Wainwright confirmed that this personal 'threshold' was something that each man carried around with him:

He couldn't change it and, if you forced him, blackmailed him, beyond that threshold of terror you were sending him and his crew to near-certain death. Because he would do something he shouldn't do … or not do something he should do. He'd freeze. He'd lose control. He'd be a useless vacuum, within a crew of which he was a part.[151]

Wainwright, in fact, had his own experience of the LMF taboo. After his aircraft was shot up and crash-landed on the runway, he was hospitalised

---

148 Yates, *Luck and a Lancaster*, p. 48.
149 Macintosh, *Bomber Pilot*, p. 194.
150 Gray, *Ghosts of Targets Past*, p. 81.
151 Wainwright, *Tail-End Charlie*, p. 180.

with severe concussion. Having completed seventy-two operational trips, he decided that the time had come to quit flying before he succumbed to the scenario outlined above. His treatment by the RAF was markedly lacking in sympathy, and for three months he was quizzed by psychiatrists who tried to prompt him to return to flying. He subsequently lost his rank as flight sergeant and was remustered as ground crew, narrowly missing classification as LMF 'by a whisker'.[152] Grandiloquently, he declared that:

most operational air crew would have agreed, and will still agree, that it is more than likely that those three letters killed more men than German flak, or German fighters. They sent terrified men to their death; they forced men to operate when they were a menace to their own crew.[153]

Like the naval officers, bomber aircrew could recognise the point at which they posed an immediate risk to the safety of their own crew, yet according to the memoirists of Bomber Command, the threat of being branded LMF forced men to continue flying long after this point. Among these aircrew, therefore, the 'touch of human nature' certainly served to allow men to work together with their aircraft as a 'sharply honed weapon'. Yet this close-knit and finely balanced seven-part combat relationship could prove the airman's Achilles heel. The fraternal nature of this relationship posed hazards, as well as advantages, to survival in combat. Ultimately, the final gift a flyer could bestow upon his aerial 'band of brothers' was to realise when his ability to use their company as a coping mechanism had run dry. Caught in a cruel snare by the noose of LMF, however, it was entirely possible that a flyer could be forced to jeopardise the lives of his crew mates in order to safeguard his own identity. With some irony, destroyer captain Roger Hill expressed envy of the bombers' system of tours, perceiving that it meant that 'there was no agonising decision to give up and be thought a coward to yourself or others.'[154] The reality, as these aircrew narratives testify, was rather different.

Summary

The 'touch of human nature' which Marshall thought requisite to enabling combatants to make efficacious use of their weapons in battle is thus confirmed in these veteran memoirs, which chart the importance of close human relationships and martial fraternity within their units. Ironically, however, the tightly knitted 'band of brothers' paradigm could

[152] Ibid., p. 178.
[153] Ibid., p. 178.
[154] Hill, *Destroyer Captain*, p. 154.

also serve to undermine broader military objectives on occasion. As Richard Holmes notes, 'a system which bonded men firmly into tribal groups might work to the disadvantage of the army as a whole'.[155] In the Army, the Salerno mutiny of September 1943 proved this, as did a more minor, albeit no less murky, episode recounted by Bowlby, who asserted that a miniature rebellion had taken place shortly before he joined his unit at Alexandria in 1944. According to the author, when Tunisia fell, the 2nd Battalion of the Rifle Brigade were outraged to find that a suggestion, generated by the Army's rumour mill, that Montgomery was to take the whole Eighth Army back to Britain for a well-earned rest was in fact false. At that point, Bowlby recorded, the riflemen were under the impression that they were to stay on in Tunisia. Admittedly basing his account on hearsay (but which he assured his audience was entirely truthful and could be corroborated by other sources), he reported that 'it was more than they could stomach. Groups of riflemen went round wrecking the camp. Their officers were unable to stop them.'[156] Such was the depth of group solidarity that by the time Bowlby joined the battalion, the punishment allegedly meted out to the unit – the repatriation of all its pre-war regulars and effective dismantlement of the unit – had left the mood of the remnants 'bitter'. In this instance, combatants displayed disgruntlement at orders imposed upon their own unit, yet other anecdotes from the naval and flyer memoirs suggest that the bonds of 'brotherhood' extended into a fraternal martial community that lay far beyond the immediate small group. Hill's destroyer, HMS *Ledbury*, formed part of the escort group for convoy PQ17. Upon receiving the order to 'scatter' from the Senior Escort Officer, Hill and the other five escorting destroyers sped off to intercept an anticipated attack from the German battleship, *Tirpitz*, leaving the scattering convoy of merchant ships and naval anti-submarine trawlers, anti-aircraft ships, and minesweepers to fend for themselves. Hill recorded that 'I can never forget how they cheered us as we moved out at full speed to the attack and it has haunted me ever since that we left them to be destroyed.'[157] He displayed still-raw rancour against the Admiralty, who were culpable for the situation in which the convoy was annihilated and the rigidity of naval orders that prevented the close escort group from returning to protect the remnants of the convoy once it became apparent that the *Tirpitz* was far away. He reported that 'Everyone was bloodyminded with the bitter memory of PQ17 and the most respectable members of the ship's company had

[155] Holmes, 'The Italian Job', p. 212.
[156] Bowlby, *Recollections*, p. 8.
[157] Hill, *Destroyer Captain*, p. 51.

broken their leave' in protest against the catastrophic Admiralty error of judgement.[158] In less mutinous but still bitter terms Bushby wrote of a collective resentment against RAF procedure when a young air gunner at OTU Finningley was ceremoniously stripped of rank for slipping off to sort out a serious domestic problem. The Station Commander decided to make an example of the gunner, and mustered a parade of all the airmen on the OTU to witness the punishment. Standing in a hollow square, these men witnessed the gunner marched out under guard, and forced to stand still whilst his sergeant's stripes and flying brevet were ripped from his tunic. Bushby recorded that this scene of 'pure pathos' was a 'major psychological error', as it had a wholly unintended effect among the witnesses:

What [the Station Commander] had failed to take into account in his arrogant pre-World War One thinking was that every aircrew member on that parade was a volunteer; and that by making us participate in another's degradation he had tacitly implied that in his opinion any one of us was likely to commit the same offence at any time. This we resented to a man.[159]

These more negative workings of the 'band of brothers' construct provide illustrations of Strachan's observation that fraternal martial loyalties could amount to a 'divorce' of combatants from the collective goals of higher military organisations.[160] Nevertheless, as an earlier chapter in this book highlighted, it was the strength of veterans' desire to remember and celebrate their wartime 'band of brothers' that frequently motivated them to write their memoirs in the first place.

[158]   Ibid., p. 53.
[159]   Bushby, *Gunner's Moon*, p. 92.
[160]   Strachan, 'Training, Morale and Modern War', 213.

7   Selfhood and Coming of Age
in Veteran Memoir

> [N]o man goes through a war without being changed by it, and in
> fundamental ways ... Change – *inner* change – is the other motive
> for war stories: not only what happened, but what happened to *me*.[1]

As Samuel Hynes recognises, war memoirs frequently possess an indicative interiority that opens up veteran processes of drawing out personal
meaning from their wartime experiences. Indeed, Hynes' own military memoir of flying more than 100 combat missions as a US Marine
pilot against the Japanese in the Pacific war, is succinctly summarised
as proffering an eloquent account of 'the sensations he experienced in
his rites of passage from untrained cadet to war-weary aviator, from
youthful innocence to manhood.'[2] Other published memoirs of Second
World War warriors also stand testament to a process of profound inner
change within their authors that was triggered and shaped by the experience of the war itself. In his study of Winston Churchill's six loosely
autobiographical volumes of the Second World War, David Reynolds
remarks that at times the great man's narratives 'became an attempt at
self-knowledge'.[3] The humbler narratives of Churchill's soldiers, sailors,
and airmen performed as equally valuable tools of self-contemplation for
those who sought to enlarge understanding of their own wartime past,
and thus provide the historian of war and memory with a unique insight
into the military veteran's self-assessment of the personal impact of war.

As Georges Grusdorf suggests in his work on the conditions and limits
of autobiographical writing, the construction of personal narratives offers
a second reading of experience, adding consciousness to experience
itself.[4] Unlike more diurnal forms of written personal testimony such as

---

[1] Hynes, *The Soldiers' Tale*, p. 3.
[2] Samuel Hynes, *Flights of Passage: Reflections of a World War II Aviator* (London: Bloomsbury,
1988).
[3] David Reynolds, *In Command of History: Churchill Fighting and Writing the Second World
War* (London: Allen Lane, 2004), p. xxiv.
[4] Grusdorf, 'Conditions and Limits of Autobiography', p. 38.

letters or diaries, published war memoirs unfold a fluid and unchipped story in which the natural irrelevancies or interruptions that accompany immediate writing have been virtually polished out. The veterans' tale is sequential, progressive, and orderly: it has a beginning, a middle, and an end. This is not to suggest that gaps, deficiencies, inconsistencies, contradictions, and so forth do not occur in the published war memoir, merely that any fissures are held shut with invisible stitches and rough spots filled and buffed out so far as possible in the private and commercial editing processes. Not all memoirs adopt the same structure or the same chronology: some recount the veteran's life as it is lived right through from birth to provide the 'whole picture', whilst others simply begin the veteran's tale at a self-designated salient point in the war experience. Yet both types of memoir provide a continuous narrative of experience in which the veteran delineates where he started from, where he went, where he thought he ended up, and what personal changes he sustained along the way. Of course, in speaking of the veterans' tale as a collective, it is needful to recognise that in the same way that no man's experiences and memories of war are ever exactly the same, there is no 'one size fits all' process of inner change to be located in the memoirs of former servicemen. Nor should one be imposed by external audiences. Not all war memoirists were sufficiently introspective, or even especially eager, to probe and record the intimate impact of battle on mind and character. Some, like ex-sergeant fighter pilot Bill Rolls, evidently preferred to recount their experiences of action within more emotionally restricted parameters, sticking to forthright narration of what they did in war rather than what war did to them.[5] But many other memoirists found that in relating battlefield experience and reconstructing emotional reactions to combat, linear narrative provided a mechanism of self-evaluation that enabled the various invocations of pre-war, wartime, and post-war identities. This allowed the veteran to actively review changes wrought by war upon his ideas of self.

Conscious expression of the subjective sense of self and attempted self-knowledge throughout the veterans' tale is thus the focus of this chapter, which draws together the most common shared facets of the veterans' narrative voyages of self-discovery. Returning to Jay Winter's observation that there are two essential premises for examining this kind of evidence – the 'first is that experience, refracted through memory, helps constitute identities. The second is that experience changes as subject positions shift over time' – this chapter suggests that a focus on the interiority of post-war memoirs helps us to get closer to what the

[5] Hynes, *The Soldiers' Tale*, p. 3.

veteran-memoirist, in those moments of telling, thought had happened
to him.[6] Whilst acknowledging the force of Penny Summerfield's argument that all forms of personal testimony are inter-subjective, shaped to
an extent by external discursive formulations, the intention of this chapter is less to address the situation of published military memoirs within
cultural frameworks of memory and representation than to illuminate
the specific subjectivity of British Second World War veteran memoirs.[7]
Echoing Michael Roper's analysis of autobiographical accounts written
by middle-class First World War veterans, the concern here is thus with
self-reconstruction 'as a process of reflexive looking back' on a youth
expended on war.[8]

War memoirs are coming of age stories. In his work on the formation
of self in the contemporary American novel, Kenneth Milliard suggests
that autobiographical writing ought to be regarded as closely related to
the Bildungsroman, the novel of self-development that emerged out of
eighteenth-century Germany.[9] Like the protagonists of this genre, the
war memoirist starts out as a novice, overcomes trials and hardship,
and concludes his story as a wiser, more adult character. Nevertheless,
as Milliard warns, the term 'coming of age' requires some care when
applied to life-writing. The expression technically refers to the attain-
ment of full legal status as an adult but it also carries critical implications that a person has reached emotional maturity and possesses a new
degree of knowledge about themselves. It is thus loaded with 'an impre-
cision and a cultural relativity' that must be taken into account when
interrogating the specific subjectivity of the Second World War veterans'
tale.[10] Geoffrey Wellum's memoir includes the strapline, 'The True Story
of the Boy who became a Man in the War-torn Skies above Britain',
but what meanings did the memoirist ascribe to the labels of 'boy' and
'man'? Hynes' progression from 'youthful innocence to manhood' echoes
throughout the veterans' tale, but what triggered this transition, and how
did it unfold? To approach the war memoir as both narrative of 'inner
change' and 'coming of age' story, it is vital to ask how these veteran-
memoirists understood and reconstructed ideas of masculinity, maturity,
and selfhood in relation to the experience of war.

[6] Winter, *Remembering War*, p. 117.
[7] Summerfield, *Reconstructing Women's Wartime Lives*, p. 15.
[8] Michael Roper, 'Re-remembering the Soldier Hero: The Psychic and Social Construction of Memory in Personal Narratives of the Great War', *History Workshop Journal*, 50:3 (2000), 346.
[9] Kenneth Milliard, *Coming of Age in Contemporary American Fiction* (Edinburgh: Edinburgh University Press, 2007), pp. 1–5.
[10] Ibid.

'Youthful Innocence'

In making the attempt to discover and understand the full impact of war upon his sense of self, the veteran-memoirist clearly found it useful to review his youthful expectations of war as a means of gauging the experience. The Second World War veteran who sat down to write of his military experiences thus frequently found himself facing the question of how he had initially confronted the prospect of joining this war. By and large, the veterans' tale insists, the outbreak of war was hailed enthusiastically by their younger selves, who greeted the prospect of ensuing hostilities as an imminent and exciting experience. Tim Vigors described listening with especial fervour to Prime Minister Neville Chamberlain's declaration of war whilst undergoing pilot-officer training at RAF Cranwell in September 1939:

There were about fifty cadets gathered in that ante room and, as one man, we jumped to our feet cheering with excitement. There was not one amongst us who would not have been bitterly disappointed had the declaration of war not been made.[11]

If such openly elated capers at Germany's refusal to cease military operations in Poland by 3 September 1939 were not quite common currency among the Second World War veterans' tales, the vast majority of these authors nevertheless depicted themselves as neither displeased nor surprised by the aggressive turn of events. Interestingly, ideology and politics exerted remarkably little influence over the memoirists' feelings about the outbreak of war in 1939. A number of these men had opted to enlist in the volunteer reserve branches of the British armed forces in the years immediately preceding the declaration of hostilities, but in retrospect these veterans did not attribute their decision to enlist early to any particular enthusiasm for national flag-waving or moral crusading between 1938–9. Explaining his decision to join the Territorial Army in January 1939, John Kenneally reflected that the worsening political situation on the Continent in fact posed very little concern to his younger self: 'Like a lot of young men of our generation we were not politically conscious; the only parts of a newspaper we read were the sports pages.'[12] Similarly, in May 1939, WGG Duncan Smith was based at RAF Woodley, undergoing training with the Royal Air Force Volunteer Reserve. He reported that all the trainees knew war lurked on the horizon but,

We had no interest in politics and, for that matter, had never been taught anything about the subject, much less attended any political meeting. We were amused by

---

[11] Vigors, *Life's Too Short to Cry*, p. 99.
[12] Kenneally, *The Honour and the Shame*, p. 12.

our posturing politicians and their promises of fixing Hitler and his jack-booted followers – that there would be 'peace in our time'.[13]

Echoing Kenneally, he reflected that most of the apprentice pilots 'looked forward to it in much the same way as preparing for an important rugger or cricket match', and a broadly congruent story is recounted throughout the memoirs of pre-war professionals, reservists, wartime volunteers, and conscripts alike.[14]

A strange blend of innocence tinged with a sharp edge of knowingness characterises the veterans' representations of the war they imagined they were going to fight. The 'big ideas' of jingoistic British nationalism and the mawkish 'Dulce et Decorum est' that are frequently associated with soldiers' narratives of going to war in 1914 are prominent by their absence in the Second World War veterans' tale. Among the scholarship of combatant experience and testimony of battle between 1939 and 1945, strong evidence has been presented to suggest that the ordinary serviceman of this later conflict regarded the war much more philosophically. There was a job that needed to be done, and so he simply got on with it.[15] Arguably this generation of memoirists knew sufficient of the First World War's wastage of human life to fight shy of any sentiment akin to the rhetoric on which the nation had crested to war in 1914. A distinctive and enduring iconography of mud, blood, and barbed wire became widely embedded into the national consciousness during the interwar period, and a number of Second World War memoirists were clearly familiar with the trench literature that emerged from the Western Front. Veterans from middle-class backgrounds were more likely to have encountered this slew of poetry, fiction, and non-fiction during the course of either their education or personal reading practices. For example, as a schoolboy during the 1930s, Peter Cochrane had been introduced to the works of Robert Graves, Siegfried Sassoon, Eric Maria Remarque, and Edmund Blunden, whilst Christopher Bulteel recorded that as a teenager, the First World War authors' 'tales of carnage made me sick. By this time, I had read Wilfred Owen and Edward Thomas, and everyone knew what had happened to *them*.'[16] In Gary Sheffield's evocative phrasing, the 'shadow of the Somme' thus loomed menacingly over youth growing up in during the 1930s, with cultural memories of the

[13] Smith, *Spitfire into Battle*, pp. 3–4.
[14] Ibid., p. 3.
[15] Hynes, *The Soldiers' Tale*; Sheffield, 'Dead cows and Tigers'.
[16] Cochrane, *Charlie Company*, p. 16; Bulteel, *Something About a Soldier*, p. 8. Sydney Jary also made a point of explaining that he had read Sassoon, Owen, and Blunden, *18 Platoon*, p. xix.

Western Front serving as a 'benchmark of the appalling nature of war'.[17] Correspondingly, the Somme's spectre lay over veteran recollections of their youthful attitude towards the outbreak of war in 1939. 'Almost every adult and child was related to or knew someone who had served in the Forces, and ended up in a sanatorium or a grave', explained Ray Ward. 'Limbless ex-servicemen were seen everywhere.'[18] Ex-airman Arthur White, whose father had served with the RASC at Mons, Ypres, and the Somme, recorded how his consciousness of the appalling nature of war had been gleaned from his father's former comrades, one of whose legs had been amputated in a German medical field station. Furthermore, he had perused letters from an uncle on active service in the trenches who wrote home about the repugnance of lice 'as big as fox terriers.' 'There is no doubt', reflected White, 'that such tales influenced me and many others', and his account exemplifies how the First World War, and especially the Battle of the Somme, did indeed operate as a 'touchstone of horror' in the Second World War veterans' tale.[19] In particular, Second World War veteran-memoirists discerned that images of the carnage of the Western Front in national and familial remembrance shaped their decision to volunteer as RAF aircrew. For example, former Lancaster pilot Peter Russell's father had won a Military Cross as Transport Officer during the earlier war, 'staggering through the mud piled around the rim of each shell-hole', an image which clearly swayed his decision to volunteer for flying duties when his own turn came.[20] In choosing to join the RAF, wrote the memoirist, 'I did not expect to have to crawl through any mud.'[21] Also a former bomber pilot, memoirist Philip Gray confessed that he had not joined the RAF out of any particular passion for either aircraft or flying: 'They just happened to be one of the more attractive alternatives offered on the day. After all, I had no desire to go charging across another Somme.'[22]

Yet although the Second World War memoirists were born of the generation that inherited cultural memories of the awfulness of the First World War, outright cynical distrust of jingoism and political rhetoric and awareness of the dreadful precedent of the earlier conflict leaves surprisingly little footprint in the veterans' collective review of how they

[17] G. D. Sheffield, 'The Shadow of the Somme: The Influence of the First World War on British Soldiers' Perceptions and Behaviour in the Second World War' in *Time to Kill*, pp. 29–30.
[18] Ward, *The Mirror of Monte Cavallara*, p. 14.
[19] White, *Bread and Butter Bomber Boys*, pp. 36–37; Sheffield, 'The Shadow of the Somme', p. 36.
[20] Russell, *Flying in Defiance of the Reich*, p. 11.
[21] Ibid., p. 25.
[22] Gray, *Ghosts of Targets Past*, p. 3.

felt about going to war as young men. Instead, what Hugh Dundas identified as a 'schoolboy approach to war' dominates, in which traditional boyish illusions of enlistment as a ticket to thrilling martial experiences suffused their recollections.[23] In spite of witnessing at first-hand the terrible lasting wounds that war branded upon the bodies of family members, Ward recorded that, upon the outbreak of hostilities, this did not affect his keenness to see battle. Although his own father-in-law had never recovered from being gassed in the trenches and his father-in-law's brother died of tuberculosis whilst serving with the Black Watch during the First World War, Ward insisted that this knowledge 'did not dispel the romantic notion' of becoming a soldier.[24] Meditating that the chief 'attraction of the army for young men was its potential to satisfy boyish delight in mischief and mayhem', he identified war as an opportune chance to perform exhilarating and daring martial exploits.[25] When Britain declared war on Germany on 3 September 1939, agreed Kenneally, 'I was on the threshold of a great adventure.'[26] Arthur White described asking fellow flyers why they had joined as bomber aircrew and finding that they had similar reasons to himself: 'Predominant was the sense of adventure and the glamour'.[27] Limited opportunities for the interwar generation to visit foreign shores meant that military service offered the tantalising prospect of experiencing travel in overseas climes where exhilarating risk must surely unfold. 'All through my young life', Ken Tout cogitated, 'my hopes had simmered slowly up to this boiling, spilling delight of foreign adventure.'[28] Bill Bellamy's narrative epitomises the almost palpable enthusiasm for war as an exciting enterprise that characterises many veteran memoirs:

I was twenty years old. I tried to conceal my excitement with a veneer of sophistication, but in reality I couldn't wait for it all to begin. To me, it seemed like a sort of game, there was a feeling of chivalry about it, almost a crusade and certainly a sense of heroism at being part of it.[29]

Warfare imagined as an alluring 'adventure' scenario was thus often distinguished by these veterans as the formative influence upon their feelings about entering the fray. The opportunity that war appeared to offer for adventure was particularly welcomed by young men who viewed their civilian career prospects with no great enthusiasm and met news of the outbreak of war with mingled joy and relief. One such youngster was

---

[23] Dundas, *Flying Start*, p. 23.
[24] Ward, *The Mirror of Monte Cavallara*, p. 27.
[25] Ibid., p. 34.
[26] Kenneally, *The Honour and the Shame*, p. 13.
[27] White, *Bread and Butter Bomber Boys*, p.37.
[28] Tout, *By Tank: D to VE Days* (London: Robert Hale, 2010), p. 10.
[29] Bellamy, *Troop Leader*, p. 19.

Tom Neil, desperately keen to join the RAF since the age of twelve, but prevented by his parents' participation in the carnage of the First World War which rendered them reluctant to allow him to enlist in the armed services. As a teenager during the summer of 1938, Neil began working for his local district bank, an event which almost five decades later he dismissed disdainfully as 'The Bank indeed!'[30] Having succeeded in joining the RAFVR, he documented that when he heard that Germany had invaded Poland on 1 September 1939, 'my heart took off. I was free. Rid of banking for ever. Thank God!'[31] Similarly, Geoffrey Page's pre-war university career was jeopardised by his love of flying with his University Air Squadron. After failing his Inter-BSc exams in his second year at Imperial College, London, he was faced with a parental ultimatum to either leave university or quit flying: 'Happily for me, or so I thought, Hitler overstepped himself.'[32] Others who were slightly older or possessed longer experience of the military looked forward to the war as a mixture of adventure and professional challenge. As members of the pre-war Royal Navy, Sam Lombard-Hobson and Sydney Hart embraced the opportunity to put their painstakingly acquired skills of seamanship into action on a wartime footing. Aged twenty-four when war was declared, Hart recorded that he was then serving in the T-class submarine HMS *Triad* and met the prospect of battle with approbation:

I was on the brink of the greatest adventure that could befall any man – war in submarines: war in a service that would not only go forth to meet the enemy, but would penetrate his sea-defences and deliver the appropriate attacks in his own lairs ... we were all keyed up by a spirit of derring-do.[33]

Lombard-Hobson also cheerfully admitted to a perception that the Second World War,

started at exactly the right moment in my lifetime: I was twenty-six years of age; I was unmarried; I was fully trained in the profession of arms; and I had not to give up a civilian job in which I was just beginning to make my mark. I may be excused, therefore, if I admit that I entered the arena with confidence, and looked forward enthusiastically to whatever part I might be called upon to play in Defence of the Realm.[34]

According to the veterans' tale, increased age was not proof against this boyish fervent desire to see military action. A similar sense of remembered excitement about the prospect of battle also infuses the narratives

---

[30] Neil, *Gun Button to 'Fire'*, p. 13.
[31] Ibid., p. 19.
[32] Page, *Shot Down in Flames*, p. 9.
[33] Hart, *Discharged Dead*, p. 31.
[34] Lombard-Hobson, *A Sailor's War*, p. 49.

of a number of older veterans who were in their late twenties or early thirties when they first saw combat, and they too yoked this enthusiasm to a combined yearning for professional challenge and a schoolboyish desire for martial adventure. Having begun his war in 1940 as an engine fitter with 1405 Met. Flight at Aldergrove in Northern Ireland, Norman Ashton lamented that this role was 'cushy' rather than stimulating. He recalled that the circulation of an Air Ministry notice inviting airmen trained as engine fitters to apply for service as flight engineers for the new heavy four-engined bombers which were being amassed offered most welcome promise of 'an exciting career'[35]: 'I wanted action and excitement'[36]. Furthermore, at the age of twenty-nine, the first thousand bomber raid on Cologne on 30 May 1942, some weeks before he perused this notice, had 'thrilled' him: 'That, thought I, was the life for a man: no phoney war, but just taking the Hun by the throat and shaking him.'[37] A year after volunteering for aircrew duties, the thirty-year-old Ashton flew his first sortie with 103 Squadron, embarking on a participation in the strategic air campaign against Germany that would last until the end of the war. Others also recalled that they took extraordinary pains to get into action. In February 1941, Charles Potts left England as a padre in the army. In *Soldier in the Sand* (1961) he documented that, although keen to enter the fray, he was refused permission to accompany any units into battle on the grounds that the Chaplains' Department felt he was indispensable.[38] Such was his desire to enter the mêlée that he resigned his chaplaincy and enlisted as a private before being commissioned into the Buffs. Despite a rule that subalterns over the age of thirty would no longer be sent up to the desert, he successfully appealed and found himself arriving among the Eighth Army at roughly the same time as Montgomery took command in 1942. Intriguingly, Potts explains that he had contemplated joining the Special Air Service, but instead opted for 'a definite chance of action with the Infantry' rather than a 'nebulous hope of being accepted for service with the S.A.S.'[39] What these accounts have in common is their expression of a clear desire to get into action, articulated in much the same fashion as their more youthful counterparts. Aged eighteen or thirty, these memoirs suggest, boyish ideas of battle retained their power to captivate and to animate. Their authors were not immune to the pull of seeing war at the sharp end and fantasies of war

[35] Ashton, *Only Birds and Fools*, p. 1.
[36] Ibid., p. 2.
[37] Ibid., p. 1.
[38] Potts, *Soldier in the Sand*, p. 2.
[39] Ibid., p. 4.

clearly retained the power to beguile long after boyhood and adolescence had ended.

These rosily romanticised associations of adventure and excitement with martial exploit are as old as war itself, and thanks to the ground-breaking work of scholars such as Graham Dawson and Kelly Boyd, it is possible to trace the constellation of cultural representations upon which late nineteenth- and twentieth-century boys and adolescents drew to fashion their ideas of war.[40] In his authoritative analysis of the fashioning of the 'soldier hero of adventure' as an archetype of idealised British masculinity, Graham Dawson outlines a long lineage of a 'popular masculine pleasure-culture of war' which critically shaped the heavily romanticised appeal combat held for generations of British boys since the late nineteenth century.[41] From the 1870s, children became a distinct market-sector in Britain, and a specific culture was created that offered boys a rich diet of war stories and images in which to immerse themselves through play and fantasy and to imaginatively develop their own sense of masculinity. Dawson suggests that the idea of war as 'adventure' – as a masculine romance of male contest and camaraderie – has provided a key form in cultures of boyhood and nation ever since the heyday of an Empire that offered an imperial playground in which to try out fantasies of heroic martial masculinity.[42] But what makes the Second World War veterans' tale particularly interesting is that the memoirists themselves drew similar conclusions about the suggestive power of the 'soldier hero' stereotype which had infused their boyhoods and adolescence. Quite independently of the comparatively recent body of scholarship which has addressed masculine culture and war, these veterans also located the foundation of their imagined knowledge of war as adventure in the specific literary, cinematic, and popular images of battle that were freely available to youth growing up during the 1920s and 1930s. Former fighter pilot Hugh Dundas recollected being 'fascinated by the idea of war from an early age.' At his preparatory school in Aysgarth, he spent many winter months sitting by a radiator reading *The Times History of the Great War* and its sister volume about the Boer War:

I gazed fascinated at the drawings and photographs of gallant Britons, engaging the enemy in every kind of situation, by land, sea and air. And in my day dreams I led a thousand forlorn hopes, died a hundred deaths in a manner which aroused the astonished admiration of the entire nation.[43]

---

[40] Graham Dawson, *Soldier Heroes*; Kelly Boyd, *Manliness and the Boys' Story Paper in Britain: A Cultural History, 1855–1940* (Basingstoke: Palgrave Macmillan, 2003).
[41] Dawson, *Soldier Heroes*, pp. 1–4.
[42] Ibid., p. 235.
[43] Dundas, *Flying Start*, p. 3.

At the age of twenty, Ken Tout joined the 1st Northamptonshire
Yeomanry and landed in Normandy in June 1944. Reflecting on his con-
scription into the army, the memoirist mused that,

it was the spirit of boyish adventure ... which made me a not-unwilling recruit.
The pages of the *Hotspur* and *The Captain* had more influence on my commit-
ment than the writings of Moses or St Paul or the foreign correspondents of *The
Times*.[44]

As his allusions to boys' papers the *Hotspur* and *The Captain* indicate,
Tout had, like many other veterans in this study, grown up reading literature designed specifically for male youth. In retrospect, the memoirist
perceived that this literature had so conditioned his youthful expectations of war that even after four long years of total war he and many
of the other young reinforcements to his regiment still envisaged the
approach of combat as,

an adventure story out of a school magazine, or the *Hotspur* or the *Wizard*. The
more literary of us even dreamed of mention on a stained glass window or an
oak-and-gold-leaf honours board in some dim school hall.[45]

The roots of these daydreams of war as adventure can be traced back
to the kind of traditional schoolboy-meets-Empire exploits that characterised so much of late Victorian and Edwardian boys' literature. The
development of technologies of military flight meant that the interwar
generation were also offered alluringly modern models of war as adventure
occurring high above the earth.[46] In retrospect, the veteran-memoirists of
Fighter and Bomber Commands unequivocally identified fictional and
non-fictional military aviator heroes of the First World War as governing
their boyish preconceptions of war. John Bushby documented that he
had grown up on a diet of air adventure stories such as those published
in the novels of Percy F. Westerman and the boys' magazine *The Modern
Boy*, with the result that 'aircraft and aviation became an abiding passion with me. It was all second-hand, of course; consisting mainly of
imagination fiction-fed from the municipal library'.[47] Favoured reading
matter for many, including Bushby, was the flying career of author WE
Johns' maverick pilot officer James 'Biggles' Bigglesworth, since dubbed
'Fighter Command's single most effective recruiting sergeant'.[48] Johns'
beloved character first appeared in popular boys' magazines during the

---

[44] Tout, *Tanks, Advance!*, p. 26.
[45] Ibid., p. 13.
[46] Michael Paris, 'The Rise of the Airmen: The Origins of Air Force Elitism, c. 1890-1918',
   Journal of Contemporary History, 28:1 (1993), 123–141.
[47] Bushby, *Gunner's Moon*, p. 8.
[48] Patrick Bishop, *Fighter Boys: Saving Britain 1940* (London: HarperCollins, 2003), p. 52.

early 1930s, and it was through the exploits of this fictional pilot officer serving with the Royal Flying Corps high above the Western Front during the First World War that many of those who served as aircrew during the Second were introduced to the enthralling and dangerously romanticised world of air combat. Cool, confident, competent, and on occasion almost suicidally courageous, the daring deeds of 'Biggles' in his high-altitude encounters with 'the Hun' caused memoirist Tim Vigors to reflect that in his own youthful inexperience he regarded flying as 'a marvellous game'.[49] Other memoirists recalled a pre-war fascination with real-life aviator heroes of the First World War. Far above the squalid, shattered landscapes of Flanders and northern France, the air war appeared to offer a welcome alternative to the pitilessness and impersonality of a land campaign that so voraciously squeezed soldiers through its vast mincing machine. Compared to the trenches which Siegfried Sassoon described so evocatively as an earthbound 'hell where youth and laughter go', aerial battle seemed to restore the finest traditions of fair play and nobility to combat.[50] Aircrew from both sides captured the attention of the adult and juvenile British publics, woven about with a satisfying myth of international aerial fraternity. Memoirist Roger Hall explained that,

My reading, since childhood, had been predominantly about flying. Immelmann, Boelke, Richthofen and Werner Voss were as familiar to me as were Bishop, Mannock, McCudden and Ball. They were all heroes to me regardless of their race or creed. In the R.F.C. I think there existed a comradeship and respect for friend and foe, born of the dangers suffered and the ecstasy experienced by all who used this new element in which to fight. I was anxious to see if the same spirit had permeated the R.A.F. to which I was so proud to belong.[51]

Among this impressive line-up of 'flying aces' who became celebrated in wartime and interwar British culture the young RFC pilot Albert Ball particularly captivated. Ball's feats in the skies above France between 1916 and 1917 earned him considerable publicity in Britain. Upon his death in 1917 his posthumous award of the Victoria Cross sealed his status as a national hero. In his memoir, Geoffrey Page mused that his own youthful idolization of Ball exerted a considerable impact upon the ways in which he perceived pilot training at RAF Cranwell during the winter of 1939:

As an officer cadet of nineteen, my thoughts were boyishly clear and simple. All I wanted was to be a fighter pilot like my hero, Captain Albert Ball … I knew

[49] Vigors, *Life's Too Short to Cry*, p. 96.
[50] Siegfried Sassoon, 'Suicide in the Trenches', in *Counter Attack and Other Poems* (New York: E.P. Dutton, 1918).
[51] Hall, *Clouds of Fear*, p. 29.

practically all there was to know about Albert Ball: how he flew, how he fought, how he won his Victoria Cross, how he died. I also thought I knew about war in the air. I imagined it to be Arthurian – about chivalry.[52]

With the rise of the cinema in interwar Britain, the silver screen further established the allure of the airman in the popular imagination. 'This', as Bushby explained to his readers, 'was the age of the Hollywood flying epic', and he devoured a number of films about the air war including *Hell's Angels* (1930) and *The Dawn Patrol* (1930).[53] The appeal of these movies is not hard to discern. As historian Malcolm Smith observes, 'War made good cinema, and air war better than most, with its opportunities for spectacular aerial photography and stories of derring-do.'[54] Together with *Wings* (1927), these classic interwar air combat films reinforced the elevated status of the flyer in popular British culture and were identified by aircrew memoirists as having played just as important a role as literature in colouring their anticipation of air warfare. Director Edmund Goulding's remake of *The Dawn Patrol* in 1938 proved immensely popular with several of the future members of Fighter Command. Starring Basil Rathbone, David Niven, and Errol Flynn – already famous for playing swashbuckling roles onscreen – this film heightened associations of heroism with the flyer. So potent was the draw of *The Dawn Patrol* remake that several memoirists recorded transposing their celluloid heroes onto actual flyers. Undergoing flight training at RAF Woodley in May 1939, WGG Duncan Smith divined a likeness between his Chief Flying Instructor and Basil Rathbone, which might well have been tinted by the fact that the young trainee had seen *The Dawn Patrol* four times.[55] Shortly before his first taste of operational flying, Hugh Dundas also pleasurably cast himself in the role of a pilot from *The Dawn Patrol*, visualising 'Errol Flynn looking over my shoulder in the mirror.'[56]

For a number of veteran-memoirists, war was thus welcomed as an opportunity to gain access to this heady realm of elitism, danger, and daring associated with the type of military adventures that exerted a continued thrall over interwar popular culture in Britain. The yearnings of memoirists like Tout, Hall, Page, Smith, and Dundas to gain induction into the ranks of real and imaginary military heroes celebrated for their valorous deeds are made plain in their narratives. Firmly tethered to these veterans' imagined knowledge of war as the stereotypical adventure so

---

[52] Page, *Shot Down in Flames*, p. 8.
[53] Bushby, *Gunner's Moon* pp. 8–9.
[54] Malcolm Smith, *Britain and 1940: History, Myth and Popular Memory* (London: Routledge, 2000), p. 20.
[55] Smith, *Spitfire into Battle*, p. 3.
[56] Dundas, *Flying Start*, p. 23.

beloved of literary and cinematic fantasy is an unshakeable assumption that battle possessed the power to convert a person from a nobody into a Somebody. As Graham Dawson has shown throughout his work on adventure narratives and imagined masculinities, war presents a valuable opportunity to try out desirable masculinities.[57] A number of veteran-memoirs suggest that the young men who fought the Second World War welcomed the prospect of combat because they confidently expected to be personally transformed by the experience. The same cultural images that proffered the war as adventure trope to an avid interwar generation of male youth also fuelled their expectations of undergoing a process of significant inner change on the battlefield. Echoing Keith Douglas, who described El Alamein as 'an important test, which I was interested in passing', the veterans' tale documents the memoirists' conviction that action would offer the ultimate proof of a man's calibre.[58] Narrating how he joined 92 Squadron at RAF Northolt in late May 1940, Geoffrey Wellum presented the forthcoming battle to stave off national invasion as a critical moment in his own formation of self: 'England is being tested and, with her, my own personal testing time is about to begin.'[59] As Owen Dudley Edwards observes, many of those young men who constituted 'the Few' of 1940 had grown up reading a wealth of juvenile literature, such as the *Magnet* or its sister paper the *Gem*, that identified 'the principal schoolboy heroes with a future destiny as air pilots'.[60] It is possible to suggest that this synonymy of adult masculinity with a martial identity in the enticing models of manly behaviour offered to the interwar generation of boys particularly conditioned the expectations of 'the Few' that aerial war would function desirably as an agent of inner change, but a similar story is told throughout the tales of veterans from the other services. Ward, a devotee of the adventure novels of John Buchan, Robert Louis Stevenson, and Sir Walter Scott, recorded experiencing elation upon receiving his commission into the Argyll and Sutherland regiment as a second lieutenant: 'I looked forward with the eagerness of youth to my first taste of travel, adventure and military glory, facing whatever challenges awaited me as a test of my manhood'.[61] The development, and subsequent incorporation into interwar boys' popular culture, of martial flight technologies represented a modern twist on an older model

[57] Dawson, *Soldier Heroes*, p. 174.
[58] Douglas, *Alamein to Zem Zem*, p. 5.
[59] Wellum, *First Light*, p. 130.
[60] Owen Dudley Edwards, 'The Battle of Britain and Children's Literature', in *The Burning Blue: A New History of the Battle of Britain* (eds.), Paul Addison and Jeremy A. Crang (London: Pimlico, 2000), p. 168.
[61] Ward, *The Mirror of Monte Cavallara*, pp. 59–60.

of adventure narrative in which the protagonist was transformed by the ordeal of battle into a heroic masculine figure.

As a result of the growth of popular imperialism during the mid-to-late nineteenth century, once the soldier became significant for his protection of the nation's imperial interests his feats were glorified in adventure stories and popular culture. The soldier therefore became celebrated as 'a quintessential figure' of heroic masculinity'.[62] Battle alone endorsed the soldier as the embodiment of heroic masculinity, since being in the field allowed him to exhibit the intense aggression, courage, and strength traditionally prized as both military qualities and manly virtues. In her work on nineteenth-century British soldiers' tales, Carolyn Steedman suggests that the soldier thus became widely regarded as 'the epitome of manhood'.[63] Whilst a considerable body of scholarship has highlighted a number of changes that the First World War wrought upon popular understandings of masculinity and the military figure, the veterans' tale of the Second World War suggests that more traditional concepts of the soldiers' robust hyper-masculinity continued to exert some influence over the aspirant combatant's fantasies of war and its impact upon constructions of personal identity. In these reflexive accounts of the memoirists' anticipation of battle, the combatant remains wishfully construed as the apogee of a manliness that encompasses extreme bravery, strength, and fortitude, and the protagonist may only attain this desirable identity through his participation in the martial enterprise. For instance, Geoffrey Wellum's depiction of pilot training at No. 6 Flying Training School at RAF Little Rissington between November 1939 and May 1940, most succinctly articulates this assumption of forthcoming masculine apotheosis. He recorded that undertaking formal instruction in the arts of war began the process of making 'not only a pilot of me but, also, a man capable of doing a man's job in a man's life.'[64] As Kelly Boyd notes in her cultural history of manliness in popular boys' literature, the martial heroes that the avid young readers were offered were seldom fully formed supermen who did not need to be initiated into or educated about manliness.[65] Rather, as Boyd observes, throughout the interwar boys' adventure genre, 'Most of the tales centred around the protagonist's development from rough approximation into fully-fledged man.'[66] The strong elements of the Bildungsroman that percolated juvenile adventure

---

[62] Dawson, *Soldier Heroes*, p. 1.
[63] Carolyn Steedman, *The Radical Soldier's Tale: John Pearman, 1819–1908*, new. ed. (Abingdon: Routledge, 2016), p. 37.
[64] Wellum, *First Light*, p. 32.
[65] Boyd, *Manliness and the Boys' Story Paper in Britain*, p. 175.
[66] Ibid., pp. 175–6.

fiction thus arguably helped to condition interwar youth to expect that war would accelerate the development of a mature masculine status.[67]

Among the veteran-memoirists' reconstructions of the ways in which they imagined the experience and impact of war as a kind of masculine romance, ordeal by battle was thus construed as the means by which to secure the type of coveted militarised masculinity embodied in the boys' adventure story. The imagined experience of forthcoming battle is presented first and foremost as a test of manly courage packaged in much the same framework of ideas as the traditional adventure narrative. Geoffrey Wellum's reported response to finding himself listed for the first time on the order of battle for the following dawn – 'I shall be either a man or a coward' – echoes the unremitting late Victorian and Edwardian emphasis upon strict codes of manly stoicism among military personnel.[68] Ideas of manly courage in connection with self-esteem were also attributed to the decisions of Peter Johnson and Norman Ashton to volunteer for operational aircrew duties. Johnson recorded that at the age of thirty-three in 1942, he was fed up with serving in RAF Training Command.[69] Having served as a pre-war fighter pilot, he accepted that he was too old to be allowed to return to this first love but rose nonetheless to the rank of Squadron Commander on a frontline bomber station. Although he acknowledged that he had made a valuable contribution to the war effort by training other aircrew, he explained that 'There had always been a sneaking feeling that I, like many others, stayed in Training Command because it was safe.'[70] Similarly, Ashton explained that his decision to swap his 'cushy' engine fitter's role for duties as a flight engineer was shaped not just by a wish for the excitement of seeing action, but also by concern that he was not exhibiting sufficiently manly behaviour. '[W]as I content', he wondered, 'to let others fight the battles or was I man enough to do my own fighting?'[71] On the whole, doing one's own fighting – or to put it another way, facing the risks of the battlefield – was clearly envisaged as the predominant benchmark of desirable manly behaviour among the veterans' tale. Constructions of manhood that were tied to the imagined identity of the combatant were bound up in traditional ideas of open displays of courage, protecting the nation, and not shirking one's duty are made apparent in the veterans' tale of how they expected war to propel them into 'manhood' and into what kind of 'men' they confidently expected to be transformed. It was thus armed with

[67] Dudley Edwards, 'The Battle of Britain and Children's Literature', p. 168.
[68] Wellum, First Light, p. 131.
[69] Johnson, The Withered Garland, p. 153.
[70] Ibid., p. 187.
[71] Ashton, Only Birds and Fools, p. 1.

a set of pleasantly fuzzy, exciting, and highly romanticised ideas about what war would bring, and confidence that they would emerge resplendent as heroes from the experience of combat, that the future veteran-memoirists of the Second World War set forth for battle, adventure, and 'manhood'.

'Manhood'

The veterans' tale thus clearly identifies a collective youthful understanding of war as an important forthcoming test of manly character. From the twin vantage points of survival and ageing, the veteran-memoirists agreed that their experiences in the armed services between 1939 and 1945 had indeed played a formative role in the process of 'growing up'. The veterans' tale therefore firmly locates the combat experience as the accelerant of processes of inner change, insisting that battle stripped away youth and innocence on a permanent basis. As a mechanism of induction into psychological and emotional maturity, these memoirs illuminate how combat operated as a rite of passage into an adult male identity. In his examination of ceremonial rituals, or 'rites of passage', ethnographer Arnold van Gennep explains that such traversion of socially constructed boundaries between identities must be accompanied by 'special acts' which serve to incorporate an individual into a new status and sense of self.[72] Within the context of frontline service during the Second World War, the kinds of 'special acts' that the memoirists identify as liminal moments in their masculine self-development were categorised into events including surviving first operational duties and proximity to violent death, gaining intimate experience of battle, overcoming fear, assuming command responsibilities, and abdicating juvenile fantasies of war as adventure. Whilst positioning the overall experience of battle as the key initiation rite into a new adult masculine status, the veterans' tale thus reveals a number of different aspects of combat that the memoirist interpreted as pivotal to his own 'coming of age'.

First experiences of operational duties are typically represented in the veterans' tale as a significant factor in this process of attaining maturity through active service. Former fighter pilot Geoffrey Page announced of his own introductory taste of action in May 1940, 'My first sortie over enemy-held territory was over. I had grown a little older.'[73] Yet the veterans' tale posits that this metamorphosis of self-bore very little similarity

---

[72] Arnold van Gennep, *The Rites of Passage*, trans. Monika B. Vizedom and Gabrielle L. Caffee (London: Routledge & Kegan Paul, 1960), p. 3.
[73] Page, *Shot Down in Flames*, p. 40.

to the transformative impact of experiencing battle that was enshrined with such confident expectation in the 'schoolboy approach' to war. Instead, these veteran memoirs report that the formerly held juvenile easy assumption that war *ipso facto* transformed combatants into the paradigmatic soldier-hero of adventure often received an early blow when the memoirist first joined his unit in the line. Several veterans recorded how early encounters with more experienced new comrades who seemed oddly reticent and separate provided an unwelcome early consciousness that war might not facilitate the shedding of youth quite so lightly as previously envisaged. Newly arrived on 92 Squadron at RAF Kenley in May 1940, Geoffrey Wellum watched as the rest of the squadron took off to protect the beaches of Dunkirk. This was their first operation. He explained that the return of the others to the Mess later on 'gave me my first intimation of what war is all about. These pilots were no longer young men with little care in the world, they were older mature men.'[74] Enquiries as to what aerial combat was really like were 'frowned upon': 'My fellow pilots, now battle experienced ... do not talk shop when off duty in the Mess. I retain, therefore, this feeling that I am not really accepted at the moment.'[75] In diagnosing why he felt like an outsider in his new squadron, the memoirist reflected that 'It must be that I am young and, as yet, still immature'.[76]

Although at eighteen years old Wellum was certainly among the youngest of the veteran-memoirists when he joined his unit, other authors who were some years older when they became operational also portrayed a similar sense of feeling like a juvenile outsider in the company of more battle-experienced new comrades. Aged twenty-four and twenty-six respectively at the beginning of active service, 'Johnnie' Johnson and Edward Young also clearly bracket themselves in the 'young and naïve' category at the outset of their wartime experiences. Their testimonies indicate that the veterans' retrospective self-perception of immaturity was bound up in the possession of the unformed emotional sensibilities, beliefs, and attitudes that are typically associated with the young. Significantly, 'youth' is thus understood in the veterans' tale as being both an emotional and physical status upon which battle stamped various changes. In relating encounters as martial novices with comrades who had already survived active duties, both memoirists recorded a perceived sense of difference and lack of belonging in the alien realm of military men similar to that described by Wellum. After completing a six-week training course at the submarine

---

[74] Wellum, *First Light*, p. 100.
[75] Ibid., p. 107.
[76] Ibid.

school HMS *Dolphin* in Gosport in September 1940, Young and two classmates whom he identifies as Lionel Dearden and Jock Tait were appointed to a pair of H-class submarines working off the north coast. Assigned to *H49* operating out of Harwich, Dearden immediately set out on his first patrol whilst the others continued travelling to join *H28*, then refitting at Sheerness. A week later, *H28* had also moved down to Harwich, and several days before he was due to set sail on his own first patrol Young eagerly watched the return of Dearden's submarine from operations in the North Sea:

In the mess that evening Jock and I pumped him for all we were worth to tell us what it had been like; but though we had been in the same training class there was a gulf fixed between us: he had completed a war patrol and we had not.[77]

Johnson too was painfully conscious of being yet to undergo the hazardous initiation ritual of battle. In late August 1940, he reported to 19 Squadron at Duxford with only 205 hours of flying time in his logbook, a scant twenty-three of which were on the Spitfires flown by his new squadron. Joining up with two other newcomers, he watched the rest of the squadron scramble for action, an event which occasioned 'a gloomy silence': 'On paper we were members of 19 Squadron, but a great gulf separated us from the handful of pilots who had disappeared into the infinite southern horizon.'[78] Like Wellum and Young, Johnson's eager efforts to 'pump' others who held combat experience to learn of the details of battle were met with considerable reticence. Between late July and August 1940, the memoirist had learnt to fly Spitfires at RAF Hawarden under the instruction of 'a seasoned bunch of fighter pilots' who had seen action in the Battle of France and over Dunkirk.[79] Although Johnson recorded that he and the other trainee pilots 'longed for' the knowledge of what aerial combat was really like, the instructors remained mostly tight-lipped:

I left Hawarden with anything but a clear-cut idea of what happened when Spitfire met Messerschmitt. Perhaps there was no short-cut, no easy way, to the lessons that could be learnt by hard experience alone.[80]

The unwillingness of these memoirists' comrades to discuss the graphic details of battle undoubtedly stemmed from the same inability to communicate the sensory details of 'what it was like' that typically characterised many veterans' conversations with civilians after the war.

---

[77] Young, *One of Our Submarines*, p. 29.
[78] Johnson, *Wing Leader*, p. 34.
[79] Ibid., p. 30.
[80] Ibid.

An invisible boundary composed of the pain, fear, and violence of battle separated the initiated from the uninitiated. The significance attached to this silence in the veteran-memoirists' tale underpins the concept that crossing this boundary and gaining first-hand knowledge of operational duties represented a crucial liminal moment in the 'coming of age' between 1939 and 1945. In order to be inducted into this elite community of martial manhood, the veterans' tale reports, it rapidly became apparent that the only route to membership was for the young serviceman to endure battle for himself. Cruelly, whilst an interwar masculine 'pleasure culture of war' led the young memoirists to suppose confidently that they 'knew' what this experience was going to be like, the 'gulf' that Wellum, Young, and Johnson identified between their freshly minted uniformed selves and their exhausted, uncommunicative, operationally experienced comrades voices the dawning of understanding that combat might prove a more daunting and isolating ordeal than boyish anticipation imagined.

Understanding and managing fear was particularly represented as a crucial aspect of the veteran-memoirist's rite of passage. Although the interwar generation of male youths who devoured popular boys' story papers were offered literary models of military men who acknowledged and controlled fear in a rational manner, the veterans' tale testifies that the more traditional, dauntless, devil-may-care soldier-hero of adventure continued to exercise a considerable appeal for impressionable young minds during this period. Recognition of the fact that fear immutably accompanied combat – comprising the 'eighth passenger' in a seven-man aircrew, as one veteran-memoirist wryly indicated – was thus bound into the veterans' tale as an integral element of developing maturity.[81] These literary audits of self illustrate how difficult it was to fit the experience of terrible, gut-clenching fear in battle into the schoolboy's paradigm of war as adventure. Former Lancaster pilot Philip Gray narrated a conversation with a girl friend who wanted to know what was operational flying was really like. The response that the memoirist recorded is enlightening: 'If you think it all comes out as the square-jawed hero stuff we see in the movies, then Lady, I have news for you.'[82] Gray went on to explain to his companion that 'all the human touches of realism' were omitted from most cultural representations of combatants, being altogether 'bad for the image' since they belied the heroic

---

[81] Tripp, *The Eighth Passenger*.
[82] Gray, *Ghosts of Targets Past*, p. 139.

masculine image promoted in popular culture.[83] He identified these bodily manifestations of fear as

the bits where the mouth is so dry that it seems even our chewing gum has turned to sawdust; where sweat cascades down the small of the back, and bubbles out of the palms of both hands; the bit where you can feel the contents of your bowels turning to water, and your stomach nerves are doing somersaults.[84]

'Just as I told you', he concluded his explanation, 'nothing at all like Hollywood, was it?'[85] Gray presents this illumination of fear as a simple conversation with a girl friend he had taken out for a drink, but throughout his memoir, he repeatedly employs a narrative trick of discussing intimate and emotional subjects through questionably clunky constructions of dialogue with an external audience. This was a technique that Richard Hillary also developed in *The Last Enemy* (1942). His narrated dialogue with the character of Peter Pease about the meaning and ethics of the war may be read at the level of a public conversation with his readership, and an intimate discussion at the level of his private self. In the context of exploring the emotional subjectivities of veteran-memoirists, such reconstructed conversations operate as an immensely valuable window into the memoirist's own dialogue at the level of the private self. This is particularly visible in the famous final chapter, in which Hillary recounts his participation in the rescue of an elderly woman from a bombed building. Displaying considerable courage throughout her ordeal, the old lady finally looks up into the terribly burned face of Hillary, remarking poignantly, 'I see they got you too'.[86] Whilst this anecdote is now widely accepted as an event that only ever occurred within the pages of Hillary's book, the memoirist crafted the incident and its accompanying conversation as a mechanism of relating a critical transformation in his own attitude towards the war. Arguably the dubious veracity of this little story is less important than the memoirist's desire to explain how he reached a new state of personal enlightenment with regard to the war, coming to understand it not simply as an exciting diversion for his own amusement, but as a moral crusade against evil. For memoirists who shied away from displaying too much open introspection, the same narrative device offered a more comfortable method of holding an intimate dialogue with the private self under the guise of a multi-party conversation with an external audience. Via another constructed dialogue, this time with his wireless operator, Gray could admit to both himself and

---

[83] Ibid., p. 140.
[84] Ibid.
[85] Ibid., p.141.
[86] Hillary, *The Last Enemy*, p. 244.

his external audience that he had lapped up the 'epics of dawn patrols' of the earlier conflict: 'seen the films, read the accounts ... In the air, at least, World War One had been a much more honourable affair than this rumble in which we were now engaged.'[87] As Gray's account exemplifies, fear became an embodied emotion for the combatant, and it is evident that the experience of one's 'bowels turning to water' in the air did not live up to the gallant images of which the 'schoolboy approach' to war was composed.

As Emma Newlands explores in her work on the attempts of wartime military authorities to counter physiological effects of fear among the British army, under the demanding conditions of combat, the male body at the 'sharp end' could rapidly become unruly and difficult to control.[88] Yet gaining control over the serviceman's bodily and emotional responses to battle in order to drive him forward in combat was not just the preserve of military authorities. Fundamentally it was a self-imposed task for each individual. The veterans' tale thus identified managing terror as a personal epoch, redefining fear in relation to the masculine self as an important part of their 'coming of age'. Although Michael Roper has deftly shown how the impact of the First World War created more nuanced perceptions of fear and manliness among middle-class, inter-war Britain, the Second World War veterans' tale again positions older and more traditional tenets of military manly behaviour as highly resilient at the outset of the memoirists' war.[89] Reflecting Edwardian military ideals of stoic endurance and disregard of fear as normative masculine behaviour in uniform, the Second World War veterans set up their pre-combat juvenile understandings of fear and courage as mutually exclusive qualities, an irreconcilability that Geoffrey Wellum epitomised in his early belief that a combatant could only be 'either a man or a coward'.[90] Since fearlessness in battle was thus construed as the ultimate manly virtue by the veteran-memoirists' younger selves, it was inevitable that anxieties about exhibiting fear should underpin their narratives of going to war. Wellum's plaintive declaration that 'I'm afraid of being a coward' resounds throughout the veterans' tale.[91] Stuart Hills recorded that as a second lieutenant in the Nottinghamshire Sherwood Rangers Yeomanry, 'My greatest fear [was] to be thought a coward by the men

[87] Gray, *Ghosts of Targets Past*, p. 79.
[88] Emma Newlands, *Civilians into Soldiers: War, the Body, and British Army Recruits 1939–1945* (Manchester: Manchester University Press, 2013), p. 155.
[89] Michael Roper, 'Between manliness and masculinity: the "war generation" and the psychology of fear in Britain, 1914–1970', *Journal of British Studies*, 44:2 (2005), 343–62.
[90] Wellum, *First Light*, p. 131.
[91] Ibid., p. 131.

I commanded. I can honestly say that I would have preferred to die than to let that happen'.[92] Serving on 222 Squadron in 1940, Tim Vigors' first operational flight took place above Dunkirk's beleaguered beaches. 'For the first time in my life I understood the meaning of the "taste of fear"', he remembered:

I suddenly realised that at long last the moment had arrived. We were going into action. Within an hour I could be battling for my life being shot at with real bullets by a man whose sole intent was to kill me. Up till now it had been something of a game; like a Biggles book, where the heroes always survived and it was generally only the baddies who got the chop. Now it was real war. I was dead scared and knew I had somehow to control this fear and not show it to my fellow pilots.[93]

Whilst the veteran memoirs convey the combatant's anxieties about maintaining appropriate masculine standards in public, they particularly document the combatant's increasing recognition that battle represented 'a struggle which also had to be ceaselessly fought at the level of the private self'.[94] Wellum recorded that he became particularly aware of this inner tussle when he watched the rest of 92 Squadron returning from their first operation in May 1940 and detected a new sense of maturity etched into their faces: 'These chaps have won their private battles and these are battles that they will have to go on winning'.[95] Although the concept of battle as a test of manly character is visible in veteran memoirs from across the services, the fighter pilot memoirs represent the test of self as especially acute. After returning safely from his first encounter with the Luftwaffe, Vigors explained that his anxieties about exhibiting fear publicly took on a new identity:

I was worried ... about deadly scared I had been when I first saw those enemy bullets streaming past my wing tip. I had never known fear like that before in my life and knew that I was likely to experience it many times again in the near future. Flying home that morning I just hoped fervently that I would be able to keep my fear under control.[96]

The character of air fighting during the Battle of Britain period dictated the enormous pressures that fighter pilots were under to control their fear. Defensive aerial combat during the summer and autumn of 1940 was short, sharp, and brutal. With aircraft reaching speeds of up to 350 miles per hour, dogfights whirled across the heavens, causing

[92] Hills, *By Tank into Normandy*, p. 228.
[93] Vigors, *Life's Too Short to Cry*, p. 152.
[94] Francis, *The Flyer*, p. 130.
[95] Wellum, *First Light*, p. 100.
[96] Vigors, *Life's Too Short to Cry*, p. 157.

many fighter pilots to become familiar with emerging out of a manoeuvre to find the surrounding sky emptied of aircraft. In his lonely cockpit, the fighter pilot was thus repeatedly offered a tempting opportunity to become legitimately displaced from battle that had to be constantly resisted, sometimes several times in the same day. As Tony Bartley noted, the men of Fighter Command did not benefit from the same kind of military structures and traditions that might provide emotional props for soldiers:

We had no comrades marching shoulder to shoulder. No pipes or drums, and the loneliness was sometimes more frightening than the bullets. If one lost one's nerve, it was easy to run away. The sky is a big place to get lost in.[97]

Hugh Dundas' memoir documents a particular struggle with the temptation to 'run away'. Narrating his first sortie in May 1940, Dundas described himself as 'close to panic in the bewilderment and hot fear of that first dog fight.'[98] Quoting a Churchillian maxim that a 'sincere desire to engage the enemy' was the benchmark by which the quality of fighting men may be judged, he explained that matters were not quite so clearcut in combat:

I found out that day, 28 May 1940, over Dunkirk, in my first close encounter with Britain's enemies, how hard it is to live up to that criterion. When it comes to the point, a sincere desire to stay alive is all too likely to get the upper hand. Certainly, that was the impulse which consumed me at that moment that day. And that was to be the impulse which I had to fight against, to try and try and try again to overcome, during the years which followed.[99]

Although the impulse to 'run' was far from confined to the men of Fighter Command, the veterans' tale of 'the Few' implies that the unique nature of aerial combat in 1940 intensified the fighter pilot's struggle to conquer his fears. Coming to terms with the fact that this private battle with fear was a vital part of the fight against the enemy meant that the relationship between courage, cowardice, and military masculinity became re-drawn in the ex-fighter pilots' tale. Roger Hall of 152nd (Nizam of Hyderabad) Squadron explained that having experienced the severe physical and psychological pressure of serving in Fighter Command, 'those who censure it or connect it with cowardice are those who have never had to undergo a similar strain.'[100] Whilst the 'coward' epithet still clearly held meaning for flyers – and was indeed enshrined in the RAF hierarchy's LMF soubriquet – the fighter pilots' tale suggests that first-hand experience

[97] Bartley, *Smoke Trails in the Sky*, p. 59.
[98] Dundas, *Flying Start*, p. 2.
[99] Ibid., p. 2.
[100] Hall, *Clouds of Fear*, p. 132.

of battle had transformed the uncompromising 'man or a coward' attitude of the 'schoolboy approach' to war into a more self-compassionate,
nuanced, and mature recognition of fear and courage as shared points
on a continuum.

The interiority of the fighter pilots' tale offers a special insight into
these veteran-memoirists' retrospective identification of combat as a rite
of passage.[101] Although the fighter pilots' tale is studded with anecdotes
of sexual encounters with women, it is significant that Bartley – whose
own memoir proudly documents a plethora of hedonistic wartime sexual relationships – identified his progression into manhood in terms of
developing an emotional response to fear rather than the loss of virgin-
ity more conventionally associated with male rites of passage. Indeed,
Bartley discerned that 'We were fit and fearless, in the beginning. By the
end, we were old and tired, and knew what fear was. I had taken a life
before I had taken a woman.'[102] Martin Francis has reflected that these
flyers underwent a 'singular, not to say bizarre, progression into manhood'.[103] As this historian notes, the wartime fighter pilot belonged to 'a
distinct fellowship of youth, albeit one in which youth had been violently
deformed by experience.'[104] In describing his first experience of battle
whilst participating in a fighter sweep over northern France during the
summer of 1940, Geoffrey Page recorded that:

For us young airmen winging our way over the Channel, life had abruptly
taken on a new meaning ... All that remained of youth in those swiftly moving
Hurricanes were the physical attributes of our bodies, the minds were no longer
carefree and careless. The sordid reality of all that our task implied banished
lighter thoughts for the time being. Those of us who had returned safely would
don the mantle of youth once again and carry on with the roistering as if no
interruption had taken place.[105]

Combat thus transformed youth into a quality that was never again fully
integrated into the emotional self, even if a semblance of boyishness
could be shrugged on and embodied through the display of high spirits
and schoolboy pranks in public. Consequently, the veterans' tale indicates that the public persona of the fighter pilot caused severe problems
for his constructions of self, both in wartime and during the post-war

[101] Frances Houghton, 'Becoming "A Man" during the Battle of Britain: Combat,
Masculinity and Rites of Passage in the Memoirs of "The Few"' in *Men, Masculinities
and Male Culture in the Second World War*, (eds.) Juliette Pattinson and Linsey Robb
(London: Palgrave Macmillan, 2018), pp. 97–117.
[102] Bartley, *Smoke Trails in the Sky*, p. 58.
[103] Francis, *The Flyer*, p. 40.
[104] Ibid., p. 40.
[105] Page, *Shot Down in Flames*, p. 38.

years. As Mark Connelly notes in his study of British cultural memories of the Second World War, ever since 1940 the nation has embraced a particular image of 'the Few': 'As Britons we know that fighter pilots were young gods leading carefree lives who positively enjoyed giving the Luftwaffe a richly deserved thrashing.'[106] Whilst this cultural representation has proved almost indestructible over the last seventy years, the British public's attachment to the image of young and fresh-faced heroes as saviours of the nation arguably served to trap 'the Few' within the same construct of heroic masculinity that had lured them into the RAF in the first place. Poignantly discussing the fighter pilots' loss of youth in 1940, Geoffrey Page explained that

beneath this safety valve of rowdiness were stretched the jagged nerves of young boys, old before their time. Instead of a legacy of peaceful playing fields and happy contented hours, ours was the heritage of blazing streaks marring the summer skies while tortured flesh bled for those at home.[107]

The fighter pilots' tale thus suggests that the flyer's rite of passage into manhood was complicated by the gulf between his painfully acquired knowledge of the harsh realities of danger and fear in the air, and the romantic fantasies of aerial combat that belonged to the uninitiated. As explored in an earlier chapter of this book, the predominant absence of idealised masculine codes of chivalry in the air war, frequently combined with a sense of unease at their identities as killers and a new awareness of the terrible physical and psychological toll exacted by war, served to excise any self-referential hints of heroism within these memoirs. Indeed, Bartley's memoir consistently documents a level of self-doubting subjectivity which situated his 'heroic' public image as being at odds with the emotional damage sustained by his wartime self:

In the eyes of the public, I was a hero of Dunkirk and of the Battle of Britain and had helped 'sweep' the skies over Northern Europe; a double DFC and once commander of two crack squadrons. Yet ... I remembered the pathetic faces of the young pilots I had seen at the LMF Centre at Sheppey, and remembered thinking at that time, that there but for the grace of God, perhaps my then insensitivity, I might have been.[108]

At the end of his memoir, the veteran enquires nakedly, 'Am I the hero that I've been made out to be?'[109]

The language of martial heroism which suffused the cultural representations of battle out of which the veterans' 'schoolboy approach' to

---

[106] Connelly, *We Can Take It!*, p. 96.
[107] Page, *Shot Down in Flames*, p. 38.
[108] Bartley, *Smoke Trails in the Sky*, p. 142.
[109] Ibid., p. 199.

war was constructed was deliberately excised from the Second World War memoirists' review of self. A number of veterans recorded that the kinds of valorous military deeds which had appealed so entrancingly when experienced vicariously through the pages of popular boys' literature or the cinema took on an entirely new perspective in real battle. Romantic visions of extreme valour as normative martial behaviour rapidly gave way to something far more pragmatic. According to the veterans' tale, there was simply no room on the battlefield for the type of 'death or glory' attitude to combat that was so beloved of interwar popular culture. Indeed, Alex Bowlby recorded these exact words being spoken to him when he joined the Rifle Brigade in 1944. He was offered the following chastening advice by an older and more experienced member of his new platoon: "'Remember, Alec,' he said. "Keep your nut down. Death or glory boys don't last."[110] Self-conscious attempts to fulfil juvenile fantasies of performing glorious military feats are portrayed with impatience in the veterans' tale as offering proof of just how naïve and immature their younger selves remained at the start of their war experience. During the North African campaign, Ray Ward attempted to embody his beloved soldier-hero of adventure in his first encounter with the enemy. Ordered mid-battle to take the place of an officer whom he identifies as a 'Lieutenant Moncur', a platoon commander who had just been killed whilst attempting to capture an enemy-held ridge, Ward narrated that he

sprinted across the valley and dashed up the hill, exhilarated even when bullets from an enemy outpost whistled past my ears as I ran. I imagined myself the hero of a John Buchan adventure story engaged in a daring military exploit.[111]

Since wartime casualty rates proved that the position of young platoon commander was one of the most dangerous of battlefield roles, even before inexperience and eagerness were added into the mix, Ward later acknowledged that he had been incredibly fortunate to survive:

I must have been oblivious to the risk. I could have approached the hill more prudently but I was keen as mustard to prove myself, and intoxicated with virility and by the violence. Later, I realised that I was lucky to have survived that first foray and not been a statistic like poor Moncur.[112]

The mood of the memoirist here is revealing, as though the veteran were looking back in avuncular exasperation at a much loved but irresponsible nephew whose actions he cannot now quite comprehend. The same tone percolated Hugh Dundas' account of subscribing to an air of quite

---

[110] Bowlby, *Recollections*, p. 26.
[111] Ward, *The Mirror of Monte Cavallara*, p. 104.
[112] Ibid., p. 105.

unfounded heroism when returning from his first sortie, an event which forty years later the veteran described as a distinctly 'inglorious story'.[113] Upon encountering a formation of German aircraft over Dunkirk on 28 May 1940, the young flyer – who only minutes before had confidently imagined himself as Errol Flynn's comrade-in-arms at Rochford airfield – was taken aback by 'the bewilderment and hot fear of that first dog fight'. He faced additional alarm when he realised that he had lost track of his course over Dunkirk and did not know where he was. Across the years, Dundas reflected, 'I can conjure up in my mind and in the pit of my stomach the nasty sickening feel and taste of my first real experience of fear. This unheroic introduction to war was very different from the way I had imagined it would be'.[114] Having suffered further panic by getting lost on his way back to Rochford, the memoirist reported that as soon as it became apparent that he was safely home again, the young Dundas' attitude was,

transformed, Walter Mitty-like: now a debonair young fighter pilot, rising twenty, proud and delighted that he had fired his guns in a real dog-fight, even though he had not hit anything, sat in the cockpit which had been so recently occupied by a frightened child and taxied in to the dispersal point, where excited ground crew waited to hear the news of battle.[115]

According to the veteran, his younger self confidently believed that he had undergone the much-anticipated transition to the manly military character of boyish fantasy. The rueful 'Walter Mitty' reference, however, indicates that from the vantage point of some forty years later, this assumed inner change was as much a fantasy as Errol Flynn's pilot character. When placed into context with Dundas's confession of his constant struggle with fear, this identification of his younger self as a 'Walter Mitty' – a fictional character famed for indulging in fantasies of martial heroism – is offered up as testimony that despite surviving his first battle, the memoirist had yet to truly come of age by abandoning juvenile illusions of battle's transformative power.

Even a veteran-memoirist who received the Victoria Cross for demonstrating near-suicidal courage in order to save the lives of his comrades opted not to discuss his undeniable valiance on the field in performative terms of military glory. In late April 1943, the Irish Guards captured a portion of enemy-held territory in Tunisia, repeatedly fending off counter-attacks by the German forces. On 28 of April, Lance-Corporal John Kenneally of 1 Company, 1st Battalion Irish Guards, launched a

---

[113] Dundas, *Flying Start*, p. 3.
[114] Ibid., p. 3.
[115] Ibid., p. 3.

solo assault against the massed enemy forming up to attack the company's position. Single-handedly, Kenneally charged down a slope towards the enemy firing his Bren gun as he ran, an exploit which so unnerved the Germans that their attack formation broke up and they retreated in disorder. Two days later, Kenneally and a sergeant repeated this astonishing feat. Despite sustaining wounds, the memoirist refused to surrender his Bren gun in order to receive medical treatment, claiming that only he understood the weapon properly, and continued to fight throughout the day.[116] Despite his consistent performance of breathtaking bravery, even shooting from the hip in the best tradition of the hero of the adventure narrative, Kenneally refused to represent himself as the paradigmatic soldier-hero. Although the official citation of Kenneally's actions applauded his 'magnificent gallantry' and lavishly portrayed the soldier as a military superman, the veteran's own account is matter of fact, downplaying any sense of having performed any particularly special feat. His relation of these battles is humble, unassuming, and presents the survival of 1 Company as a team effort, choosing to quote from the Battalion's War Diary rather than unfold his own tale in his own words.[117] To some extent, of course, this modest recounting might have owed something to the dislike of 'shooting a line' that famously characterised British military culture between 1939 and 1945. Yet Kenneally's narrative documents a continued distaste for casting himself as a martial hero. The title of the 1997 revised edition of his memoir, *The Honour and the Shame*, conveys the veteran's struggle to reconcile his own constructions of self with the public and military label of war hero.[118] Kenneally, in fact, was not wholly thrilled in the first place to have been awarded the VC, since the publicity which surrounded his medal threatened to uncover his closely guarded secret that he had been born Leslie Robinson in 1921, the illegitimate son of Neville Blond (future chairman of the English Stage Company) and an eighteen-year-old girl who became a high class prostitute. Furthermore, Kenneally was concerned that his unorthodox entry into the elite Irish Guards regiment would be unmasked, since he had deserted the Royal Artillery to join their ranks. Although clearly a maverick, Kenneally did not view himself as woven out of particularly heroic fabric. Acknowledging that he had indeed shown extraordinary courage under fire, he preferred to construe his award in terms of passing a private ordeal by combat: 'The only pride I felt was that intimate personal pride of every soldier in the fact that he had been tried and tested

---

[116] TNA/WO/98/8/789, No. 2722923 Lance-Corporal John Patrick Kenneally, Irish Guards' citation.

[117] Kenneally, *The Honour and the Shame*, p. 77.

[118] Initially published as *Kenneally VC* (London: Kenwood, 1991).

in battle and not found wanting.'[119] Like Tony Bartley, the memoirist reported that his public image as a 'hero' was not an identity that his younger self embodied comfortably. When the 1st Battalion of the Irish Guards returned home in April 1944, he wrote,

I suddenly found myself a celebrity. War-weary Britain was looking for heroes and I found myself a 'pop star' of my generation. There were invitations for this, that and the other, press reporters wanted interviews and lots of mail came in. It was much too early for me; I did not want to know. All I wanted was to retreat behind the anonymity of an ordinary Guardsman. I was only just twenty-three, I badly needed sound advice and there was no one to guide me.[120]

The language of martial heroism could thus leave men feeling isolated and unsure of themselves. The self-confessed unease of Kenneally and the veteran-memoirists of 'the Few' at achieving the schoolboy's dream of being elevated so publicly to the status of military hero uncovers a painful and ironic disconnect between the emotional impact of war as it was experienced first in imagination and subsequently in reality. As experience and survival rapidly taught the impracticality of indulgence in adolescent fantasies of martial behaviour on the battlefield, and the serviceman became aware of the psychological and emotional cost of war, the imagined martial hero of adventure became an unlamented casualty of battle in the veterans' tale.

The demise of the soldier-hero of adventure in these memoirs is symptomatic of a much wider abdication of juvenile fantasies of war as adventure. Rather predictably, fighting bore very little resemblance to anything that the memoirists had imagined as pre-war youngsters, and the veterans' tale charted the ways in which they felt their attitudes towards the experience of battle had significantly changed. 'Before I had ever been in action', explained Charles Potts, 'I had looked forward to it as an exciting adventure: now I regarded it as revolting business, a fearful penance that had to be endured for a good cause.'[121] At the end of August 1940, Tony Bartley and the rest of 92 Squadron were sent to Biggin Hill, an airfield lying south-east of London which found itself in the front line of defence against the marauding Luftwaffe. The night before he arrived at Biggin Hill, recalled the memoirist, was spent in eager anticipation of the thrilling battles that surely lay ahead:

I was too excited to sleep much, and spent most of the night in speculating what the future might hold in store for me. It never entered my head that I could be

[119] Kenneally, *The Honour and the Shame*, pp. 116–117. Awarded the VC in Tunisia, late April 1943.
[120] Ibid., pp. 161–162.
[121] Potts, *Soldier in the Sand*, p. 109.

killed. All I could imagine was shooting the Luftwaffe out of the sky, with the boys beside me, and winning honour and glory for myself and the squadron.

In retrospect, I realise how pathetically naïve we were in the supreme confidence of youth which would never countenance any thought or possibility of defeat.[122]

Other veterans frequently cited constant exposure to the physical and psychological pain that accompanied killing and wounding in battle as a key cause in their loss of 'the supreme confidence of youth' that imagined war to be a delightful adventure. After sustaining minor wounds when his Spitfire was shot down, Hugh Dundas returned to join his squadron in mid-September 1940 when they moved to the Duxford sector to operate with 12 Group. The memoirist reported that by this stage, only a matter of weeks after first engaging the enemy, his former 'schoolboy approach' to war had been utterly dismantled:

I viewed the prospect of combat with real inner fear. The memory of what had happened last time crowded back in on me. The juvenile desire for glory which had been uppermost in my mind … had been driven out altogether by the fear of death and the personal knowledge of the unpleasant form in which it was likely to come.[123]

In Ken Tout's memoir, his pre-combat image of war as 'a sort of game, there was a feeling of chivalry about it, almost a crusade and certainly a sense of heroism at being part of it' was redrawn by violence:

all the more romantic notions about soldiering have been blown out of my brain by the incessant explosions of shells. Visions of medals and honours have become tarnished by the memory of the greying faces of the dead and the haunted eyes of the wounded.[124]

Memoirists from all three services recorded the similar erosion of the youthful war as adventure ideal and its replacement with a knowledge of war and self that was far less tinged with rosy-hued romanticism. According to William King, a 'thrill' that he identified at being piped aboard his first submarine command became corroded by the constant proximity to violent death and the fatigue of prolonged operational duties at sea. By 1941, two years after assuming command first of HMS *Snapper*, and subsequently HMS *Trusty*, he portrayed himself as physically and emotionally debilitated by his wartime experiences:

now I was tired to the bone. I knew that I hated killing. I hated sinking, burning and drowning, and after two years of almost incessant under-sea action I thought

---

[122] Bartley, *Smoke Trails in the Sky*, p. 25.
[123] Dundas, *Flying Start*, p. 47.
[124] Tout, *Tanks, Advance!*, p. 208.

I'd been depth-charged enough. I desperately wanted to cease hunting ships. I also wanted to cease being hunted myself.[125]

A similar significant shift in sensibility was also recounted by Sydney Hart, who noted that after a lengthy spell of sea time the 'filth of submarine atmosphere seemed to be corroding our souls.'[126] The veteran who had declared with such brio at the beginning of his tale that 'I was on the brink of the greatest adventure that could befall any man – war in submarines' also learned that the experience of grieving bitterly for lost comrades triggered a profound inner change in his emotional response to war. In his narrative, the memoirist set out the emotional bonds of comradeship that tethered him to the crew of HMS *Triad*, a group of men that he described fondly as 'a pretty good crowd to go anywhere with'.[127] Having been sent ashore for a short stay in hospital when *Triad* reached Malta in 1940, Hart narrowly avoided being killed with his former crewmates when the submarine was lost on patrol in the Mediterranean in the October of that year. Upon being released from hospital, the submariner insisted upon being drafted to an operational ship, explaining that 'From now on I had a private war on my hands – a war in which to wreak vengeance on the enemy on my shipmates' behalf.'[128] A similar kind of transition from boyish enthusiasm for battle as an adventure to a painful awareness of combat's ability to corrupt the emotional sense of self was also documented by Geoffrey Page. In retrospect, the former fighter pilot wrote that his idolisation of the First World War ace, Albert Ball, had proved insufficient preparation for the battles that lay ahead:

I also thought I knew about war in the air. I imagined it to be Arthurian – about chivalry.

Paradoxically, death and injury had no part in it. In the innocence of youth, I had not yet seen the other side of the coin, with its images of hideous violence, fear, pain and death. I did not know then about vengeance. Neither did I know about the ecstasy of victory. Nor did I remotely suspect the presence within my being of a dormant lust for killing.[129]

As Francis pertinently observes of the wartime RAF, the flyer experienced his youth in 'the most peculiar and testing of circumstances. If he managed to survive, his youthful freshness and naïve idealism were unlikely to remain equally resilient.'[130] These narratives collectively testify that the same sentiment applied equally to the men who experienced

[125]   King, *The Stick and the Stars*, p. 102.
[126]   Hart, *Discharged Dead*, p. 64.
[127]   Ibid., p. 50.
[128]   Ibid., p. 61.
[129]   Page, *Shot Down in Flames*, p. 8.
[130]   Francis, *The Flyer*, p. 39.

life 'at the sharp end' throughout the other armed services. Veterans thus employed their memoirs to measure the extent to which their first-hand knowledge of war had transformed their boyish illusions of war as an exciting adventure into an experience which wrought a potentially much more sinister impact upon their constructions of self.

Nevertheless, despite this rather brutal dismantling of the 'schoolboy approach' to war as romantic adventure, loss of fantasy is not represented with any particular sense of bitterness or disillusionment in the veterans' tale. The process of learning that war bore little resemblance to the glorious, gung-ho *Boy's Own* style of narratives that had shaped the memoirists' imagined battles is depicted instead as an inherently normative aspect of 'coming of age' in the front lines. Ray Ward described his geographical journey with the wartime army as a valuable voyage of the self, an 'odyssey from the Pyramids to the Po.'[131] 'I was no longer the callow young man who had left home to join the Argylls in 1940', he explained. 'But I was alive and well, a little older and perhaps wiser.'[132] Like the fighter pilots, the soldier-memoirists initially assessed their identities as freshly minted combatants against those of men who had already been seasoned by battle, identifying the experience of battle as an important bridge in crossing the 'gulf' between inexperienced immaturity and a more mature adult masculine identity. Among the army veteran-memoirists, however, the remembered sense of their comparative youth and immaturity at the outset of wartime service was frequently connected to holding new rank and heightened by their inexperience of leading more tried and tested men into battle. As a newly promoted troop leader, Bill Bellamy remembered being particularly concerned about taking over his new unit:

The new members of my troop had experienced the loss of comrades in battle already, and I felt that their morale would not be improved by the appointment of an inexperienced troop leader.[133]

Nicholas Mosley also documented that his youth and inexperience rendered his assumption of command a formidable experience. Having volunteered to join the army before his nineteenth birthday in June 1942, in December 1943, he was commissioned in the 2nd Battalion London Irish Rifles who were then serving at Taranto, a duty which he found daunting:

I, aged twenty, and with no war experience, was due to take charge of a platoon of men mostly considerably older than myself who had been fighting for

[131] Ward, *The Mirror of Monte Cavallara*, p. 367.
[132] Ibid., p. 372.
[133] Bellamy, *Troop Leader*, p. 48.

a year through North Africa, Sicily, and a third of the way up Italy, and were exhausted.[134]

Looking back as a middle-aged veteran, Sydney Jary commented that,

I would never wish to change places with the shy, hesitant boy whom circumstances had put in command of 18 Platoon. Aged twenty I was far too young and inexperienced to appreciate that an infantry platoon was the finest command in the Army and that the success or failure of a battle so often lay solely in the hands of a young officer.[135]

All three memoirists identified their wartime experiences of serving as junior officers as a catalyst in their sense of self-development. By the end of the war, mused Bellamy, 'I had undoubtedly matured a great deal and had lost much of my 'schoolboy' image'.[136] As the product of a well-cushioned albeit somewhat unconventional upper-class upbringing, Mosley recorded that when he first joined his new unit, his outlook remained conditioned by the social and cultural constraints of prep and public school:

I was still appallingly priggish in my diary: I seemed to disapprove of anyone who was not of the type of my precious coteries from Ranby or Eton. I took refuge in admiring the beauty of the landscape; and on Boxing Day I recorded that I read the whole of *Chrome Yellow*.[137]

Clearly attaching some significance to the fact that he chose to spend Boxing Day reading Aldous Huxley's first satirical novel (1921), whose protagonist was a naïve and introverted young poet, the veteran-memoirist was unimpressed with his youthful former attitude:

In old age I find it difficult to acknowledge the awfulness of my diary at this time. However, insofar as it seems to have taken the war to knock some of this out of me, this is part of the story.[138]

More specifically, Jary identified the responsibilities of commanding 18 Platoon in battle as triggering his own sense of self-development into maturity. 'When I had joined them on 31st July, I was naïve and gauche', the veteran explained:

Due to a narrow upbringing, except for a passionate love of music, my intellect and emotions were unstimulated. My achievement at school had been abysmal, my mind was undisciplined and confidence in myself nil. This was rapidly swept away, probably within three weeks …

[134] Mosley, *Time at War*, p. 44.
[135] Jary, *18 Platoon*, p. 123.
[136] Bellamy, *Troop Leader*, p. 233.
[137] Moseley, *Time at War*, p. 45.
[138] Ibid., p. 45.

Discovering an ability to command a group of men, some frightened and bewildered, produced a new-found confidence, particularly since I seemed to be able to achieve it quietly and without acrimony or fuss.[139]

Through learning the trade of a junior officer in a light infantry platoon, Jary explained that a 'new world' had opened up for him, in which skills of 'forethought', 'planning', and 'imagination' were demanded. This, he stated, 'was the making of me.'[140]

Far less introspective than the memoirs of their counterparts in the RAF and the army, the naval veterans tended not to display the same intimate level of subjectivity in their narratives. Whether this comparative lack of interiority was due to the fact that a number of these men had already experienced peacetime service in the Royal Navy and perhaps felt more professionally accustomed to the emotional impact of service life, or was simply a product of the 'stiff upper lip' emotional climate of the 1950s during which many of these accounts were written, is ultimately unclear. Nevertheless, the sailors' tale recorded its own version of the development of the self through war, in which assuming the responsibilities of commissioned rank stood out as a special event. Since most of the naval memoirists were former officers, among the sailors' tale assumption of the responsibilities that come with rank was also defined as an important part of the maturing process. Having come up through the ranks of the Royal Navy by way of serving first as an Ordinary Seaman, and then as a CW rating before receiving his commission, Harry Foxcroft gave some thought as to how the experience of scrving as a 'hostilities only' officer had influenced his sense of self-development:

On reflection, I had missed out on that period of life extending from the late teens to the middle twenties ... with its dances, tennis clubs and the like which charted the gradual growth into adulthood pre-war. In their place I had experienced a life at sea and an early acceptance of responsibility which otherwise would never have been my lot. In that process I had matured rapidly and, more importantly for me, I had shared with all seafarers a unique privilege. That of living in daily contact with nature on the one timeless, unchanging, unspoilt element of all; the sea in all its moods of simple, often savage, beauty.[141]

In the same way that the natural environment of the ocean conditioned the seaman's relationship with his fellow sailors and his ship, it also arguably worked upon his sense of self and manhood. The burden of shouldering responsibility for himself and others in duelling both the sea and the human enemy was perceived as rapidly fomenting a special degree

[139] Jary, *18 Platoon*, p. 122.
[140] Ibid., p. 122.
[141] Foxcroft, *Hostilities Only 1940–1945*, p. 178.

of maturity in the young naval officer. The war at sea was understood as causing young officers to grow up quickly, a fact which the Navy marked with due pomp and circumstance when these men were elevated to the status of commanding officers. The sailors' narratives suggest that a liminal moment for the young naval officer arrived when he took command of his first ship, assuming charge of not only the lives of his men in battle but also the ship which housed and protected his crew throughout their time at sea. In May 1939, William King took command of the S-class submarine HMS *Snapper*. Describing this moment, he wrote that

Every young fellow must feel a thrill when he first obtains command of his own ship and finds himself being piped on board great warships along with the older captains of destroyers, cruisers and aircraft-carriers.[142]

The Royal Navy's tradition of piping aboard commanding officers on official business is therefore represented in the naval veterans' tale as an epoch in the memoirist's own sense of self-development. The first time a freshly appointed captain was piped ceremoniously onto his ship thus represented both a symbolic moment and a reassuring statement of official confidence in the individual that, in retrospect, the naval veteran portrayed as being deeply meaningful. Appointed to command HMS *Guillemot* in July 1941, Sam Lombard-Hobson recorded that this represented 'a thrilling, though awe-inspiring, moment.'[143] The Royal Navy thus cleverly tapped into centuries of tradition and ceremony in order to instil a sense of self-confidence in its commanding officers right from the very beginning. Reflecting on this practice, Denys Rayner noted that 'The psychology of the Navy is excellent.'[144] In carrying on this tradition the Navy thus linked new commanding officers to centuries of sea captains who had gone before:

There are few new captains who can feel such self confidence that, in their inmost thoughts, there does not lie a fear that they may prove unworthy of their charge. It is remarkable how the customs of the Navy aid one. When you come to think of it the surest way to help a man is to remind him continually of his position, and of what the men whom he has been called to join expect of him.[145]

For the naval memoirists, the conference of rank and assuming the responsibilities of command at sea were clearly identified as key moments in the veteran's reconstruction of selfhood. As befitting of Britain's Senior Service, the occasion was invested with a degree of pomp and

---

[142] King, *The Stick and the Stars*, p. 27.
[143] Lombard-Hobson, *A Sailor's War*, p. 119.
[144] Rayner, *Escort*, p. 64.
[145] Ibid., p. 64.

circumstance, a ceremonial tradition which also served as an induction into the ranks of centuries of great British seamen.

Ceremony, however, is distinctly lacking among the veteran-memoirs of Bomber Command. With only the odd exception, the bombers' tale of inner change was primarily bound up in trying to reconcile their wartime duties with a hostile post-war culture of criticism. Arguably, the bombers' trade never quite lent itself to the 'war as adventure' scenario in quite the same manner that other forms of armed service appeared to. Lacking the personal agency of the fighter pilot, the naval traditions of the sailor, and the tight-knit regimental ties of the soldier, the bomber airman was seldom offered opportunities to imagine or perform comparable acts of derring-do in the face of the enemy. As discussed earlier in this chapter, a number of bomber memoirists recorded that they had volunteered as aircrew based on the same ideals of the aviator-hero that motivated the fighter pilots. There, however, the 'war as adventure' fantasy stops point blank in the memoirs of Bomber Command. Instead, these memoirs document a struggle to resolve their own understandings of selfhood amid a barrage of post-war criticism which labelled the Bomber Command flyers at best as victims, and at worst, as villains. The exigencies of domestic politics during 1945, Cold War propaganda during the 1950s, and old wartime anxieties about the ethics of area bombing renewed by the Vietnam war and resurrected yet again first during the 1990s and subsequently by the 2003 Anglo-American bombing of Baghdad, meant that veterans of Bomber Command perceived that they were constantly publicly cast in the mould of either winged lions sacrificed by blue-uniformed donkeys, or as bloody-handed war criminals who had callously immolated tens of thousands of women and children in Hamburg and Dresden. With many bomber-memoirists feeling that they had been stigmatised by their wartime service, their narrative reconstructions tend to focus on trying to reconcile their own understandings of self with a perceived public persona of despicability. Peter Johnson recorded that he became deeply upset after buying a book of drawings of London during the Blitz, needing reassurance that 'I couldn't be what this book says, a murderer, a killer of women and children, a member of Bomber Command.'[146] Yet despite expressing sadness and anger that his wartime service left him feeling 'branded for life' in peacetime Britain, Frank Musgrove still believed that 'my period with Bomber Command remains the most important time of my life.'[147] Although the post-war veteran-memoirist of Bomber Command was, even if he were so inclined,

---

[146] Johnson, *The Withered Garland*, p. 192.
[147] Musgrove, *Dresden and the Heavy Bombers*, pp. 74–75.

arguably robbed of any chance to identify himself as an aviator-hero long
before he lifted pen to paper, there are some marked similarities between
his tale of self-development and those of veterans from other services.[148]
Musgrove reflected that

> I have said that I have never gained from my war service in any material sense.
> In fact, the opposite has been the case; but there were significant non-material
> gains. I was young and learned a great deal about myself, especially the extent
> and limits of my courage, which I had considerably over-estimated in 1941. I
> learned something also of my intellectual limitations (but was pleased I could
> continue to function quite well under fire).[149]

Similarly, Arthur Gamble documented that by the time he was demobilised from the RAF in March 1946, he had undergone a complete change
in character:

> I had entered the service a very immature and naïve eighteen-year-old youth
> from a semi-rural community, a simple 'swede basher' if ever there was one,
> and now, here was I, leaving the service as a twenty-four-year old, self-confident
> adult, with a wealth of experience behind him, looking forward to taking up a
> fresh challenge of life back in civvy street.[150]

Although hostile political and cultural post-war discourses made reas-
sembling images of self infinitely more difficult and upsetting for the
bomber memoirist, the same ideas of war as a rite of passage into a
mature, more self-enlightened, adult masculine status that characterise the rest of the veterans' tale also dominate the memoirs of Bomber
Command.

Summary

Taking into account all of these aspects of inner change that the memoirists identified in their tales, it is possible to draw some conclusions across
the veterans' tale as a collective review of self. Whilst the idea of war
functioning as a male rite of passage is ageless, these narratives testify
that war itself caused important shifts in the ways in which adult masculine status was constructed and experienced. Overall, there remains
considerable work still to carry out with regard to military veterans'
constructions of self and masculinity, and no attempt is made here to

---

[148] However, pre-Dresden wartime cultural discourses and propaganda certainly sought
to invest the bombers' war with heroic virtues, not least because until 1943, Bomber
Command was the only branch of the British armed forces carrying the war directly to
the enemy in Europe.

[149] Musgrove, *Dresden and the Heavy Bombers*, p. 77.

[150] Gamble, *The Itinerant Airman*, p. 157.

claim more than an effort to shine an exploratory light upon the ways in which a self-selecting group of individuals deployed linear prose to assess the impact of war upon their own sense of masculine selfhood. What this study does propose, however, is that it is possible to trace the emergence of different scripts of masculinity in the veterans' tale which can be linked to new understandings of managing the self and its limits in response to battle. In so clearly jettisoning the traditional soldier-hero of adventure as a mechanism of understanding the relationship between war and the self, the veteran-memoirists collectively turned to a different template of masculinity which emerged during the Second World War itself. Sonya Rose has demonstrated how a wartime shift towards celebrating the understated, good-humoured, kindly, and self-deprecating courage of the 'little man' led to the emergence of a model of 'temperate heroes' in constructions of British masculinity between 1939 and 1945.[151] Whilst continuing to value the physical and mental bravery, strength, and fortitude that characterised traditional military ideals of manliness, the more nuanced and less hyper-masculine template of manly courage could be expanded to include civilians on the home front. This elasticity between civilian and martial masculine virtue arguably sought to offer an element of reassurance that soldiers would not return home as psychotic killers but would be able to readjust to civilian masculine identity without too much effort. The experience of learning to manage fear, exhaustion, privation, pain, and extremes of violence is proffered in the veterans' tale as the cornerstone of a process of maturing into an adult male identity that might serve as both valuable and acceptable in the veteran's post-war civilian life.

It is clear that the ideal of the 'temperate hero' influenced the post-war veteran-memoirist's composure of masculine self in his narrative. They felt that they had emerged from war with greater maturity, confidence, and self-awareness, and were willing to acknowledge the great disparity between the imagined and lived experiences of battle. The 'schoolboy approach' through which so many veterans had sought to envisage war as very young men was resurrected, not as a lens of bitterness through which to scrutinise the difference between fantasy and reality, but as a tool with which to identify and measure process of war-related inner change. It was thus that the veterans' tale insists that the soldier-hero of adventure was left behind on early battlefields and bidden a fond and occasionally rueful farewell, as the veterans metamorphosed into

---

[151] Sonya O Rose, 'Temperate heroes: Concepts of Masculinity in Second World War Britain', in *Masculinities in Politics and War: Gendering Modern History*, (eds.) Stefan Dudink, Karen Hagemann and John Tosh (Manchester: Manchester University Press, 2004), pp.177–95.

men who had witnessed and experienced the best and worst of human nature in wartime. Ultimately, it is to a highly toned-down and restrained version of military masculinity that the post-war veteran memoirs subscribe, emphasising manly martial behaviour as bravery without bravado, humour without hubris, and compassion without cowardice. These memoirs portrayed an individual's courage as that of the 'ordinary man', whose mettle lay in accepting as opposed to denying the fear, pain, and extreme violence that accompany war. Through meeting and managing these facets of battle with quiet resolve and a new tolerance of the limits of the emotional self, a rite of passage into a more tempered and valuable form of manhood was thus understood to have taken place on the battlefield.

8   History, Cultural Memory, and the Veteran-Memoirist

[T]he published war memoir therefore became a valuable weapon in the 'unending battle' for the ways in which [servicemen] should be remembered.[1]

Publishing a memoir immediately transformed the British Second World War veteran into a self-appointed, sometimes belligerent, spokesman within the public domain. For many former servicemen this genre of life-writing proffered an irresistible opportunity not only to contribute to long-running debates over wartime strategy but, perhaps more importantly, also to air personal grievances about contemporary scholarly and cultural representations of 'their' war. This chapter examines three case studies in which the published post-war memoirs of veterans from the Army, RAF, and Royal Navy became placed at the centre of critical disputes about how the Second World War should be represented and remembered. Alex Bowlby's *The Recollections of Rifleman Bowlby*, Miles Tripp's *The Eighth Passenger*, and Jack Broome's *Convoy is to Scatter* offer particularly striking examples of how veteran-memoirists deployed their narratives to challenge other representations of wartime experience that they perceived as unsatisfactory. The public function of memoir has been somewhat neglected by historians but the testimonies of Alex Bowlby, Miles Tripp, and Jack Broome individually and collectively make an important contribution towards understanding how veteran narratives were frequently intended to operate in public as an authoritative and definitive record.

These three memoirs illustrate that post-war veteran-memoirists often exhibited a shared desire to exert a degree of control over contemporary and future public understandings of the conflict. As Jay Winter notes, the process of remembering is an inherently performative act which involves varying degrees of active reconstruction of lived

---

[1] Houghton, 'The "Missing Chapter"', p. 170.

experience.[2] Furthermore, the post-war veterans' tale was not written in a cultural vacuum, but was created within what Maurice Halbwachs defines as a 'social framework' of dominant shared public and historical memories of the Second World War.[3] Veteran memory, however, was not a sponge which passively absorbed external representations of war and then squeezed them out again in prose. Although initially created as a work of private recollection, by virtue of its publication the war memoir fundamentally represented a decision to act in public, to engage in some way with shared social memories or historical representations of conflict. War memoir thus operated as an important site from which to contest wider scholarly and cultural modes of remembrance.

Many veteran-memoirists wrote with the objective of fleshing out scholarly or official histories, which they insisted conveyed only a misleading skeletal outline of battle in the dispassionate form of dates, manoeuvres, and casualties. Their antipathy towards unsatisfactory sources of knowledge production about war experience also extended to cultural representations generated by popular films and fictional literature. The self-confessed desire of these former servicemen to broadcast 'the full story' of combat on the front line unequivocally situates their military memoirs as 'vectors of memory'. Identified by Henri Rousso as 'any source that proposes a deliberate reconstruction of an event for a social purpose', such 'carriers of memory' may be designated as official (ceremonies, monuments, regular or irregular celebrations organised by national or local governments); scholarly (including school textbooks and academic works); and cultural (in which individual interpretations of the past are expressed in a variety of popular media, such as film, television, or literature).[4] Rousso's theory offers a valuable critical framework within which to unravel published veteran memoirs. As 'carriers' of memory, these documents facilitated the transmission of veterans' understandings of the Second World War to a public audience. The war memoir thus offered the veteran a conduit of memory through which he could publicly revise or challenge displeasing representations of wartime experience. Bowlby, Tripp and Broome, along with many other veteran-memoirists, took full advantage of this public platform to defend the actions of their unit, the strategy of their senior officers, or simply their own tactical decisions.

---

[2] Winter, *Remembering War*, p. 3.
[3] Halbwachs, *On Collective Memory*, p. 38.
[4] Rousso, *The Vichy Syndrome*, pp. 219–220.

The Recollections of Rifleman Bowlby versus the Army

In each of these case studies, the question of who held authority to speak of wartime experience became a centralised and heated issue. In the autumn of 1969, *The Recollections of Rifleman Bowlby* appeared in print. Recounting the experiences of a Radley-educated 'gentleman ranker' serving with the 2nd Battalion Rifle Brigade during the Italian campaign in 1944, this account was remarkable because it constituted one of the very first voices from the ranks to be published. It was also remarkable for having been rejected for publication on seventeen occasions, including at Longmans where it had crossed the desk of its eventual publisher Leo Cooper before he left to set up on his own. When Cooper established his own publishing firm in the late 1960s, Bowlby's memoir was one of the first five books that he brought out.

In many ways, *Recollections* carried a whiff of the Great War canon of subaltern trench literature in that its author lovingly conveyed an unimpeachable camaraderie of ordinary soldiers whilst excoriating the strategic decisions made by the wartime Army's higher echelons. It was the latter attitude, in the book's introduction, that triggered a ferocious spat that nearly ended in the libel courts. Bowlby had joined the battalion at Alexandria during the spring of 1944. His new unit had previously been deployed in the desert campaigns of North Africa, fighting as the motorised infantry wing of an armoured division. The 2nd Battalion had enjoyed a well-earned record for outstanding service in the desert, particularly for their actions at Snipe during the battle of El Alamein in October 1942, for which their CO, Colonel Vic Turner, received the VC. In May 1943, after the fall of Tunisia, the 2nd Battalion was stationed outside Tunis. It was here that discontents within the unit caused a most unsatisfactory situation to arise. There were men in the battalion who had been overseas with the unit since the late 1930s and were desperate to go home. As Sergeant R. L. Crimp, noted sourly in his wartime diary, the initials 'MEF' (Mediterranean Expeditionary Force) which still comprised the battalion's address, were popularly held as abbreviations for 'Men England Forgot'.[5] Horace Frederick 'Harry' Suckling, another member of the battalion, recalled the circulation of rumours that the men were to be trained in amphibious warfare, a prospect that he viewed with considerable disapprobation.[6] The mood of the battalion after the fall of Tunisia was not at all happy. Having supposed that they would be allowed to return home once the desert campaign was successfully

[5] IWM Documents 5659, 96/50/1, Private Papers of R. L. Crimp, Diary for 13 May 1943 to 28 April 1944.
[6] IWM Sound Archive, Horace Frederick 'Harry' Suckling, 21588/6/5-6.

concluded, it came as a blow to learn that this was not the case. A surprise visit by the King was met with boos from the men, for which the battalion was punished by being sent off on multiple route marches. Major RW Hastings' history of the Rifle Brigade during the Second World War records that the 2nd Battalion then led 'an even more varied existence, since it moved first to Tripoli, thence after an interval to the Delta, to Syria, Palestine, the Delta, Syria again, the Delta', before finally embarking with the 7th Battalion for Italy in April 1944.[7] Having rested and trained in an air of anti-climax, further problems followed once the battalion was sent to Italy. Since the terrain was unsuited to vehicles, the unit was stripped of its Bren gun carriers and anti-tank guns, and downgraded from a motor battalion to ordinary infantry. Riflemen who were accustomed to fighting from rapidly moving vehicles were reduced to fighting on foot.[8] Additionally, the battalion arrived in Italy minus some of its most experienced and popular members, as the 1937 regulars had been repatriated before the unit embarked for Europe. This unhappy state of affairs led Bowlby to deduce that by the time he arrived in the spring of 1944, he had joined at a particularly sore point in the battalion's wartime history. The memoirist perceived a distinctly 'bitter' mood among his new battalion, and it was to this that he attributed the unit's later failure to achieve the same battle rating in Italy as it had enjoyed in North Africa. Nonetheless, to the young ex-public schoolboy, the battalion quickly became a source of comfort and familiarity. His memoir thus broadcasts a marked devotion to his former Company, which Bowlby asserted provided the 'only real sense of security I ever had.'[9] This self-sworn fealty to the Rifle Brigade ultimately landed Bowlby and his publisher, Leo Cooper, in considerable trouble in 1969.

On 31 October 1969, shortly after the release of the first edition of *Recollections*, Cooper received a letter from a Lieutenant Colonel Patrick Boden, who had served with some distinction as second-in-command of the 2nd Battalion whilst it was in North Africa. Boden wrote to complain about an extract from Bowlby's memoir which he perceived as a 'grave and damaging inaccuracy'.[10] He strenuously objected to the fourth paragraph of the author's 'Foreword', which described the battalion's reaction to the news, after the fall of Tunisia, that the unit would be staying in

---

[7] Major R. H. W. S. Hastings, *The Rifle Brigade in the Second World War 1939–1945* (Aldershot: Gale & Polden, 1950), p. 238.
[8] David Lee, *Up Close and Personal: The Reality of Close-Quarter Fighting in World War II* (London: Greenhill 2006), p. 182.
[9] Bowlby, *Recollections*, p. 169.
[10] UoR, LC/ A/2/79, Colonel Patrick Boden to Leo Cooper, 31 October 1969.

the area, rather than embarking for Britain, as had been rumoured. The offending passage read thus:

When the Rifles heard the news it was more than they could stomach. Groups of riflemen went round wrecking the camp. Their officers were unable to stop them. Next day the word went round that machine-gunners from the 56th Division were being sent up to restore order. The riflemen ringed the camp with anti-tank guns. After three days the men cooled off. They'd had their show. All that remained was to see what G. H. Q. would do by way of retaliation. For a while they did nothing. It isn't difficult to imagine their problem: how to discipline the Battalion without burning their fingers in the process. They solved it only too well. The 1937 regulars were due for repatriation. They sent them home, leaving the rest of the Battalion in North Africa.[11]

Although the memoirist stopped just shy of using the ugly word 'mutiny', it was nevertheless implicit in his description of the battalion's actions. Considerably upset, Boden protested that there was 'no truth whatsoever' in this insinuation. According to his own recollections, the troops had in fact behaved 'with admirable restraint in very trying circumstances'.[12] He warned Cooper that former officers and troops who had been with the Battalion at this time would undoubtedly feel 'some justifiable indignation at the false charges made' in this paragraph.[13] With the spectre of a potential libel action menacing his newly established publishing business, Cooper hastened to contact Bowlby, who maintained that the incident had indeed occurred. In fact, conscious that his account might prove controversial, Bowlby informed his publisher that he had already deliberately softened his representation of events by 'stressing the humour element' of the situation rather than pointing accusing fingers at specific members of the regiment.[14] Nevertheless, it appeared that this distinction had not successfully translated into print, and the battle lines between memoirist, publisher, and senior officer were rapidly drawn up.

   The dispute was clouded by the fact that Bowlby himself had not actually been present at the 'mutiny', only joining the battalion shortly after it was supposed to have taken place. His description of this alleged incident, therefore, was wholly based on second-hand accounts and hearsay. The sequence of events which led to Bowlby believing that he had the full facts of the matter at his disposal is regrettably somewhat clouded. According to the author, the account of the disturbance at Tunis had been passed along to him in 1949 by an unnamed officer of the regiment who, at the time of the incident, had been a Regimental Sergeant Major

---

[11] Bowlby, *Recollections*, p. 8.
[12] UoR, LC/ A/2/79, Colonel Patrick Boden to Leo Cooper, 31 October 1969.
[13] Ibid.
[14] UoR, LC/ A/2/79, Alex Bowlby to Leo Cooper, 16 February 1969.

in the 2nd Battalion. When Bowlby met this man after the war, he was serving as a Quartermaster in 21 SAS, a Territorial regiment that Bowlby had also joined in 1948. Affirming that this man's version of events only confirmed in detail other stories Bowlby had heard circulating during the war, the memoirist was puzzled when, upon meeting him again some years later and informing him of his intention to write a book, his erstwhile source categorically denied having told him anything about the 'mutiny' at Tunis.[15] However, Bowlby darkly reassured his publisher, he possessed a 'long memory' and could remember the name of the soldier who had supposedly taken charge of setting up the anti-tank guns. When the identity of this man, an NCO named J. Swann, was put to the former RSM, the memoirist reports that the latter was forced to acknowledge that 'something silly' had indeed occurred.[16] Bowlby, therefore, firmly refused to be swayed from his own portrayal of the 'mutiny', unshakeable in the belief that his source had provided him with the full facts. He explained that he was convinced of the veracity of the latter's information, as it tallied with the version of events he himself had obtained after he joined the 2nd Battalion. According to Bowlby, therefore, the RSM had been able to provide him with both the identity of the ringleader and the duration of the incident.[17] The memoirist also chose to place his faith in the RSM's version of events because he trusted his source on a personal basis, noting that he was a 'very level-headed chap'.[18] Bowlby was thus confident that his information was accurate, and refused to back down.

The veracity of the 'mutiny' described by the memoirist is also difficult to ascertain. Certainly the official battalion war diaries and the regimental history made no mention of these events. The waters of investigation here are also further muddied by the fact that Joe Swann, the sergeant whose name was given to Bowlby as the man who illegally set up the anti-tank guns, was a hero of the Regiment who was decorated for his valiance in commanding a troop of anti-tank guns during the Snipe action of October 1942. When interviewed by the Imperial War Museum in 1982, Swann himself made no mention of the alleged events of 1943.[19] Yet whilst there is no official record of mutiny in Tunisia during the summer of that year, accounts from other non-ranking soldiers of the battalion lend some weight to Bowlby's story. According to 'Harry' Suckling and RL Crimp, feelings of discontent among the men of the

[15] UoR, LC/ A/2/79, Alex Bowlby to Leo Cooper, 4 November 1969 (1 of 2).
[16] Ibid.
[17] Ibid.
[18] UoR, LC/ A/2/79, Alex Bowlby to Leo Cooper, 4 November 1969 (2 of 2).
[19] IWM Sound Archive, Joe Swann, 27437 and 27438.

2nd Battalion were running so high in May 1943 that they all signed a 'round-robin' petition to the CO, setting forth their grievances. To this, Suckling added that the men were subsequently surrounded by a corps of machine gunners and instructed that they would be shot if they attempted to leave the immediate area.[20] Similar rumours of mutinous rumblings and actions outside Tunisia were also reported by men from the 1st and 7th Battalions. Whilst none of this directly substantiates the chain of events as narrated by Bowlby, there is sufficient corroborating evidence of discontent among the riflemen to infer that there was certainly something in the wind. Whether the full-blown refusal of orders and setting up of anti-tank guns ever actually occurred in the manner described by Bowlby may never be entirely settled, but the testimonies of Suckling and Crimp suggest that the men at least made their dissatisfaction known to their senior officers.

The timing of the altercation between former officers and soldiers of the Rifle Brigade in the late 1960s was particularly awkward for all concerned. The first print run of *Recollections* was selling quickly in the autumn of 1969 and a re-print run was imminent, with negotiations already under way with Corgi to issue the book in paperback. It was essential, therefore, for all parties to resolve the dispute as rapidly as possible in order to make a decision on whether or not future editions of the memoir would have to be altered to excise all mention of the alleged mutiny. Battle was joined in a rapid exchange of correspondence between Boden, Bowlby, and Cooper in late October and early November. Both sides began to marshal lists of supporters who might bear out their conflicting recollections of the 'mutiny'. Boden remarked that there were 'fortunately large numbers of survivors' from the period whom he believed would be willing to lend their voices to his version of events and contradict the 'manifest falsehood' that Riflemen had assembled anti-tank guns around the camp. Commenting that some witnesses might also be drawn from other units, including the 1st Kings Royal Rifle Corps and the 7th Battalion Rifle Brigade, he observed that 'anyone' who had been near Tunis at the time and had read Bowlby's foreword would know that there was little truth in it.[21] Bowlby swiftly followed Boden's lead, informing his publisher that there were 'plenty' of other witnesses who would remember what happened at Tunis and recommended that a 'gathering of the clans' may be necessary to settle the dispute.[22] In mustering his defences, he remained quite adamant that his was the correct

---

[20] IWM Sound Archive, Suckling, 21588/6/5-6.
[21] UoR, LC/ A/2/79, Colonel Patrick Boden to Leo Cooper, 31 October 1969.
[22] UoR, LC/ A/2/79, Alex Bowlby to Leo Cooper, 4 November 1969.

version, and remarked that he was 'quite prepared to take time on I.T.V.' to send out a message to former members of the 2nd Battalion who were aware of the events at issue.[23]

Senior commanders were also reluctantly drawn into this wrangle, and at least one found himself caught in an unenviable position. Lieutenant General Sir Richard Fyffe, then Deputy Chief of Defence Staff at the MoD, had served as a Major with the 10th Battalion Rifle Brigade in North Africa during the spring campaigns of 1943. Due to his long-standing post-war connections with the regiment, Fyffe had already been involved with *Recollections* since May 1969, when Cooper submitted the proof of the memoir to him for a 'personal and private view'.[24] Fyffe returned a cordial reply to the publisher, commenting that he welcomed the book because it was evident that Bowlby had the interests of the regiment 'deeply at heart'. He was sufficiently pleased with *Recollections* that a proposal was made to consider Bowlby for authorship of a history of the 95th Rifles for Cooper's rapidly expanding 'Famous Regiment Series', and Fyffe also offered to suggest to the next Regimental Committee Meeting that a small 'History Committee' be appointed to help Bowlby in such ways as they could, and direct him to sources.[25] Bowlby and his memoir had clearly acquired the backing of Fyffe and the Regimental Committee, but despite the amiability with which these proceedings were conducted, there had been some warning signs of potential trouble ahead. At the height of the brouhaha with Boden in November 1969, Bowlby suggested that even as far back as the summer there had been several ripples of dissatisfaction with his account of the fracas at Tunis. Upon first reading the proof of *Recollections*, the memoirist argued that Fyffe had 'queried my veracity'.[26] Bowlby, it seems, had long suspected that the reaction of the 2nd Battalion's officers at Tunis might cause problems. With some perspicacity, he predicted that their response to his book – 'that chap's dug up what we wanted kept quiet' – would not be instantly favourable.[27] Nevertheless, he felt that the matter could easily be put to rest once these officers discerned his line of reasoning and realised that it was 'likely to become equally plain to anyone who reads the book from a detached angle, i.e. someone not in the regiment.' To

[23] UoR, LC/ A/2/79, Alex Bowlby to Leo Cooper, undated.
[24] UoR, LC/ A/2/79, Leo Cooper to Lieutenant General Sir Richard Fyffe, 29 May 1969.
[25] UoR, LC/ A/2/79, Lieutenant General Sir Richard Fyffe to Leo Cooper, 3 June 1969. Some months later, Bowlby turned down the offer of writing the history of the 95th for the 'Famous Regiment Series', as he was struggling with ill health and described himself as too dispirited to take on the task.
[26] UoR, LC/ A/2/79, Alex Bowlby to Leo Cooper, 16 November 1969.
[27] UoR, LC/ A/2/79, Alex Bowlby to Leo Cooper, 2 June 1969.

this end, he insisted upon sending a draft explanation of his account to General Fyffe:

He [Bowlby] is confident that his information regarding the Tunis fracas is accurate. And he would be glad to let any of the regimental committee who were present at Tunis read the passage and comment on it (if none of the committee were present then any senior officer who was). A.B. has taken soundings from a cross-section of all ranks regarding the causes that led up to the trouble and the general opinion is that the battalion should never have been left behind in the way it was. Had the battalion been kept together i.e. had it left North Africa with all its regulars there is no doubt it would have continued to be a great one. As the committee must know the battalion's rating in Italy differed considerably from its rating in North Africa. A.B. considers that the events surrounding Tunis were directly responsible for this and it is for this reason alone that he has touched on them.[28]

As a sop towards preserving the integrity of the regiment, he also offered to disguise the identity of the 2nd Battalion, camouflaging it as a fictional 3rd Battalion. This attempt to mask the identity of the 2nd Battalion did not survive for long, however. Although Bowlby suspected that a review in the *Sunday Times* was the culprit, it is more probable that the narrative's explicit commentary on locations and actions brought about its own downfall in this respect. This appeared to soothe any early doubts the Regimental Committee might have harboured towards the intentions of his account. Indeed, as Cooper later informed Colonel Boden, 'No voice was raised in protest' at this time.[29] Inevitably, this all made matters very awkward when the Boden dispute blew up several months later. From the perspective of Bowlby and Cooper, the manuscript had in effect been fully approved by Fyffe and the Regimental Committee. From the opposite view, however, the insinuation of mutiny was ugly and the row threatened the reputation of both the regiment and Colonel Boden, an outstanding officer who had been awarded a Military Cross whilst commanding a company of the 2nd Battalion in early 1942.

In the end, the storm blew over and was resolved to the mutual satisfaction of all parties. Bowlby and Cooper sought legal advice from the solicitors firm of Rubinstein, Nash & Co, and a compromise was worked out, although the solicitor privately warned Cooper that on no account was concession to be allowed to be interpreted as an admission that the material complained of was erroneous, as this would leave wide open future opportunities for Colonel Boden and/or other senior officers to sue publishers of war memoir for libel.[30] This involved the insertion of a publisher's note into unsold copies of the first edition of *Recollections*,

[28] Ibid.
[29] UoR, LC/ A/2/79, Leo Cooper to Colonel Patrick Boden, 5 November 1969.
[30] UoR, LC/ A/2/79, Michael Rubinstein to Leo Cooper, 14 November 1969.

together with a rewording of the dust-jacket blurb. Bowlby would also re-draft the problematic paragraphs, and the amended version would appear in the re-print and any forthcoming editions. In his revised account, any allusion to 'mutiny' was to be removed and he was to confine himself to describing the mood of the battalion as 'restless', a term which Boden himself had used in reference to his men.[31] This, explained Cooper's solicitor Michael Rubinstein, posed an 'admirable' solution to the legal difficulties, and the matter was quietly dropped.[32]

The clash over *The Recollections of Rifleman Bowlby* thus hinged upon competing narratives of veteran memory, and the manner in which rank was dragged into the question of which former soldiers held the most author-ity to speak lent the affair an unpleasant edge. Indeed, Bowlby suspected former senior officers of the Rifles of launching 'Operation Whitewash' in order to erase a potentially embarrassing incident from future remem-brance.[33] He clearly viewed Boden's scepticism over the veracity of the RSM's testimony as impugning the honour of the lower ranks. Ironically, both sides in this clash attempted to use the memoir as a vehicle through which to salvage the reputation of the 2nd Battalion of the Rifle Brigade. From the perspective of Boden, Bowlby's suggestion of a mutiny would cement in the historical record an episode which he denied had ever occurred, and if indeed it had, would reflect badly on the entire regiment. From the perspective of Bowlby, he was keen to include the incident out of a wish to illuminate the contempt with which his beloved Rifles felt they had been treated after the successful conclusion of the North African campaign, and to explain why the unit's battle rating dropped during the subsequent Italian campaign. As a site of contest, therefore, *Recollections* functioned as a 'vector of memory' for two veterans who desired to defend, in very different ways, the reputation of their battalion.

The Eighth Passenger versus Popular Remembrance of Bomber Command

The next case study illustrates veteran deployment of memoir in order to defend the wartime record of Bomber Command and attempt to redraw unsatisfactory public memories of the strategic bombing cam-paign, which many former aircrew felt effectively branded them as war criminals. In 1969, Heinemann published one of the first memoirs of ordinary British bomber aircrew under the rather mysterious title of *The*

---

[31] UoR, LC/ A/2/79, Colonel Patrick Boden to Leo Cooper, 31 October 1969.

[32] UoR, LC/ A/2/79, Michael Rubinstein to Leo Cooper, 14 November 1969.

[33] UoR, LC/ A/2/79, Alex Bowlby to Leo Cooper, 4 November 1969 (2 of 2).

Eighth Passenger. The allusion to fear (the so-called 'eighth member' of a Lancaster crew) that memoirist Miles Tripp's title carried was maintained throughout the book. Indeed, Tripp's memoir acquired, as his literary agent noted, something of a 'cult status' due to the ways in which he portrayed the horrors experienced by the seven-man crews of the heavy bombers in the later years of the war.[34] As one of the first bomber memoirs to recount the author's participation in the infamous Allied attack on Dresden on 13 February 1945, Tripp's book also became embroiled in the increasingly acrimonious post-war debates on the ethics of this raid. In fact, excerpts from his narrative appear in various scholarly accounts of the Dresden operation, including Alexander McKee's *Dresden 1945: The Devil's Tinderbox* (1982) and Frederick Taylor's *Dresden: Tuesday 13 February 1945* (2004). These works, alongside the now-disgraced David Irving's *The Destruction of Dresden* (1963), have played an important role in shaping troubled cultural representations of the raid in Britain. Linked to this, in the decades since it originally appeared in print *The Eighth Passenger* has been reborn in three different editions, each of which reflect the memoirist's changing dialogue with scholarly and popular understandings of the Dresden attack. Whilst Tripp's account of his personal experiences remains the same in each of these editions, his own analysis and interpretation of the role he played in the destruction of Dresden possess a somewhat shifting quality. Chameleon-like, *The Eighth Passenger* repeatedly adapted itself to its contemporary cultural surroundings.

The central and unchanging feature of Tripp's memoir is arguably the author's vivid description of his actions over the target of Dresden on the fateful night of 13 February 1945. The author's account of this operation in the 1969 Heinemann first edition of *The Eighth Passenger* told an unusual tale in which he as bomb aimer took a private – and highly unofficial – decision not to drop his bombs in order to avoid contributing to the firestorm enveloping the city centre below. Tripp asserted that the crews had been informed at a briefing of the presence of 'a million' refugees in Dresden, and it was this knowledge, combined with his memory of watching newsreel footage of Belgian refugees being attacked earlier in the war, that informed his decision over the target.[35] According to Tripp, once his Lancaster had reached the already blazing target, over the radio there was no sound of the Master Bomber instructing the crews where to place their bombs. With the authority invested in the bomb aimer to direct the aircraft whilst in the vicinity of the target, he instructed his pilot to steer a course for the south of the city. He narrated

[34] UoR, LC/ A/2/681, Michael Sissons to Leo Cooper, 28 July 1992.
[35] Miles Tripp, *The Eighth Passenger* (London: Heinemann, 1969), pp. 80–3.

pressing the bomb release just beyond the fringe of the fires, in the hope
that they would fall 'harmlessly in fields'.[36] Lest his audience attributed
this decision to a conscientious act of rebellion, however, Tripp insisted
that he was not guilty of mutiny, maintaining that if the Master Bomber
had given instructions, he would have obeyed. Under no circumstances,
therefore, did he wish to be regarded as a 'heroic figure who deliberately
disobeyed orders'.[37]

Unfortunately for Tripp, this desire was not to be granted. His tale
was later seized upon by a number of historians whose own analyses of
the Dresden raid implied that there was much for Bomber Command
to be ashamed of. For instance, a graphic account published in 1982
by Alexander McKee, which spared few details of the suffering of the
German civilians, made use of extracts from Tripp's memoir to illustrate the former's own condemnation of the raid. McKee, in particular,
incurred the veteran's wrath through the following aside: 'Miles Tripp
wrote that there was no sound of the master-bomber on R/T controlling
the attack. Perhaps Miles was deaf in both ears as Nelson was in one
eye.'[38] The memoirist, was distinctly unflattered by the allusion, remarking tartly that 'I don't care for it and it is not true. Had there been a
master-bomber on the air it is most likely that I should have obeyed
instructions.'[39] How, he enquired, did McKee suppose that he would
have explained his actions to the rest of the crew had there been orders
transmitted over the radio? Was he expected to have indulged in a moral
debate whilst in the target area?[40] Although his decision to release the
bombs away from the city centre was legitimately open to query, the
veteran nonetheless wanted to make it clear that his actions should not
be interpreted as a criticism of Bomber Command.[41] In other historiography, however, this was exactly how his narrative was appropriated.
Frederick Taylor's supposedly revisionary account of the Dresden raid
also incorporated Tripp's description of placing his bombs away from the
centre of the target. Although Taylor's work did not relish the horror of
the attack's aftermath to the extent of McKee, Tripp's account was left
to stand alone without benefit of context, analysis, or counter-narrative
to tell the story of the hundreds of crews who did bomb on target. This
skewed implication therefore served to falsely imply that many crews of

[36] Ibid, p. 87.
[37] Tripp, *The Eighth Passenger* (1993), p. 169.
[38] Alexander McKee, *Dresden 1945: The Devil's Tinderbox* (London: Souvenir Press, 1982), p. 102.
[39] Miles Tripp, *The Eighth Passenger*, rev. ed. (London: Macmillan Papermac, 1985), p. 189.
[40] Ibid, p. 189.
[41] Frederick Taylor, *Dresden: Tuesday 13 February 1945* (London: Bloomsbury, 2004), p. 323.

Bomber Command were struck by intense qualms about conducting the Dresden raid.

The use to which Tripp's original account had been put by some historians was deplored by a later Bomber Command memoirist, Frank Musgrove. As a former navigator who had also flown on the Dresden raid, Musgrove's own memoir, *Dresden and the Heavy Bombers* (2005), formed part of a newly emerging stream of bomber narratives which began to appear in the early 1990s.[42] As the commemorative cycle of fiftieth anniversaries of the Second World War shifted into gear, public debates over the role of the Allied strategic air offensive intensified to new levels of ferocity. Responding to what many former aircrew perceived as unfounded, vicious, and seemingly downright ungrateful criticism of their wartime efforts, the published memoirs of Bomber Command crew started openly to contest popular condemnation of the war, springing particularly to the defence of their late Commander-in-Chief, Sir Arthur Harris, and his pursuit of the area bombing campaign during the latter war years. Musgrove, like many of his then elderly former comrades, perceived that Bomber Command occupied a place of opprobrium in British popular and scholarly remembrance of the Second World War that was deeply hurtful to surviving aircrew. In his own memoir, Musgrove recorded that he was thus 'saddened' to encounter Tripp's tale in Frederick Taylor's recent historical work, which seemed to indicate that the bomber crews had serious qualms about the raid on Dresden.[43] Despite saluting the earlier memoirist's 'great courage', Musgrove explained that he did not find Tripp's tale of consciously dropping his bombs away from the conflagration 'credible'. He concluded that the bomb aimer may well have come to believe in his narrative himself, but that it had probably been produced as a direct result of widespread public condemnation of the raid in the late 1960s.[44] The misgivings of Musgrove that his counterpart had experienced a 'crisis of memory', defined by Susan Suleiman as 'a moment of choice, and sometimes of predicament or conflict, about remembrance of the past'.[45] The later memoirist thus conveyed a suspicion that Tripp's memoir merely reflected rather than sought to correct public memories of the strategic air offensive during the late 1960s. Significantly, however, Musgrove did not censure Tripp for apparently shattering codes of loyalty to Bomber Command by breaking rank so publicly.

---

[42] Houghton, 'The "Missing Chapter"', pp. 155–157.
[43] Musgrove, *Dresden and the Heavy Bombers*, p. 108.
[44] Ibid p. 108.
[45] Susan Suleiman, *Crises of Memory and the Second World War* (Cambridge (MA): Harvard University Press, 2006), p. 1.

Rather, he regretted that the earlier memoirist had been forced by social
pressure into giving this version of the raid:

It is a gloss on events by a man carrying the burden ... of guilt, for a situation that
was certainly not of his making. There is no shame in putting his bombs dead
centre in the marked target area. The shame is the nation's, that a very brave man
should have to say that he didn't.[46]

Musgrove's dark suspicion that in 1969 a former bomb aimer had publicly rewritten his own memories underscores the veteran's perennial
temptation to compose what historian Alistair Thomson identifies as a
'safe memory', or a memory which fits reassuringly with public myths.[47]
A 'crisis of memory' in Tripp's first edition is impossible to either prove
or disprove, but certainly this part of his narrative remained unaltered
throughout all of *The Eighth Passenger's* subsequent incarnations. Although
Tripp remained adamant that his actions in dropping the bombs away
from the blazing city had been prompted by his knowledge that there
were helpless German refugees in Dresden, evidence that crews were
briefed on this specific is not easy to find. Of Tripp's own crew, only one
other member could remember being informed about the presence of refugees at briefing on 13 February 1945. Expanding the search outwards
to the many oral testimonies of former aircrew, the question of whether
crews learned of their possible presence before or after the raid remains
unsatisfactorily answered.[48] Examining the subject of aircrew morale during and after the Dresden raid in 1963, the Head of the Air Historical
Branch recorded that he could not find any evidence in the Bomber
Command Operational Record Book (ORB), Group ORBs, or Squadron
ORBs that aircrew were particularly uneasy about the raid because of
moral scruples.[49] His overall impression from these accounts was that, to
the aircrew involved, the operation was only different from countless others because of the unusually long distance travelled to the target, the fact
that Dresden had not been attacked before, and the spectacular success
of the raid.[50] This impression tallies with the evidence presented in the
published war memoirs and oral accounts of Bomber Command aircrew.

Tripp's memoir, however, needs to be situated among a specific climate
of antagonism towards area bombing into which it was born in 1969.

[46] Musgrove, *Dresden and the Heavy Bombers*, p. 108.
[47] Thomson, *Anzac Memories*, p. 10.
[48] IWM Sound Archive, Sam Lipfriend, 31462; Frank Tolley, 29049; Joseph Vivian
Williams, 15471; Rex Oldland, 20918; Harold Davis, 9194. These interviews represent
just a few of the many oral testimonies of former Bomber Command aircrew which insist
that Dresden was a legitimate target.
[49] TNA/AIR/19/1028, Loose Minute, 30 April 1963.
[50] Ibid.

By the late 1960s, increasingly aggressive public discourses on the Allied fire-storming of Dresden were circulating. With overall responsibility for the attack having been quietly elided by the British government in the immediate post-war period, the raid had also become an important tool in Cold War politics.[51] Blame for the devastating attack was therefore popularly heaped onto Arthur Harris and, by extension, Bomber Command. As Musgrove noted, 'Dresden has been invested with huge symbolic significance; and a number of well-publicised books have highlighted its awfulness.'[52] Several key scholarly and popular works came into publication in the 1960s, which emphasised the raid's dreadful aftermath and served to further sensationalise the attack on Dresden in cultural remembrance. In particular, a then up-and-coming young historian named David Irving had stirred up veteran resentment by publishing an inflammatory account of the attack in the early 1960s which excoriated the RAF. Irving later became notorious as a Holocaust denier, but long before the Lipstadt libel trial of 2000, his methodologies as a historian were scrutinised and questioned. When his book *The Destruction of Dresden* was published in 1963, it had a critical and long-lived impact on popular memories of the raid, as it inflated the casualty statistics by over 100,000.[53] Although Irving later recounted these figures, the damage had been done. As LA Jackets, the Head of the Historical Air Branch, noted bitterly in 1966, 'It is practically impossible to kill a myth of this kind once it has been widespread'.[54] This sensationalised figure formed a key trope in Cold War propaganda and subsequently became entrenched in British popular culture, being trotted out by the media at every available opportunity.[55] The horrors of the Dresden raid were reinforced by the publication in 1968 of Kurt Vonnegut's cult novel, *Slaughterhouse Five*. This appeared at the same time as wider public debate raged over the United States' use of napalm to bomb Vietnam. It was in this context of controversy and censure that *The Eighth Passenger* made its first appearance in print.

The various revisions which Tripp's narrative underwent in subsequent editions in 1985 and 1993 highlight the veteran's desire to employ his published memoir to reshape popular memories of the air war. A key feature of the second edition, published in 1985 by Papermac, was the insertion of Tripp's account of participating in a recent German

---

[51] Richard Overy, 'The Post-War Debate', in *Firestorm: The Bombing of Dresden 1945*, (eds.) Paul Addison and Jeremy A. Crang (London: Pimlico, 2006), p. 132.
[52] Musgrove, *Dresden and the Heavy Bombers*, p. 2.
[53] David Irving, *The Destruction of Dresden* (London: William Kimber & Co, 1963), p. 7.
[54] TNA/AIR/19/1028, L. A. Jackets, memo 20 July 1966.
[55] Most current studies now agree that the accepted total of casualties in Dresden was approximately 35,000.

television documentary about the bombers' war in an epilogue. In September 1983, he was invited by a German producer to contribute to a five-part documentary called *Der Krieg der Bomber*, the last episode of which would focus on the attack on Dresden. Sir Arthur Harris and Sir Leonard Cheshire VC had also been invited to take part, so Tripp would be in distinguished company. After a rather stiff opening exchange with the producers, in which Tripp stipulated that if he was 'expected to express remorse, [he] would not do so', and neither would he criticise the men of Bomber Command who had flown on the Dresden raid, the programme began to take shape.[56] An episode that occurred during filming is reported in this edition, which assumes considerable significance when the 1985 edition is compared with its 1993 successor. On the first day of filming on location in Britain, the memoirist recollected, the producer took Tripp and other former aircrew out to a hotel lounge to discuss the next day's schedule. The memoirist narrated that the meeting was about to end 'in good humour', when an embarrassing incident occurred. Their conversation had been overheard by other guests in the lounge and one addressed himself to Tripp and his comrades, announcing loudly that he had been in London when the V2 bombs had been dropped: 'gentlemen', he declared, 'if you had dropped twice as many bombs on Germany as you did, I, for one, would have been very glad.'[57] After a nasty silence, 'a babble of voices broke out – and they were our voices, British voices. The Germans said nothing.' Apologizing for 'the rudeness of a compatriot', the memoirist was relieved that the producer remained sanguine about the interruption. Nevertheless, this incident did not appear in the third edition of *The Eighth Passenger* in 1993. This reflected a changing *zeitgeist* among former Bomber Command veterans, who were at that time beginning to adopt a ferociously protective public stance towards their perceived status in popular remembrance.

In fact, the 1993 edition of *The Eighth Passenger* explicitly revealed a hardening of its author's attitude towards unfavourable cultural memories of Bomber Command. With a new and updated epilogue to replace the 1985 version, Tripp's anecdote of the scene in the hotel lounge was replaced by a fervent defence of his Commander-in-Chief. Describing instead 'the old warrior's' speech in the German documentary, Tripp mused that Harris's words were:

uttered with stubborn conviction. Others, their freedom made safe by the sacrifices of a former generation, might occupy the moral high ground and indulge in fashionable criticism, but his foundations remained as firm as the abandoned

---

[56] Tripp, *The Eighth Passenger* (1985), p. 186.
[57] Ibid., p. 187.

concrete runways in the eastern counties of England down which bomb-laden aircraft had once roared on their way to take-off for Germany.[58]

Tripp's editorial change chimed with the emerging effort of veterans at this time to defend the record of Bomber Command. By the early 1990s, old debates on the wartime actions of Bomber Command had been reignited and acquired a startling new ferocity. The furore that raged over the erection and vandalising of a commemorative statue to Harris in 1992, in addition to incendiary television documentaries of the same year such as *The Valour and the Horror*, seemed to indicate to many of Bomber Command's surviving aircrew that the wartime bomber was being publicly presented for remembrance in extreme and highly unsatisfactory terms of either victim or villain.[59] At the same time as this apparent public misrepresentation of their efforts, many were further incensed that there appeared to be very little sign of any open commemoration of their 55,000 fallen comrades.[60] Together with an enduring absence of any national form of recognition of the contribution these men had made to Victory in Europe – the lack of any official commemorative medal for aircrew remained a bitter bone of contention. Overall, to former aircrew it appeared that British culture and remembrance were actively determined to vilify the men of Bomber Command.[61] The issue of Bomber Command in British popular remembrance remained a very sore subject for the former flyer, and was in fact reflected throughout a new wave of aircrew memoirs which appeared in the 1990s and 2000s. Notably, Tripp specifically stated in his 1993 edition that although the bulk of the narrative remained in its original form, it was now geared toward mustering a defence of all of Bomber Command's men. The addition of a new appendix illustrating the courage of aircrew strengthened his argument that the men of Bomber Command had not been fully appreciated by officialdom, scholars, or the public. Adding that there was much he would like to include about the area bombing campaign, the mood of *The Eighth Passenger* had become palpably steelier.

Of the wartime strategic air offensive itself, Tripp commented that it 'has been adversely criticized and its effects detrimentally exploited by those intent on minimizing the attempts of Bomber Command to finish a war in which combatants and civilians on both sides were suffering.'[62]

---

[58] Tripp, *The Eighth Passenger* (1993), p. 186.
[59] A representation which a cohort of British and Canadian veterans fruitlessly attempted to challenge through the courts during the early 1990s.
[60] It was not until 2012 that an official Bomber Command memorial was erected in London's Green Park.
[61] Houghton, 'The "Missing Chapter"', pp. 161–70.
[62] Tripp, *The Eighth Passenger* (1993), p. xi.

Yet he remarked cryptically that these were 'matters for another time, a different book.'[63] Further to this, in a letter he wrote to his literary agent in January 1992, Tripp explained that he was planning a new work – the aforementioned 'different book' alluded to in the 1993 edition of *The Eighth Passenger* – which would explore more fully the 'use and misuse' of aircrew and airpower during the Second World War.[64] Although this new book never made it into publication, the reasons Tripp gave for tackling this fresh project help to contextualise the revisions he made to his third edition. In his new work he planned to include a chapter on Dresden to be entitled 'in mitigation of the raid'. The purpose, he explained, of this lay in the 'extremely adverse publicity' of the bombers' war – 'an opposite view', he deemed, 'has seldom been expressed.' Moreover, he announced a belief that 'the Dresden raid is now being exploited by neo-Nazis and has been the subject of hatchet jobs by David Irving and Alexander McKee.'[65] Tripp's personal reaction to the former historian in 1992 is also noteworthy, as it communicates his increasing concern about adverse popular remembrance of the Dresden raid. In 1963, he was interviewed for Irving's *The Destruction of Dresden*, yet by early 1992 Tripp had informed his agent that he was 'worried by the plaudits' that Irving had recently received in Germany as a 'revisionist' historian.[66] This followed shortly after Irving had made a series of infamous, and highly publicised, remarks asserting that Dresden had been a worse atrocity than Auschwitz. This all added up to a very unsavoury method of writing history that Tripp did not appreciate. Against this, Tripp affirmed that the third edition of *The Eighth Passenger* was intended to proffer 'a reasoned plea in mitigation such as might be delivered by a counsel for the defence.'[67] The final revisions to the 1993 edition of *The Eighth Passenger* were thus a direct response to the memoirist's perceptions of increasing official, scholarly, and public condemnation of Bomber Command at a time when there were increasingly few left to guard the honour of Harris and his men.

Convoy is to Scatter versus the Court of Historical Opinion

The final case study explores the veteran's use of published life-writing to mount a strong defence of his own actions as a combatant. Captain Jack Broome's narrative of wartime service in the Royal Navy arose out

[63] Ibid., p. xi.
[64] UoR, LC/ A/2/681, Miles Tripp to Michael Sissons, 26 January 1992.
[65] Ibid.
[66] Ibid.
[67] Ibid.

of most unusual circumstances as it was published in 1972, emerging out of his role as the successful litigant in a particularly public and vicious libel case that raged in January 1970. One of the defendants was the publishing house Cassell & Co. The other was David Irving. As mentioned earlier, during the late 1960s Irving was still regarded as a reasonably creditable and promising young historian, albeit one with an emergent uncanny flair for whipping up controversy. The ensuing court case between historian and historical subject was vicious and attracted considerable attention in the British press. In stirring up the ancient murk which had just settled around the carcase of PQ17, Irving found himself in the sights of Broome, to whom his book attached much of the blame for the loss of the convoy. As the victor in the case of *Broome v. Cassell & Co.*, the naval veteran was awarded £40,000 damages. At that point in time, this constituted the highest damages for defamation awarded in British legal history. What followed was a battle of the books which demonstrates the critical importance that a number of veteran-memoirists attached to their narratives as a mechanism of controlling the historical record of their wartime experiences.

The imbroglio centred upon the former naval officer's actions in scattering PQ17, that ill-starred Allied Arctic convoy which was destroyed in 1942 only to be exhumed and 'dragged back from the fringe of living memory' in a court of law three decades later.[68] PQ17 remains indelibly marked in the annals of seafaring catastrophe. When disaster descended upon the convoy on 4 July 1942, only eleven out of thirty-five British and American merchant ships survived to limp into Russian ports. Attacks from German U-boats and bombers scattered the rest, along with their precious cargo of war materials, across the bottom of the icy Barents Sea. Although various other wartime convoys suffered similarly heavy losses in terms of tonnage and lives, PQ17 was granted special infamy by the circumstances under which the convoy was destroyed. As Senior Officer of the Close Escort for the merchantmen (1st Escort Group), Commander Broome and his destroyer HMS *Keppel* were charged with ensuring that the convoy reached its destination safely. However, on 4 July 1942, the Admiralty sent out orders for the convoy to scatter, believing that an attack by heavy German surface forces, including the dreaded battleship *Tirpitz*, was imminent. Meanwhile, convinced by a prior series of signals received from the Admiralty that the supposedly looming *Tirpitz* constituted an immediate threat to the scattering convoy, Broome decided to attach his destroyers to a covering force of cruisers under the command of Rear Admiral Louis Hamilton, in anticipation of engaging the

[68] Broome, *Convoy is to Scatter*, p. 15.

expected enemy. Left to their own devices, the fragmented convoy and remaining escort vessels became easy targets for the pursuing U-boats and aircraft, with disastrous results. The tragedy of PQ17 was deepened by the fact that the entire affair stemmed from a tangle of miscommunication between the Admiralty and surface forces and poor reconnaissance. The Admiralty's information that the pride of the German navy was at sea was based on negative, rather than positive, intelligence and the *Tirpitz* remained snugly berthed at Altenfiord, Norway, throughout the hunting and destruction of PQ17. The expected battle with the enemy's heavy surface forces never materialised.

   In 1968 Irving's inflammatory account of these events, *The Destruction of Convoy PQ17*, attributed the loss of the convoy to Broome's poor and hubristic tactical decisions. Having surreptitiously obtained a copy of the manuscript, Broome was outraged by this slur and began legal proceedings against Irving and his publisher Cassell & Co. for libel. Following his well-publicised victory in the law courts, the veteran published *Convoy is to Scatter* (1972), which clearly sought to broadcast to an even wider audience his own 'true' version of events, and to place his own narrative on popular, as well as legal, record. The first half of Broome's memoir offers a comparatively innocuous account of the war at sea which is similar to the other naval narratives explored in this study. The second half, however, pointedly assembles a justification of the author's tactical decisions relating to convoy PQ17 as if the author were still making a case to defend his actions in court. Broome synthesised his conventional linear narrative of the convoy's voyage with accompanying explanations of the evidence Broome and his legal team presented in court, throwing into sharp relief a concrete link between book and the trial to clear Broome's name. This emphasises the veteran's intention to use his published memoir to ensure that reminders of the exculpation of both himself and the wartime Royal Navy remained available to current and future audiences who were interested in the fate of convoy PQ17. Its origins in the law courts might be unique but Broome's memoir particularly embodies a common theme of a power struggle between veteran and history, proffering a valuable insight into the processes by which an extremely angry veteran crafted a published personal narrative into an essential tool to correct a mendacious scholarly account of 'his' war.

   In many respects, *Convoy is to Scatter* is an intensely self-conscious text, perhaps unsurprisingly, as it was designed with the specific intention of publicly challenging Irving's historical interpretation of the fate of PQ17. A strong seam of self-justification therefore runs throughout the memoir. In particular, Broome believed that more credence should be given to the views of those present at the event in question, rather than those of distant commentators:

> One object in writing this book is to keep ramming home this basic fact which no improvement in 'communications' can alter: the situation confronting the man on the spot will *never* be exactly the same as that visualized anywhere else.[69]

Shoehorned into the narrative at every possible opportunity, this recurrent assertion was used repeatedly to demolish criticism of his actions. Broome continually placed his reader in the position of the jurors in his court case, drawing repeated analogies between the two. For instance, he pointedly enjoins his readers to 'remind ourselves yet again, as the jury was constantly being reminded' that

> the text of a signal is for ever keyed to information available to the sender up to the moment that signal was sent. It might predict, instruct, cancel, amend, but it can't foresee – nor, unlike history, can it be sullied by hindsight.[70]

His use of the original signals as a literary device through which to tell the 'true' story of PQ17 lends considerable weight to Broome's argument. Using the signals from which 'Bundle 11' of the courtroom evidence was compiled, Broome sought to lay to rest three key criticisms of his conduct by Irving. The first of these centred upon the easterly course on which Broome had re-routed the convoy. On 3 July 1942, the Admiralty sent out a signal instructing the convoy to pass at least fifty miles to the north of Bear Island. Having received an earlier report from the Admiralty that the summer limit of the Arctic ice edge was further north than previously anticipated, Hamilton proposed that Broome take advantage of the increased sea room and route the convoy further to the north, which would take it further out of range of the German bombers stationed along the Norwegian coast. Instead, Broome opted to pursue a more easterly route; a decision which Irving's account condemned as disobedience of Hamilton's instructions, asserting that the destroyer captain had deliberately 'chosen not to carry out' his instructions.[71] Although the historian did not go quite so far as to use the term 'mutiny', his appraisal indicted Broome as a maverick commander. Under naval discipline, ignoring an order was among the most serious of charges, and Broome's memoir thus took especial pains to justify his actions. Much of this defence rested on the difficulties of navigation in such close proximity to the Arctic Circle, which led to some positional discrepancies.

---

[69] Ibid., p. 52.
[70] Ibid., p. 93.
[71] Churchill Archives Centre (hereafter CAC), The Papers of Jackie Broome, BRME 5/1, Statement of Claim Against David Irving, 11 May 1970.

In addition, Broome was reluctant to amend course too far northward, as every eight miles that the convoy travelled in this direction would add another two hours onto the voyage time: 'our target', he acerbically commented, 'was Archangel, not the North Pole'.[72] In his view, any lengthening of the voyage significantly increased the risk to the convoy. Broome further explained that, with regard to the potential threat of enemy aircraft, he had exercised his own judgement:

with long endurance shadowers present to home attacking aircraft it seemed to me to make very little difference from the point of view of air attack whether an 8-knot convoy was 300 or 500 miles from enemy aerodromes.[73]

He also maintained that escort commanders had 'learnt the hard way' when to take the advice of senior 'spectators', and that all these thoughts had been in his mind when routing the convoy past Bear Island on 3 July.[74] Immediately, therefore, his memoir set in motion the former officer's defence that reliance upon his own judgement was central to ensuring the safety of the convoy.

Irving's second criticism revolved around a sequence of three Admiralty signals received within the space of half an hour by PQ17 and its covering cruiser force. These were the messages that, in Broome's words, 'between them changed PQ17 from a convoy with its chin well up, into a shambles.'[75] The critical signals read thus:

9.11 pm. MOST IMMEDIATE: Cruiser Force withdraw to westward at high speed.

9.23 pm. IMMEDIATE: Owing to threat from surface ships convoy is to disperse and proceed to Russian ports.

9.36 pm. MOST IMMEDIATE: Convoy is to scatter.

Irving contended that the third signal was 'essentially a correction' of the second and did not imply an immediate German surface force threat.[76] However, read in conjunction with previous information transmitted to PQ17 about the Admiralty's concern that German heavy surface forces might have put to sea to intercept the convoy, the effect of each these signals implied to Broome that his shore-based superiors expected the masts of the *Tirpitz* to appear on the horizon at any second. Furthermore, Broome noted that whilst entirely logical for scholarly histories to group the three signals together in order to examine their aggregate effect, this approach bore little relation to how the officer at 'the sharp end'

---

[72] Broome, *Convoy is to Scatter*, p. 130.
[73] Ibid., p. 130.
[74] Ibid.
[75] Ibid., p. 173.
[76] CAC, BRME 5/1, Statement of Claim Against David Irving, 11 May 1970.

interpreted their meaning: 'while cumulative effects are in the making', he emphasised, 'you don't know what is coming next.'[77] *Convoy is to Scatter* especially maintained that due to contemporary naval discipline and policy, the historian's latter reading of the signals was not feasible:

> The order to SCATTER is the prerogative of the senior man on the spot when, and only when, an overwhelming force attacks his convoy, which would be more difficult to massacre spread out than if it remained concentrated. It is the last straw, the 'sauve qui peut' [every man for himself] and it is, of course, irrevocable.[78]

Broome described the effect of receiving this 'scatter' order as like 'an electric shock'.[79] He explained that the signals conveyed a 'crescendo of priority' that implied that the Admiralty knew for certain that the merchant ships would be safer alone than remaining with the convoy. Despite recalling that the shock of the order rendered him 'hot and angry', he nevertheless maintained that he saw no reason to question the signals.[80] According to his memoir, he was quite simply left with no other option than to trust that the Admiralty had sufficient reason to give this order. Broome therefore asserted that Irving's conclusion that he had misinterpreted the signals was extraordinarily unfair, given that the prevailing circumstances did not allow for a different reading.

The third, and most damning, criticism of Broome's conduct in Irving's account centred upon the former's conduct once the convoy had initiated the process of scattering. Irving was extremely critical of Broome's decision to take his six destroyers to join Hamilton's cruiser force, leaving the rest of the escort and the merchantmen to fend for themselves. His censure was founded upon the signal Broome sent to the rest of his escort group and the convoy: 'Convoy to scatter and proceed to Russian Ports. Escorts, negative Destroyers, proceed independently to Archangel.' According to Irving, instructing the remaining escort vessels to proceed independently meant that the merchant ships were thus 'stripped of their last protection' and so abandoned to their fate.[81] Broome strongly objected to the historian's representation of this

---

[77] Broome, *Convoy is to Scatter*, p. 179.
[78] Ibid., p. 182. Instructions to 'disperse' and to 'scatter' were two very different procedures. To 'disperse' meant that the merchant ships would break formation and proceed onward, but would remain close together for a time. To 'scatter' meant that the convoy would instantaneously break out into a pre-arranged pattern – in the case of PQ17 this was fanwise – and put as much distance between each other as rapidly as possible in order to present less of a target to the enemy surface forces. The 'scatter' order was very much a last resort.
[79] Broome, *Convoy is to Scatter*, p. 182.
[80] Ibid., p. 182
[81] CAC, BRME 5/1, Statement of Claim Against David Irving, 11 May 1970.

so-called 'terrible mistake', and his memoir provides a very different portrayal of events.[82] He argued that the situation which confronted the 1st Escort Group had never been envisaged, and so it was unclear precisely what the escort was supposed to do. 'They couldn't', he reasoned, 'be left mooning around the Barents Sea with no convoy to escort.'[83] He thus insisted that in the context of naval doctrine in 1942, the order to 'proceed independently' in this sense meant to 'proceed independently of *Keppel*' as opposed to independently of the remnants of the convoy. Thereafter, the rest of the merchant ships would come under the command of the most senior escort ship remaining.[84] Meanwhile, the six destroyers were instructed to join *Keppel* and link up with Hamilton's cruisers in order to engage the supposedly approaching surface forces. It was at this juncture that the close proximity of the covering cruiser force to the escort group became, explained Broome, something of a problem. Rapidly picking up speed and turning to the south-west, Hamilton's cruisers gave the distinct impression that they were racing to intercept the enemy. According to Broome, his next and most criticised signal was triggered entirely by this sudden movement of the cruisers. Described by the Commander as 'more an instinctive act on my part than a cold-blooded decision', he sent a signal to Hamilton: 'Propose Close Escort Destroyers join you', which was curtly accepted. The rationale behind this signal, Broome expounded, was that there seemed little point in wasting precious time by watching the cruisers head off to meet the enemy, and then have to catch up with them to help out. This, he believed, would also have the effect of neutralising the threat to the scattering convoy.

Five hours after the convoy was ordered to scatter, the Admiralty sent a further signal announcing that it was now not certain that the German heavy ships were at sea. Although the merchant ships were by then thoroughly distributed across the Barents Sea, Broome expected that Hamilton would order *Keppel* and the other destroyers back to round up as many remnants of the convoy as they could find, hinting to the Admiral that this was where the destroyers' duty lay.[85] Hamilton, however, maintained radio silence for almost eighteen hours, during which time Broome argued that the dispersing convoy became irretrievable: 'Had we been sent back an hour – or even two – after scattering, with sheep-dog aggression and cunning we stood a chance of revoking the irrevocable order to scatter.'[86] When Hamilton broke his lengthy silence,

[82] Ibid.
[83] Broome, *Convoy is to Scatter*, p. 191.
[84] Ibid., p. 191.
[85] Ibid., p. 213
[86] Ibid., p. 214.

Broome requested to go back and salvage what he could of the remnants of the convoy, even though he estimated that he was now some 400 miles from the scattering position and each merchant ship must have travelled about 150 miles from it following a variety of individual courses.[87] Nevertheless, he insists that he was willing to attempt to recover the convoy: 'to all of us at the time', he wrote, 'it seemed the obvious next move.'[88] Irving, however, further impugned Broome's actions and honour here, claiming that the latter only wanted to return to collect the other escort vessels – there was, Irving declared, 'no mention of the merchant ships'.[89] Yet Broome's memoir conveys a deep sense of anguish at being forced to leave the rest of PQ17 behind and he records his distress at hearing over the radio 'the pathetic cries for help which continued to come limping in from dying merchant ships.'[90]

Irving continued his attack on Broome, contending that he alone bore responsibility for the fate of the convoy:

the point of no return was at Commander J.E. Broome's withdrawal of his escort destroyers on his own initiative, and not in Hamilton's refusal to send them back to what would have been almost certain destruction.[91]

The Commander strongly countered that he never, 'as some Historians' stated, 'withdrew' from PQ17.[92] The description of his actions as 'withdrawing' from the merchant ships, thus implying that he abandoned them, particularly stung the memoirist. This representation, he argued, was 'misleading': under threat of heavy surface attack, the destroyers switched from a defensive to an offensive role. The convoy itself had ceased to exist the instant the 'scatter' order was received.[93]

Abiding by the principle that the best defence is a good offence, Broome put forward his own trenchant views of where culpability for the destruction of PQ17 lay. In contrast to Irving's account, his memoir refuted that either of the officers 'on the spot' ought to bear the overall blame for the disaster. The absolute faith that naval officers were required to place in their senior shore-based commanders was, he proposed, a far more integral component of the destruction of PQ17 than the actions of those at sea. Indeed, on 25 June 1942, he had received a signal which asserted that since commanders afloat were unlikely to possess much depth of information about the enemy's movements, it would therefore

[87] Ibid., p. 215.
[88] Ibid.
[89] CAC, BRME 5/1, Statement of Claim Against David Irving, 11 May 1970.
[90] Broome, *Convoy is to Scatter*, p. 215.
[91] CAC, BRME 5/1, Statement of Claim Against David Irving, 11 May 1970.
[92] Broome, *Convoy is to Scatter*, p. 214.
[93] Ibid., p. 214.

be necessary for the Admiralty to exercise shore-based control over those of the convoy.[94] The reins of command of PQ17 were thus in the firm grip of Admiralty hands, and officers at sea were forced to assume that their distant superiors were better appraised of a situation than they could be. For the senior officers to whom the immediate safety of the convoy was entrusted this was a most uneasy situation, and Broome's narrative insists that this was where responsibility for the tragedy should rightfully be allocated: 'PQ17 was just another splendid convoy, ploughing along with no claim whatever to history or fiction until those signals arrived from the Admiralty.'[95] He believed, however, that the latter had never been held fully accountable: 'A lot of whitewash and criticism has followed in the wake of this disaster, with the whitewash mainly confined to the end of the story carrying the Top Brass.'[96] Reiterating that his conviction that it was the 'Convoy is to Scatter' signal which triggered the doom of PQ17, the memoirist avowed that the 'responsibility for what actually did happen must therefore rest on the shoulders of the man who gave that order and his advisers.'[97] Broome plainly felt he had been cast unfairly as a scapegoat for the demise of the convoy. Despite winning his legal battle over scholarly representation of PQ17, the veteran revealingly opted to further broadcast his defence in the form of a war memoir that he clearly viewed as a powerful public platform. By putting his side of the story in the public domain, Broome visibly hoped that *Convoy is to Scatter* would cement his good name into the popular record, and permanently close the case of PQ17 in the court of historical opinion.

Summary

As the three narratives in these case studies demonstrate, memoir was deployed as a public site of contest from which to challenge unsatisfactory representations of a war which many veterans regarded through a lens of distinct possessiveness. Each of these veteran-memoirists crafted their memoirs with the specific intention of salvaging the reputations of individuals, units, and strategies that they felt history, the authorities, and collective memory had maligned. Bowlby's *Recollections* proffers an insight into an aspect of wartime regimental history that remained untraceable in more official accounts. The convoluted history of *The Eighth Passenger* outlined a common predicament which all veteran-memoirists faced. In the post-war decades, survivors were confronted

[94] Ibid., pp. 110–11.
[95] Ibid., p. 229.
[96] Ibid.
[97] Ibid., p. 230.

with a multitude of shifting cultural and historical frames within which to articulate their memories and representations of combat. Ultimately, the Tripp affair as a whole illustrates the inherently symbiotic nature of veteran relationship with public and private memories of war. The dramatic origins of Broome's *Convoy is to Scatter* confirm that published memoir was viewed as a potent vehicle through which to challenge history itself. As 'vectors of memory', these memoirs also functioned as the ultimate 'survivor's song'. By virtue of his own combat role and survival, the memoirist could lay claim to a singular authority to speak for a conflict which he perceived as 'his'. Through a process of self-selection, therefore, veteran-memoirists such as Bowlby, Tripp, and Broome assumed a role as gatekeepers of military memory in the public domain. So far as each veteran was concerned, his military memoir should constitute a final word on the subject of combatant experience during the Second World War.

Conclusion

> [W]e all need help understanding the most vital and valuable documents available about the human experience of war and the military.[1]

As Rear-Admiral Rupert Sherbrooke recognised in Graeme Ogden's narrative, *My Sea Lady*, by depicting the combatant's 'personal reactions' to war, veteran memoirs proffer unique accounts of the medley of 'human factors' which comprised the experience of battle.[2] Here, he echoed the sentiments of SLA Marshall, who wrote in 1947 that during the Second World War 'we learned anew that man is supreme, that it is the soldier who fights who wins battles, that fighting means using a weapon, and that it is the heart of man which controls its use.'[3] He claimed that the post-war world was already on the point of forgetting the importance of the man as combatant. In 1997, John Keegan also lamented that, habitually, the 'military historian's man in uniform bore no resemblance to the man in the street. He was a being without family or friends, without future or past, without values ... The traditional military historian's *homo pugnans* seemed a being different and separate'.[4] The British Second World War veterans' tale suggests that their authors felt the same way. Overwhelmingly, they desired to cement the human identity of combatants into the historical record. Whilst acknowledging that the grander narratives of military historians are to some degree inevitably 'dehumanised' due to the sheer scale of their purview, George Macdonald Fraser commented that 'With all military histories it is necessary to remember that war is not a matter of maps with red and blue arrows and oblongs, but of weary, thirsty men with sore feet and aching shoulders wondering where they are'.[5] Similarly, Ray Ward expressed

---

[1] Vernon, *Arms and the Self*, p. x.
[2] Sherbrooke, foreword to *My Sea Lady*, p. 9.
[3] Marshall, *Men Against Fire*, p. 23.
[4] Keegan, 'Towards a Theory of Combat Motivation', p. 5.
[5] Macdonald Fraser, *Quartered Safe Out Here*, pp. xi–xii.

doubts about the value of official histories of campaigns and battles which were often written by 'expert' former high-ranking officers. Noting that he had written his own memoir with the specific intention of providing a counter-narrative to these types of accounts, Ward remained sceptical about the ability of the latter to convey the reality of experience on the frontline accurately:

Official histories, written by senior commanders who may have had a troubled conscience about some incidents, and encounters so disturbing that they were sanitised, or overlaid by a false or mistaken interpretation more acceptable to self-esteem, rarely tell the full story. What strikes me is their frequency of bald references ... No mention of the fear and panic, the pain and suffering, the blood and guts – realities that tend to be taboo in such accounts, as they are in the officers' mess, and at the Cenotaph on Remembrance Day. Only those who were on the spot – junior officers, non-commissioned officers and ordinary soldiers – know the full horror between the lines of such laconic, evasive statements: the horror that haunts every infantryman who survived it.[6]

War memoirs are thus special. They capture the man inside the uniform, his own understanding of his physical and psychological performance in the field, and his emotional responses to various dimensions of the combat experience including landscape, weaponry, comrades, and the enemy. By rights, Macdonald Fraser mused, 'each official work should have a companion volume in which the lowliest actor gives his version ... it would at least give posterity a sense of perspective.'[7] The tales of Second World War veterans serve proudly as these 'companion volumes', focusing upon that 'simplest and most complex topic in the military art – man himself as a figure on the field of combat.'[8] In so doing, they confer flesh and life upon the skeleton of battle.

These memoirs are thus to be prized because, as Samuel Hynes observes, 'If we would understand humankind's most violent episodes, we must understand them humanly, in the lives of individuals.'[9] The post-war narratives written by British veterans tell us not only 'what war was like', but also how battle appeared from the perspective of former combatants. In so doing, they offer a new depth of window into the experience of battle as it endures in a veteran's mind throughout his lifetime. Through its focus on the veteran-memoirists' representations of the landscapes in which they operated, the machines with which they fought, and the men against, and alongside, whom they did battle, *The Veterans' Tale* suggests that this grants an invaluable insight into the ways

[6] Ward, *The Mirror of Monte Cavallara*, pp. 17–18.
[7] Macdonald Fraser, *Quartered Safe Out Here*, p. xi.
[8] Marshall, *Men Against Fire*, p. 26.
[9] Hynes, *The Soldiers' Tale*, p. xvi.

in which ex-aircrew, sailors, tank crew, and infantrymen retrospectively interpreted their own emotional responses to combat. The language and images selected by these memoirists to describe their war experiences reveal how that wartime experience came to be remembered, understood, and defined by the veteran. In its assessment of the recorded 'personal reactions' of former combatants to battle during the Second World War, this book has sought to further understandings of the multitude of ways in which that war lived on in the recollections of its veterans. It also suggests that individually and collectively veteran memoir tells a particular tale. In essence, these books relate the story of war that an old soldier wanted to put on record.

Pursuing questions of 'why' and 'how' veterans made the decision to turn their 'remembered war' into a published narrative, new understandings of the lasting import of battle to combatants have opened up. Perhaps it is self-evident to conclude that the experience of fighting in the Second World War had been so significant to these men that they quite simply did not want their war to be forgotten, but it is such a fundamental truth that it bears reiterating. As seen earlier, former rear air gunner Jim Davis voiced the sentiments of many veteran-memoirists when he proclaimed that 'we all have to make an imprint and, if possible, have to leave behind us a memory of ourselves, or something we have accomplished in the minds of other people.'[10] Similarly, in an interview with BBC Radio 4 in 2008, Geoffrey 'the Boy' Wellum proclaimed poignantly, 'I think the thing that we want is to be remembered.' 'We're not heroes,' insisted the former Battle of Britain pilot, 'don't give us medals, just remember us.'[11] Through using published narrative form to inscribe the experience and legacy of battle, these veterans were able to make a wider-reaching and permanent 'imprint' of their experiences. Their memoirs were consequently designed to operate in several specific ways in the public domain. They were driven by an imperative to create a historical record that would serve as a literary memorial to the fallen, but also to inform 'those who wanted to know what it was like'.[12] The veterans' tale was thus intended simultaneously to educate, to entertain, and to warn against repeating the folly of war. Perhaps most importantly, the veterans' tale also transformed war memoirists into guardians of memory, operating as sites from which these former servicemen could claim a degree of control over scholarly, official, and cultural remembrance of the Second World War.

[10] Davis, *Winged Victory*, p. 85.
[11] IWM Sound Archive, Geoffrey Wellum (BBC Radio 4 Interview, 2008), 31715.
[12] Bowlby, *Recollections*, p. 222.

Alongside their public function, the veterans' tale also operated on an intensely private level. Writing allowed memoirists to process their war experiences and they could either relive enjoyable moments of comradeship, or seek catharsis and a measure of solace from grief or psychological trauma. Furthermore, the veterans' tale possesses an interiority which charts the memoirists' own perceptions of undergoing a fundamental process of inner change through experiencing battle. Ray Ward articulated the sentiments of many fellow memoirists when he recorded that the Second World War,

was the most momentous experience in my life, and in the lives of my comrades in arms. It had an enduring influence far beyond our muddled and immature appreciation of it at the time. It was only later we came to realise the effect our war service had on our subsequent lives and careers.[13]

Like many of his fellow veteran-memoirists, Ward's testimony explicitly engaged in self-contemplation in an effort to understand and communicate the impact of active frontline service on the selfhoods of himself and his fellow wartime combatants. In his narrative, the veteran's recollection of the battle experience was firmly connected to a symbolism of mirrors. Although republished as *With the Argylls* (2014), in its original edition the title of *The Mirror of Monte Cavallara* offers a telling association of ideas of war, memoir, and self-reflection. In the first instance, this mirror/war symbolism was drawn from a metaphor in Keith Douglas's memoir, in which the young tank commander memorably asserted that entering battle was comparable to stepping through a 'looking glass' into an inverted reality. In turn, Douglas had borrowed his imagery from Lewis Carroll's tales of a child's adventures in the fictitious 'Wonderland', drawing upon the novelist's symbolism to describe his own transition to warrior in a bizarre world of distorted familiarity where nothing quite made sense:

it is exciting and amazing to see thousands of men, very few of whom have much idea why they are fighting, all enduring hardships, living in an unnatural, dangerous, but not wholly terrible world, having to kill and be killed, and yet at intervals moved by a feeling of comradeship with the men who kill them and whom they kill, because they are enduring and experiencing the same things. It is tremendously illogical – to read about it cannot convey the impression of having walked through the looking-glass which touched a man entering battle.[14]

In this strange martial environment, the combatant's own identification of self also became jumbled. War forced the combatant to set aside his

---

[13] Ray Ward, letter written in 1995 to sons, included in *The Mirror of Monte Cavallara*, p. 13.
[14] Douglas, *Alamein to Zem Zem*, p. 6. Douglas kept a treasured copy of *Alice in Wonderland* amid his baggage in the desert. Indeed the full quotation is inserted into Ward's narrative as an epigraph, p. 9.

normative peacetime identity, divesting himself of 'a learned and deeply embodied set of physical impulses regarding his relation to any other person's body.' Through consenting to kill for the nation, the soldier's identity became fragmented. War unmade his sense of self.[15] Once he stepped back through the 'looking glass' from the battlefield into peacetime civilian life, memoir functioned as another mirror in which to reassemble the pieces. Like Ward, the veteran-memoirists of the Second World War were clearly well aware that autobiographical writing offered a valuable opportunity to reconstruct shattered notions of masculine self into a coherent and meaningful image.

The veteran-memoirists of the Second World War sustained physical injury, psychological damage, and occasionally suffered from cultural stigmatisation. Heightened emotional responses to violence were also common. After driving his Sherman tank through the grotesque carnage of the Normandy countryside in June 1944, Stuart Hills recorded that witnessing the mass destruction of human and animal life left an enduring emotional residue: 'to this day I have a detestation of scenes involving blood and wounds.'[16] Sydney Jary also reflected that the devastation of war had inculcated a new personal attitude in which he placed a premium upon all human and animal life: 'Hunting revolts me.'[17] But the veteran-memoirists of the Second World War had found their wartime experiences exciting, thrilling, and enjoyable. Keen to relate their exploits to an external audience of family, friends, and interested strangers, as well as to make a record for their own private consumption, undoubtedly these men would have been disappointed if their narratives were to be read through a lens of bodily and psychological damage and disillusionment. Despite experiencing loss, grief, and fear, the veteran-memoirists of the Second World War firmly maintained that it had all been worthwhile. Indeed, Geoffrey Page, one of the original members of the wartime Guinea Pig Club for airmen who sustained disfiguring injuries, avowed that despite 'being badly burned, sustaining bullet wounds and a fractured back, I would not want to change one moment of those wonderful, youthful years.'[18] Furthermore, there is not one memoir among all the narratives examined in this book that did not insist upon the ultimate justification of the fight against fascism between 1939 and 1945. 'There could', declared John McManners, who became a clergyman and a historian of religion in peacetime, 'be no question about the justice and the necessity of the war.' He went to explain that 'It was

---

[15] Scarry, *The Body in Pain*, p. 122.
[16] Hills, *By Tank into Normandy*, p. 91.
[17] Jary, *18 Platoon*, p. 129.
[18] Page, *Shot Down in Flames*, p. 176.

the first and last definition of the wars of history that were "just wars" within the Christian definition.'[19] Charles Potts also pondered the ethics of 'whether or not it is un-Christian to kill a man'. He too remained adamant that the Second World War had been a 'good' war:

I consider that, if in the ordinary course of life I were to see a dangerous lunatic at large and attacking a child, I would do everything in my power to stop him, even if I had to shoot and kill him. In my opinion Hitler was a dangerous lunatic, and his lunacy had infected a whole nation. It was our duty to protect the children, the weaker nations of Europe, that were being scourged and enslaved by these dangerous lunatics.[20]

Recording how he shot down a German aircraft over Dunkirk, Tim Vigors was keen to ensure that his reader understood that his actions were justifiable:

I was aware that I had killed a fellow human being and was surprised not to feel remorse ... But the way I saw it then was, 'Poor son of a bitch. He was probably a nice guy and we would probably have got on well had we met. But he was on the wrong side. He shouldn't have signed up with that bastard Hitler!' The fact was, and remains to this day, Germany was wrong in every way allowing itself to be bamboozled by one of the most evil monsters the world has ever seen.[21]

He went on to explain that the 'deaths of my friends and companions, and for that matter my own death should it happen, were justified in order to fight for that cause. The sacrifice, no matter how frightful it might be, was worthwhile.'[22] Equally, despite articulating self-doubt about the public label of 'hero' that had been pinned to his person, Tony Bartley considered that, in summary of his wartime experiences, 'I would say that I fought for what I believed was right to the limit of my capacity.'[23] Whilst willing to explore and recount the horrors of battle within their narratives, the veteran-memoirists thus remained enormously proud of their wartime roles at 'the sharp end' of the Second World War.

Finally, the veterans' tale represents a most precious asset to cultural-military investigation of warfare. Separately and collectively, these memoirs relate the cyclical story of men at war, charting the serviceman's transition from civilian to combatant to veteran and his return to civilian. As has been argued in this book, recognition of this allows us to evaluate published military memoirs as an important source of evidence about what Hynes terms the 'two stories of war': 'the things men do in war'

[19] McManners, *Fusilier*, p. 21.
[20] Potts, *Soldier in the Sand*, p. 110.
[21] Vigors, *Life's Too Short to Cry*, p. 136.
[22] Ibid., p. 233.
[23] Bartley, *Smoke Trails in the Sky*, p. 198.

and the 'things war does to them'.[24] Through his construction of a narrative account that imposed order, shape, and coherency upon experience, the veteran reveals the legacy of combat upon his body, mind, and self-identity. Beyond the historical value of such testimonies, it is also clear that they have a wider cultural resonance. In recent years, public awareness of the plight of veterans from recent wars has steadily expanded, thanks to a diverse variety of institutions including the ceaseless efforts of charities such as the Royal British Legion and 'Help for Heroes'. There remains, however, still considerable work to do in terms of understanding how the experience of war may endure in the minds of these servicemen and women, and the psychological and emotional ways in which memories of warfare will make themselves felt across their lifetimes. It is therefore surely incumbent upon us to understand and cherish 'the most vital and valuable documents available about the human experience of war and the military.' Ultimately, *The Veterans' Tale* establishes that published veteran memoirs offer a new way of understanding the lived, remembered, and recorded experience of war. As the generation of Second World War veterans dies out, it is more vital than ever to understand and learn from their personal records of experience.

[24] Hynes, *The Soldiers' Tale*, p. 3.

Bibliography

Archives

Archive of British Publishing and Printing, Special Collections, University of Reading.
Churchill Archives Centre, Churchill College, Cambridge.
Imperial War Museum, London.
Imperial War Museum Sound Archive, London.
National Archives, Kew.

Published Military Memoirs and Personal Narratives

Allen, H. R., *Battle for Britain: The Recollections of H. R. 'Dizzy' Allen DFC* (London: Arthur Barker Ltd., 1973).

Anscomb, Charles, *Submariner* (London: William Kimber, 1957).

Ashton, J. Norman, *Only Birds and Fools: Flight Engineer, Avro Lancaster, World War II* (Shrewsbury: Airlife, 2000).

Bailey, Jim, *The Sky Suspended: A Fighter Pilot's Story* (London: Bloomsbury, 2005).

Bartley, Tony, *Smoke Trails in the Sky*, rev. edn. (Wilmslow: Crecy Publishing, 1997).

Bellamy, Bill, *Troop Leader: A Tank Commander's Story* (Stroud: Sutton Publishing, 2005).

Bowlby, Alex, *Recollections of Rifleman Bowlby* (London: Leo Cooper, 1969).
Recollections of Rifleman Bowlby, rev. edn. (London: Leo Cooper, 1989).

Broome, Frank, *Dead Before Dawn: A Heavy Bomber Tail Gunner in World War II* (Barnsley: Pen & SwordAviation, 2008).

Broome, Jack, *Convoy is to Scatter* (London: William Kimber, 1972).

Bulteel, Christopher, *Something about a Soldier: The Wartime Memoirs of Christopher Bulteel M.* (Shrewsbury: Airlife, 2000).

Bushby, John, *Gunner's Moon: A Memoir of the RAF Night Assault on Germany* (London: Ian Allan, 1972).

Cochrane, Peter, *Charlie Company: In Service with C Company, 2nd Queen's Own Cameron Highlanders 1940–44* (London: Chatto & Windus, 1977).
Charlie Company: In Service with C Company, 2nd Queen's Own Cameron Highlanders 1940–44, rev. edn. (Stroud: Spellmount, 2007).

Cooper, Leo, *All My Friends Will Buy It: A Bottlefield Tour* (Staplehurst: Spellmount, 2005).

Currie, Jack, *Lancaster Target*, 2nd edn. (London: Goodall Publications, 1981).

Davis, Jim, *Winged Victory: The Story of a Bomber Command Air Gunner* (Ditton: R.J. Leach & Co, 1995).

Dickens, Peter, *Night Action: MTB Flotilla at War* (London: P. Davies, 1974).

Donald, William, *Stand by for Action: A Sailor's Story* (London: William Kimber, 1956).

Douglas, Keith, *Alamein to Zem Zem* (London: Editions Poetry, 1946).

Alamein to Zem Zem, rev. edn. (London: Faber and Faber, 2008).

Dundas, Hugh, *Flying Start: A Fighter Pilot's War Years* (London: Stanley Paul and Co., 1988).

Farrell, Charles, *Reflections 1939–1945: A Scots Guards Officer in Training and War* (Bishop Auckland: The Pentland Press, 2000).

Foley, Cedric John, *Mailed Fist: With a Tank Troop through Europe* (London: Panther Books, 1957).

Forty, George (ed.), *Tanks Across the Desert: The War Diary of Jake Wardrop*, rev. edn. (Stroud: Sutton Publishing, 2003).

Foxcroft, Harry, *Hostilities Only 1940–1945* (Weymouth: Miller-Lee Books, 1999).

Gamble, Arthur, *The Itinerant Airman* (Ilfracombe: Arthur H. Stockwell, 2003).

Gibson, Guy, *Enemy Coast Ahead* (London: Michael Joseph, 1946).

Gillman, Ronald, *The Shiphunters* (London: J. Murray, 1976).

Grace, Edward, *The Perilous Road to Rome and Beyond: Fighting Through North Africa and Italy*, rev. edn. (Barnsley: Pen & Sword Military, 2007).

The Perilous Road to Rome via Tunis (Tunbridge Wells, Parapress, 1993).

Graves, Robert, *But It Still Goes On: An Accumulation* (London: Jonathan Cape, 1930).

Gray, Philip, *Ghosts of Targets Past: The Lives and Losses of a Lancaster Crew in 1944–45*, 3rd edn. (London: Grub Street, 2005).

Gretton, Peter, *Convoy Escort Commander* (London: Cassell, 1964).

Hall, Roger, *Clouds of Fear* (Folkestone: Bailey Brothers and Swinfen Ltd, 1975).

Hampson, Norman, *Not Really What You'd Call a War* (Caithness: Whittles Publishing, 2001).

Harris, Arthur, *Bomber Offensive* (London: Collins, 1947).

Hart, Sydney, *Discharged Dead: A True Story of Britain's Submarines at War* (London: Odhams Press, 1956).

Hill, Roger, *Destroyer Captain* (London: William Kimber, 1975).

Hillary, Richard, *The Last Enemy*, rev. edn. (London: Pimlico, 1997).

Hills, Stuart, *By Tank into Normandy* (London: Cassell, 2002).

Horsfall, John, *The Wild Geese are Flighting* (Kineton: The Roundwood Press, 1976).

Hughes, Robert, *Through the Waters: A Gunnery Officer in H.M.S. Scylla 1942–43* (London: William Kimber, 1956).

Hynes, Samuel, *Flights of Passage: Reflections of a World War II Aviator* (London: Bloomsbury, 1988).

Jary, Sydney, *18 Platoon* (Carsholton Beeches: Sydney Jary Limited, 1987).

18 Platoon, rev. edn. (Winchester: Light Infantry Office, 2009).

Johnson, J. E. 'Johnnie', *Wing Leader* (London: Chatto & Windus, 1956).

Johnson, Peter, *The Withered Garland* (London: New European Publications, 1995).

Johnstone, Sandy, *Enemy in the Sky: My 1940 Diary* (London: William Kimber, 1976).

Kenneally, John, *The Honour and the Shame* (London: Headline Review, 2007).

King, William, *The Stick and the Stars* (London: Hutchinson, 1956).

Leakey, Rea, *Leakey's Luck: A Tank Commander with Nine Lives* (Stroud: Sutton Publishing Ltd, 1999).

Lombard-Hobson, Sam, *A Sailor's War* (London: Orbis Publishing, 1983).

Macdonald Fraser, George, *Quartered Safe Out Here*, rev. edn. (London: Harper Collins, 2000).

Macintosh, Don, *Bomber Pilot* (London: Browsebooks, 2006).

Macintyre, Donald, *U-Boat Killer* (London: Weidenfeld and Nicholson, 1956).

Mackenzie, K. W., *Hurricane Combat: The Nine Lives of a Fighter Pilot* (London: William Kimber, 1987).

Mars, Alistair, *Unbroken: The Story of a Submarine* (London: Frederick Muller, 1953).

McManners, John, *Fusilier: Recollections and Reflections 1939–1945* (Norwich: Michael Russell, 2002).

Messer, Herbert J., *Able Seaman RNVR* (Braunton: Merlin, 1989).

Monsarrat, Nicholas, *Three Corvettes*, 10th edn. (London: Mayflower, 1972).

Life is a Four Letter Word, Vol. 2 (London: Cassell & Company, 1970).

Mosley, Nicholas, *Time at War* (London: Weidenfeld and Nicholson, 2006).

Musgrove, Frank, *Dresden and the Heavy Bombers: An RAF Navigator's Perspective* (Barnsley: Pen & Sword Aviation, 2005).

Naydler, Merton, *Young Man You'll Never Die* (Barnsley: Pen & Sword Aviation, 2005).

Neil, Tom, *Gun Button to 'Fire'* (London: Kimber, 1987).

Gun Button to Fire: A Hurricane Pilot's Dramatic Story of the Battle of Britain, rev. edn. (Stroud: Amberley Publishing, 2010).

Nesbit, Roy Conyers, *Woe to the Unwary: A Memoir of Low Level Bombing Operations* (London: William Kimber, 1981).

Ogden, Graeme *My Sea Lady: The Story of H.M.S. Lady Madeleine From February 1941 to February 1943* (London: Hutchinson, 1963).

Oxspring, Bobby, *Spitfire Command* (London: William Kimber, 1984).

Page, Geoffrey, *Tale of a Guinea Pig* (London: Pelham Books, 1981).

Shot Down in Flames: A World War II Fighter Pilot's Remarkable Tale of Survival (London, Grub Street, 1999).

Passmore, Richard, *Blenheim Boy* (London: Thomas Harmsworth, 1981).

Picot, Geoffrey, *Accidental Warrior: In the Front Line from Normandy till Victory* (Lewes: The Book Guild, 1993).

Potts, Charles, *Soldier in the Sand* (London: P.R.M. Publishers, 1961).

Powell, Geoffrey, *Men at Arnhem*, rev. edn. (Barnsley: Pen & Sword, 2003).

Rayner, D., *Escort: The Battle of the Atlantic* (London: William Kimber, 1955).

Renaut, Michael, *Terror by Night: A Bomber Pilot's Story* (London: William Kimber, 1982).

Roach, Peter, *The 8.15 to War: Memoirs of a Desert Rat* (London: Leo Cooper, 1982).

Rolls, Bill, *Spitfire Attack* (London: William Kimber, 1987).
Russell, Peter, *Flying in Defiance of the Reich: A Lancaster Pilot's Rites of Passage* (Barnsley: Pen & Sword Aviation, 2007).
Sims, James, *Arnhem Spearhead: A Private Soldier's Story* (London: Imperial War Museum, 1978).
Smith, Ron, *Rear Gunner Pathfinders* (London: Goodall Publications, 1987).
Smith, W. G. G. Duncan, *Spitfire into Battle*, rev. edn. (London: John Murray, 2002).
Spooner, Tony, *In Full Flight* (London: Macdonald & Co., 1965).
In Full Flight, rev. edn. (Canterbury: Wingham Press, 1991).
Sutherland, Donald, *Sutherland's War* (London: Leo Cooper, Secker & Warburg, 1984).
Thesiger, Wilfred, *Arabian Sands*, rev. edn. (London: Penguin Books, 2007).
Tout, Ken, *Tank!* (London: Robert Hale, 1985).
Tanks, Advance! Normandy to the Netherlands, 1944 (London: Robert Hale, 1987).
By Tank: D to VE Days (London: Robert Hale, 2010).
Tripp, Miles, *The Eighth Passenger* (London: Heinemann, 1969).
The Eighth Passenger, rev. edn. (London: Macmillan, 1985).
The Eighth Passenger, rev. edn. (London: Leo Cooper, 1993).
Vigors, Tim, *Life's Too Short to Cry: The Compelling Memoir of a Battle of Britain Ace* (London: Grub Street, 2006).
Wainwright, John, *Tail-End Charlie* (London: Macmillan, 1978).
Ward, Ray, *The Mirror of Monte Cavallara: An Eighth Army Story* (Edinburgh: Birlinn, 2006).
Wellum, Geoffrey, *First Light* (London: Viking, 2002).
White, Arthur, *Bread and Butter Bomber Boys* (Upton on Severn: Square One Publications, 1995).
White, Graham, *The Long Road to the Sky: Night Fighter over Germany* (Barnsley: Pen & Sword Aviation, 2006).
Wilson, Andrew, *Flamethrower* (London: William Kimber and Co., 1956).
Wingfield, R. M., *The Only Way Out: An Infantryman's Autobiography of the North-West Europe Campaign August 1944–February 1945* (London: Hutchinson, 1955).
Woollcombe, Robert, *Lion Rampant* (London: Chatto & Windus, 1955).
Yates, Harry, *Luck and a Lancaster* (Shrewsbury: Airlife, 1999).
Young, Edward, *One of Our Submarines* (London: Rupert Hart-Davis, 1952).

Secondary Sources

Allport, Alan, *Demobbed: Coming Home after the Second World War* (New Haven: Yale University Press, 2009).
Anderson, Linda, *Autobiography* (London: Routledge, 2001).
Barr, Niall, *Pendulum of War: The Three Battles of El Alamein* (London: Jonathan Cape, 2004).
Bierman, John and Colin Smith, *Alamein: War Without Hate* (London: Viking, 2002).

Bishop, Patrick, *Fighter Boys: Saving Britain 1940* (London: HarperCollins, 2003).

Bomber Boys: Fighting Back 1940–1945 (London: HarperPress, 2007).

Bond, Brian, *Survivors of a Kind: Memoirs of the Western Front* (London: Continuum, 2008).

Bourke, Joanna, *An Intimate History of Killing: Face-to-Face Killing in Twentieth-Century Warfare* (London: Granta Books, 1999).

Fear: A Cultural History (London: Virago, 2005).

'Fear and Anxiety: Writing about Emotion in Modern History', *History Workshop Journal*, 55 (2003), 111–33.

Bowlby, Alex, *Countdown to Cassino: The Battle of Mignano Gap, 1943* (London: Leo Cooper, 1995).

Boyd, Kelly, *Manliness and the Boys' Story Paper in Britain: A Cultural History, 1855–1940* (Basingstoke: Palgrave Macmillan, 2003).

Brooks, Stephen, *Montgomery and the Eighth Army: A Selection from the Diaries, Correspondence and Other Papers of Field Marshal the Viscount Montgomery of Alamein, August 1942 to December 1943* (London: Bodley Head for the Army Records Society, 1991).

Bruss, Elizabeth, *Autobiographical Acts: The Changing Situation of a Literary Genre* (Baltimore: Johns Hopkins University Press, 1976).

Buckley, John, *British Armour in the Normandy Campaign 1944* (New York: Routledge, 2004).

Bungay, Stephen, *The Most Dangerous Enemy: A History of the Battle of Britain* (London: Aurum Press, 2000).

Alamein (London: Aurum, 2002).

Butler, R. N., 'The Life Review: An Interpretation of Reminiscence in the Aged', *Psychiatry*, 26 (1963), 65–76.

Calder, Angus, 'The Battle of Britain and Pilots' Memoirs', in *The Burning Blue: A New History of the Battle of Britain*, (eds.) Paul Addison and Jeremy A. Crang (London: Pimlico, 2000), 191–206.

Cecil, Hugh, *The Flower of Battle: British Fiction Writers of the First World War* (London: Secker & Warburg, 1995).

Churchman, Laurie, *The Art of Boat Names: Inspiring Ideas for Names and Designs* (New York: International Marine/McGraw-Hill, 2009).

Conley, Mary A., *From Jack Tar to Union Jack: Representing Naval Manhood in the British Empire, 1870–1918* (Manchester: Manchester University Press, 2009).

Connelly, Mark, *Reaching for the Stars: A New History of Bomber Command in World War II* (London: IB Tauris, 2001).

We Can Take It! Britain and the Memory of the Second World War (Harlow: Pearson Education, 2004).

Copp, Terry, '"If this war isn't over, and pretty and damn soon, there'll be nobody left, in this old platoon …": First Canadian Army, February–March 1945', in *Time to Kill: The Soldier's Experience of War in the West 1939–1945*, (eds.) Paul Addison and Angus Calder (London: Pimlico, 1997), 147–58.

Dawson, Graham, *Soldier Heroes: British Adventure, Empire, and the Imagining of Masculinities* (London: Routledge, 1994).

Deer, Patrick, *Culture in Camouflage: War, Empire, and Modern British Literature* (Oxford: Oxford University Press, 2009).

Edwards, Owen Dudley, 'The Battle of Britain and Children's Literature', in *The Burning Blue: A New History of the Battle of Britain*, (eds.) Paul Addison and Jeremy A. Crang (London: Pimlico, 2000), 164–90.

Ellis, John, *The Sharp End of War: The Fighting Man in World War II* (London: David & Charles, 1980).

'Reflections on the "Sharp End" of War', in *A Time to Kill: The Soldier's Experience of War in the West 1939–1945*, (eds.) Paul Addison and Angus Calder (London: Pimlico, 1997), 12–18.

Engen, Robert, 'Killing For Their Country: A New Look at "Killology"', *Canadian Military Journal*, 9:2 (2008), 120–8.

Feather, John, *A History of British Publishing*, 2nd edn. (Abingdon: Routledge, 2006).

Fennell, Jonathan, *Combat and Morale in the North African Campaign: The Eighth Army and the Path to El Alamein* (Cambridge: Cambridge University Press, 2011).

Foley, D., 'Why We Call A Ship A She', *Naval History*, 12:6 (1998).

Francis, Martin, *The Flyer: British Culture and the Royal Air Force, 1939–1945* (Oxford: Oxford University Press, 2008).

Frankland, Noble, *History at War: The Campaigns of an Historian* (London: Giles de la Mare, 1998).

Freedman, Jean, *Whistling in the Dark: Memory and Culture in Wartime London* (Kentucky: University Press of Kentucky, 1999).

Freeman, Mark, *Rewriting the Self: History, Memory, Narrative* (London: Routledge, 1993).

French, David, 'Discipline and the Death Penalty in the British Army in the War Against Germany during the Second World War', *Journal of Contemporary History*, 33:4 (1998), 531–45.

Raising Churchill's Army: The British Army and the War against Germany 1919–1945. (Oxford: Oxford University Press, 2000).

Fussell, Paul, *The Great War and Modern Memory*, rev. edn. (Oxford: Oxford University Press, 2000).

Garber, Marjorie, *Shakespeare After All* (New York: Anchor Books, 2004).

van Gennep, Arnold, *The Rites of Passage*, trans. Monika B. Vizedom and Gabrielle L. Caffee (London: Routledge & Kegan Paul, 1960).

Gill, D. C., *How We Are Changed by War: A Study of Letters and Diaries from Colonial Conflicts to Operation Iraqi Freedom* (New York: Routledge, 2010).

Gittins, Diana, 'Silences: The Case of a Psychiatric Hospital', in *Narrative and Genre*, (eds.) Mary Chamberlain and Paul Thompson (London: Routledge, 1998), 46–62.

Grossman, Dave, *On Killing*, rev. edn. (New York: Back Bay Books, 2009).

'S.L.A Marshall Revisited ...?', *Canadian Military Journal*, 9:4 (2008), 112–13.

Grusdorf, Georges, 'Conditions and Limits of Autobiography', in *Autobiography: Essays Theoretical and Critical*, (ed.) James Olney (Princeton: Princeton University Press, 1980), 28–48).

Halbwachs, Maurice, *On Collective Memory*, trans. Lewis Coser (Chicago: University of Chicago Press, 1992).

Harari, Yuval Noah, *Renaissance Military Memoirs: War, History, and Identity, 1450–1600* (Woodbridge: Boydell Press, 2004).

'Martial Illusions: War and Disillusionment in Twentieth-Century and Renaissance Military Memoirs', *Journal of Military History*, 69:1 (2005), 43–72.

'Military Memoirs: A Historical Overview of the Genre from the Middle Ages to the Late Modern Era', *War in History*, 14:3 (July 2007), 289–309.

The Ultimate Experience: Battlefield Revelations and the Making of Modern War Culture, 1450–2000 (Basingstoke: Palgrave Macmillan, 2008).

'Armchairs, Coffee, and Authority: Eye-Witnesses and Flesh-Witnesses Speak about War, 1100–2000', *Journal of Military History*, 74:1 (2010), 53–78.

Hastings, Max, *Bomber Command*, 3rd edn. (London: Pan Books, 1999).

Hastings, R. H. W. S., *The Rifle Brigade in the Second World War 1939–1945* (Aldershot: Gale & Polden, 1950).

Holmes, Richard, 'The Italian Job: Five Armies in Italy, 1943–45', in *A Time to Kill: The Soldier's Experience of War in the West 1939–1945*, (eds.) Paul Addison and Angus Calder (London: Pimlico, 1997), 206–20.

Hough, Richard and Denis Richards, *The Battle of Britain: The Jubilee History* (London: Hodder & Stoughton, 1989).

Houghton, Frances, 'Becoming "A Man" during the Battle of Britain: Combat, Masculinity and Rites of Passage in the Memoirs of "The Few"', in *Men, Masculinities and Male Culture in the Second World War*, (eds.) Juliette Pattinson and Linsey Robb (London: Palgrave Macmillan, 2018), 97–117.

'The "Missing Chapter": Bomber Command Aircrew Memoirs in the 1990s and 2000s', in *British Cultural Memory and the Second World War*, (eds.) Lucy Noakes and Juliette Pattinson (London: Bloomsbury, 2013), 153–70.

'"To the Kwai and Back": Myth, Memory and Memoirs of the "Death Railway" 1942–1943', *Journal of War and Culture Studies*, 7:3 (2014), 223–35.

Hunt, Nigel C., *Memory, War and Trauma* (Cambridge: Cambridge University Press, 2010).

Hunt, Nigel C. and Ian Robbins, 'Telling Stories of the War: Ageing Veterans Coping with Their Memories through Narrative', *Oral History*, 26:2 (1998), 57–64.

Hynes, Samuel, *The Soldiers' Tale: Bearing Witness to Modern War* (London: Pimlico, 1998).

'Personal Narratives and Commemoration', in *War and Remembrance in the Twentieth Century*, (eds.) Jay Winter and Emmanuel Sivan (Cambridge: Cambridge University Press, 1999), 205–20.

Irving, David, *The Destruction of Dresden* (London: William Kimber & Co, 1963).

Iveson, Tony, and Brian Milton, *Lancaster: The Biography* (London: Andre Deutsch, 2009).

Jalland, Pat, *Death in War and Peace: Loss and Grief in England, 1914–1970* (Oxford: Oxford University Press, 2010).

Jenkings, K. Neil and Rachel Woodward, 'Communicating War through the Contemporary British Military Memoir: The Censorships of Genre, State, and Self', *Journal of War & Culture Studies*, 7:1 (2014), 5–17.

'Practices of Authorial Collaboration: The Collaborative Production of the Military Memoir', *Cultural Studies <-> Critical Methodologies* 14:4 (2014), 338–50.

Jones, Edgar, '"LMF": The Use of Psychiatric Stigma in the Royal Air Force during the Second World War', *Journal of Military History*, 70 (2006), 439–58.

Jones, Edgar and Neil Greenberg, 'Royal Naval Psychiatry: Organization, Methods and Outcomes, 1900–1945', *The Mariner's Mirror*, 92:2 (2006), 190–203.

Keegan, John, *Six Armies in Normandy: From D-Day to the Liberation of Paris June 6th-August 25th, 1944* (London: Jonathan Cape, 1982).

'Towards a Theory of Combat Motivation', in *Time to Kill: The Soldier's Experience of War in the West 1939–1945*, (eds.) Paul Addison and Angus Calder (London: Pimlico, 1997), 3–11.

Kennedy, Catriona, *Narratives of the Revolutionary and Napoleonic Wars: Military and Civilian Experience in Britain and Ireland* (Basingstoke: Palgrave Macmillan, 2013).

Koestler, Arthur, 'The Birth of a Myth: In Memory of Richard Hillary', *Horizon* (April 1943), 227–43.

LaCapra, Dominick, *Writing History, Writing Trauma* (Baltimore: Johns Hopkins University Press, 2001).

Lavery, Brian, *In Which They Served: The Royal Navy Officer Experience in the Second World War* (London: Conway, 2008).

Lawrence, D. H., *Apocalypse and the Writings on Revelations*, (ed.) Mara Kalnins (Cambridge: Cambridge University Press, 2002).

Lee, David, *Up Close and Personal: The Reality of Close-Quarter Fighting in World War II* (London: Greenhill 2006).

Lejeune, Philippe, *On Autobiography* (Minneapolis: University of Minnesota Press, 1989).

Linder, Ann P., *Princes of the Trenches: Narrating the German Experience of the First World War* (Colombia: Camden House, 1996).

Luminet, Olivier and Antonietta Curci (eds.), *Flashbulb Memories: New Issues and New Perspectives* (New York: Psychology Press, 2009).

Mahan, Alfred Thayer, *Types of Naval Officers Drawn from the History of the British Navy: With Some Account of the Conditions of Naval Warfare at the Beginning of the Eighteenth Century, and of Its Subsequent Development During the Sail Period* (London: Sampson Low, Marston & Company, 1902).

Mansell, Tony, 'Flying start: Educational and Social Factors in the Recruitment of Pilots of the Royal Air Force in the Interwar Years', *History of Education*, 26:1 (1997), 71–90.

Marcus, Laura, *Auto/Biographical Discourses: Theory, Criticism, Practice* (Manchester: Manchester University Press, 1994).

Marshall, S. L. A., *Men against Fire: The Problem of Battle Command*, rev. edn. (Oklahoma: University of Oklahoma Press, 2000).

McCarthy, John, 'Aircrew and "Lack of Moral Fibre" in the Second World War', *War & Society*, 2:2 (1984), 87–101.

McKee, Alexander, *Dresden 1945: The Devil's Tinderbox* (London: Souvenir Press, 1982).

McManners, Hugh, *The Scars of War* (London: HarperCollins, 1993).

Middlebrook, Martin, *The Nuremberg Raid, 30–31 March 1944* (London: Allen Lane, 1973).

Milliard, Kenneth, *Coming of Age in Contemporary American Fiction* (Edinburgh: Edinburgh University Press, 2007).

Moran, Lord Anthony, *The Anatomy of Courage*, rev. edn. (London: Constable & Robinson, 2007).

Moran, Christopher, *Classified: Secrecy and the State in Modern Britain* (Cambridge: Cambridge University Press, 2012).

Morris, Richard, *Guy Gibson* (London: Viking, 1994).

Muhlhahn, Klaus, 'Remembering a Bitter Past: The Trauma of China's Labor Corps, 1949–1978', *History & Memory*, 16:2 (2004), 108–39.

Neillands, Robin, *The Battle of Normandy* (London: Cassell, 2003).

Newlands, Emma, *Civilians into Soldiers: War, the Body, and British Army Recruits 1939–1945* (Manchester: Manchester University Press, 2013).

Newsome, Bruce, 'The Myth of Intrinsic Combat Motivation', *Journal of Strategic Studies*, 26:4 (2003), 24–46.

Noakes, Lucy, '"War on the Web": The BBC's "People's War" Website and Memories of Fear in Wartime in 21st Century Britain', in *British Cultural Memory and the Second World War*, (eds.) Lucy Noakes and Juliette Pattinson (London: Bloomsbury, 2013), 60–76.

Nolan, Mary, 'Air Wars, Memory Wars', *Central European History*, 38:1 (2005), 7–40.

Olney, James, *Metaphors of Self: The Meaning of Autobiography* (Princeton: Princeton University Press, 1972).

Overy, Richard, 'The Post-War Debate', in *Firestorm: The Bombing of Dresden 1945*, (eds.) Paul Addison and Jeremy A. Crang (London: Pimlico, 2006), 123–42.

Paris, Michael, 'The Rise of the Airmen: The Origins of Air Force Elitism, c. 1890–1918', *Journal of Contemporary History*, 28:1 (1993), 123–41.

Pascal, Roy, *Design and Truth in Autobiography* (London: Routledge & Keegan Paul, 1960).

Plamper, Jan, *The History of Emotions: An Introduction*, trans. Keith Tribe (Oxford: Oxford University Press, 2015).

Prysor, Glyn, *Citizen Sailors: The Royal Navy in the Second World War* (London: Viking, 2011).

Ramsey, Neil, *The Military Memoir and Romantic Literary Culture, 1780–1835* (Farnham: Ashgate, 2011).

Rawlinson, Mark, *British Writing of the Second World War* (Oxford: Oxford University Press, 2000).

Redding, Tony, *Life and Death in Bomber Command*, rev. edn. (Stroud: Fonthill Media, 2013).

Reynolds, David, *In Command of History: Churchill Fighting and Writing the Second World War* (London: Allen Lane, 2004).

Ricoeur, Paul, *Memory, History, Forgetting* (Chicago: University of Chicago Press, 2004).

Rimmele, Ulrike, Lila Davachi, Radoslav Petrov, Sonya Dougal, and Elizabeth A. Phelps, 'Emotion Enhances the Subjective Feeling of Remembering, Despite Lower Accuracy for Contextual Details', *Emotion*, 11:3 (2011), 553–62.

Roper, Michael, 'Between Manliness and Masculinity: the "War Generation" and the Psychology of Fear in Britain, 1914–1970', *Journal of British Studies*, 44:2 (2005), 343–62.

'Re-remembering the Soldier Hero: The Psychic and Social Construction of Memory in Personal Narratives of the Great War', *History Workshop Journal*, 50:3 (2000), 181–204.

Roper, Michael and John Tosh (eds.), *Manful Assertions: Masculinities in Britain since 1800* (London: Routledge, 1991).

Rose, Sonya O., 'Temperate heroes: Concepts of Masculinity in Second World War Britain', in *Masculinities in Politics and War: Gendering Modern History*, (eds.) Stefan Dudink, Karen Hagemann, and John Tosh (Manchester: Manchester University Press, 2004), 177–95.

Rosenwein, Barbara H., 'Problems and Methods in the History of Emotions', *Passions in Context: International Journal for the History and Theory of Emotions*, www.passionsincontext.de/?id=557

Roskill, S. W., *The War At Sea 1939–1945*, Vol. 1 (London: Her Majesty's Stationary Office, 1954).

Ross, David, *Richard Hillary: The Definitive Biography of a Battle of Britain Fighter Pilot and Author of The Last Enemy* (London: Grub Street, 2000).

Rousso, Henri, *The Vichy Syndrome: History and Memory in France Since 1944*, trans. Arthur Goldhammer (Cambridge, MA: Harvard University Press, 1991).

Scarry, Elaine, *The Body in Pain* (Oxford: Oxford University Press, 1985).

Schneider, James. J, 'The Theory of the Empty Battlefield', *Military Science*, 132:3 (1987), 37–44.

Sheffield, G. D., *Leadership in the Trenches: Officer-Man Relations, Morale and Discipline in the British Army in the Era of the First World War* (Basingstoke: Macmillan, 2000).

Sheffield, Gary, 'Dead cows and Tigers: Some aspects of the experience of the British soldier in Normandy, 1944', in *The Normandy Campaign 1944: Sixty Years On*, (ed.) John Buckley (London: Routledge, 2006), 118–30.

'The Shadow of the Somme: The Influence of the First World War on British Soldiers' Perceptions and Behaviour in the Second World War', in *Time to Kill: The Soldier's Experience of War in the West 1939–1945*, (eds.) Paul Addison and Angus Calder (London: Pimlico, 1997), 21–39.

Shephard, Ben, *A War of Nerves* (London: Jonathan Cape, 2000).

Shils, Edward and Morris Janowitz, 'Cohesion and Disintegration in the Wehrmacht in World War II', *Public Opinion Quarterly*, 12 (1948), 280–315.

Smith, Michael, *Britain and 1940: History, Myth and Popular Memory* (London: Routledge, 2000).

Snape, Michael, *God and the British Soldier: Religion and the British Army in the First and Second World Wars* (London: Routledge, 2005).

Stanley, Liz, *The Auto/Biographical I: The Theory and Practice of Feminist Auto/Biography* (Manchester: Manchester University Press, 1992).

Steedman, Carolyn, *The Radical Soldier's Tale: John Pearman, 1819–1908*, new edn. (Abingdon: Routledge, 2016).

Stouffer, Samuel (ed.), *The American Soldier: Combat and Its Aftermath* (Princeton: NJ, 1949).

Stout, T. and M. Duncan, 'War Surgery and Medicine', in *Official History of New Zealand in the Second World War* (Wellington: Historical Publications Branch, 1954).

Strachan, Hew, 'Training, Morale and Modern War', *Journal of Contemporary History*, 41:2 (2006), 211–27.

Sturrock, John, *The Language of Autobiography: Studies in the First Person Singular* (Cambridge: Cambridge University Press, 1993).

Suleiman, Susan, *Crises of Memory and the Second World War* (Cambridge, MA: Harvard University Press, 2006).

Summerfield, Penny, 'Divisions at Sea: Class, Gender, Race, and Nation in Maritime Films of the Second World War, 1939–60', *Twentieth Century British History*, 22:3 (2011), 330–53.

Reconstructing Women's Wartime Lives: Discourse and Subjectivity in Oral Histories of the Second World War (Manchester: Manchester University Press, 1998).

Tall, Jeff, 'RN Submarines in World War II', in *100 Years of the Trade: Royal Navy Submarines Past, Present & Future*, (ed.) Martin Edmonds (Lancaster: Centre for Defence and International Security Studies, 2001), 52–7.

Taylor, Frederick, *Dresden: Tuesday 13 February 1945* (London: Bloomsbury, 2004).

Terkel, Studs, *'The Good War': An Oral History of World War Two* (New York: Pantheon, 1984).

Terraine, John, *The Right of the Line: The Royal Air Force in the European War 1939–1945* (London: Hodder & Stoughton, 1985).

Thomson, Alistair, *Anzac Memories: Living With the Legend* (Oxford: Oxford University Press, 1994).

Anzac Memories: Living with the Legend, rev. edn. (Monash: Monash University Publishing, 2013).

Trott, Vincent Andrew, 'Remembering War, Resisting Myth: Veteran Autobiographies and the Great War in the Twenty-first Century', *Journal of War and Culture Studies*, 6:4 (November, 2013), 328–42.

Vernon, Alex, 'No Genre's Land: The Problem of Genre in War Memoirs and Military Autobiographies', in *Arms and the Self: War, the Military and Autobiographical Writing*, (ed.) Alex Vernon (Kent: Kent State University Press, 2005), 1–40.

Watson, Alexander, 'Self-Deception and Survival: Mental Coping Strategies on the Western Front, 1914–18', *Journal of Contemporary History*, 41:2 (2006), 247–68.

Wessely, Simon, 'Twentieth-Century Theories on Combat Motivation and Breakdown', *Journal of Contemporary History*, 41:2 (2006), 269–86.

Winter, Jay, *Remembering War: The Great War Between Memory and History in the Twentieth Century* (New Haven: Yale University Press, 2006).

'Thinking about Silence', in *Shadows of War: A Social History of Silence in the Twentieth Century*, (eds.) Efrat Ben-Ze'ev, Ruth Gino, and Jay Winter (Cambridge: Cambridge University Press, 2010), 3–31.

Winter, Jay and Emmanuel Sivan, 'Setting the Framework', in *War and Remembrance in the Twentieth Century*, (eds.) Jay Winter and Emmanuel Sivan (Cambridge: Cambridge University Press, 1999), 6–39.

Wood, Nancy, *Vectors of Memory: Legacies of Trauma in Postwar Europe* (Oxford: Berg, 1999).

Woodward, Rachel and K. Neil Jenkings, 'Soldiers' bodies and the contemporary British military memoir', in *War and the Body: Militarisation, Practice and Experience*, (ed.) Kevin McSorley (London: Routledge, 2013), 152–64.

Unpublished Thesis

Barnacle, Gemma Elizabeth, 'Understanding Emotional Memory: Cognitive Factors' (University of Manchester, 2016).

Newspaper Articles

'Mud and Larks', *Times Literary Supplement*, 13 November 1969.

Rustin, Susanna, 'Hello to All That', *The Guardian*, 31 July 2004.

Van der Merwe, Pieter, 'Ask a Grown-Up: Why are Boats Called She', *The Guardian*, 1 February 2014.

Pettie, Andrew, 'Geoffrey Wellum: The Terrible Beauty of Flying a Spitfire at the Age of 18', *The Telegraph*, 10 September 2010.

House, Christian, 'The 89-year-old Boy', *The Spectator*, 17 July 2010.

Films

Desert Victory, (dir.) Roy Boulting. Army Film Unit, 1943.

Ice Cold in Alex, (dir.) J. Lee Thompson. Associated British Picture Corporation, 1958.

In Which We Serve, (dirs.) Noel Coward and David Lean. British Lion Film, 1942.

The Cruel Sea, (dir.) Charles Frend. GDF, 1953.

Plays

Shakespeare, William, *Henry V*, in *William Shakespeare: The Complete Works*, (ed.) W. J. Craig (London: Magpie Books, 1993).

Novels

Monsarrat, Nicholas, *The Cruel Sea* (London: Cassell & Co., 1951).

Vonnegut, Kurt, *Slaughterhouse Five* (New York: Delacorte, 1969).

Poetry

Hampson, Norman, 'Corvette', reproduced in *The Terrible Rain: The War Poets 1939–1945*, (ed.) Brian Gardner (London: Methuen, 1966).

Kipling, Rudyard, *A Book of Words: Selections from Speeches and Addresses Delivered Between 1906 and 1927* (London: Macmillan and Co., 1928).

Owen, Wilfred, *The Poems of Wilfred Owen*, (ed.) Owen Knowles (Ware: Wordsworth Editions, 2002).

Sassoon, Siegfried, 'Suicide in the Trenches', in *Counter Attack and Other Poems* (New York: E.P. Dutton, 1918).

Websites

www.killology.com

Index